THE ETHICS OF ARMED
INTERVENTION

The question of military intervention for humanitarian purposes is a major focus for international law, the United Nations, regional organizations such as NATO, and the foreign policies of nations. Against this background, the 2011 bombing in Libya by Western nations has occasioned renewed interest and concern about armed humanitarian intervention (AHI) and the doctrine of responsibility to protect (RtoP). This volume brings together new essays by leading international, philosophical, and political thinkers on the moral and legal issues involved in AHI, and contains both critical and positive views of AHI. Topics include the problem of abuse and needed limitations, the future viability of RtoP and some of its problematic implications, the possibility of AHI providing space for peaceful political protest, and how AHI might be integrated with post-war justice. It is an important collection for those studying political philosophy, international relations, and humanitarian law.

DON E. SCHEID is Professor of Philosophy, Emeritus, at Winona State University. He is co-editor (with Deen K. Chatterjee) of the anthology *Ethics and Foreign Intervention* (Cambridge, 2003).

THE ETHICS OF ARMED HUMANITARIAN INTERVENTION

DON E. SCHEID

CAMBRIDGE
UNIVERSITY PRESS

CAMBRIDGE
UNIVERSITY PRESS

University Printing House, Cambridge CB2 8BS, United Kingdom

Cambridge University Press is part of the University of Cambridge.

It furthers the University's mission by disseminating knowledge in the pursuit of
education, learning, and research at the highest international levels of excellence.

www.cambridge.org
Information on this title: www.cambridge.org/9781107610675

First published 2014

Printed in the United Kingdom by Clays, St Ives plc

A catalogue record for this publication is available from the British Library

Library of Congress Cataloguing in Publication data
The ethics of armed humanitarian intervention / edited by Don E. Scheid.
          pages   cm
Includes bibliographical references and index.
ISBN 978-1-107-03636-9 (hardback) – ISBN 978-1-107-61067-5 (pbk.)
1. Humanitarian intervention–Moral and ethical aspects.   2. Just war
doctrine.   3. Intervention (International law)   I. Scheid, Don E., editor of compilation.
JZ6369.E74 2014
172′.4–dc23
2013041797

ISBN 978-1-107-03636-9 Hardback
ISBN 978-1-107-61067-5 Paperback

CONTENTS

Notes on contributors   *page* vii
Preface and acknowledgments   xi
List of abbreviations and acronyms   xii

PART I   **Intervention and debate**   1

1   Introduction to armed humanitarian intervention   3
DON E. SCHEID

2   Revisiting armed humanitarian intervention: a 25-year retrospective   26
GEORGE R. LUCAS, JR.

3   The responsibility to protect and the war in Libya   46
TZVETAN TODOROV, TRANSLATED BY KATHLEEN A. JOHNSON

PART II   **Moral perspectives**   59

4   The moral basis of armed humanitarian intervention revisited   61
FERNANDO R. TESÓN

5   All or nothing: are there any "merely permissible" armed humanitarian interventions?   78
NED DOBOS AND C.A.J. COADY

6   Judging armed humanitarian intervention   95
HELEN FROWE

7   Bombing the beneficiaries: the distribution of the costs of the responsibility to protect and humanitarian intervention   113
JAMES PATTISON

PART III   **Ideas and reconsiderations**   131

8   The costs of war: justice, liability, and the Pottery Barn rule   133
MICHAEL BLAKE

v

9 Armed humanitarian intervention and the problem of
abuse after Libya   148

LUKE GLANVILLE

10 The responsibility to protect and the problem of
regime change   166

ALEX J. BELLAMY

11 Law, ethics, and the responsibility to protect   187

MICHAEL W. DOYLE

12 Responsibility to protect and the language of crimes:
collective action and individual culpability   209

JENNIFER M. WELSH

13 Post-intervention: permissions and prohibitions   224

BRIAN OREND

14 Rethinking responsibility to protect: the case for human
sovereignty   243

DAVID RODIN

Select bibliography   261
Index   274

CONTRIBUTORS

ALEX J. BELLAMY is Professor of International Security at the Griffith Asia Institute/Centre for Governance and Public Policy, Griffith University, Queensland, Australia. He is also Non-Resident Senior Adviser at the International Peace Institute, New York, United States. He is co-editor of the journal *Global Responsibility to Protect*, and he serves on the editorial board of the journal *Ethics & International Affairs*. His recent books include: *Massacres and Morality: Mass Killing in an Age of Civilian Immunity* (2012); *Global Politics and the Responsibility to Protect: From Words to Deeds* (2011); *Understanding Peacekeeping*, 2nd edn., with Paul D. Williams and Stuart Griffin (2010).

MICHAEL BLAKE is Professor of Philosophy and Public Affairs at the University of Washington, in Seattle, Washington, United States. He is Director of the Program on Values in Society. Recent publications include: *Justice and Foreign Policy* (2013); "We Are All Cosmopolitans Now," in Gillian Brock (ed.), *Cosmopolitanism versus Non-cosmopolitanism: Critiques, Defenses, Reconceptualizations* (2013); and "Does International Law Make a Moral Difference? The Case of Preventive War," in Deen K. Chatterjee (ed.), *The Ethics of Preventive War* (2013).

C.A.J. (TONY) COADY is Professor of Philosophy at the University of Melbourne, Victoria, Australia. Professor Coady's books include: *Morality and Political Violence* (2008); *Messy Morality: The Challenge of Politics* (2008); *Terrorism and Justice*, co-editor with Michael O'Keefe (2003); and *Testimony: A Philosophical Study* (1992).

NED DOBOS is Lecturer in Applied Ethics at the University of New South Wales, Canberra, Australia. He is also an Adjunct Fellow at the Centre for Applied Philosophy and Public Ethics at Charles Sturt University. He is the author of *Insurrection and Intervention: The Two Faces of Sovereignty* (2012). Other publications include: "International Rescue and Mediated Consequences," *Ethics & International Affairs* (2012); and "On Altruistic War and National Responsibility: Justifying Humanitarian Intervention to Soldiers and Taxpayers," *Ethical Theory and Moral Practice* (2010).

MICHAEL W. DOYLE is the Harold Brown Professor of International Affairs, Law, and Political Science at Columbia University, New York, United States, and the Chair of the UN Democracy Fund. Professor Doyle's major works include: *Liberal Peace: Selected Essays* (2012); *Striking First: Preemption and Prevention in International Conflict*, with commentaries (2008); *Making War and Building Peace: United Nations Peace Operations*, with Nicholas Sambanis (2006); and *Ways of War and Peace* (1997).

HELEN FROWE is Director at the Stockholm Centre for the Ethics of War and Peace and a Wallenberg Academy Fellow, Department of Philosophy, Stockholm, Sweden. Previously, she was a Senior Lecturer in Philosophy at the University of Kent, UK. Her publications include: *The Ethics of War and Peace: An Introduction* (2011); "Self-defence and the Principle of Non-Combatant Immunity," *Journal of Moral Philosophy* (2011); "The Justified Infliction of Unjust Harm," *Proceedings of the Aristotelian Society* (2009); and "A Practical Account of Self-Defence," *Law and Philosophy* (2009).

LUKE GLANVILLE is a fellow in the Department of International Relations at the Australian National University, Canberra, Australia. He is a co-editor of the quarterly journal *Global Responsibility to Protect*. His most recent book is *Sovereignty and the Responsibility to Protect: A New History* (2014). His other recent publications include: "The Myth of 'Traditional' Sovereignty," *International Studies Quarterly* (2013); "Intervention in Libya: From Sovereign Consent to Regional Consent," *International Studies Perspectives* (2013); "The Responsibility to Protect Beyond Borders," *Human Rights Law Review* (2012).

KATHLEEN A. JOHNSON is a freelance translator and editor for translation agencies in the United States, United Kingdom, Austria, France, Germany, and Portugal. She has done extensive translation work in a number of fields, including: legal and commercial documents, construction reports and specification documents, World Health Organization reports and environmental studies, newspaper and magazine articles. Her translations of a more literary nature include: Francine Muel-Dreyfus, *Vichy and the Eternal Feminine* (2001); Philippe de la Genardière, "Lesson of the Incipits," *Review of Contemporary Fiction* (Summer 1988); and Philippe Boyer, "Topographies," *Review of Contemporary Fiction* (Summer 1988).

GEORGE R. LUCAS, JR. holds the "Distinguished Chair in Ethics" in the Vice Admiral James B. Stockdale Center for Ethical Leadership at the US Naval Academy (Annapolis, MD). He is also Professor of Ethics and Public Policy at the Graduate School of Public Policy at the Naval Postgraduate School in Monterey, California. His most recent book is *Anthropologists in Arms: The Ethics of Military Anthropology* (2009), and he has a commissioned work on military ethics in preparation. Other publications include: "Industrial Challenges of Military Robotics," *Journal of Military Ethics* (December 2011); and "The Strategy of Graceful Decline," *Ethics & International Affairs* (Summer 2011).

BRIAN OREND is Director of International Studies and Professor of Philosophy at the University of Waterloo in Canada. He has been Distinguished Visiting Professor of Human Rights at the University of Lund, Sweden. He is best known for his book, *The Morality of War* (2006; revised 2nd edn. 2013) and its emphasis on post-war justice. His other books include: *Introduction to International Studies* (2012); *On War: A Dialogue* (2009); and *Human Rights: Concept and Context* (2002).

JAMES PATTISON is Senior Lecturer in Politics at the School of Social Sciences, University of Manchester, UK. His book, *Humanitarian Intervention and the Responsibility to Protect: Who Should Intervene?* (2010), was awarded a Notable Book Award in 2011 by the International Studies Association. He recently published *The Morality of Private War: The Challenge of Private Military and Security Companies* (2014) and edited the four-volume *Humanitarian Intervention* (2013). His other recent publications include: "The Legitimacy of the Military, Private Military and Security Companies, and Just War Theory," *European Journal of Political Theory* (2012); and "The Ethics of Humanitarian Intervention in Libya," *Ethics & International Affairs* (2011).

DAVID RODIN is Senior Research Fellow at the University of Oxford in the UK where he directs the Oxford Institute for Ethics, Law, and Armed Conflict. He is also Senior Fellow at the Carnegie Council for Ethics in International Affairs in New York, United States. He is a regular lecturer at the UK Joint Services Command and Staff College where he provides ethics training for senior officers. He is co-director of the Oxford Institute for Ethics, Law, and Armed Conflict. His first book was *War and Self-Defense* (2005), and his other publications include: "Terrorism and Torture," in John Skorupski (ed.), *The Routledge Companion to Ethics* (2010); *Just and Unjust Warriors: The Moral and Legal Status of Soldiers*, co-editor with Henry Shue (2008); and *Preemption: Military Action and Moral Justification*, co-editor with Henry Shue (2007).

DON E. SCHEID is Emeritus Professor of Philosophy at Winona State University in Minnesota, United States. Recent publications include: "Replies to Commentaries" (Exchange: Don Scheid on Indefinite Detention of Mega-Terrorists), *Criminal Justice Ethics* (April 2011); "Indefinite Detention of Mega-Terrorists in the War on Terror," *Criminal Justice Ethics* (April 2010); and *Ethics and Foreign Intervention*, co-editor with Deen Chatterjee (2003).

FERNANDO R. TESÓN is the Tobias Simon Eminent Scholar at Florida State University College of Law in Florida, United States. He is a permanent visiting professor at Universidad Torcuato Di Tella, Buenos Aires, Argentina. His publications include: *Rational Choice and Democratic Deliberation*, with Guido Pincione (2006); *Humanitarian Intervention: An Inquiry into Law and Morality*, 3rd edn. (revised) (2005); and *A Philosophy of International Law* (1998).

TZVETAN TODOROV is Honorary Director of Research at the Centre National de la Recherche Scientifique in Paris, France. He is the author of 30 or more books, translated into many languages. Among his many publications translated into English are: *The Totalitarian Experience* (2011); *The Fear of Barbarians* (2010); *Torture and the War on Terror* (2009); *The New World Disorder: Reflections of a European* (2005); *Hope and Memory: Lessons from the Twentieth Century* (2003); and *Imperfect Garden: The Legacy of Humanism* (2002).

JENNIFER M. WELSH is Professor and Chair in International Relations at the European University Institute in Florence, and co-director of the Oxford Institute for Ethics, Law, and Armed Conflict. She is an editorial board member for the journals *Ethics & International Affairs* and *Global Responsibility to Protect*, and for the Cambridge University Press BISA series on International Relations. Professor Welsh is the author, co-author, and editor of several works on international relations, the evolution of the Responsibility to Protect, and the ethics of military force. Among recent publications are: *Just and Unjust Military Interventions: European Thinkers from Vitoria to Mill*, co-editor with Stefano Recchia (2013); "Who Should Act? Collective Responsibility and the Responsibility to Protect," in Andy Knight and Frazer Egerton (eds.), *The Routledge Handbook on the Responsibility to Protect* (2012); and "Implementing the 'Responsibility to Protect': Where Expectations Meet Reality," *Ethics & International Affairs* (Winter 2010).

PREFACE AND ACKNOWLEDGMENTS

The 2011 bombing in Libya by Western nations occasioned renewed debate and concern about armed humanitarian intervention and the doctrine of "Responsibility to Protect" (RtoP). This book is a collection of chapters on many of the important moral and legal issues involved. All the chapters are original contributions, written specifically for this volume. The chapters are by leading international thinkers from Australia, Canada, France, the United Kingdom, and the United States.

The question of military intervention for humanitarian purposes has become a major focus for international law, the United Nations, regional organizations such as NATO, and the foreign policies of nations. The chapters reflect the latest ideas of the authors on this timely international issue – one that continues to evolve in the quest for reasonable global governance.

A number of the chapters present perspectives on the moral rationale for armed humanitarian intervention (AHI). Others focus on normative aspects of the practice – including critical views of AHI, the problem of abuse and needed limitations, the future viability of RtoP and some of its problematic implications, the possibility of AHI providing space for peaceful political protest, and how AHI might be integrated with post-war justice.

I wish to thank all the authors for their contributions to this volume and, in some cases, their work on revisions. Special thanks go to Hilary Gaskin of Cambridge University Press and to her assistant, Anna Lowe, for their advice, patience, and valuable help in the preparation of this volume. I am especially grateful to my wife, Dr. Mary Ann Scheid, for her support – and quiet tolerance during episodes of absentmindedness or grouchiness.

ABBREVIATIONS AND ACRONYMS

AHI	armed humanitarian intervention
AU	African Union
BRICS countries	Brazil, Russia, India, China, South Africa
CDF	Canadian Defence Force
CIA	Central Intelligence Agency (US)
DDE	doctrine of double effect
ECOWAS	Economic Community of West African States
EU	European Union
GA	General Assembly (UN)
G-8	Group of Eight (governments of eight countries: Canada, France, Germany, Italy, Japan, Russia, UK, United States; also represented is the European Union)
G-77	Group of 77 (at the UN, a loose coalition of developing countries)
ICC	International Criminal Court
ICISS	International Commission on Intervention and State Sovereignty
ICJ	International Court of Justice
ICTY	International Criminal Tribunal for the former Yugoslavia
ISAF	International Security Assistance Force (Afghanistan)
KFOR	Kosovo Force (NATO-led international peacekeeping force responsible for establishing a secure environment in Kosovo, beginning in June 1999)
KLA	Kosovo Liberation Army
LTTE	Liberation Tigers of Tamil Eelam
MOOTW	military operations other than war
NATO	North Atlantic Treaty Organization
NGO	non-governmental organization
NTC	National Transition Council (of Libya)
ROE	rules of engagement
RPF	Rwandan Patriotic Front
RtoP or R2P	Responsibility to Protect
SC	Security Council (UN)
UAE	United Arab Emirates

UK	United Kingdom
UN	United Nations
UNAMIR	United Nations Assistance Mission in Rwanda
UNDUTCHBAT	United Nations Dutch battalion
UNOCI	United Nations Operation in Côte d'Ivoire
UNPROFOR	United Nations Protection Force
UNSC	United Nations' Security Council
USSR	Union of Soviet Socialist Republics (Soviet Union)

PART I

Intervention and debate

1

Introduction to armed humanitarian intervention

DON E. SCHEID

The chapters in this volume address normative issues concerning military interventions for humanitarian purposes. The modern debate about such interventions moved to a high point in the 1990s with a series of interventions and non-interventions, including Somalia (1993), Rwanda (1994), Srebrenica/ Bosnia (1995), and Kosovo (1999). This debate led to the development of a promising doctrine called "Responsibility to Protect" (RtoP). The RtoP rationale was implemented in 2011 when the UN Security Council approved military intervention in Libya, and this intervention again spurred debates about armed humanitarian interventions. The intervention in Libya provides the reference point for many of the chapters in the present collection.

Terminology and the concept of armed humanitarian intervention

The phrase "armed humanitarian intervention" (AHI) denotes a military intervention into the jurisdiction of a state by outside forces for humanitarian purposes. The humanitarian goal is to protect or rescue innocent people (i.e., non-combatants) from ongoing or imminent, grave, and massive human-rights violations – that is, from mass atrocities. The rationale is not punishment for past wrongs, but prevention. The intervention is conceived to be a last resort for averting or stopping atrocities such as genocide, crimes against humanity, or mass expulsions.

Any of a variety of military actions can be armed humanitarian interventions, such as: supplying arms and military advisors to opposition forces, conducting secret raids, maintaining a naval blockade, protecting safe havens or enforcing no-fly zones, destroying stockpiles of chemical and biological weapons, bombing military installations, or introducing a full-scale ground invasion.

The term "intervention" is sometimes employed in a benign sense to mean simply a "coming between," as when a military peacekeeping force is placed along a ceasefire line between warring armies. "Intervention" in the context of international affairs, however, usually refers to an action by an outside party that significantly affects the internal affairs of a state without that state's permission or even grudging acquiescence. The term "armed humanitarian intervention" is usually extended to apply to military actions by outside forces in a failed state even though there is no legal authority to give or withhold consent. Many types of actions, besides strictly military ones, can count as "interventions," for instance: transmitting unauthorized radio programs into a country; jamming state-run radio or TV broadcasts; interrupting economic relations (e.g., freezing a state's international financial assets, imposing trade embargoes); carrying out espionage; providing financial aid to subversive movements within a country; sabotaging infrastructure; conducting cyber attacks; and so on.

The term "humanitarian aid" normally refers to non-military aid. Hence, the term "humanitarian intervention" can refer to a non-military intervention for humanitarian purposes. International relief organizations, for example, often seek to provide food and medicine to people in a foreign state without that state's permission. Such actions are clearly interventions for humanitarian purposes, but just as clearly, they are not military interventions. Thus, strictly speaking, "humanitarian intervention" should be distinguished from "*armed* humanitarian intervention."

All the authors in the present collection discuss intervention in the military sense, but they often use the term "humanitarian intervention" – as do many other writers. The shorter expression is less awkward and, in the context, understood to mean what is more accurately expressed by: "armed humanitarian intervention," "humanitarian military intervention," "intervention for human-protection purposes," "military campaign of rescue," and the like. There is no harm in using the shorter expression, of course, so long as the distinction is borne in mind.

In earlier times, military conquests in the Americas were often justified as efforts to Christianize and civilize the heathens. In more recent times, military interventions have been justified as a way of overthrowing a noxious regime, promoting communism, installing an Islamic theocracy, or supporting a democratic form of government. While some of these may be laudable goals, none is part of the concept of armed humanitarian intervention. The defining purpose of AHI is solely the immediate one of protecting or rescuing innocent people. Paradigmatically, AHI is strictly neutral with regard to the parties to any conflict. Where a government is attacking its own citizens, for instance, the aim of AHI is only to stop the carnage; it does not include the further goal of overthrowing the offending government or taking sides in a civil war.[1]

Admittedly, states that undertake armed humanitarian interventions usually do so in pursuit of both humanitarian and strategic goals. Indeed, goals of national interest are easier than altruistic ones for political leaders to sell to their domestic constituencies. Nevertheless, for definitional purposes, in order

---

[1] Military interventions to rescue a state's own citizens abroad might be thought of as humanitarian operations. Nevertheless, they are traditionally considered to be cases of *national self-defense*, not cases of AHI.

to be truly an armed *humanitarian* intervention, the predominant, immediate goal of the intervention must be humanitarian. Thus, neither the US-led war against the Taliban and Al Qaeda in Afghanistan (2001), nor the US-led invasion of Iraq (2003) can be considered an instance of AHI – even though humanitarian concerns and justifications became more prominent as those wars continued.

Moral terrain

The key issue concerning the possible moral basis for armed humanitarian intervention is: What responsibility do individuals, or their state, have for the protection or rescue of foreigners?

Does morality apply?

There is the view that moral responsibilities are limited in scope to members of one's own kin group or tribe. In the modern context, it is sometimes maintained that individuals have moral obligations only to their compatriots and that the state itself has obligations only to its own citizens; neither the state, nor its citizens as individuals, have any moral responsibilities toward foreigners or other states.

This view mirrors that of the Political Realist according to which international relations are an anarchistic state of affairs wherein each state pursues its own "state interests" and where morality does not really apply. The term "state interest" is ambiguous, allowing for narrower and wider, objective and subjective, meanings.[2] But in a narrow and objective sense, the term refers to those interests, or needs, that are essential to the existence and basic welfare of the state. In this sense, it functions to exclude the interests of outsiders. In pursuing its "state interests," a state is not concerned with the interests of any group outside its own jurisdiction – except to the extent that they affect its own vital interests.

The far more usual view is that morality applies to all human beings (some would include animals) and that moral responsibility does not stop at state borders. Memberships in a particular state and most associations (e.g., church, union, corporation, military unit) undoubtedly create special duties to fellow

---

[2] "Objective interests" are states of affairs important for the actual existence or well-being of the state. Such interests include: the prerequisites of physical survival, military preparedness, economic well-being, and political independence. "Subjective interests" are whatever interests the state wishes to pursue (by its leadership, or by the democratic majority) and could include purely altruistic aid to foreign peoples that has absolutely no effect on the existence or well-being of the state in question. Hans Morgenthau criticized US foreign policy for sometimes putting idealistic moral ventures (subjective interests) above its true (objective) interests.

members – because of particular role-based duties, for example – but these do not preclude moral responsibilities to all others.

What is the nature of AHI responsibilities to foreign peoples?

Allowing that morality must encompass all of humanity, what responsibilities are owed to distant strangers? This, it turns out, depends on a wide variety of moral theories.

At one end of a possible continuum is universal utilitarianism. Actions or government policies are right in so far as they promote the greatest good worldwide. All persons are of equal moral standing; the same interests (e.g., to not be killed) are of equal weight for all people. Sacrifice by a person or state is required whenever a greater good for others can be achieved anywhere in the world.[3] At the other end of the continuum might be a theory that assigns only a very few basic rights to strangers, while assigning more, and more stringent, rights to some preferred category of persons (e.g., family and friends, or compatriots). Strangers may have rights not to be physically harmed, killed, or enslaved, but not much else, for example. Even when a favored person and a stranger have the same right, that of the favored person is treated as the more stringent. This idea is reflected in the claim that the life of a fellow citizen is "worth more" than that of a foreigner.[4] Within this general approach, the relationship between favored persons and strangers may be worked out in a variety of ways.[5]

---

[3] Universal utilitarianism is represented in the archetypal article by Peter Singer in "Famine, Affluence, and Morality," *Philosophy & Public Affairs* 1, no. 3 (Spring 1972). See also: Peter Singer, *One World*, 2nd edn. (New Haven and London: Yale University Press, 2004).

[4] This moral/political view was famously expressed by Samuel Huntington:

> [I]t is morally unjustifiable and politically indefensible that members of the [US] armed forces should be killed to prevent Somalis from killing one another.

S.P. Huntington, "New Contingencies, Old Roles," *Joint Forces Quarterly* 2 (Autumn 1993), 38–44, 42.

[5] There are at least two possible ways of differentiating moral status between favored persons and strangers (and many permutations):

(1) Favored persons may have more rights, while strangers are assigned an extremely minimal set of rights.

(2) Favored persons may not only have more rights, but the rights they have in common with strangers can be more stringent or have more weight. In any conflict situation where a favored person and a stranger both have X as a right, the favored person's right prevails.

These differences in moral status were reflected in an analogous legal scheme of early slave laws in the United States. Unlike killing an animal, killing a slave was murder; hence, slaves had a legal right not to be killed. Nevertheless, in practice, a slave's right not to be killed was much less stringent than the same right for a freeman, as reflected in the much lighter sentences (or acquittals) killers received for killing a slave than for killing a freeman. Of course,

We cannot consider here all the possibilities that different moral theories might generate. It must suffice to notice only the most prominent views about responsibilities to foreigners in connection with AHI.

The duty of non-maleficence. Some take the view that a state and its citizens have only "*negative*" obligations toward the rest of humanity: the duty to leave others alone. One may not kill foreigners (e.g., wars of conquest), nor harm them (e.g. dumping pollution in their backyard), nor use them for one's own advantage (e.g., slavery); but one has no positive obligation toward them. That is, the obligations to people outside of one's own state are only duties of non-maleficence.

On this view, one incurs a "*positive*" duty only under "special circumstances," such as when:

(1) one causes the peril the strangers find themselves in (e.g., rapacious economic exploitation of one state by another); or

(2) positive obligations have been explicitly undertaken (e.g., duties under a treaty); or

(3) a special relationship has been established that gives rise to the expectation of positive obligations (e.g., possibly the relationship between a principle power and a former colony).

In the absence of any such particular action, commitment, or relationship, the duty toward strangers is simply to refrain from harming them. Special circumstances apart, then, there is no duty to aid or rescue strangers. On the other hand, some writers argue that given the interconnections of all peoples in our globalized world, special circumstances often, or even always, *do exist*.

Third-party self-defense. Many have suggested that AHI should be viewed as a case of "third-party self-defense" or "other-defense." The basic idea is that if party A is justified in fighting B in self-defense, then any third party C may aid A in A's defense against B. For example, if some part of a state's civilian population is being unjustly attacked by its government forces, then another state (a third party) may intervene militarily to defend the population under attack. That is, outside forces may defend the population from the internal onslaught, just as foreign powers may come to the aid of a state that is suffering aggression from another state – provided for as "collective self-defense" in Article 51 of the UN Charter. Third-party rescue is normally thought of as *permissible* but not *obligatory*.[6]

---

slaves had far fewer rights than freemen over all; and they obviously did not have a legal right not to be enslaved.

[6] There is also the view that the bystander (the third party) must, *as a matter of duty*, go to the defense of a person being unjustly attacked – at least, if he can do so at little cost to himself. This is a minority view; but it is seen to be implied by the duty of beneficence and Good Samaritanism, principles that support a general duty to rescue. While the person under

The duty of beneficence. Many thinkers believe that, even apart from any special circumstances, helping or rescuing strangers is a positive duty, at least in some limited circumstances.

A number of writers have suggested that AHI is a moral duty deriving from the notion of beneficence. While the duties of non-malevolence say only that we should refrain from inflicting evil or harm on others, the "duty of beneficence" says that we must do good for others. The duty of beneficence includes actively preventing evil, stopping ongoing evil, rendering aid, and providing positive benefits. In the context of AHI, emphasis is on a duty to prevent, mitigate, or stop evil.

There are two features normally associated with the duty of beneficence. First, the duty is qualified with a cost proviso: we have a duty to do good only when we can do so at little or no cost to ourselves. This is sometimes referred to as the "duty of easy rescue." A standard example involves a small child drowning in a pond. If a person on shore can easily wade in and save the child, he has a moral duty to do so, even if this means getting his shoes and trousers muddy. On the other hand, if the child is in the middle of a raging river at high flood and the person on shore could easily drown if he tried to save the child, then he has no duty to rescue.[7]

The second associated feature is that the duty of beneficence is usually taken to be a so-called "imperfect duty." Imperfect duties do not give rise to correlative rights in any particular person or persons. Under the duty of beneficence, one may have a duty to help others, but nobody may demand of that person that he or she be helped as a matter of right. Each benefactor may pick and choose his or her beneficiaries, but no potential beneficiary has any right to demand help from the would-be benefactor. One has a general duty toward humanity to help others, but the particular occasions of performing this duty are left up to the individual. How much time and resources one should spend helping others is also unspecified – some say 10 percent, thus tithing in churches, from "tithe" meaning tenth.

Imperfect duties are sometimes translated into perfect ones by assigning them to particular institutions or individuals. For example, while the duty to rescue may be an imperfect one, rescuing a drowning swimmer may be specifically assigned to a lifeguard.

Starting with a duty of beneficence, the state may have a general duty to undertake armed humanitarian interventions – whether the principle is thought to apply directly to the state or derivatively through the citizens as moral agents who make up the state. As an *imperfect* duty, however, it would

---

attack has the option of defending him/herself or not, there is no option for the bystander. The bystander has a duty to defend the victim against unjust attack.

[7] Another view is *graduated risk*. While we have a duty to save one person only when it will be at little risk to ourselves, we have a duty to save many people even if it will be a much greater risk to ourselves. But this is decidedly a minority view of the duty to aid strangers.

be up to the state to decide on which occasions it would perform this duty. International institutional arrangements could be set up, of course, to assign which states should undertake which interventions at what costs.

The Good Samaritan. Some thinkers find appealing the story of the Good Samaritan and take it as an appropriate model for determining our obligation to aid or rescue those in distress. In the story, a Samaritan comes upon a man who has been beaten and robbed and is lying by the side of the road half dead. The Samaritan bandages the man, transports him to an inn, and prepays the innkeeper.[8] The story suggests that a would-be rescuer has a duty to aid a victim, even if no special circumstances obtain between them.

The story has other implications as well. The Samaritan does not do anything that seriously endangers himself and, presumably, was not required to do so. He is not called upon to fight off the robbers, for instance, or to hunt them down. The Samaritan sees to it that the victim is left in a safe place, but the Samaritan does not acquire a duty to provide for the victim indefinitely or to become the victim's bodyguard, for instance. Neither does he have a duty to patrol the road seeking to apprehend robbers or looking for other robbery victims.

The Good Samaritan may be understood to have a *perfect* duty to render assistance – not an imperfect duty – because he is there, can give aid at little cost to himself, and no one else is present to help. It's up to him! But the duty is limited by time and place to the immediate crisis he happens upon. His duty is a narrowly circumscribed instance of the duty of beneficence. On the other hand, this duty arises each and every time he is confronted by an emergency where he can help at little cost to himself.[9]

The duties of universal moral rights. Yet another line of thought involves the notion of universal moral rights. The theory is that everyone in the world has a specific set of basic moral rights, and everyone has a right to enforce his/her own basic rights against all others. Beyond this, all people in the world have a duty to see to it that these rights – rights they all have – are always both respected and enforced. Everyone must respect the rights of others by refraining from interfering with them, and everyone has a duty to help protect and enforce the rights of others. Somewhat like the practice of the "Hue and Cry" of old English Common Law, everyone in the (global) village has an obligation to help catch the villain. All have a duty to protect and enforce the rights of all. Hence, when the rights of some groups are violated, it is the duty of all others in

---

[8] *The New Testament,* Luke 10: 30–37.

[9] The two qualifications associated with the duty of beneficence (cost proviso and imperfect duty) might come into conflict. The duty of easy rescue arises *each and every time* one is confronted with an easy rescue. Yet the idea of an imperfect duty implies that one may pick and chose on which occasions to render aid. This conflict might be resolved by distinguishing levels of need. Perhaps one must always rescue a person in dire need if it is possible to do so at little cost to oneself, but one may pick and choose whom to aid when the aid required is less significant.

the world, by themselves or through their institutions, to enforce those rights of the victim group.

This theory of universal moral rights obviously lends itself to an analogous line of reasoning about the universal human rights in international law. The international community has an obligation to both respect and enforce human rights. All people and their states, have duties (1) to refrain from violating anyone's human rights, and (2) to protect and enforce everyone's human rights against violations.

Moral conditions for AHI

Assuming there is a moral case for AHI, certain conditions are normally thought to govern such a military campaign. Most thinkers insist upon all or most of the standard conditions from the just-war tradition, namely: *right authority, right intention, last resort, reasonable prospects,* and *proportionate means.* Ragtag groups may not go off half-cocked. Any AHI must be conducted under a unified command authority that acts with careful deliberation and circumspection. A body needs a head for coherent action. The immediate intended action must be the humanitarian one of protection or rescue. The intervention must be a last resort, all other measures having been tried or seen to be clearly hopeless. In prospect, the intervention must have a reasonably high probability of success. The intervention must be no more destructive than absolutely necessary to achieve its goal; and, overall, it must be the case that more good than harm will have been achieved by the intervention (i.e., more harm will have been prevented than caused by the intervention).

Political philosophy and international law

Sovereignty and human rights

The concept of sovereignty has undergone major changes over the last 400-odd years. It arose and developed along with the rise of the nation-states of Europe and their challenge to the universalist claims of the Catholic Church and the Holy Roman Empire.

Jean Bodin (1530–1596) – often credited as father of the theory of sovereignty – conceived of sovereignty as an indivisible, single locus of ultimate power and authority over a state. It was absolute, slightly constrained only by divine and natural law. Monarchs were the sovereign rulers who were established as God's lieutenants to command all human beings.[10] The sovereign could treat his own people as he saw fit and make war on other states whenever he was so inclined.

---

[10] Jean Bodin, *Six Books of the Commonwealth* (written in 1576), Book I, chap. 8, available at: www.constitution.org/bodin/bodin_.htm. According to Bodin, major attributes of

With the growth of democratic movements in the seventeenth and eighteenth centuries, the idea developed that the people were properly the source of sovereignty and not a king. At the same time, the idea of *internal* unitary sovereignty began to break down with the concept of the separation of powers (executive, legislative, judicial). Moreover, the American scheme featured a dual sovereignty, with some governmental functions delegated to the federal government while others were reserved to the individual states.[11] Nevertheless, the *external* aspect of sovereignty remained: there was no higher authority over the state, and a state could act as it saw fit in its relations with other states.

In the nineteenth and twentieth centuries, it became apparent that unlimited sovereignty in the international arena was incompatible with any hope of a world free from the devastations of war. International law began to become more prominent in international relations. After countless peace proposals, especially in the eighteenth and nineteenth centuries, and the failed League of Nations in the early twentieth century, an astonishing series of developments in international law took place following World War II – especially the creation of the United Nations (1945) and the Geneva Conventions (1949). States, or at least their leaders, could be held liable for grave breaches of the laws of war (e.g., Nuremberg and Tokyo trials); and, most importantly, all wars, except those of self-defense, were made illegal. With these developments, the concept of a divided *external* sovereignty emerged. Most issues concerning international relations remained under the control of the individual state, but some things began to come under the control of international society.

Finally, from the latter half of the twentieth century to the present, another concern, besides war between states, has arisen to challenge and modify the concept of state sovereignty: universal human rights. This was first reflected in the Universal Declaration of Human Rights (1948), and then in a series of treaties and conventions.[12]

The ascent of human rights has lead to further change in the concept of state sovereignty. Sovereignty still embodies the idea that states are politically equal, independent, and self-governing (autonomous) entities. A condition of state

sovereignty are the power: (1) to make and unmake law, (2) to make war and peace, (3) to appoint the officers of the state, (4) to be the final resort of appeal from all courts, including the power to pardon convicted persons, (5) to make and regulate currency, and (6) to levy taxes and impose dues. For Bodin, all the attributes are essentially contained within the main attribute of making and unmaking law.

[11] James Madison refers to this feature as the "compound republic of America" Number 51 of the *Federalist Papers*. See Alexander Hamilton, James Madison, and John Jay, *The Federalist Papers*, edited by Clinton Rossiter (New York: Penguin Group, 1961), Paper No. 51, 320.

[12] Key treaties establishing human rights include: the Genocide Convention (1948); the four Geneva Conventions (1949); the International Covenants on Civil and Political Rights, and on Social, Economic, and Cultural Rights (1966); and the Convention Against Torture (1987).

The 20-plus human-rights accords signed during the last half of the twentieth and early twenty-first century cover slavery, refugees, women, racial discrimination, children,

sovereignty is the state's obligation to respect the sovereignty of every other state; and from this, arises the norm of non-intervention. There may be international constraints on a state's right to go to war; but the sovereign state still maintains a monopoly on the legitimate use of force within its own territory and has the right to the exclusive control of its territory and population. The norm of non-intervention means that no state may intervene in the internal affairs of another state. But AHI challenges this because it assumes that outside powers *have a right* (or possibly even a duty) to intervene in another state to protect people from severe and widespread violations of their human rights.

The UN Charter's requirement of threat to "international peace and security"

The UN Charter allows for the use of armed force in two situations: (1) cases of self-defense or collective security measures under Chapter VII (Article 51), and (2) with the authorization of the Security Council when "necessary to maintain or restore international peace and security" (Article 42). Provisions in Chapter VII strongly imply that a threat to "international peace and security" is a prerequisite to the Security Council's authorization of any use of armed force. At the end of World War II, armed conflicts within a country were regarded as entirely domestic matters. Nevertheless, it was widely accepted that the Security Council could authorize armed interventions under Chapter VII in response to humanitarian emergencies so long as they presented a threat to *international peace and security*. In the most obvious case, an internal conflict could affect international peace and security when it spilled over into neighboring states.

With the growing emphasis on human rights, the question arose as to whether the Security Council could authorize AHI even in a case where no particular threat to international peace and security existed. Certainly, the UN Charter does not provide for AHI as such. Throughout the 1990s, the problem was skirted by expanding interpretations of the key phrase, "international peace and security." For example, one claim was that the flow of refugees into neighboring countries could be considered a threat to international peace and security.[13]

Conditional sovereignty

Expanding the category of situations that count as threats to international peace and security was one way of handling the conflict between the enforcement of

indigenous peoples, migrant workers, persons with disabilities, forced disappearance, etc. Unfortunately, there are few effective enforcement mechanisms.

[13] British Prime Minister Tony Blair, speaking shortly after the beginning of the NATO campaign in Kosovo in 1999, remarked: "[W]hen oppression produces massive flows of refugees which unsettle neighboring countries, they can properly be described as 'threats to international peace and security.'" Tony Blair, "Doctrine of the International Community," Speech to the Economic Club of Chicago, Hilton Hotel, Chicago (April 22, 1999).

human rights and the state-sovereignty norm of non-intervention. But the real solution to the conceptual logjam came with the idea of *conditional sovereignty*. Now, human rights are regarded as the most basic principle of world order. The sovereignty of the state is *conditional*: a state's legitimacy and the enjoyment of its sovereignty depends on the protection it provides for the human rights of its population. A state is thought of as something like a trustee for the people committed to its care. Whenever a state seriously violates the human rights of its population (e.g., because of a tyrannical, corrupt, or incompetent government) it loses legitimacy, thus forfeiting its claim to full sovereignty and non-intervention. At this point, outside forces may intervene to halt present, and prevent imminent, grave human-rights violations. This concept of conditional sovereignty became embodied in the doctrine of Responsibility to Protect, as we shall see.

Responsibility to Protect

Armed humanitarian intervention had been controversial both when it happened – as in Somalia (1993), Bosnia (1995), and Kosovo (1999) – and when it failed to happen, as in Rwanda (1994). These and other cases indicated the need for a comprehensive reassessment of AHI. In a series of writings and addresses at the end of the 1990s, UN Secretary-General Kofi Annan raised questions about the extent of state sovereignty, the place of human rights in international relations, and the possible role of AHI.

Annan set out the case for AHI at a Ditchley Foundation conference in Britain in 1998. Among other things,[14] he argued that the Security Council had the authority "to decide that the *internal* situation in a state is so grave as to justify forceful intervention."[15] In a 1999 report to the UN General Assembly entitled "Two Concepts of Sovereignty," Annan contrasted state sovereignty with "individual sovereignty," noting a "spreading consciousness of individual rights." Annan asserted that states "are now widely understood to be instruments at the service of their peoples, and not vice versa." Annan declared that

---

[14] Annan noted that the Genocide Convention put all states under an obligation to "prevent and punish" that most heinous of crimes. But, since genocide is almost always committed with the connivance or participation of the state authorities, he argued, it is difficult to see how the United Nations could prevent it without intervening in a state's internal affairs. Annan claimed that state borders "should no longer be seen as watertight protection for war criminals or mass murderers." And, he asserted, "The fact that a conflict is 'internal' does not give the parties any right to disregard the most basic rules of human conduct."

[15] Kofi Annan, "Intervention," 35th Annual Ditchley Foundation Lecture, The Ditchley Foundation, Ditchley Park, UK (June 26, 1998), available at: www.ditchley.co.uk/conferences/past-programme/1990–1999/1998/lecture-xxxv.

Kofi Annan, *Interventions: A Life in War and Peace* (New York: Penguin Press, 2012), 89–97.

the international community had to reach a consensus on the proposition that massive and systematic violations of human rights must be stopped wherever they take place, but also on the means for deciding what action is necessary, when, and by whom.[16]

In response to the ideas and challenges set out by Kofi Annan, an ad hoc commission was formed: the International Commission on Intervention and State Sovereignty (ICISS). It was founded in 2000 by Gareth Evans, former Foreign Minister of Australia, and Mohamed Sahnoun, a former senior Algerian diplomat, under the auspices of the Canadian government. The result of the commission's work was a report in 2001 entitled *The Responsibility to Protect*, which laid out an alternative approach to that of the much-criticized interventions of the 1990s.[17] The principles outlined in the report constitute the doctrine of Responsibility to Protect (R2P or RtoP).

Although RtoP is not itself law, it is worth reviewing salient parts of the doctrine because it has become a normative framework for action by the United Nations and the international community. The doctrine of RtoP reflected a decisive shift in the conception of sovereignty: from the *rights* of sovereignty to the *duties* of sovereignty – or, as the ICISS report has it, from *sovereignty as control* to *sovereignty as responsibility*.[18] The Commission maintained that all members of the community of states have a responsibility to protect both their own citizens *and those of other states*.[19] According to the Commission, the international community's "responsibility to protect" consists of three essential responsibilities, as follows.

(1) The Responsibility to Prevent. Each state has primary responsibility for preventing deadly conflict within its own jurisdiction. But for prevention to succeed, strong support from the international community is often indispensable; and the international community must shift its mindset from a culture of reaction to a culture of prevention.[20] When a state is unable to fulfill its responsibility, it may ask for help from other members of the international community.

Efforts at prevention must address *root causes* of deadly conflict by attending to a country's longer-term political, economic, legal, and military needs and address *direct causes* in the same categories to avert immediate crises. Under

[16] Kofi A. Annan, "Two Concepts of Sovereignty," *The Economist* (September 16, 1999); Annan, *Interventions*, 115–116. See also Annan's Millennium Report to the General Assembly in 2000: *We The Peoples: The Role of the United Nations in the Twenty-first Century* (New York: UN Dept. of Public Information, March 2000).

[17] Report of the International Commission on Intervention and State Sovereignty, *The Responsibility to Protect* (Ottawa: International Development Research Centre, 2001), available at: http://responsibilitytoprotect.org/ICISS%20Report.pdf.

[18] *Ibid.*, chap. 2, para. 2.14.   [19] *Ibid.*, chap. 2, para. 2.27, emphasis added.

[20] *Ibid.*, chap. 3, paras. 3.2–3.3, 3.42.

each heading, the ICISS report describes a number of measures that might be taken.[21]

(2) The Responsibility to React. Here, the concept of *conditional sovereignty* comes into view. A state's right to control its territory and population comes with the responsibility to protect the people within its borders and to uphold their human rights. If a state is unwilling or unable to meet this responsibility, as in a case of mass killings, its sovereignty is suspended, and the responsibility to protect the vulnerable population shifts to the international community.[22]

Armed humanitarian intervention ("intervention for human protection purposes" as it is called in the ICISS report) must be a last resort. Less intrusive measures should be considered before more coercive ones, and various types of coercive political and economic sanctions should be tried before military intervention.[23]

The kind of violence sufficient to trigger a military intervention overriding the non-intervention principle must be severe and widespread. In the Commission's view, AHI may be allowed in only two circumstances:

(1) It is necessary to halt or avert large-scale loss of life, which is the product of deliberate state action, state neglect or inability to act, or a failed state.
(2) It is necessary to halt or avert large-scale "ethnic cleansing," whether carried out by killing, forced expulsion, acts of terror, or rape.

The Commission emphasizes that human-rights violations that fall short of outright killing or ethnic cleansing are *not* sufficient to justify AHI, even if they are serious and widespread. For example, systematic racial discrimination, or the systematic imprisonment of political opponents would not be enough to justify AHI.[24]

In addition to these basic conditions, any AHI must also conform to what the ICISS report calls "Precautionary Principles." These, in fact, are simply the standard conditions of the just-war tradition, which we noted above.

(3) The Responsibility to Rebuild. The international actors must remain in the state in question long enough to ensure sustainable reconstruction and the installation of good governance. The responsibility to rebuild requires a commitment to full assistance in addressing the causes of the humanitarian crisis the intervention was intended to halt in the first place.

The three most crucial areas of this responsibility are security, justice, and economic development. Again, the report describes any number of measures that might be taken in each of these areas.[25] Past experience has shown that, if

---

[21] *Ibid.*, chap. 3, paras. 3.21–3.24, 3.26, 3.28–3.31.
[22] *Ibid.*, chap. 2, paras. 2.29–2.31.
[23] *Ibid.*, chap. 4, paras. 4.1–4.3, 4.6–4.9.
[24] *Ibid.*, chap. 4, paras. 4.18–4.22, 4.25.   [25] *Ibid.*, chap. 5.

security is not maintained, old habits and structures will prevail and under-mine post-conflict, peace-building efforts. The immediate aftermath of any internal war spawns organized crime, revenge attacks, arms proliferation, and looting. The ICISS report states unequivocally, "coalitions or nations act irre-sponsibility if they intervene without the will to restore peace and stability, and to sustain post-intervention operation for as long as necessary to do so."[26]

As is evident from this brief review, RtoP is a broad doctrine. Although the authors in the present collection naturally focus on its provision for military inter-vention, the doctrine of RtoP encompasses much more. Indeed, even under "The Responsibility to React," any number of non-military actions are contemplated.

Legal authority

Establishing a *legal* right to militarily intervene in another state must require authorization from some legal authority. This is important if for no other rea-son than deciding whether the state intervened upon has a right of self-defense. Suppose there is a morally justifiable case for AHI in state X but that the inter-vention has not been approved by the proper authority. In that circumstance, state X would arguably have the legal right to defend itself militarily. The ICISS report proposed a graduated set of authority preferences.[27]

Setting aside the approach of the ICISS, the most prominent views on legal authority are the following:

A. In spite of growing acceptance of the idea of conditional sovereignty, some continue to insist on the sanctity of state sovereignty and non-interven-tion. They would prohibit AHI altogether and believe it is and should remain illegal. Small states argue that the norm of non-intervention is the only pro-tection they have. Many, with the memory of colonialism, fear that AHI can easily be used as pretext for aggression and neo-colonialism. Another concern is that allowing legitimate cases of AHI will encourage other, illegitimate cases of military intervention.

B. There is a moral right (or imperative) to intervene, even without official legal authorization, in extreme humanitarian emergencies. The US-led mili-tary intervention in Kosovo is the determinative case. That intervention was technically illegal because it lacked Security Council authorization. Yet a com-mission of experts later held that the intervention was "illegal but legitimate."

The idea behind this approach is that violation of present law is one way customary international law evolves. AHI in morally appropriate cases might

---

[26] *Ibid.*, chap. 7, para. 7.40.
[27] *Ibid.*, chap. 6.
   The ICISS report maintained that authorization from the UN was to be greatly preferred. In the first instance, authorization was to be sought from the Security Council. Failing that, potential interveners were to approach the General Assembly under the Uniting for Peace mechanism; and failing that, they were to work through regional organizations.

eventually establish a new international norm that then becomes part of customary international law. Hence a kind of "civil disobedience" is justified both morally and as a means of "legislation" in international law.

C. Military interventions in response to atrocities may be lawful, but only if authorized by the UN Security Council. On this view, NATO's unauthorized intervention in Kosovo (1999) constituted a violation of Article 2(4), while NATO's authorized intervention in Libya (2011) was legal. Most states agree that AHI is legal only if authorized by the Security Council. They do not subscribe to the view (immediately above) that unauthorized intervention may be legitimate in exceptional circumstances.

It is now more or less settled that AHI can be authorized only by the UN Security Council; and this was reaffirmed at the 2005 UN World Summit, which we take note of below.

Adoption and implementation of RtoP

Adoption

Many ICISS recommendations were adopted by Kofi Annan's High-level Panel in their report, *A More Secure World: Our Shared Responsibility* (2004)[28] and by his later report, *In Larger Freedom: Towards Development, Security and Human Rights for All* (2005).[29] These, in turn, provided material for consideration by the 2005 World Summit at the United Nations in New York. In this way, aspects of RtoP were adopted at the World Summit – the largest-ever gathering of heads of state and government – and subsequently endorsed by both the General Assembly and Security Council.[30]

The key provisions in the *2005 World Summit Outcome Document* were paragraphs 138 and 139 – which are set out in full in Chapter 11 in this volume. In these paragraphs, states commit themselves to the protection of their own populations from four specific crimes: genocide, war crimes, ethnic cleansing,

---

[28] *A More Secure World: Our Shared Responsibility*, Report of the Secretary-General's High-level Panel on Threats, Challenges and Change (New York: United Nations, 2004). It states:

> The report endorses the emerging norm of a *responsibility to protect* civilians from large-scale violence – a responsibility that is held, first and foremost, by national authorities. When a State fails to protect its civilians, the international community then has a further responsibility to act, through humanitarian operations, monitoring missions and diplomatic pressure – and with force if necessary, though only as a last resort. And in the case of conflict or the use of force, this also implies a clear international commitment to rebuilding shattered societies. (Executive Summary, p. 4)

[29] *In Larger Freedom: Towards Development, Security and Human Rights for All*, Report of the Secretary-General, UN document A/59/2005 (March 21, 2005).

[30] The World Summit was held September 14–16, 2005. The General Assembly's adoption of the *2005 World Summit Outcome Document* is UN document A/60/L.1 (September 20, 2005). The Security Council reaffirmed the key provisions in a resolution of its own in Resolution 1674, UN document S/Res/1674 (April 28, 2006).

and crimes against humanity. As an international community, they also commit themselves to protect populations and, with Security Council authorization, to take military action when "peaceful means are inadequate and national authorities are manifestly failing to protect their populations."

Implementation

In 2009, UN Secretary-General Ban Ki-moon released a report, *Implementing the Responsibility to Protect*, calling for the implementation of RtoP; and he has continued to seek to develop ways of implementing RtoP since then.[31] The 2009 document outlines a "three-pillar strategy" (not to be confused with the three responsibilities of the 2001 ICISS report), as follows.

Pillar One: The Protection Responsibilities of the State. Each state has primary responsibility to protect its own populations – whether citizens or not – from genocide, war crimes, ethnic cleansing, and crimes against humanity, and from their incitement.

Pillar Two: International Assistance and Capacity-building. The international community is committed to assisting states in meeting their Pillar One responsibilities. This commitment seeks to draw on cooperation from member states, regional and sub-regional arrangements, civil society, and the private sector, as well as the agencies of the United Nations. When a state is unable to fully meet its Pillar One responsibility, the international community is expected to assist the state in meeting this core responsibility.[32]

Pillar Three: Timely and Decisive Response. Member states have a responsibility to respond collectively in a timely and decisive manner when a state is manifestly failing to provide the protections required of it under Pillar One. A timely response could involve any of a broad range of "tools" available to the United Nations and its partners, including: pacific measures under Chapter VI of the UN Charter, coercive ones under Chapter VII, and/or collaboration with regional arrangements under Chapter VIII. Armed forces may be used, but they must be authorized by the Security Council and must be a measure of last resort.[33]

[31] *Implementing the Responsibility to Protect*, Report of the Secretary-General, UN document A/63/677 (January 12, 2009). Further discussion of "gaps and capacities" and "next steps" are provided in *Early Warning, Assessment and the Responsibility to Protect*, Report of the Secretary-General, UN document A/64/864 (July 14, 2010).

[32] A vast variety of possible measures come under this heading, for instance: fact-finding missions; early-warning to identify and resolve existing conflicts; cross-regional conflict training programs; building judicial capacities by training police, prison, and judicial officials; building preparedness and planning for both natural disasters and conflict; and so on.

[33] *Implementing the Responsibility to Protect*, Report of the Secretary-General, UN document A/63/677 (January 12, 2009). See also UN Secretary-General Ban Ki-moon's address in Berlin, "Responsible Sovereignty: International Cooperation for a Changed World," UN Dept. of Public Information, SG/SM/11701 (July 15, 2008).

This three-pillar scheme, and Pillar Three in particular, provided the framework for the UN Security Council resolutions on both the sanctions (Resolution 1970) and AHI (Resolution 1973) in the 2011 Libyan conflict.

Intervention in Libya

The NATO intervention in Libya is an example of AHI under the general rationale of RtoP. It can be an important case study for those who want to explore in detail the social/political dynamics that can trigger AHI and that can cause an intervention to move beyond its UN mandate. Here, however, we restrict ourselves to a few notable items and events referred to in the chapters in this volume.

In February 2011 – inspired by the mostly nonviolent revolutions in Tunisia and Egypt – calls went out on Internet social networks for demonstrations for greater freedoms in Libya. People were urged to take to the streets in a planned "Day of Rage" on February 17, a date associated with opposition to the Libyan regime.[34]

On the "Day of Rage," tens of thousands took part in marches and demonstrations throughout the country. Meanwhile, state media showed pro-government supporters in Tripoli waving green flags and shouting in support of Libyan ruler Muammar Gaddafi.

In many cases, demonstrations escalated into violent confrontations. Demonstrators threw rocks and Molotov cocktails; police used tear gas, water cannons, and rubber bullets. Some protesters set police stations and other government buildings afire; regime security forces fired live rounds into the crowds. Scores were arrested. In all, the demonstrations resulted in between 20 and 50 protesters being shot and killed.[35] Human Rights Watch, Libya's Muslim Brotherhood, and other groups condemned the government security forces for using live ammunition to disperse protesters. Following the Day of Rage, mass protests erupted across the country with ever-more lethal clashes between protesters and security forces.

In the weeks and months that followed, several government officials, diplomats, military officers, tribal leaders, and ordinary soldiers deserted the Gaddafi regime.[36] Some military units mutinied. As individual soldiers and military

---

[34] On February 17, 1987, nine people were executed on national television after being charged with plotting against the regime. On the same day in 2006, government security forces killed at least ten people in the course of suppressing a riot outside the Italian consulate. The riot itself arose because an Italian minister wore a T-shirt displaying an indecent cartoon of the Islamic prophet Muhammad.

[35] "HRW Says 24 Killed in Libyan 'Day of Rage' Protests," *Voice of America* (February 17, 2011); "Deadly 'Day of Rage' in Libya," *Aljazeera* (February 18, 2011).

[36] "Gaddafi's Friend Turns Foe," *Aljazeera* (March 1, 2011).

units defected, the Gaddafi regime augmented its forces with mercenaries from other African countries.[37]

While regime security forces had resorted to firing live ammunition, military defections made possible weapons looting from military garrisons; and protesters armed themselves. There were gun battles with deaths on both sides. From the beginning, the major eastern city of Benghazi was the center of the political opposition; but violent protests erupted in the other eastern cities simultaneously with ones in Benghazi. Violent protests also took place in some western cities, most notably the port city of Misratah.

By February 20, Human Rights Watch, citing interviews with hospital staff and witnesses, reported that the number of people killed in the various protest actions across Libya since February 15 was at least 233. Peaceful marches and demonstrations had quickly turned into an armed insurrection.

Calls for Gaddafi's resignation, sanctions

On February 22, Gaddafi appeared on national television and delivered a long, rambling harangue. He denied responsibility for the previous deaths at the hands of his security forces and accused protesters of being "rats" and "gangs of drugged cockroaches." He vowed never to step down, stating: "I am not going to leave this land, and I will die here as a martyr." At the end of his speech, Gaddafi threatened that he and "millions from the Sahara ... will cleanse Libya inch by inch, house by house, home by home, alleyway by alleyway, person by person, until the country is cleansed of dirt and scum."[38]

Two of the most important to defect were: Mustafa Abdul Jalil, the Minister of Justice, and Mahmoud Jibril, the head of the Economic Development Board. They became leading figures in the National Transitional Council.

Two Libyan Air Force fighter pilots defected on February 21 by flying their jets to Malta and requesting asylum there.

A number of senior military officials defected to the opposition. Major General Abdel Fatah Younis al-Obeidi was the Libyan Interior Minister and a former army officer who had participated in Gaddafi's 1969 coup. He joined the revolt after his cousin was shot in the protests; Younis then served as a military commander for the rebel forces.

Staff from a number of Libya's diplomatic missions resigned. Libya's ambassadors to the Arab League, European Union, and United Nations resigned. Libya's ambassador to India, Ali al-Issawi, resigned his post and called for Gaddafi to step down. Libya's ambassador to the United States, Ali Aujali, resigned in protest.

Libyan Prosecutor General, Abdul-Rahman al-Abbar, resigned his position and joined the opposition. Oil Minister Shukri Ghanem and Foreign Minister Moussa Koussa fled Libya.

[37] Handbills urging support for Gaddafi and his regime and advertising large financial payments for mercenaries were sent out to many countries throughout Africa.

[38] "Libya Protests: Defiant Gaddafi Refuses to Quit," *BBC News – Middle East* (February 22, 2011); Dan Murphy, "Qaddafi Speech: More Saddam Hussein than Mubarak," *The Christian*

Gaddafi's threat to go *"dar dar, zanga zanga"* (from house to house, alley to alley) to cleanse the country of the "rats" and "cockroaches" was taken by many to be a harbinger of an all-out assault on rebel strongholds like Benghazi.[39]

In Tripoli on February 25 – in one of many similar incidents – uniformed forces shot directly into unarmed crowds to disperse thousands of protesters who streamed out of mosques after Friday prayers to mount protest demonstrations. Dozens were killed. The same day, French President Nicolas Sarkozy became the first state leader to call for Gaddafi's departure, declaring: "France's position is clear, Mr. Gaddafi must go."[40] The next day, in a speech to the UN Human Rights Council in Geneva, US Secretary of State Hillary Rodham Clinton stated: "Gaddafi has lost the legitimacy to govern and it is time for him to go without further violence or delay."[41]

UN Resolution 1970. The UN Security Council condemned the crackdown in Libya and passed Resolution 1970 on February 26. The Council noted the widespread attacks taking place against the civilian population and the refugees forced to flee the country. It demanded an immediate end to the human-rights violations, reminding Libyan authorities of their "responsibility to protect" their population. The Council also referred the situation in Libya to the International Criminal Court for investigation into reports of crimes against humanity. The Resolution authorized UN member states to: (1) impose an arms embargo on all weapons being sold to or being transferred to Libya, (2) impose a travel ban on Gaddafi, his family, and a number of key members of his government and military, and (3) impose a freeze on Gaddafi's financial assets and those of his immediate family.[42]

In accordance with UN Resolution 1970, the European Union imposed a travel ban on Gaddafi and others connected with his regime. It also implemented an arms embargo and froze the assets held by Libya's sovereign-wealth fund and central bank. Australia, Canada, Switzerland, the United Kingdom, and the United States all unilaterally undertook similar sanctions.[43]

Undeterred by these measures, Gaddafi dispatched the national army to mount a counter-offensive to crush the uprising, using aircraft, tanks, and

---

Science Monitor (February 22, 2011). See also Lindsey Hilsum, *Sandstorm: Libya in the Time of Revolution* (New York: Penguin Press, 2012), 39.

[39] "Gaddafi Comments Signal Genocide," *Press TV* (February 23, 2011), available at: http://edition.presstv.ir/detail/166602.html; David Scheffer, "No-fly Zone: Putting a Leash on Kadafi," *Los Angeles Times* (March 18, 2011).

[40] Alaa Shahine, Zainab Fattah, and Benjamin Harvey, "Gaddafi Rallies Supporters in Libya as Sarkozy Calls for Ouster," *The Washington Post* (February 25, 2011).

[41] "Remarks at the Human Rights Council," US Dept. of State (February 28, 2011).

[42] UN Security Council Resolution 1970, UN document S/Res/1970 (February 26, 2011).

[43] President Obama authorized US military planes to help carry the tens of thousands of non-Libyan refugees who had fled to Egypt or Tunisia back to their home countries. He directed that humanitarian-assistance teams be sent to the Libyan border to help with

artillery, as well as troops. The revolt lost momentum in March, and the Gaddafi regime regained control of many of the rebellious cities.[44]

Armed humanitarian intervention

Opposition leaders requested outside help in the form of weapons and a no-fly zone; but they were opposed to any other foreign intervention for fear of losing ownership of their revolution. Abdul Hafiz Ghoga, a human-rights lawyer who was Vice Chairman for the newly formed National Transitional Council (NTC),[45] expressed the sentiment: "We are completely against foreign intervention. The rest of Libya will be liberated by the people and Gaddafi's security forces will be eliminated by the people of Libya."[46]

In early March, the opposition claimed that Gaddafi forces were poised to massacre the citizens of Benghazi and pleaded for international help. In fact, a siege on Benghazi began on March 17 with a series of airstrikes near Benghazi's airport.

UN Resolution 1973. The UN Security Council adopted Resolution 1973 on March 17. After reiterating the Libyan authorities' responsibility to protect the Libyan population, the Security Council demanded an immediate ceasefire and an end to all attacks against civilians. It reaffirmed the provisions of Resolution 1970, including the freeze on assets and the arms embargo. Resolution 1973 authorized UN member states: (1) to establish a no-fly zone over Libya, and (2) "to take all necessary measures ... to protect civilians and civilian populated areas under threat of attack in [Libya], including Benghazi, while excluding a foreign occupation force of any form on any part of Libyan territory." Thus, it authorized an armed humanitarian intervention.[47]

---

delivery of food and other needed supplies. He announced a unilateral freeze on $30-billion worth of assets of the Libyan government. Massimo Calabresi, "Obama Refines Talk of Libya Intervention," *Time* (March 4, 2011), available at: www.time.com/time/nation/article/0,8599,2057191,00.html.

[44] Abigail Hauslohner and Vivienne Walt, "The War Between the Libyas," *Time* (March 21, 2011), 30.

[45] On February 26, opposition leaders declared an interim government, the National Transitional Council (NTC), to be headed by the former Justice Minister, Mustafa Abdul Jalil. Omar el-Hariri, a former military officer who had been imprisoned for his role in an attempted coup in 1975, was named the defense minister. "Time to Leave," *Economist* (February 22, 2011).

[46] Mohammad Abbas, "Libya Rebels Form Council, Oppose Foreign Intervention," *Reuters* (February 27, 2011); "No Foreign Intervention, Libyans tell West," *Agence France-Presse* (March 1, 2011).

[47] UN Security Council Resolution 1973, UN document S/Res/1973 (March 17, 2011).
There were no opposing votes on the 15-member Council; but Brazil, China, Germany, India, Russia, and South Africa all abstained from voting for Resolution 1973.
Resolution 1973 also: strengthened the arms embargo that applied to both sides by allowing for forcible inspections of ships and planes; imposed a ban on all Libyan-designated

On March 18, Gaddafi's government announced it would comply with the resolution and implement a ceasefire; but it quickly became apparent that no ceasefire was to be observed, as artillery and sniper attacks on Misratah and other cities continued, and regime forces continued approaching Benghazi.[48] Tank fire and airstrikes began hitting Benghazi's southernmost neighborhoods on March 19.

Coalition forces started their military intervention on the same day. French fighter jets began patrolling the skies to enforce the no-fly zone and then immediately destroyed four or five tanks in a column of armored vehicles nearing Benghazi. British and US ships and submarines fired over 110 Tomahawk cruise missiles at more than 20 air-defense targets throughout Libya, including anti-aircraft systems, early warning radar sites, and communications facilities. In the following days, US and UK militaries also bombed Libyan military depots and airbases and set up a naval blockade to enforce the arms embargo. The coalition forces destroyed most of the 70 or so military vehicles headed toward Benghazi on the coastal highway between Ajdabiyah and Benghazi. Regime forces retreated to Ajdabiyah on March 20. Thus, this initial intervention succeeded in stopping Gaddafi forces in their assault on Benghazi; and, in Western eyes, it thereby averted a horrendous massacre.

NATO took control of the entire military mission at the end of March, and it was then thought that the Gaddafi regime would topple in a matter of weeks; but the civil war continued for another seven months.[49]

Regime change, taking sides

Coalition air power was accused of supporting the rebel forces in Benghazi and Misratah and then later in Tripoli, Sert, and other loyalist locations. The fact that some Western powers had called for Gaddafi to step down well before Security Council Resolution 1973 led many to believe that, from the beginning,

flights; imposed a freeze on assets owned by Libyan authorities; extended the travel ban and assets freeze of the earlier Resolution 1970 to additional individuals and Libyan entities; and established a panel of experts to monitor and promote implementation of the sanctions.

[48] There is some debate as to whether the rebels were willing to begin a ceasefire on their side.

[49] March 27, NATO agreed to take control of the entire military mission in Libya, including protection of the civilian population with airstrikes against Libyan ground targets, as well as control of the no-fly zone and the naval blockade. The actual takeover of operational control came a few days later.

Fourteen of NATO's 28 members contributed forces to the NATO operation: Belgium, Britain, Bulgaria, Canada, Denmark, France, Greece, Italy, the Netherlands, Norway, Romania, Spain, Turkey, and the United States. Four non-NATO states joined the operation: Jordan, Qatar, Sweden, and the United Arab Emirates.

NATO ended operations on October 31, thus drawing to a close the military intervention – despite a plea by the NTC chairman, Mustafa Abdul Jalil, for it to remain until the end of the year.

the unspoken coalition mission had been to remove Gaddafi from power. China and Russia severely criticized NATO, accusing it of pursuing regime change under the guise of "humanitarian intervention."

Many complained that US and European forces overstepped the UN mandate and provided close air support to the rebels instead of merely establishing a no-fly zone or protecting civilians. The Secretary-General of the Arab League, Amr Moussa, for example, said he deplored the broad scope of the coalition's bombing. He said the Arab League's approval of a no-fly zone was based on a desire to prevent Gaddafi's air force from attacking civilians and was not intended to embrace the intense bombing and missile attacks on Tripoli and on Libyan ground forces.[50]

Criminal acts

In accordance with UN Resolution 1970, ICC Prosecutor, Luis Moreno-Ocampo, launched an investigation in Libya, and reported in April evidence that "civilians were attacked in their homes; demonstrations were repressed using live ammunition, heavy artillery was used against participants in funeral precessions, and snipers placed to kill those leaving the mosques after the prayers." On June 27, the ICC Prosecutor issued arrest warrants for crimes against humanity for Muammar Gaddafi, his son Saif al-Islam, and chief of military intelligence, Abdullah al-Senussi, stemming from the first two weeks of the uprising.

The African Union "rejected" the ICC arrest warrants for Gaddafi and the others because they "seriously complicated" efforts to find a political solution to the crisis.

Amidst intense fighting on October 20, Gaddafi and his bodyguards tried to flee his hometown of Sert, when a NATO airstrike hit their convoy just outside of town. Shortly thereafter, Gaddafi and others were found hiding in a large concrete drainage pipe under a roadway. Gaddafi was captured alive but soon killed. His son, Mutassim, also captured alive, was killed a few hours later.

During the war, France transferred light arms, rocket launchers, and anti-tank missiles to rebel groups, thus violating the arms embargo of the UN resolutions. Qatar supplied anti-tank missiles, as well as pickup trucks to the rebels; and a number of countries reportedly supplied small arms to the rebel forces during the last months of the war.

War crimes and crimes against humanity were committed by both sides during the civil war, but by far the greater number and the more systematically conducted were committed by Gaddafi forces. Rebel groups were reported to have tortured and killed captured Africans who were suspected of being Gaddafi

---

[50] Edward Cody (*The Washington Post*), "Arab States May Now Want to Rethink Approval," *Star Tribune* (Minneapolis/St. Paul; March 21, 2011).

mercenaries. In September, the International Committee of the Red Cross reported that mass graves had been found containing the bodies of executed rebels. The following month, Human Rights Watch reported that the bodies of 53 Gaddafi supporters had been found, apparently executed by rebel militias.

In the end, at least 50,000 Libyans were killed and unknown numbers wounded in the civil war.

2

Revisiting armed humanitarian intervention

A 25-year retrospective

GEORGE R. LUCAS, JR.

The use of military forces either for the purpose of halting or impeding a humanitarian disaster, or for providing relief and restoring order in the aftermath of one, is hardly a new phenomenon. What is genuinely new about the recent record of humanitarian military interventions during the past 25 years, however, is that such efforts have become the principal justification (beyond national self-defense) for maintaining and deploying national military forces.[1] The militaries of Canada, Australia, and the United Kingdom, as well as of France, and the combined forces of the NATO alliance (under the lead of Danish, Dutch, and Belgian forces), all have such peacekeeping and stabilization operations among their core missions (alongside defense of the homeland).[2] The United States, meanwhile, since 1991, has increasingly defined

---

[1] This apparent shift from conventional *jus ad bellum* to a new justification for the use of force that I termed *jus ad pacem*, was the new state of military affairs by the end of what I term in this chapter the "second wave" of humanitarian crises in the 1990s. See George R. Lucas, Jr., "From *Jus ad Bellum* to *Jus ad Pacem*: Re-thinking Just-war Criteria for the Use of Force for Humanitarian Ends," in Deen K. Chatterjee and Don E. Scheid (eds.), *Ethics and Foreign Intervention* (Cambridge University Press, 2003), 72–96.

[2] This commitment to international peacekeeping and humanitarian operations as a collective responsibility of the international community pervades the current mission literatures of all of these services, including the United States.

The Canadian Defence Force (CDF), as a leading sponsor and participant in the International Commission on Intervention and State Sovereignty (2001), is perhaps most explicit in identifying military intervention in humanitarian crises as a key component of its overall mission, by "remaining engaged internationally in everything from humanitarian assistance to peace-keeping operations," as part of the CDF's overall mission "to support freedom, democracy, and the rule of law around the world." See also Jennifer Welsh, *At Home in the World: Canada's Global Vision for the 21st Century* (New York: HarperCollins, 2004).

Meanwhile, "Peace Support and Humanitarian Missions" is fourth among several core responsibilities listed for the UK Defence Force, while AHI missions constitute more than half of the list of "Global Operations" in which the Australian Defence Force is now, or has recently been, involved (www.defence.gov.au/op/index.htm) and virtually all those involving the Defence Forces of the Netherlands (www.defensie.nl/english/tasks/missions). Similar statements and summaries may be found in the mission literature of the other allied military forces: e.g., the Army of France's discussion of the primacy of humanitarian

its role in international relations in terms of such missions, while sequestering an astonishingly large, and ever-increasing logistical stockpile to support them.[3] Although armed humanitarian intervention (AHI) in fact has a relatively long and somewhat blinkered history,[4] merely reciting that history is of little but mild antiquarian interest, however, unless something substantive can be learned from it concerning what this recent and dramatic inversion or reordering of conventional military priorities portends for the future of international conflict and military professionalism.

In this chapter, accordingly, I propose to examine the dramatic transformation of international priorities governing the purpose and principal uses of military force over the past 25 years. I will first distinguish the broader historical background of armed humanitarian intervention prior to 1989 (what we might term "first-wave" AHI) from two subsequent, distinctive phases: a "second wave" of humanitarian crises and responses during the 1990s, and a more recent "third wave" of ethical analysis, dominated by proposals for new political arrangements that would govern collective decision-making by the international community when faced with the question of whether to deploy their military forces for the prevention or cessation of humanitarian crises.

Using such terminological distinctions, I propose to set a context for evaluating the so-called "Responsibility to Protect" (R2P or RtoP) as the "third wave" in this larger historical context. While RtoP currently dominates political and philosophical discussions of the future of humanitarian intervention (and of the use of military forces, in particular, for this purpose), it addresses questions and problems arising principally in the second wave of AHI, which RtoP has now

---

intervention and peacekeeping in "Winning the Battle: Building Peace," Doctrine 13 FT-01 (October 2007) (www.cdef.terre.defense.gouv.fr/publications/doctrine/doctrine13/version_us/doctrine13_us.pdf) and the Danish Armed Force's manual on "International Perspectives," p. 10.

[3] Essential mission and operational doctrines on this topic are included in "Peacekeeping and Stability Operations," *US Army Field Manual 3–07* (2008) (http://downloads.army.mil/docs/FM_3-07.pdf) and in "Joint Tactics, Techniques, and Procedures for Foreign Humanitarian Assistance," *US Joint Forces Doctrine, JP 3–07.6.*

   US forces have pre-positioned enormous stockpiles of emergency food and housing resources in Okinawa, for example, at Kadena Air Force Base and at Camp Butler, home of the III Marine Expeditionary Force, from which positions both rapid-response military forces and emergency supplies can be quickly deployed throughout Southeast Asia and other far-flung areas in the Pacific rim.

   See Aruna Apte, "Humanitarian Logistics: A New Field of Research and Action," *Foundations and Trends in Technology, Information and OM* 3, no. 1 (2009), 1–100; and J. Salmeron and A. Apte, "Stochastic Optimization for Natural Disaster Asset Prepositioning," *Production and Operations Management* 19, no. 5 (2010), 561–575.

[4] See Nicholas G. Onuf, "Humanitarian Intervention: The Early Years," *Symposium on the Norms and Ethics of Humanitarian Intervention*, Center for Global Peace and Conflict Studies (Irvine, California: University of California-Irvine, May 2000).

largely supplanted. The well-known problems experienced during the second wave stemmed, in turn, from the dominant set of presuppositions regarding military interventions that had formed only gradually, over centuries, during the first wave of AHI. Mine is simply a proposal to analyze RtoP in terms of these earlier waves of humanitarian crises that empirically framed some of the questions to which RtoP now represents one controversial answer. I believe that this procedure will ultimately illuminate some of the daunting challenges that any future operationalization of the present international policy itself now presents.

Historical narratives of complex and disturbing events such as AHI, how-ever, often compete as well as overlap. It is therefore important to attend to the distinct narrative perspectives of the principal actors in the recent history of AHI: in this case, the diplomats and political leaders who order (or fail to order) such military interventions, the military forces that carry them out, and the pundits and philosophers who evaluate the outcome and aftermath – not to mention the victims of the crises, whose voices are sometimes drowned out in this competition. Each historical wave of AHI, in principle at least, could be narrated from several of these perspectives. In forging positions on these com-plex questions, it often matters deeply which of these competing narratives we may unconsciously privilege.

I

The wider background history, or "first wave," of AHI is of early and long-standing duration, encompassing attempts by nations and empires in the eight-eenth and nineteenth centuries to justify military intervention in sovereign states on allegedly humanitarian grounds (e.g., Hungary in 1848, or delibera-tions among political rivals in England about intervening in the pending US Civil War).[5] Both of these particular illustrations were the occasion of John Stuart Mill's provocative essay, "A Few Words on Non-intervention" (1859),[6] decrying the excessive reliance on "national self-interest" as the sole justi-fication for deciding such policy questions. This lengthy historical first wave would, importantly, also encompass *failures to initiate* humanitarian interven-tions, such as the Armenian genocide immediately prior to World War I, or

---

[5] In addition to Michael Walzer's brief discussions of these historical events in his treat-ment of armed humanitarian intervention in *Just and Unjust Wars: A Moral Argument with Historical Illustrations* (New York: Basic Books, 1977), 102–108, see Martha Finnemore, "Constructing Norms of Humanitarian Intervention," in Peter J. Katzenstein (ed.), *The Culture of National Security: Norms and Identity in World Politics* (New York: Columbia University Press, 1996), 161–172.

[6] Reprinted in *Dissertations and Discussions*, vol. III (London: Longmans, Green, Reader, and Dyer, 1867).

the Holocaust during World War II, when other nations *failed to intervene* to prevent the ensuing disasters.

This is the armed humanitarian intervention about which Michael Walzer writes in the first edition of *Just and Unjust Wars* (1977), and toward which he exhibits such suspicion and antipathy. Legitimate examples of humanitarian intervention are "very rare," he observes since, as with the Holocaust, "the lives of foreigners don't weigh that heavily in the scales of domestic decision-making."[7] If we allow Walzer's analysis to serve as a summary of the harsh lessons learned during this first wave, we might conclude that nations and empires tend to use AHI (when they engage in it at all) as a cloak for self-interested aggression, so that presumably righteous calls for AHI should be viewed with deep skepticism. Meanwhile prospects for genuine, legitimate, and morally justifiable AHI usually go unaddressed, inasmuch as it is invariably the case (in Mill's caustic phrase) that "no English interests are involved."[8]

The second wave of AHI developed in the aftermath of the collapse of communism and the fall of the Berlin Wall in 1989. Rather than issuing in the triumph of democracy and the beginning of what US President George H.W. Bush called "a new world order," the end of the bipolar, superpower, nuclear rivalry during the Cold War instead begat a wave of ethnic and religious conflict, especially (but by no means exclusively) in the regions of the former Warsaw Pact. The beginning of this second wave of AHI, referred to fleetingly as "the Golden Age" of humanitarian diplomacy,[9] is usually thought to occur with the US military intervention in Somalia in late 1992 (undertaken in the waning days of the administration of George H.W. Bush, and continued by the newly elected president, William Jefferson Clinton). This simmering crisis, in which desperate victims faced starvation largely as a result of fierce rivalries among competing "warlords" in that collapsing nation, was in fact preceded by the ominous growth in tensions between Orthodox Serbs, Catholic Croats, and Muslims – tensions that began almost immediately after 1989, and quickly culminated in the rise of Serbian nationalism and concomitant military efforts at "ethnic cleansing" and genocide among the diverse populations of the former Yugoslavia.

The variety of humanitarian crises and genocidal tragedies that so unexpectedly occurred in Somalia, Rwanda, Bosnia, Srebrenica, and Kosovo, confronted the wider international community with the dilemma of how to respond. This second wave of AHIs, which occurred in rapid succession, spawned early

---

[7] Walzer, *Just and Unjust Wars*, p. 102. Most such interventions proceed, according to Walzer, from mixed motives, unless the intervention is undertaken to rescues a state's own citizens (as at Entebbe, 1976). This is not (says Walzer) an argument against intervention itself, so much as a reason to be skeptical about the reasons a state may be willing to undertake it.

[8] Mill himself denounces this "realist" justification for AHI as constituting a "morally shabby refrain." *Dissertations and Discussions*, vol. III, 153f.

[9] For example, by the eminent international human-rights lawyer: Richard Falk, "Humanitarian Intervention: A Forum," *The Nation* (July 14, 2003).

attempts by moral philosophers and scholars in international relations, from roughly 1990 through 2004, to understand the moral and political complexities of these crises and failures by various sectors of the international community to respond effectively to them. This scholarly reflection during the second wave encompassed the published work of figures like Stanley Hoffman, Michael Walzer, James Turner Johnson, Anthony Coady, Henry Shue, David Luban, Allen Buchanan, and John Lango, among others.[10] These debates and discussions inaugurated, from a variety of disciplinary backgrounds, reflections on the limits of sovereignty, "territorial integrity," and denunciations of conceptions of national sovereignty that appeared to grant nations (as Henry Shue passionately and eloquently phrased it at the time) "a right to do unlimited wrong" within the confines of one's own borders.[11] They also analyzed the frustrating limitations of international institutions, grounded in, and organized according to these fundamental presuppositions of the so-called "Westphalian paradigm."[12]

---

[10] These are only a selection of commentators on AHI during this period, and an only partial list of the many essays on this subject by these and other scholars. Walzer featured the rise of armed humanitarian intervention during the preceding decade in his preface to the third edition of *Just and Unjust Wars* (2000). See also, for example, Stanley Hoffman, *The Ethics and Politics of Humanitarian Intervention* (South Bend: Notre Dame University Press, 1996); Fernando Tesón, *Humanitarian Intervention: An Inquiry into Law and Morality* (New York: Transnational Publishers, 1997); James Turner Johnson, *Morality and Contemporary Warfare* (New Haven: Yale University Press, 1999); John W. Lango, "Is Armed Humanitarian Intervention to Stop Mass Killing Morally Obligatory?" *Public Affairs Quarterly* (July 2001), 173–192; David Luban, "Intervention and Civilization: Some Unhappy Lessons of the Kosovo War," in Ciaran Cronin and Pablo de Greiff (eds.), *Global Justice and Transnational Politics: Essays on the Moral and Political Challenges of Globalization* (Cambridge, Massachusetts: MIT Press 2002), 79–115; C.A.J. Coady, *The Ethics of Armed Humanitarian Intervention*, no. 45 (Washington, DC: United States Institute of Peace, 2002); Henry Shue, "'Let Whatever Is Smoldering Erupt'? Conditional Sovereignty, Reviewable Intervention, and Rwanda 1994," in Albert Paolini, Anthony Jarvis, and Christian Reus-Smit (eds.), *Between Sovereignty and Global Governance: The State, Civil Society and the United Nations* (New York: St. Martin's, 1998), 60–84; "Eroding Sovereignty: The Advance of Principle," in Robert McKim and Jeff McMahan (eds.), *The Morality of Nationalism* (New York: Oxford University Press, 1997), 340–359; Allen Buchanan and Robert O. Keohane, "The Preventive Use of Force: A Cosmopolitan Institutional Proposal," *Ethics & International Affairs* 18, no. 1 (2004), 1–22.

[11] Henry Shue, "Conditional Sovereignty," *Res Publica* 8, no. 1 (1999), 8–9.

[12] So named in reference to the putative origins of present notions of state sovereignty as first outlined in the "Peace of Westphalia" (1648) – equivalent, essentially, to what Michael Walzer terms the "legalist paradigm," according to which states, rather than persons, are the entities whose basic rights, including sovereignty and territorial integrity, are protected under international law. My point is that this stipulation trades upon an inherent equivocation: international human-rights law pertains to the rights of biological individuals, while most other international law, including the Law of Armed Conflict, outlines the rights and responsibilities of states.

Increasingly over its duration, the second wave of AHI also began to encompass the often-tragic narratives of those military forces who were deployed to carry them out, for example: Mark Bowden's journalistic account of Somalia from the standpoint of the intervening forces and General Anthony C. Zinni's dramatic rebuttal of Bowden's charge of "mission creep" as sowing the seeds of failure in that initial humanitarian campaign;[13] the memoirs of Canadian General Roméo Dallaire, describing the UN-sanctioned military force's helplessness and bureaucratic impasse in Rwanda[14] (captured in the tragic dilemma of Belgian Army Captain Luc Lemaire and his contingent of 90 soldiers guarding the Don Bosco school compound); and US Army General Wesley Clark's account of his frustrations during the Kosovo campaign.[15] The military accounts are often sharply critical of diplomats, political leaders, and policymakers for their inconsistent and often incoherent directives and seemingly ad hoc mission constraints, or for their pursuit of ineffectual and outmoded peacekeeping policies. Such policies usually ended up leaving it to the prudent judgment of the ground forces themselves to sort out the confusion and solve problems piecemeal on the ground (as General Zinni, in particular, so eloquently documents). The narrative voices of the political leaders and diplomats themselves, by contrast, are deafening in their comparative silence during this "second wave." That silence was dramatically broken, beginning in 2001, however, with the onset of what would quickly become the third wave of AHI, in the form of the "RtoP" movement.

My own purpose in briefly revisiting this history is decidedly not to attempt to add further to the already detailed analysis, for example, of the initial use of military force by the United States solely for the purpose of protecting

---

[13] Mark Bowden, *Blackhawk Down* (New York: Grove Press, 1999); Gen. Anthony C. Zinni, USMC (ret.), "The Case of Somalia," in G.R. Lucas, Jr., *Perspectives on Humanitarian Intervention* (Berkeley Public Policy Institute, 2001), 53–63.

Zinni's account of the mission in Somalia is that, in hindsight, its ultimate failure stemmed less from any deliberate or increasingly unwise partisanship on the part of US and UN forces as the occupation time lengthened (as Bowden alleges), but was instead attributable to the nature of the mission itself, as needs and challenges on the ground (such as the need to establish civilian legal and judicial institutions in the gradual reconstruction of civil society within this failed state) inevitably continued to evolve. This "soldier's narrative" squares more directly with the International Security Assistance Force (ISAF) experience in Afghanistan: The longer a peacekeeping mission endures, the greater the complexity of the reconstruction problems it will face, and the greater the likelihood of wearing out the welcome of the interveners in the humanitarian crisis.

[14] Lt. General Roméo Dallaire, *Shake Hands with the Devil: the Failure of Humanity in Rwanda* (New York: Carroll & Graf Publishers, 2003). The case of the Belgian Army contingent at Don Bosco is recounted in many places. An impartial account of the dilemma of the Belgian Army forces can be found in G.R. Lucas and W. Rubel (eds.), *Case Studies in Military Ethics*, 3rd edn. (Upper Saddle River, New Jersey: Pearson, 2010).

[15] Gen. Wesley K. Clark, US Army (ret.), *Waging Modern War: Bosnia, Kosovo, and the Future of Combat* (New York: Public Affairs Press, 2001).

humanitarian aid and famine relief workers from harassment by local warlords in Somalia, nor to retrace the gradual evolution of this humanitarian mission into the full-scale military conflict that ultimately collapsed and failed. Neither do I wish – nor could I – add further detail or analysis to the inconceivable tragedy that was Rwanda. What I intend to portray, instead, is how those debates at the time reflected the genuine confusion and mixture of motives that influenced decision-making in those early "second wave" experiences, and perhaps account for the wildly inconsistent approaches taken to the succession of crises during this period.

Some of these instances of AHI, like Somalia, were purely humanitarian and involved (at least at first) no discernible national self-interest whatsoever.[16] Somalia in particular represented, at least initially, a decisive rebuttal of the underlying cynicism of the first-wave narratives. Other subsequent interventions, such as Haiti in 1994, however, seemed to involve a congruence of national interest with humanitarian sympathies (e.g., a practical and self-interested desire to halt the refugee problem, while genuinely providing relief of the human suffering that was causing this migration to American soil). Still others, like Bosnia and Kosovo, entailed mixed motives largely of the sort that Michael Walzer's first-wave narrative had earlier decried with suspicion.[17] And, of course, the abject failure of the international community to intervene in the tragic genocide in Rwanda in 1993–1994 was reminiscent of the wider community's moral failures with respect to Armenia, and subsequently to Eastern Europe under German rule in the earlier part of that century, and eerily echoed John Stuart Mill's condemnation, more than a century before, of those nations who would refuse to offer aid simply because no "vital national interests" were at stake.

By the end of the decade, a number of analyses had been provided to help organize and clarify the moral and political terrain of the second wave.[18] Michael Walzer's acknowledgment, by the year 2000, of the radical transformation of the background assumptions that had informed his earlier magisterial study was especially telling: On one hand, he blandly opined, nothing had changed sufficiently over the ensuing quarter-century to require a substantive revision of his original book; and yet, somehow (he admitted), everything had

---

[16] This is the consensus of opinion in the aftermath of this campaign. See, for example, Walter Clarke and Jeffrey Herbst, *Learning from Somalia: The Lessons of Armed Humanitarian Intervention* (Lexington, Massachusetts: Westview Press, 1997).

[17] Thus, Gen. Wesley Clark's account concludes that the "real" purpose of the Bosnian and Kosovo campaigns was to re-establish NATO's credibility as a defensive alliance, rather than to come to the aid of the victims of these tragedies. Clark, *Waging Modern War*.

[18] In "The Reluctant Interventionist" (1999), I sought to encompass the contributions of many of these earlier studies and summarize their collective findings within the framework of conventional just-war doctrine. See Lucas, *Perspectives on Humanitarian Intervention*, 1–13.

changed.[19] AHI had now risen from a secondary consideration to the sole justification for a nation's continuing to train and equip a military force: To protect innocent victims of violence and injustice, wherever these might be encountered, and to serve as an international peacekeeping and stabilizing force for law and order.

After the terrorist attacks on the Pentagon and World Trade Center in September of 2001, I was unable to persist without qualification in my own earlier accounts of AHI as the new military-mission priority. Even so, I tried simultaneously to show how AHI motives infused even military efforts at anti-terrorism and counter-insurgency.[20] Significantly, in lieu of the ominous rhetoric of "preemptive self-defense" in June 2002 that led up to the US war of intervention in Iraq the following spring, the actual March 2003 invasion was accompanied by formal justificatory decrees that cited only Iraq's numerous violations of established UN resolutions, together with the continuing de facto state of war that had existed since 1991, especially with respect to attacks on allied aircraft enforcing a UN-mandated "no-fly" zone in the region. Most significantly, as Brian Orend subsequently observed, these unilateral and internationally unauthorized declarations of war cited the desire to bring humanitarian relief to the long-suffering citizens of Iraq.[21] The doctrine of "preemptive self-defense" as the putative justification for the invasion (as Deputy Secretary of Defense, Paul Wolfowitz, dismissively and condescendingly remarked on numerous subsequent occasions) was *nowhere invoked* in support of the actual invasion when it finally transpired. Such was the morally compelling rhetoric of AHI at the end of the second wave, that even the contentious debate over the plausibility of pre-emptive self-defense was subsumed within its wider purview.

The chief conceptual issue during this period (and never fully resolved in evaluations of the crises of the second wave) was the gap between a "right" of intervention (the prevalent second-wave term of art, but sometimes also the "permission" to intervene, which was increasingly sought from the United Nations or the international community out of an overriding concern for sovereignty) on one hand, and, on the other hand, what a few of us at the time were coming to recognize as a presumptive *"duty" or obligation to intervene*. Only the

---

[19] This is my summary account of Walzer's comments on the evolution of armed humanitarian intervention in his Preface to the third edition of *Just and Unjust Wars* (2000).

[20] This was the opening confession in my contribution, "From *Jus ad Bellum* to *Jus ad Pacem*," 72–73.

[21] Orend offers a summary of the various justifications cited, an analysis of the final resolution accompanying the 2003 invasion, and a pointed critique of the dubious tactic of attempting multiple and diverse justifications for a given armed conflict. Finally, he believes, the case for armed humanitarian intervention was, and would have been, the strongest justification for the invasion. See Brian Orend, *The Morality of War* (Peterborough, Ontario: Broadview Press, 2006).

latter designation seemed to capture precisely the nature of the dilemma that bystander nations faced in the midst of a humanitarian crisis or ongoing genocide. Sovereignty itself should no longer be regarded as an inviolable absolute, and certainly should not serve to provide a license granting governments or powerful ethnic majorities (again, in Henry Shue's telling phrase) the "right to do unlimited wrong" to one's own fellow citizens within the confines of one's sovereign borders.

But *how*, exactly, was this duty of intervention to be understood and exercised, and what would be the consequence for the prevailing international legal norms of sovereignty and territorial integrity (sacrosanct since the Peace of Westphalia in 1648)? By the end of the second wave, many of us were led to acknowledge what was termed an "imperfect duty" of military intervention, which must inevitably lead to the erosion of the Westphalian paradigm on behalf of a more cosmopolitan, law-governed international order – one in which human beings, as the only authentic individuals, would remain the sole bearers of rights (as international humanitarian law implied they were), rather than ambiguously sharing such rights with (and even subordinating them to) artificial constructs like "nation-states" (as enshrined in the Westphalian paradigm underlying the provisions of the UN Charter itself). This is the evolution of what David Rodin, in his own more recent work on AHI, describes as the rise of "conditional sovereignty."[22]

II

Against the simmering backdrop of repeated failures of UN peacekeeping missions, from Rwanda to Srebrenica, a "Committee of Eminent Persons" assembled in Ottawa in 2001 under the auspices of the Canadian government to formulate what came to be known as "The Responsibility to Protect" (R2P or RtoP).[23]

This "third wave" of AHI owes its own initial formulation in 2001, and the subsequent formal adoption by the United Nations of a "Responsibility to Protect" in 2005,[24] to the ruminations of diplomats and policy-makers who

[22] See Chapter 14, this volume. See also Shue, "Conditional Sovereignty," 8–9; Jennifer M. Welsh and Serena K. Sharma, *Operationalizing the Responsibility to Prevent* (Oxford Institute for Ethics, Law and Armed Conflict, April 2012), available at: www.elac.ox.ac.uk/downloads/elac%20operationalising%20the%20responsibility%20to%20prevent.pdf.

[23] Gareth Evans and Mohamed Sahnoun (co-chairs), *The Responsibility to Protect*, Report of the International Commission on Intervention and State Sovereignty (Ottawa: International Development Research Centre, December 2001). See also Gareth Evans and Mohamed Sahnoun, "The Responsibility to Protect," *Foreign Affairs* 81, no. 6 (November/December 2002), 99–110.

[24] UN Security Council Resolution 1674 (adopted on 28 April 2006, but affirmed in principle in a plenary session of the General Assembly in September 2005) constituted the first official attempt to define a procedural response to humanitarian crises, and to affirm the principle of "conditional sovereignty," in which the rights of sovereignty and territorial integrity

were themselves frustrated and largely stymied in their attempts, during the previous decade, to manage the numerous tragic instances of ethnic cleansing and genocide successfully. This third wave of attention to AHI also inspired a new generation of scholars, who, for the most part, welcomed this new development and explored the wider moral and political implications of RtoP as an international policy. Here I include the work of scholars like Alex Bellamy, Jennifer Welsh, James Pattison, David Rodin, Michael Doyle, Brian Orend, and Michael Blake, to name only a few.[25]

The differences between the second and third wave of AHI, however, are more than merely generational. The second-wave analysis, spawned literally in the midst of the actual crises themselves, undertook to understand AHI operations primarily from the perspective of the military forces charged with carrying them out. Second-wave accounts thus tended to favor the "soldier's narrative" of AHI, in contrast to what, in the third wave, would become the narratives of international diplomats, representatives of national governments, and lawyers and philosophers reflecting on the impact of AHI on international law.

Recall that one of the chief puzzles during the second wave was whether nations had a "right" (or at least, permission) to override sovereignty for the sake of protecting basic human rights. By contrast, the third-wave scholars attempted to analyze a somewhat different problem generated by the political declarations of international diplomats, like the Brussels "Crisis Group" president at the time, Australian Ambassador-at-large, Gareth Evans. Third-wave diplomats and statesmen simultaneously sought to preserve the underlying conception of sovereignty (inherent in the present nation-state system and presupposed in the UN Charter), while nevertheless asserting an obligation on the part of the collective international community of states (rather than a "right" or permission) to protect the endangered human rights of vulnerable victims within sovereign borders.

are linked to a nation's willingness and capacity to provide security and basic rights to its own citizens. Resolution 1674 was the culmination of efforts by Ambassador Evans and the International Crisis Group, who prepared a full report for the UN General Assembly on this effort in 2004: *A More Secure World: Our Shared Responsibility*, Report of the Secretary-General's High-level Panel on Threats, Challenges, and Change (New York: United Nations, 2004).

[25] See, for example, Alex J. Bellamy, *A Responsibility to Protect* (Malden, Massachusetts: Polity Press, 2009); Jennifer M. Welsh (ed.), *Humanitarian Intervention and International Relations* (Oxford University Press, 2003); David Rodin, "The Responsibility to Protect and the Logic of Rights," in Oliver Jütersonke and Keith Krause (eds.), *From Rights to Responsibilities: Rethinking Interventions for Humanitarian Purposes*, PSIS Special Study 7 (Geneva: Programme for Strategic and International Security Studies, 2006); James Pattison, *Humanitarian Intervention and the Responsibility to Protect* (Oxford University Press, 2010); Michael Blake, "Reciprocity, Stability and Intervention: The Ethics of Disequilibrium," in Chatterjee and Scheid, *Ethics and Foreign Intervention*, 53–71; Brian Orend discusses AHI and RtoP at length as justifications for use of military force in his book *The Morality of War* (2006: 2nd edn. 2013).

The difficulty with this conception of an international political obligation of beneficence and protection, as the subsequent "Arab Spring" revolutions in Libya and Syria quickly illustrated, is its coherence and consistency. If there is (as Walzer, Coady, Shue, and others variously asserted during the second wave) some sort of "imperfect duty" of humanitarian military intervention, well beyond what Stanley Hoffman had championed in the early 1990s as a "right" of intervention, then such an imperfect duty would inherently defy any attempt to precisely define, legislate, or otherwise institutionalize it. Imperfect duties are so called because they attempt to describe the obligations of agents (including nations?) to act beneficently in the absence of precise designation either of the recipients of that beneficence, or of the actions owed them. Imperfect duties, by their very nature, do not qualify as what Immanuel Kant had carefully defined as "duties of justice";[26] that is, they cannot be formally institutionalized or legislated. Yet RtoP, as befitted its origins in the deliberations of diplomats, is "legislative" to the core. It seeks to define, legislate, and institutionalize precisely what Kant claimed inherently cannot be so formulated: a "duty" to do good, as well as to prevent or restrain evil. Nonetheless, a legal and procedural formulation of RtoP is exactly what diplomats and statesmen, like Australia's Garth Evans or Canada's Linda Ponds (who organized the initial "Committee of Eminent Persons" at the beginning of the second wave), aimed to achieve through formal or procedural authority under international law.

These different avenues of approach to the problem of armed humanitarian intervention reflect an underlying tension, finally, between the two sources of international law themselves: the publicist, intellectual tradition of philosophers and political theorists (dominant in the second wave), versus the procedural authority of diplomats and legislators (that is prominent and problematic in the third wave, in which the work of scholars and the earlier experience of military practitioners is largely subordinated).[27] The two sources of law do not always agree; and these two "waves" of AHI reflection themselves, in any case, yield somewhat divergent advice about who we can help, when we can help,

---

[26] This distinction is first made in Kant's *Groundwork of the Metaphysics of Morals* (1783), but elaborated far more precisely in his later work, *The Metaphysics of Morals* (1795), in which "perfect" duties become the material of legislation and justice (*Rechtslehre*), while "imperfect" duties are assigned to the realm of individual moral virtue (*Tugendlehre*). For a detailed account of these distinctions and their significance for ethics generally, see G.R. Lucas, Jr., "Moral Order and the Constraints of Agency: Toward a New Metaphysics of Morals," in Robert C. Neville (ed.) *New Essays in Metaphysics* (Albany, New York: State University of New York Press, 1987), 117–39. See also G.R. Lucas, Jr., "Agency After Virtue: A Defense of Kantian Constructivism," *International Philosophical Quarterly* 28, no. 3 (September, 1988), 293–311.

[27] I owe this distinction to the work of Anthony F. Lang, Jr. at St. Andrews University on the problem of authority and jurisdiction in international law. Anthony F. Lang, Jr., "International Authority: Theory and Practice in International Relations" (Fife: St. Andrews University, 2011), unpublished paper.

and most significantly how we collectively decide and act in the international political arena.

I have found all this a bit exasperating; and I have criticized the third-wave effort, not for its good intentions, but for its blindness, lack of attention to the immediate past, and studied unwillingness to listen and learn from the hard-won lessons of the second wave. There is, among those who work on this problem at present, no awareness or incorporation of an earlier generation of insights into both the concept of "conditional sovereignty" and, even more problematically, the conceptual ambiguities of a widely discerned "imperfect duty" of AHI. Paradoxically, sovereignty itself is still held by diplomats authoring various RtoP formulations as largely sacrosanct. There is little or no attempt to recognize or resolve the tension between the Westphalian paradigm, grounded in inviolable state sovereignty, and this alleged collective responsibility or duty of the international community that inherently threatens to override the primacy of national sovereignty. In making this critical blunder, we also find a kind of headstrong formal or procedural authority exerting its presumed jurisdictional supremacy to trump (and utterly ignore) the earlier findings of the publicist tradition, grounded in the intellectual authority of scholars and military practitioners, consideration of which would have resulted in a stronger, more consistent and enforceable policy.

As a result, RtoP, as finally formulated in the UN Security Council resolution of 2006, is profoundly flawed and deficient. On the one hand, RtoP is an explicit acknowledgment of the inherent weakness of the first attempt to "criminalize" genocide and ethnic cleansing in the "Genocide Convention" of 1948 (that merely commits states to assist in the interdiction of Holocaust perpetrators and to not provide them with asylum or diplomatic immunity), and represents a much-needed attempt to move beyond its limited scope. But, on the other hand, by failing to incorporate the findings and experience of practitioners in the 1990s and the earlier, second-wave analysis of the difficulties they encountered, RtoP has unnecessarily resulted in an incoherent and ultimately unworkable doctrine. It fails to provide for any substantive means of adjudicating between the claims of sovereignty and the claims of (in)justice. It seeks to impose RtoP, instead, as what Kant termed a "strict duty" (of justice), even though lacking a clear procedural specification of the obligor, or of the precise means and methods for fulfilling that obligation on the part of (undefined) obligees. These latter difficulties, however, are fundamental features of imperfect duties, which (as Kant had originally discerned) ultimately render them inappropriate and unsuited to law or regulation, since the requisite features of effective governance (precisely relations between obligor and obligee) are inherently absent.

Practically speaking, RtoP also suffers from political flaws. RtoP was the doctrine most recently invoked by the UN General Assembly as the justification for the UN-sanctioned NATO intervention in Libya. Indeed, this violent civil war might be said to have provided the first test case of the adequacy of the doctrine. Russian and Chinese support for the Security Council resolution authorizing the NATO air campaign was grudgingly obtained from those two reluctant members only in the interests of protecting victims caught in the crossfire and of preventing the contending forces in a de facto civil war from committing humanitarian atrocities with impunity. Theirs was not a vote in favor of partisanship in that civil war, let alone wholesale regime change. The demands of strict impartiality on the part of intervening forces, which formed the key restriction in second-wave formulations of the imperfect duty of AHI,[28] however, were quickly set aside in favor of partisan regime change, aimed at deposing an admittedly unjust tyrant. The results, however, as most recently illustrated by the murder of US Ambassador Chris Stevens in Benghazi (September 2012), were to empower in Gaddafi's place a cabal of Islamic extremists, consisting largely of Al Qaeda operatives returning from Afghanistan, as well as souring full Security Council support for intervention of any sort in the even more deadly civil war in Syria. This could hardly have been the objective of AHI, and must be reckoned among the serious failures of this first UN attempt to formulate international policy on the basis of RtoP.

III

The manner in which the history of armed humanitarian intervention is narrated is strongly dependent upon the perspectives from which AHI efforts themselves were experienced. The underlying philosophies of these three waves of AHI interpretation thus implicitly embody their proponents' visceral reactions to a variety of distinct events.

First-wave narratives, from Mill to Walzer, reflected the bitter lessons of nineteenth-century imperial *realpolitik* coupled with the moral devastation that was the twentieth century's Holocaust. The harsh lesson that both experiences taught is that, in the absence of cynical political interests on the part of prospective intervening forces, no others really care, let alone put themselves out to come to the aid of vulnerable victims of injustice. The ultimate failure of the US-led humanitarian intervention in Somalia in 1992, by contrast, demonstrated that nations might, after all, be willing to attempt to rescue such victims if their plight was sufficiently grave, and the immediate moral experience of it inescapable.

Coupled with memories of the earlier disastrous experiences of Vietnam (in retrospect, perhaps the first historical instance of a modern AHI), the "soldier's narrative" of these second-wave humanitarian exercises came to portray

---

[28] Absence of self-interests or partisanship sufficient to constitute a conflict of interest on the part of intervening forces in any AHI operation constitutes "right intention" on the part of those authorizing and conducting the intervention. See Lucas, "From *Jus ad Bellum* to *Jus ad Pacem*," 86–87.

AHI itself as a morally ambiguous, messy, and largely unsatisfactory enterprise. Lacking the moral and legal clarity of conventional war, humanitarian interventions (the preeminent example of what military doctrine at the time classified as "MOOTW" (military operations other than war)), should only to be undertaken with the greatest reluctance.[29] Indeed, military reflections on the failures of Vietnam in particular had, by the mid 1980s, resulted in a consensus among US policy-makers that military forces should not be half-heartedly or reluctantly deployed for morally ambiguous purposes. The so-called "Weinberger–Powell" doctrine[30] attempted to stipulate that military forces should only be deployed with the fully informed consent and unwavering support of the governed, and even then only on behalf of clearly defined national interests, and only with the commitment of substantial resources toward a clearly defined objective whose attainment would constitute grounds for successful termination of hostilities (and, presumably, a recall of deployed troops). All of the military interventions proposed or carried out for humanitarian purposes in the 1990s, however noble their intent, violated every single provision of that doctrine. This, in turn, regrettably seems to demonstrate that an essential property of AHI is that all such interventions fail to satisfy conventional just-war doctrine's requirement of a "reasonable probability of success."

RtoP, as we saw, is essentially a narrative of guilt on the part of dissident former-UN diplomats, frustrated by failures of UN Assistance Mission in Rwanda (UNAMIR), and also in Bosnia and Kosovo (where NATO forces were obliged to supplant the UNPROFOR's utterly failed efforts to restore order or keep peace).[31] The corrective that diplomats and statesmen in this third wave proposed as their remedy for these failures, however, is their formulation of

---

[29] Hence the title of my 1997 presentation for a seminar on the future of warfare, sponsored by the Carnegie Council for Ethics in International Affairs, "The Reluctant Interventionist." See Lucas, *Perspectives on Humanitarian Military Intervention*, chap. 1.

[30] So named after US Secretary of Defense, Casper Weinberger, who outlined these principles in a major policy speech for the National Press Club during the Reagan administration; the text was published the same day in the *New York Times* (November 29, 1984), A5.

Because the doctrine was frequently cited by General Colin Powell, Chairman of the Joint Chiefs of Staff, during the run-up to the first Gulf War in 1991, journalists began to refer to this position, demanding both clarity of purpose and the use of military force only as a last resort, as the "Weinberger–Powell" doctrine.

[31] The United Nations Protective Force in Bosnia (UNPROFOR-Bosnia). Paolo Tripodi's moving and thoroughly documented case study of the UN Dutch battalion (UN DUTCHBAT) and the massacre at Srebrenica illustrates that those failures, as was also the case with Belgian Army forces under UN command in Rwanda, stemmed less from cowardice and dereliction of duty (as was charged at the time) than from persistent bureaucratic and leadership failures throughout the poorly organized and politically cumbersome and ineffective UN chain of command. Tripodi's case is included in Lucas and Rubel, *Case Studies in Military Ethics*.

a morally and legally binding "duty of intervention," obligating (unspecified) members of the international community collectively to come to the aid of vulnerable victims of intrastate violence. Scholars during the second wave, to be sure, had sought to discern a more orderly procedure for deliberation and action in the midst of humanitarian emergencies;[32] but RtoP went well beyond those nascent efforts at reformulating just-war doctrine to guide such decisions. In attempting to craft legislation that would unambiguously define this responsibility to protect and commit the members of the international community to it, the RtoP movement attempted to do what Kant originally had demonstrated could not be done: to stipulate a moral obligation in the form of law in the absence of clearly defined obligees, obligors, or even the precise nature of the obligation itself.[33]

If the first-wave narratives might be characterized as bitter acceptance of the overwhelming propensity to "turn the other way" in the face of injustice, second-wave AHI efforts, and the narrative of scholars interpreting them, embody the well-intentioned moral reaction to that propensity: "Never again!" As with individuals, so with the community of nations: Intuitively, there just does seem to be some kind of duty to help the vulnerable victims of cruel injustice or unspeakable acts of violence, national self-interest notwithstanding. But what kind of duty is this? Second-wave narratives glumly acknowledge, for their part, that, in spite of our sympathetic concern, we do not know precisely whom we must help, what exactly we must do, nor even how it comes to be "we" (rather than others more connected to the victims or more advantageously positioned to help) who are obligated to do it.

The third-wave concern for AHI likewise represents a determination "never again" to abandon those in need of rescue from violent harm, coupled with a resolve to repair the inadequacies of existing international institutions and arrangements in order to operationalize that moral determination more effectively. The exercise of the "formal authority" of diplomats and political leaders, however, invariably takes the form of law-like, "black letter," or "bright-line" statutory arrangements. After all, this is primarily what diplomats, statesmen, and political leaders do: They proclaim, they proscribe, and they legislate. By proceeding to do so in this instance, however, the RtoP movement unwittingly ignored the most important insight of the second wave that – in a manner

---

[32] These new guidelines, reflecting proposals made by most of the principal participants in the second-wave discussions, were collectively referred to at the time as *jus ad pacem*, intended as both an analogue to, and a replacement for, conventional just-war doctrine in these novel circumstances. See Lucas, "From *Jus ad Bellum* to *Jus ad Pacem*."

[33] Kant's having said this was so does not make it so, of course. Mine is not simply an argument from authority. It is, rather, a recognition that these substantive deficiencies (namely, of precisely defined obligee, obligor, and substantive obligations) certainly do constitute formidable, if not irresolvable, obstacles to any legislative attempt to "operationalize" the perceived (imperfect) duty of intervention.

similar to the difficulties experienced with "Good Samaritan" legislation within a domestic legal framework – this noble objective can prove extremely difficult, if not impossible, to achieve.

The second wave of AHI did have one positive outcome. The behavior of nations, however imperfect in execution, decisively refuted the claim of *realpolitik*, that those same nations would *never* undertake an intervention in which national interests were not somehow involved. Indeed, even in failure, as in Rwanda, the concerns and the moral outrage expressed suggested that, in some sense, the notion of "national self-interest" had itself evolved to recognize, perhaps more explicitly than ever before, that the ultimate guarantor of substantive, practical interests of individuals (or of nations) lies in assurance of the well-being and security of all. In some instances, such as Somalia, no other interests on the part of intervening nations could be, or ever have been, successfully identified. In other cases, such as the US humanitarian intervention in Haiti in 1994, even though underlying national interests (such as control over refugees and unauthorized immigration) were at stake, these interests seemed either subordinate to, or inextricably bound up with, genuine humanitarian anguish.

To be sure, the tragic failures in Rwanda in 1993, and the European and United Nations' reluctance and bungling in Bosnia, are often cited by advocates of *realpolitik* to disparage this hopeful assessment. I regard that as a mistaken inference, however; it was less the absence of clearly defined national self-interests on the part of prospective intervening nations that led to these well-publicized failures than it was the absence of a clearly defined procedure for assigning specific nations the responsibility for deploying adequately resourced and sufficiently well-led military forces to enable the intervention to succeed. And it was precisely this deficiency that, to its credit, the International Commission on Intervention and State Sovereignty originally sought to address. That the resulting RtoP movement seems finally (in my estimation) to fall short in this well-intended effort is due less to the need to address serious legislative lacunae in the current nation-state system, than to the need to acknowledge the insight from the second wave, that imperfect duties of beneficence are not easily amenable to legislative remedies.

IV

If our understanding of AHI is affected by our unconscious narrative stance, it is influenced just as much or more by the conscious choice of metaphors and analogies we use to describe it. In this, it shares a problem with other non-conventional uses of military force, as in pre-emptive or preventive self-defense. The choice of metaphor, and the drawing of close, accurate analogies, are crucial to the proper analysis of these various forms of conflict that differ substantially from conventional warfare. But there are no canons or principles (other, perhaps, than relative plausibility and verisimilitude) that we can systematically apply to these choices.

In AHI, the metaphors of choice were and are most frequently "Good Samaritan" scenarios, in which individuals in dire need or distress (drowning children, starving homeless persons, victims of rape or robbery under vicious assault, or victims dying by the roadside) are brought forcefully to our attention, prompting a felt need to render aid as the only morally decent response. We morally condemn those who do not recognize this obligation, and commend as virtuous those who attempt to respond in a credible and competent fashion.

Such metaphors seem to capture accurately the moral dilemma members of the international community find themselves in following an immense natural disaster, like the 2006 Indonesian tsunami. Although these metaphors capture the "bystander's dilemma" of what to do or when to intervene in providing assistance, I would argue that they fail to capture the complexity of the most pressing cases of massive killing associated with genocide. These, instead, are more akin to domestic analogies involving one's immediate neighbors, who might be suffering spousal or child abuse, and include within their purview the appropriate response of domestic police to reports of the abuse.

Knowledge of what is occurring prompts discomfort on the part of concerned neighbors and generates a felt need, either on their part or on the part of law-enforcement officials whom they might summon, to override the sovereignty of home and family in the interests of justice. But what does this mean, or how precisely is that domestic intervention effectively carried out, either by neighbors or by the police? Intervention by either may serve to halt the injustice temporarily; but, in the absence of sustained and substantial structural intervention in the family, the unjust treatment will resume as soon as the police or the neighbors leave. The neighbors, for their part, ideally should avoid "taking sides," or becoming a partisan in the quarrel, lest the effectiveness or sincerity of their concern become suspect by either of the parties in the conflict. Furthermore, neighbors or police involved in the intervention will quickly recognize that, unless they remain involved over the longer term to help address the underlying structural problems or other fundamental defects in the family relationship, their intervention will have no long-term effect. Yet what capabilities do they possess, or from whence do they derive either the right or the requisite expertise to restructure the neighbor's family in order to prevent future violence?

These problems in the domestic case are well-known, widely recognized, and invariably prove all but intractable. Caring persons or their community authorities cannot, on the one hand, leave the vulnerable spouse or child to be beaten or killed, but neither can they infallibly determine, let alone supervise, the requisite jurisdictional and structural issues necessary to address the underlying problems of the family. They are obliged, rather, to do the best they can under the circumstances. Repeated instances of such social problems, especially on the part of domestic police forces, can prove devastating to morale, as they try their best to assist, frequently fail, and are often impeded in their desire to do even more.

AHI, with all its attendant complexities and difficulties, is this problem writ large. RtoP does little, in itself, other than to clarify the nature of the burden already imperfectly felt in this regard. It does nothing; nor did its formulators begin to possess the relevant experience and expertise to formulate substantive procedures to address such deep-seated structural questions. Plato famously observed in the *Republic* that the state is "man, writ large." Hegel went further in drawing a more apt social analogy, namely, that the state is, in essence, the family writ large. What this romantically idealized notion failed to encompass, however, is that a great many families are deeply dysfunctional. The enduring moral challenge of AHI arises precisely from this stubborn and recalcitrant fact of international relations: Just as with actual, biological families, a disturbingly large number of these metaphorical "state families" are likewise dysfunctional.

As with the demoralizing impact of these intractable domestic disputes on the police who intervene, we might likewise wonder about the impact of humanitarian missions upon those military personnel whom we ask to undertake them. The foregoing domestic metaphor of the dysfunctional and abusive family finally puts us in a position to assess what likewise frequently turns out to be the indelible, tragic, and destructive impact of AHI missions on military personnel and on their sense of professional purpose.

Imagine, in the domestic case above that, besides the difficulty with devising and imposing structural remedies for the long-term problem of domestic violence, we added the proviso that, when summoned, the domestic authorities are, in addition, forbidden to act. That is, having been called, the police are forced to stand by silently while the abuse continues, hoping that their mere presence will help to deter the violence, but absolutely forbidden by their own supervising authorities to physically intervene, or to use the force at their command, to protect the victims or restrain the perpetrators. Domestic police, at least, have the right to forcibly halt the immediate violence until everyone involved "calms down." Summoning them in the first place would make little sense if they did not. One might well imagine the profoundly destructive psychological effects such frustrating impediments would have on their own morale and professional demeanor, were they to be constrained in such a ridiculous fashion. Their work in domestic-abuse cases is difficult and demoralizing enough as it is.

Military personnel, deployed in the midst of a humanitarian intervention, however, are routinely obliged to operate under such constraints (known in the military as "rules of engagement" or ROE). In the standard variation of ROE for armed humanitarian intervention, not only are the intervening military forces obliged to witness and despair at the grinding poverty and cruelly violent conditions under which a large share of the world's population is forced to exist, but, under a paradoxical application of the twin doctrines of strict neutrality and "force protection," they are often prohibited from doing anything substantial to address these conditions. In conventional warfare, the doctrine of "force protection" simply obligates commanding officers to avoid subjecting those under their command to excessive or pointless risk of harm in the pursuit of reasonable military objectives. In AHI, however, in the absence of both compelling national-security interests and conventional military objectives against which to balance such concerns, reasonable risk aversion is transformed into wholesale casualty aversion or "radical" force protection, in which command authorities warn their troops, in effect, that "none of these victims is worth the loss of a single one of your lives." In Kosovo, for example, radical force protection in the name of casualty aversion frequently led to the much-criticized tactic of high-altitude bombing, which paradoxically led to the infliction of disproportionately high casualties in the civilian population – hardly the goal of the intervention.[34] In Haiti, returning US troops despaired over their inability to come to the aid of political prisoners or victims of political violence during the episodic street violence between rival factions. Their own disparaging metaphor for the perverse rules of engagement under which they were deployed was "a self-licking ice cream cone." Perhaps no frustration at such restrictions was more palpable, profound, or personally and professionally damaging, however, than that described by General Dallaire in Rwanda.

The doctrine of force protection in AHI can thus lead either to a perverse offloading of risk of harm to the civilian population or to preventing professional military personnel from doing what they otherwise see clearly as their job, namely, to assist. The imposition of casualty aversion by senior leadership on many such missions during the 1990s was roundly denounced by the rank and file, led by US Army Colonel Don Snider of West Point, as a profound threat to, and erosion of, what he first termed "the professional military ethic."[35] Compelling armed and well-trained military personnel to "stand around and watch" the violence and criminality unfold around them (as in Rwanda) has an even greater destructive impact on that sense of professionalism. Yet that is what we frequently do in such missions, out of concern for the welfare of those we send to conduct them. Little thought has been given to addressing this problem, and no provisions of any sort are made for the impact of such perverse policies on military personnel in the RtoP legislation. This remains one

[34] See Martin L. Cook, "Immaculate War: Constraints on Humanitarian Intervention," *Ethics & International Affairs* 14 (2000), 55–65. Michael Ignatieff criticizes high-altitude bombing in particular as a violation of the "warrior's ethic" in Michael Ignatieff, *Virtual War: Kosovo and Beyond* (New York: Metropolitan Books, 2000).

[35] See Don M. Snider, John A. Nagl, and Tony Pfaff, *Army Professionalism, Military Ethics, and Officership in the 21st Century* (Carlisle, Pennsylvania: Army War College Strategic Studies Institute, 1999).

of the most serious challenges impeding successful AHI, and it is extremely unfortunate that it is a topic about which that much-touted legislative remedy is entirely silent.

Military practitioners often used to claim that "our job is to kill people and break things when ordered to do so, until someone else *orders us* to stop." In the recent era of AHI, by contrast, there is no shortage of enemies of civilization already fully engaged in killing people and breaking things. What has evolved as the principle mission of professional military personnel, by contrast, is to interpose themselves between such people and their intended victims, and *order them* to stop. We citizens who impose such missions on our militaries, accordingly, must do a much better, more coherent job in the future than we have in the immediate past to fully understand and support their efforts and to recognize the profound impact such missions can have upon their morale and professional comportment.

3

The responsibility to protect and the war in Libya

TZVETAN TODOROV,
TRANSLATED BY KATHLEEN A. JOHNSON

A new chapter in the history of international relations was inaugurated in 1999 when NATO military forces intervened in Yugoslavia to defend ethnic Albanians in the province of Kosovo, over the objections of Yugoslavia. It is no coincidence that the intervention occurred after the end of the Cold War; the Soviet Union no longer existed, and Russia was not ready for a confrontation. The Western nations that initiated the intervention had not obtained a formal decision from any international organization, like the United Nations – which, in any event, does not have its own military branch.[1] This intervention was founded on a doctrine formulated a few years earlier. At the outset (1988), this was a simple demand to be able to provide humanitarian assistance to populations in distress; but it was progressively transformed (1991) into a proclamation of the right to intervene militarily in a country in crisis. The revelation of the Rwandan genocide (1994) seemed to argue in its favor, and since that time people have spoken of a "right of intervention." Subscribing to this doctrine amounts to claiming that if human-rights violations occur in a country, then other countries around the world have the right to intervene through force to protect the victims and to prevent the aggressors from acting.

In Yugoslavia, the application of these principles revealed a number of problems inherent in the doctrine. Some concern doubts about information: Each of the two opposing forces has an interest in inflating the number of its victims and in concealing its own attacks (the manipulation of data is a shared temptation). In this regard, the Albanian minority was more effective than the Serbian majority; they succeeded in convincing American diplomats and NATO that they were the main victims of the violence (it is also possible that the choice was

---

[1] There was general consensus in the UN Security Council that forces of the Federal Republic of Yugoslavia (FRY) were primarily responsible for an imminent humanitarian catastrophe in Kosovo (i.e., ethnic cleansing), and that this posed a threat to international peace and security. But there was no consensus on the use of force. The Security Council never authorized the use of force; Russian and Chinese positions made it clear that they would veto any attempt at such authorization. See: Independent International Commission on Kosovo, *Kosovo Report* (Oxford University Press, 2000), pp. 141–142.

made even before the manipulation of information began).[2] A second problem stems from the necessarily selective application of the principle. Human-rights violations are, unfortunately, quite numerous, and intervening everywhere is impossible; so one tends to spare political friends and to unleash forces against those who are pursuing a policy contrary to one's own interests.[3] As a result, the impartiality of the choice is jeopardized. A third problem arises from the very form of the interference, namely, a war with its inevitable consequences: bombings, destruction of the country and its inhabitants, countless sorrows.

To these particular problems we can add a general consideration to which countries that were formerly colonized or subjugated by Western powers were sensitive: The new situation was a bit too reminiscent of the old world before decolonization in which the Big decided the fate of the Small. At the beginning of the twenty-first century, the concept of a "right of intervention" was discredited and rejected by the majority of the countries in the world.

The latest of the Western interventions intended to bring Good to the other countries of the world was the war in Libya, launched in March 2011 and brought to a victorious end in August of the same year. Many commentators from the countries involved in this operation claimed that, unlike the Iraq and Afghanistan campaigns that had occurred before, the campaign in Libya was a formidable success: The goal was achieved, the dictator was overthrown, the allied forces did not suffer any damage and withdrew at the end of the intervention. This was, in short, an operation that could serve as a model for the future. For this reason, it deserves close examination.

One obvious difference between this war and those that preceded it was that this time there was a UN Security Council resolution authorizing the

---

[2] The "epistemic problem" (knowing exactly what is happening) is especially severe in the context of vast social conflicts. Every political leader and military commander faces the epistemic problem in the fog of war. During the Kosovo conflict, reports by the Kosovo Liberation Army (KLA) and the Federal Republic of Yugoslavia (FRY) varied widely in their assessments of both KLA and FRY combat deaths. Reports on various aspects of the conflict by purportedly neutral NGOs also varied. Throughout 1998, Secretary-General Kofi Annan's monthly reports to the UN Security Council included the disclaimer that since the UN had no active presence in the region, he was entirely dependent on second-hand information. *Ibid.*, 90–91, 141; see especially "The Role of the Media," 215–224. See also Stig A. Nohrstedt, Sophia Kaitatzi-Whitlock, Rune Ottosen, and Kristina Riegert, "From the Persian Gulf to Kosovo – War Journalism and Propaganda," *European Journal of Communication*, 15, 3(2000), 383–404.

[3] This selectivity objection to a doctrine of armed humanitarian intervention has been expressed many times by many commentators. The objection is especially pressing in the context of UN Security Council resolutions, as discussed herein. See for example: J. L. Holzgrefe, "The Humanitarian Intervention Debate" in J. L. Holzgrefe and Robert O. Keohane (eds.), *Humanitarian Intervention: Ethical, Legal, and Political Dilemmas* (Cambridge Univeristy Press), 46–47. For a discussion addressing this problem, see Chris Brown, "Selective Humanitarianism: in Defense of Inconsistency," in Deen K. Chatterjee and Don E. Scheid (eds.), *Ethics and Foreign Intervention* (Cambridge University Press, 2003), 31–50.

intervention, whereas there was no such resolution in preceding cases.[4] Furthermore, this resolution was justified by a new principle, summarized by the expression "responsibility to protect." Nevertheless, despite appearances, and also despite the solemn invocations of noble principles like freedom, democracy, human rights, and respect for people, the situation was not all that different. As a starting point, let us examine these two innovations.

"Responsibility to protect" (RtoP) is a recently coined phrase and doctrine.[5] Since the expression "right of intervention" does not inspire trust in the rest of the world, a substitute had to be found for it. "Responsibility to protect" seemed to be a more prudent expression, and the principle was adopted by a vote of the UN General Assembly in 2005.[6] The underlying idea is that if a government lacks the ability or the will to protect its civil population, the United Nations has the right to intervene in the country without seeking that government's permission. Since Colonel Gaddafi had ordered the bloody repression of Libyan citizens who were demanding his departure, the principle of protection appeared to be applicable.

It is entirely possible that the initial designers of the doctrine, Responsibility to Protect, were driven by pure and generous intentions.[7] However, as we know, good intentions do not suffice to guarantee a good policy. To begin, the meaning of the expression itself is not clear. Are we to understand it in the minimal sense as the introduction of humanitarian aid? Or should we accept that it means this aid may also be protected by military force? Or should we understand it to imply the destruction of the armed forces that are threatening the civilian population? Or should we adopt a maximalist interpretation, the overthrow of the government responsible for the crisis and its replacement with another government deemed preferable by the interveners? Depending on the response given to these questions, we obviously end up with very different situations. In principle, the military option is presented as a last resort, once all the opportunities for reaching a peaceful solution to the conflict have been exhausted. But there are no clear criteria for distinguishing these different interpretations, which opens the way for all kinds of manipulation. And as soon as this "protection" no longer merely involves simple

---

[4] UN Security Council Resolution 1973, UN document S/Res/1973 (adopted March 17, 2011).

[5] Under the auspices of the Canadian government, the ad hoc International Commission on Intervention and State Sovereignty (ICISS) produced a report in 2001 entitled *The Responsibility to Protect* outlining principles that constitute the doctrine. See Garth Evans and Mohamed Sahnoun (co-chairs), *The Responsibility to Protect*, Report of the International Commission on Intervention and State Sovereignty (Ottawa: International Development Research Centre, December 2001); available at http://responsibilitytoprotect.org/ICISS%20 Report.pdf.

[6] UN document A/60/L.1 (September 20, 2005), General Assembly adoption of the *2005 World Summit Outcome Document*.

[7] Garth Evans, former Foreign Minister of Australia, and Mohamed Sahnoun, a former senior Algerian diplomat, founded the commission that produced the report, *The Responsibility to Protect*.

humanitarian assistance but the military intervention of another state, it is difficult to see how it differs from the "right of intervention" brandished previously.

Whether a doctrine of armed humanitarian intervention (AHI) should become a permanent feature of international law is greatly to be doubted so long as its interpretation and application is entrusted to the UN Security Council whose permanent members (United States, Russia, China, Great Britain, France) have a right of veto. This unconscionable privilege can be explained by the context in which the UN regulations were set up; the five countries in question were the victors of the Second World War. Sixty-five years later, does this justification still make sense? It seems unlikely. If the Security Council wants to serve as a global government, at least sporadically, it must increase its legitimacy. Therefore, it must recruit additional countries as permanent members chosen either because they are among the most populated in the world or because they would represent continents that are presently absent. Today, there is no justification for the exclusion of a country like India, Brazil, or South Africa. Yet, for now, the permanent members are not willing to give up their privileges.

The right of veto, reserved for five countries that can thus elude the common rule, is the original sin of the Security Council and of the international order it is supposed to guarantee. Having this right, the permanent members of the Council are placed from the outset above the law that they are supposed to implement: neither they nor the countries they choose to protect can be condemned! The justice in question is therefore highly selective. This explains why, despite the established suffering of the civilian populations, certain interventions will never take place. This is obvious when we think about Russia with its Chechens, China with its Tibetans, but also of other countries that carry too much weight on the international scene to consider a violent intervention that would make it possible to arrest even one of their dignitaries – countries like India, Pakistan, Saudi Arabia, or Israel. Worse still, the permanent members can decide to intervene wherever they wish *without* the authorization of the United Nations, as the United States and its allies did in Kosovo and Iraq. No sanctions were imposed on them on these occasions. The same exception applies to the countries that permanent members have chosen to protect. At the very same time that they decided to intervene in Libya, members of the Council were encouraging very different types of interference by Saudi Arabia in the neighboring countries where they intended to defend the established governments against the rebellious crowds.[8] The international order embodied by the Security Council sanctions the rule of force, not of law.

---

[8] Saudi Arabia extended refuge to President Ben Ali when the Jasmine Revolution forced him out of Tunisia. It also initially supported Mubarak in Egypt and Al Saleh in Yemen by providing financial backing; and Saudi Arabia provided billions of dollars in grants to Oman and Bahrain in an effort to support those authoritarian governments. Saudi troops and tanks entered Bahrain to assist the authorities there in putting down the mass, pro-democracy uprising. "Saudi Arabia Accused of Repression after Arab Spring," *BBC News* (December 1,

It is sometimes said, as a matter of pride, that this new world order puts an end to the sacrosanct Westphalian notion of state sovereignty – the principle that "a man's home is his castle," or in other words, that each government does what it wants at home, and it alone decides what is right or wrong. Certainly imperfect, this order is now replaced by an even older principle, that is, the principle that "might makes right" and that the powerful of this world may impose their will on the weaker. Now, it is "one man's castle is everywhere"! And in practice, this "man" is the United States and its allies.

It is not certain that the member states of the United Nations took into consideration the possible consequences of their unanimous 2005 vote. The charter of this organization, adopted when it was founded just after the Second World War, sought to prevent wars from beginning again, and for this reason declared the sovereignty of states inviolable; the Big could no longer invade the Small with impunity. It is this founding principle that was weakened by the 2005 decision. Subjecting the principle of state sovereignty to the principle of universal governance is an act that by itself establishes inequality, since the world is now divided into two groups of states: those that can do what they want at home and elsewhere (the permanent members of the Security Council who have the right of veto, as well those they protect) and those who, like the feeble-minded or the young, are placed under the supervision of the former and will be punished for any infringement of the rules.

The previous principle implied, not the imposition of the same good on all, but the acceptance of the plurality of ideals of the good and state sovereignty. This is the only principle compatible with the idea of democracy, that is, the right of each people to choose their own path, provided that they do not harm others. He who proclaims that a higher body, external to the people in question, will decide their fate is more akin to those eighteenth century regimes that were characterized as "enlightened despotism," when a strong central power, embodied by the king or the emperor (Frederick the Great in Prussia, Catherine the Great in Russia, Joseph II in Austria), imposed on the people what he or she believed was most suitable for them without bothering to consult them. Another memory also comes to mind: When today we see newspaper headlines like "The fate of Libya is being decided between London and Paris," we might think that we have gone back in time one-hundred or one-hundred-and-fifty years, when Great Britain and France, the major colonial powers, effectively ruled over parts of Africa and Asia and chose the governors of the countries subject to their oversight.

2011). John R. Bradley, "Saudi Arabia's Invisible Hand in the Arab Spring: How the Kingdom is Wielding Influence Across the Middle East," *Foreign Affairs* (October 13, 2011), available at: www.foreignaffairs.com/articles/136473/john-r-bradley/saudi-arabias-invisible-hand-in-the-arab-spring.

Now let us turn to the actual conduct of this war, which is supposed to illustrate the doctrine of Responsibility to Protect. The objective initially invoked was to loosen the stranglehold by Gaddafi's army that threatened to cause a bloodbath in the city of Benghazi. Was this a real danger or inflamed rhetoric? Without any tangible proof, the first interpretation was adopted by the insurgents, by the influential Qatari television channel, Al Jazeera (at the forefront in the fight against the non-Islamist Arab autocracies), and by the Western powers. Instead, the evidence tends to lean in the opposite direction.[9] Nevertheless, even supposing that the threat was real, the initial objective of preventing the massacre (which could be deemed a legitimate goal in itself), was achieved early on.

It was quickly necessary to face facts: The real objective of the foreign states engaged in the war was not simply to protect the civilian population, even if this protection had to be understood in an extremely broad sense. The goal of the operation was to oust the head of state and replace him with another, who would be more docile and who looked more kindly on the West. The first resolution of the Security Council (Resolution 1970) was adopted on February 26. The second (Resolution 1973), adopted on March 17, authorized the intervention of March 19. Yet, on February 24, the French Defense Minister, Alain Juppé, stated that Gaddafi must leave power. The next day, the French President confirmed this choice.[10] A bit later, the new Defense Minister, Gérard Longuet, explained the need to unify the two objectives, which stemmed from his maximalist interpretation of the new doctrine, saying, "The protection of the populations involves striking the entire chain of command." It is true that the resolution contained a phrase supporting this reading; it authorized "the protection of civilians by all necessary means," including deposing the head of state and replacing the regime.

Faced with a nascent conflict, we can seek to protect the civilian populations via one of two opposite paths: that of peace or that of war. In concrete terms, in the first case, we seek to impose a ceasefire as quickly as possible so that negotiations between the two parties can begin. Later, if necessary, a neutral international force (the UN "blue helmets") can intervene between them. According to the second option, only a complete victory, the outcome of an uncompromising war, can provide true protection. In this case, Gaddafi and the majority of the countries of the globe attempted to follow the path of peace. The day after the Security Council resolution, on March 18, the Libyan head of state proposed entering into negotiations. This proposal was rejected

---

[9] See in particular the well-documented analysis of Hugh Roberts with the International Crisis Group, "Who Said Gaddafi Had to Go?" *London Review of Books* 33, no. 22 (November 17, 2011), 8–18.

[10] French President Nicolas Sarkozy became the first head of state to call for Gaddafi's departure. Alaa Shahine, Zainab Fattah, and Benjamin Harvey, "Gaddafi Rallies Supporters in Libya as Sarkozy Calls for Ouster," *The Washington Post* (February 25, 2011).

with contempt, as were the Libyan government's subsequent attempts along these lines.

Approximately one month later, on April 14, ceasefire requests were issued by the Arab League, the African Union, the Islamic Conference, and even by the representative of the European Union, Catherine Ashton.[11] At the same time, the so-called BRICS countries (Brazil, Russia, India, China, South Africa) pleaded for the same solution and filed an official protest: The purpose of the UN resolution had been altered, and the parties involved were no longer content with an intervention of a humanitarian nature.[12] But these attempts collided with the firm resolution of the Western countries to wage war until they had achieved complete victory. For them, the goal of the intervention had never truly been to impose a ceasefire, since the demands in this regard remained unilateral; the loyalists were asked to suspend their attacks, but the insurgents were not asked to lay down their weapons. Besides, the insurgents were hostile to the idea of a ceasefire from the beginning.[13] They preferred continuous combat until NATO had destroyed or driven out their adversary! We may wonder whether this explains why the focus of the NATO bombings quickly shifted from around the cities besieged by the loyalists to the capital, Tripoli.[14] Officially, the elimination of Gaddafi was not one of the objectives; but the alliance assiduously bombed all the locations where he might be found (command, control and communication centers). If he were killed, it would not have been intentional! It is far from clear that such a political choice is a good illustration of the spirit in which the resolution was drafted in line with the Responsibility to Protect.

Even assuming (what is far from obvious) that at the beginning, there was a crowd demonstrating peacefully under threat of repression by the regime's forces, it was soon necessary to recognize that the situation had escalated into a civil war between Gaddafi loyalists and rebels, each side supported by the

---

[11] The United Nations signed an agreement with Libya for a "humanitarian presence" in that country. The planning took place in the office of Catherine Ashton, the EU's foreign and security policy chief. Ed Pilkington, Ian Black, and Ian Traynor, "Libya: UN Will Only Request Military Support for Aid Mission 'As Last Resort,'" *The Guardian* (April 18, 2011).

[12] Edward Cody, "Arab League Condemns Broad Bombing Campaign in Libya," *The Washington Post* (March 21, 2011). John Chan, "China and Russia Criticise Libyan Bombing Campaign," *World Socialist Web Site* (March 26, 2011); available at: www.wsws.org/en/articles/2011/03/chru-m25.html. Global Research, "Russia Says NATO Strikes Violate UN Resolution" (May 14, 2011), available at: www.globalresearch.ca/russia-says-nato-strikes-violate-un-resolution/24762.

[13] According to South African President Jacob Zuma, Gaddafi had endorsed an African Union's plan on or about April 12. The proposal included a ceasefire, the establishment of safe corridors for delivery of humanitarian aid, and a dialogue on reforming Libya's political system. But Mustafa Abdul Jalil, head of the opposition's Transitional National Council, summarily dismissed the proposal, saying, "We will not Negotiate on the Blood of our Martyrs. We Will Die with Them or be Victorious." Ned Parker and Borzou Daragahi, "Libyan Rebels Reject Cease-fire Plan," *Los Angeles Times* (April 11, 2011).

[14] Ian Black, Chris McGreal, and Barry Neild, "Gaddafi Compound Hit by Coalition Air Strikes on Tripoli," *The Guardian* (March 21, 2011).

various tribes that make up the country. NATO therefore served one of the parties in this civil war. Going beyond the UN resolution that imposed an embargo on supplying arms to the two belligerents, the countries of the West and Qatar equipped the insurgents militarily and prevented any acquisition of arms by the loyalists.[15] From this perspective, the situation resembled that of Kosovo in 1999 when NATO conducted the war against Serbian rule on behalf of the Kosovo Liberation Army, the Albanian insurgent group.

The ambiguity in the objective of the NATO intervention provoked numerous questions and much resistance, which increased as the end of the war approached.[16] The intervention met with the immediate disapproval by the countries of the African Union.[17] It was also gradually disapproved of by the BRICS countries, which had abstained during the Security Council vote (and which by themselves represent half the world's population).[18] They thought that the NATO campaign went well beyond what the adopted UN resolution authorized. "Instead of protecting the populations," Jacob Zuma, the South African president stated, the intervention "allowed the group of rebels to advance."[19] Even in Europe, the intervention did not receive majority support. Only Italy, Denmark, Norway, and Belgium joined the countries leading the intervention, Great Britain and France, while other countries like Germany, Poland, and Turkey expressed their disagreement.

The West had chosen to call Gaddafi's partisans "mercenaries" or "submissive populations" and his adversaries "people," and it opted for his adversaries. The Western powers sided with Gaddafi's adversaries and favored them with qualifiers like "democratic," which were hardly justified. Based on what we know today, the forces hostile to Gaddafi were extremely heterogeneous. They included the defenders of democratic ideas, but also Islamists and Al Qaeda

---

[15] "Russia Slams France's 'Crude Violation' of Libya Arms Embargo," *France 24* (June 30, 2011). Lavrov, "European, Arab Countries Violated Libya Arms Embargo" *RIA Novosti* (September 27, 2011).

[16] For scathing objections to the NATO intervention, see for example Dennis Kucinich, "Time to End Nato's War in Libya: Whether Gaddafi goes or not, this costly intervention has thwarted peace talks and betrayed its 'humanitarian' mission," *The Guardian* (August 21, 2011). Seumas Milne, "If the Lyban War was About Saving Lives, It Was a Catastrophic Failure," *The Guardian* (October 26, 2011). For one account of civilian deaths caused by NATO bombing, see C. J. Chivers and Eric Schmitt, "In Strikes on Libya by NATO, an Unspoken Civilian Toll," *New York Times* (December 17, 2001).

[17] "African Union Demands End to Military Strikes on Libya, Skips Paris Meeting," *Sudan Tribune* (March 19, 2011).

[18] Michael Cecire, "BRICs Fall Flat on UNSC Libya Vote," *World Politics Review* (March 28, 2011).

[19] "S. Africa 'Not Happy' on Libya, Boycotts Paris Meet: Zuma," *AFP* (September 1, 2011), available at: http://beta.dawn.com/news/655955/s-africa-not-happy-on-libya-boycotts-paris-meet-zuma?view=print. See also Emsie Ferreira, "Zuma Warns Against Military Intervention in Libya," *Mail and Guardian* (March 21, 2011); "Jacob Zuma Criticises Military Action in Libya," *BBC News* (July 18, 2011).

combatants, former dignitaries of Gaddafi's regime, and Libyans who had emigrated to the West and had established strong ties with political or business circles. To give a few examples, Mustafa Abdul Jalil, the Chairman of the NTC, headed the Tripoli court of appeals for years; and he twice upheld the death sentences of the Bulgarian nurses accused of spreading AIDS in Libya. As a reward for his good services, Gaddafi named him Justice Minister, a position he held until his defection in February 2011.[20] During the uprising, the rebel armed forces were commanded for a time by General Abdel Fatah Younis, a man who had fought alongside Gaddafi from 1969 to 2011. He also had been Gaddafi's Interior Minister and head of the special troops responsible for decades of repression. He was killed under unexplained circumstances at the end of July 2011 – probably by former Islamists, because he had been in charge of their persecution.[21] The new military governor of Tripoli, Abdelhakim Belhadj, was a former Al Qaeda member and Afghanistan combatant and was arrested and tortured by the CIA before being turned over to the Libyan jailers.[22] Was not all the talk of "democracy" by Westerners a bit out of place in the context of Libya, a country that had never experienced elections, and that did not have any political parties or any equivalent of a so-called "civil society"?

Noting that the "democratic" argument does not suffice to explain the Westerners' choice of one of the belligerents to the detriment of the other, we might wonder if it would not be closer to the truth to see the initial rebellion as a coup whose leaders offered the West a deal: If the NATO forces would help them get rid of Gaddafi so they could seize power, in exchange, they would reserve for their benefactors free access to the country's natural oil and gas reserves. This strategy is all the more likely, since having a faithful ally in Tripoli could prove very useful at a time of political upheaval in the neighboring Arab countries where leaders may come to power who are less favorably disposed toward the West than the autocrats who are overthrown. The future will show us whether this suspicion is justified or not. If it is, we can say that the humanitarian cause (preventing a bloodbath) was a kind of Trojan horse, a good pretext for intervening militarily and controlling the political orientation of a state with rich energy reserves. Interventions of this type present themselves as a means of putting brute military force in the service of a noble humanitarian ideal. But the reality is altogether different: The ideal is exploited by those who hold the force. The fools are the ones who believed they were fooling the others.

---

[20] Igor Kossov, "Libya's New Rebel Leader," *The Daily Beast* (August 29, 2011), available at: www.thedailybeast.com/articles/2011/08/29/Libyan-revol-s-quiet-mastermind-mustafa-abdul-jalil.html.

[21] Jon Lee Anderson, "Killing Abdul Fattah Younes," *The New Yorker* (July 30, 2011). Trevor Mostyn, "Gen Abdel Fatah Younis Obituary," *The Guardian (July 31, 2011).*

[22] Praveen Swami, Nick Squires, and Duncan Gardham, "Libyan Rebel Commander Admits His Fighters Have Al-Qaeda Links," *The Telegraph* (March 25, 2011).

There are certainly many reasons that explain why this intervention was undertaken, even though, under very comparable circumstances, others are not. Why Libya, but not Bahrain or Yemen? The reasons may have something to do with difficulties experienced by leaders of the intervening states at a certain moment in their career, or with the political or economic interests of these states, or with alliances established previously. France supported the dictatorships in Libya's neighboring countries, Tunisia and Egypt, for a long time. By choosing to support the insurgents in Libya, it could hope to be on the right side of history. At the same time, France demonstrated the effectiveness of its weapons, which placed it in a position of strength in future negotiations. But beyond specific justifications, there remains a common framework.

In his address on March 28, 2011, delivered at the National Defense University in Washington, DC, the United States president, Barack Obama, provided a global rationale for the intervention, much like the one he had given previously for the war in Afghanistan. Well aware that the security of the United States was not at issue in Libya (this was not a war of self-defense), he invoked the unique role incumbent on his country to maintain international order. The United States, in its role "as an anchor of global security and as an advocate for human freedom," has a unique responsibility to lead the rest of the world. It must therefore often intervene when a natural disaster strikes in any corner of the globe, but also when intervention is necessary for "preventing genocide and keeping the peace; ensuring regional security, and maintaining the flow of commerce" (the economic interests of the United States are not forgotten by Obama). The nature of this mission is also specified; it is neither divine nor the result of a consensus of nations, but simply stems from the status of the United States "as the most powerful nation in the world." This is how force cloaks itself in the colors of law! And Obama concluded by applying the theory to this particular case: Gaddafi must give up power.[23]

The intervention in Libya confirms a messianic plan familiar to Western democracies. Because of their technological, economic, and military successes, they are convinced of their moral and political superiority over the other countries of the globe (men love to cloak their superior force in virtue). They therefore decide that their military power gives them the right, or even the duty, to manage the affairs of the entire world (with the exception of the other permanent members of the Security Council and those they protect). Hence, upon countries rated poorly by them, they impose the values they deem superior and the governments they deem likely to implement the appropriate policies. The case of Great Britain and France, which dominated the coalition engaged in Libya, is a little more specific. These two countries were major

---

[23] President Barack Obama, "Remarks by the President in Address to the Nation on Libya," speech at National Defense University, Washington, DC (March 28, 2011), available at: www.whitehouse.gov/the-press-office/2011/03/28/remarks-president-address-nation-libya.

colonial powers 100 or 200 years ago; but today they have become medium-sized powers that must take into consideration the will of those stronger than they. Yet with the situation in Libya, they were offered the opportunity to show their military capabilities and to enjoy the impression that they were again managing the affairs of the world. They willingly took advantage of the situation. Encouraged by the results achieved, the French president did not delay in designating the next target. On August 31, 2011, he warned Iran of the possibility of a "preventive strike" against its nuclear sites, thus adopting for his own purposes the notion of preventive war promoted by US president, George W. Bush.[24]

We could nevertheless imagine a different outcome for the Libyan crisis, an outcome that was, moreover, demanded by the other African countries – but their opinion was considered negligible. After the initial intervention that destroyed the regime's air force and halted the advance of Gaddafi's forces toward the cities that were in the hands of the insurgents, it would have been possible to impose a ceasefire on all the belligerents. Following the ceasefire, political talks could have begun, preferably under the aegis of the African Union. Gaddafi's departure could have been negotiated under these conditions. If no agreement were reached, the transformation of the country into a federation, or even its partition might have been imposed. These solutions are admittedly provisional and imperfect, but they are free of the excessiveness that drives the idea of imposing Good by force.

For the time being, the Libyan war represents the only example where the new doctrine of Responsibility to Protect has been applied, but it seems to embody its spirit well. Faced with the criticisms that the doctrine has sometimes prompted even in the West, one of its designers, Gareth Evans, former Australian Foreign Affairs Minister, defended the principle, while at the same time acknowledging shortcomings in its application as hasty and disproportionate.[25] This type of justification irresistibly recalls the ardent supporters of the communist ideal undaunted by any admission of failure in practice. They excused it by asserting that the initial intentions had been perverted or diverted.

---

[24] Speech by President Nicolas Sarkozy, 19th Ambassadors' Conference, Paris (August 31, 2011), available at: www.franceonu.org/france-at-the-united-nations/un-express-922-article/19th-ambassadors-conference-speech.

[25] Gareth Evans is the author of the book *The Responsibility to Protect: Ending Mass Atrocity Crimes Once and For All* (Washington, DC: Brookings Institution Press, 2008).
Evans answered his critics – e.g., David Rieff, "R2P, R.I.P.," *International Herald Tribune* (November 8, 2011); Alex de Waal, "How to End Mass Atrocities," *International Herald Tribune* (March 10, 2012) – in the same newspaper during the days following the publication of their texts.
See Gareth Evans, letter in response to David Rieff's article "R2P, R.I.P.," Letters column, *International Herald Tribune* (November 16, 2011); letter in response to Alex de Waal's article "How to End Mass Atrocities," Opinion, *New York Times* (March 11, 2012).

However, the disadvantages, today as in the past, stem from the doctrine itself rather than from its application.

We find an immoderate messianic ambition in the plan to permanently cure humanity of its ills, a plan to which the subtitle of Evans' book bears witness: "Ending Mass Atrocity Crimes Once and For All."[26] Knowledge of past history suggests the search for more modest objectives than the one that consists in saving humanity, a new utopianism that is no less threatening than the previous one.[27] What characterizes the current moment of history is that we apparently no longer like to present war as it is, namely, the imposition of the will of the strongest; instead, we prefer to disguise it with reassuring labels such as "humanitarian intervention," "protection of the population," or "defense of human rights." Here, again, the current form of political messianic zeal recalls that of the colonial period, when conquests were justified by the fight against cannibalism, slavery, and other savage practices, and when war against insurgents was called "pacification."

One could reply to my protests that, in any event, the relationships between nations have always obeyed only the dictates of force and self-interest, unlike the relationships that are established within each country. In this case, why bother becoming indignant before each new example of this law of power politics? We will never succeed in changing the way in which countries conduct themselves with one another, it will be said; they do not obey the principles of morality. The only choice left to us is that between a frank presentation of our political choices and a hypocritical (or naive) presentation. Why, then, not choose this second option? After all, according to La Rochefoucauld, is not hypocrisy the homage vice pays to virtue, and therefore at least a nominal acceptance of justice? Can we not hope that, by dint of feigning virtuous conduct, we will be progressively led to it? On the other hand, we could prefer to steer clear of the "gift wrapping" with which intervention is packaged and get closer to the truth about the acts of intervention. Otherwise, we risk sacrificing the very ideas of justice, democracy, and human rights, which now appear as a convenient disguise for actions that can procure for us greater riches or increased power. Moreover, we are

---

[26] Garth Evans, *The Responsibility to Protect.*

[27] Things like cease-fires, truces, interim political arrangements and political compromises, on-going negotiations, temporary peace-keeping operations, etc. – while incremental, messy, and slowly evolving approaches to conflict resolution – are nearly always preferable. Some have also argued that any possible legal doctrine of armed humanitarian intervention should be developed incrementally *via* customary international law, as opposed to an explicit legislative approach that promulgates a full-blown code through a UN Charter amendment or through a UN General Assembly declaration. See Jane Stromseth, "Rethinking Humanitarian Intervention: The Case for Incremental Change," in Holzgrefe and Keohane (eds.), *Humanitarian Intervention,* 232–272.

not obligated to adhere to this dark view of international relations; in the long term, it may turn out that respect for others is more advantageous than their subjugation. Realism and idealism do not necessarily conflict with one another.

Before singing an ode to the glory of a new kind of conflagration better than all the others, making it possible to eradicate Evil "once and for all," we would perhaps do well to meditate on the lessons that the great painter Goya illustrated 200 years ago from another war waged in the name of Good: depictions of the Napoleonic regiments bringing freedom and progress to the Spanish. Massacres committed in the name of democracy are no gentler than those caused by faithfulness to God or to Allah, to the Guide, or to the Party. They all lead to the same *Disasters of War*.[28]

---

[28] "The Disasters of War" is the title of a series of prints created between 1810 and 1820 by the Spanish painter and printmaker Francisco Goya (1746–1828). Most of the pictures in the series depict the terrible and fatal consequences of the military conflicts between Napoleon's French Empire and Spain. In these works, Goya rejects the heroic visions of previous Spanish war art and, instead, shows the effect of war on individuals through scenes of atrocities, starvation, degradation, and humiliation.

PART II

Moral perspectives

The moral basis of armed humanitarian
intervention revisited

FERNANDO R. TESÓN

Perhaps the most disputed issue in the vast literature on armed humanitarian intervention is its rationale: are nations sometimes justified to use military force to rescue victims of tyranny? If so, why? Answers to this question vary. The two extreme positions are absolute non-interventionism, according to which armed humanitarian interventions are never justified, and proactive interventionism, the view that military interventions are justified to remedy any situation of injustice, no matter how slight (though I do not know anyone who holds this view).

I will confine the scope of this chapter in three ways. First, I assume that the truth lies between those extremes, that is, I assume that a military humanitarian intervention is sometimes permissible. Still, war is presumptively prohibited for obvious reasons, and the burden of proof always lies on those who argue that a particular war can be justified on humanitarian grounds. Second, I confine the discussion to the permissibility of *military* intervention to protect persons against their own governments – humanitarian intervention, for short. Important as they are, I will not discuss here non-military diplomatic measures that governments may adopt to respond to humanitarian crises, although the same basic principles I propose here apply, *mutatis mutandis*, to those as well. And finally, I will address only the *moral* status of humanitarian intervention, and not its status in international law. I do this for several reasons, but the most important is that it is not clear at all that the legal status of humanitarian intervention should track the philosophical analysis. International legal rules create their own incentives that have to be considered in their design, and sometimes these considerations recommend a legal rule that will be, from the standpoint of philosophy, a second-best solution.[1]

In this chapter I make two claims. First, the rationale for humanitarian intervention, as for any war, is only the defense of persons. I here elaborate on this claim, which in my previous writings was simply stated. Second, whether a particular intervention will be morally justified depends *only* on how it fares under

---

[1] A full treatment of the law and morality of armed humanitarian intervention can be found in Fernando R. Tesón, *Humanitarian Intervention: An Inquiry into Law and Morality*, 3rd edn. (New York: Transnational Publishers, 2005).

a full-blown theory of just war. It does *not* depend on other factors, such as the legitimacy *vel non* of the regime, or on whether or not the intervention aims at solving a "supreme emergency." This claim departs from my previous views. My plan is as follows. I first discuss what constitutes a just cause for war and suggest how to think about humanitarian intervention through those lenses. I then address the question of state legitimacy and how it bears on an analysis of humanitarian intervention. I conclude by proposing a just-war canvass that tackles the notion of proportionality using a modified version of the doctrine of double effect.

Armed humanitarian intervention as defense of persons

Since humanitarian intervention is a species of war, I start with the *jus ad bellum*, that is, the legitimate *reasons* to wage war. In traditional terminology, this is the question of what constitutes a just cause for war. Any use of violence maims, kills, and destroys, and for that reason it is presumptively prohibited. Because war is the most terrifying and destructive form of violence, the presumption against it is particularly strong. War is in principle prohibited; justified wars are the exception. For that reason, humanitarian intervention, if it is to be justified at all, must meet a high threshold.

Let us start with a broadly accepted just cause for war: the defensive war against an unjustified attack, that is, against international aggression. The war to repel an aggressor is a justified war in national self-defense. While the contours of self-defense are not easy to draw, virtually everyone agrees that defensive wars are justified.[2] The just cause here is pretty obvious: The victims of the attack are defending *themselves and their compatriots*, that is, their lives and property, against the aggressor. Their government coordinates the defensive action. When we say that government must defend us against foreign attacks, we mean, I think, that *we* are entitled to defend ourselves against such attack. The government is the agency that *we* create to coordinate our defensive efforts (this does not prejudge the permissibility or otherwise of conscription). Citizens may also be defending their institutions, their way of life, or other valuable things that they may see threatened by the aggressor, but that is not necessary. Even if the defensive fighters reject their own institutions or their own government, they are confronting a risk that the aggressor foists upon *them*; and, under standard principles of self-defense, they are justified in fighting. Moreover, citizens may require that their government conduct the defense, even if the government is otherwise objectionable.

---

[2] Not quite everyone, though. David Rodin thinks that national self-defense as understood in international law is morally unjustified. David Rodin, *War and Self-Defense* (Oxford: Clarendon Press, 2002), chaps. 5, 6, and 7.

Now consider humanitarian intervention. Traditionally, writers have considered humanitarian intervention an *offensive* war.[3] Because offensive wars are in principle banned, humanitarian intervention, it is thought, should be held to a high epistemic and normative threshold, and perhaps banned alongside other forms of offensive war, such as wars of conquest and similar forms of aggression. The reason for this treatment is easy to see. Humanitarian intervention, on the traditional view, is an offensive war because the intervener attacks a sovereign *state* without itself or another state having been wronged by that state. Neither the intervener, nor a third state, have been attacked by that sovereign state; and therefore, it is thought, the intervener has no business attacking. The same reasoning applies when the matter is seen from the standpoint of the state targeted by the intervention. A state loses its moral shield against military intervention only when it has wrongly attacked another state. Since this has not happened, the humanitarian intervention does not qualify as self-defense for obvious reasons, and does not qualify as defense of others, because the state targeted by the intervention has not attacked a third state either. On this view, humanitarian intervention is therefore an offensive act of war and must be judged harshly as such.

The traditional approach fails because it unduly personifies states. If we disaggregate the state, we can see that humanitarian intervention is a use of force *in defense of others*, namely, the *persons* who are victims of unjustified violence by their own government. The defense of others in international relations assumes two forms: defense of *third* states that are victims of aggression (what the United Nations Charter calls "collective self-defense"),[4] and defense of persons *within* a state who are attacked by their government. But in both cases, the defensive force is used to protect persons. In collective self-defense, the state that assists another state that is a victim of aggression is defending the persons whose lives are put at risk by the aggressor. Derivatively, of course, the assisting state may be defending the government and the institutions; but, again, this is not necessary. If state A attacks state B, state C may assist state B even if it thinks the institutions are worthless, because the aggression is against B's citizens, those who inhabit the invaded territory.

Just as national self-defense and defense of third states are justified as a defense of persons (myself and my compatriots in one case, the citizens of an unjustly attacked third state in the other) against an aggressor, so humanitarian intervention is justified as a defense of persons (the persons *within* the targeted state) against their government. Self-defense and humanitarian intervention have the same rationale. While there are important differences between them, it is misleading to consider self-defense as a defensive war and humanitarian

---

[3] See, for example, Rodin, *War and Self-Defense*, 130–1. It is also the standard position in traditional international law.

[4] UN Charter, Article 51.

intervention as an offensive war. Both wars in self-defense (individual or collective) and wars in defense of others (humanitarian interventions) are wars in defense of persons. The main difference between the two is that when the country is attacked the government has a *duty* to fight grounded in a fiduciary obligation to its citizens – after all, one of the *raisons d'être* of government is to defend us. A humanitarian crisis elsewhere, on the contrary, generates in principle only a *permission* to act, because the intervener is not bound to foreigners in the same way and thus cannot lightly impose costs on its citizens to save others. (However, if the cost of intervention is very low and the rights violations very severe, then the permission may morph into a moral *obligation* to intervene. For example, some observers thought that the failure of Western powers to intervene in the Rwandan genocide of 1994 was a moral failure.)

When we think about humanitarian intervention in this way, we can see the irrelevance of national borders. Consider this pair of cases. In a remote rural region of a state, an ethnic group attacks a rival ethnic group with the intent of exterminating it. The government sends troops to prevent the genocide and succeeds, after considerable cost in blood and treasure. The victims are saved. I think virtually everyone would agree that the military action was justified. Now suppose, instead, that the government is unwilling or unable to stop the genocide occurring within its own borders. The government of a neighboring nation then invades and stops the genocide, at the same cost of blood and treasure. Critics of humanitarian intervention will typically say that this invasion, unlike the military action by the state's own government, is not justified. Yet it seems to me that there is no moral difference between the rescue in the first case and that in the second case. The only difference is that in the second case the rescuing army crossed a border. Why this fact should make a moral difference is entirely mysterious, provided everything else remains equal.

Or consider this other pair of cases. A tyrannical military junta overthrows the legitimate government, suspends all constitutional guarantees and starts imprisoning, killing, and torturing people who oppose it. The democratic forces regroup and revolt against the junta. After considerable cost in blood and treasure they succeed. Again, most people would agree that the revolution is morally justified. Now suppose the democratic forces are not powerful enough to confront the superior government forces, for example, because the junta controls the weapons. They then implore their democratic neighbor to help them. The neighbor invades, joins the revolutionaries, and defeats the tyrants at a similar cost. Again, critics of humanitarian intervention will deem the invasion unjustified. And again, the moral difference between these two cases is hard to see. It seems to me that traditional thinking has assigned an exaggerated weight to national boundaries.

If opposition to humanitarian intervention is not grounded in state sovereignty but on other factors such as the impermissibility of killing innocents, then the non-interventionist cannot justify her endorsement of the use of *internal* force to stop genocide, or liberal *revolutions* to depose tyrants, because in these instances innocent bystanders also die. There is no relevant difference between the national army rescuing victims of genocide and a foreign army doing the same thing. Similarly, if a revolution is justified, foreign aid to them is too, *if* everything else remains equal. Indeed, foreign aid might be the revolutionaries' only hope for liberation. Of course, it may well be that violent action is unjustified in *all* those cases, domestic or international, because the costs are too high. But if so, the impermissibility of armed action applies to the action by the central government in the first example and the revolution in the second example. The fact that the rescuing army crosses a national boundary can hardly determine the difference between permission and prohibition. There is no moral difference between the internal political violence in these imaginary cases and the foreign interventions having identical purpose and effect.

I said that a humanitarian intervention can only be justified as a defense of persons. The applicable moral principles are known in the criminal law as *defense of others*. Persons are entitled not only to defend themselves against unjust attacks, but also to defend others who are victim of unjust attacks. Criminal law scholars use a well-known matrix: If Attacker unjustly attacks Victim, Third Party is morally permitted to defend Victim by force.[5] But when is Attacker's attack on Victim unjust? We can say that it is whenever Victim has a right not to be attacked. So if Attacker attacks Victim and Victim has a right not to be attacked, *Attacker forfeits his own right not to be attacked.* To be justified, an attack by Third Party against Attacker must presuppose that Attacker has lost its moral shield, as it were.

Now this analysis is confined to attacks by individuals against other individuals. The application of the basic matrix to humanitarian interventions, where armies and governments are involved, is not automatic, for several reasons. First, the factors that make a *government* morally protected against military attack by another government are not the same factors that make an *individual* morally protected against attacks. Individuals have a right to life and physical integrity; that is why an attack against them is impermissible. Transposing this idea to the state's structure, these rights are the ones that a tyrannical regime violates. So, the status of the *victims* of tyranny is very similar to the status of the individual victim in the classical self-defense hypothetical above: The Attacker is the government, and the Victims are the citizens unjustly assaulted by the government. The two cases are not identical, however, because governments, unlike the Attacker of the hypothetical, have a special relationship with the citizens, which makes the attack even more culpable. These attacks are unjustified because Victims had a right not to be attacked. But the analysis of *Attacker* is

[5] See Larry Alexander, "Self-Defense," University of San Diego Research Paper No. 11–065 (September 2011), 2–6. Available at: http://ssrn.com/abstract=1924513.

somewhat different. The Attacker is not a person *tout court* but a government whose powers and duties are specified by the special fiduciary relationship it has with its subjects. The government has a duty to respect the rights of the subjects, to govern within the terms of the social contract, and if it fails in that duty, *its* moral shield collapses. One can say that this moral shield is an *artificial* shield created by the *appointment* of the government by the citizens. The individual, in contrast, has a *natural* right not to be attacked, that is, a right by virtue of personhood. The government, qua government, does not have any natural rights. Its status is entirely conventional.

Second, military action almost always produces costly externalities that affect third parties, in a way that individual attacks against persons usually do not. So suppose A (a tyrannical regime) attacks B (the population or a subset of it). If C (the intervener army) invades the country to assist B, it causes significant harm to D, an innocent party such as civilian bystanders. Notice that in the examples above of defense of others the costs of acting are internalized; the third party that rescues the victims does so at his own risk. In contrast, the intervener imposes risks on non-culpable parties. Because of this problem, the transposition of the principles of defense-of-others must be done with care.

When can we say that a government attacks its own subjects? Provisionally, I define such an attack as the perpetration of *grave acts of impermissible coercion.* The idea is this. We could say that governments are in the coercion business. In order to provide the services it is supposed to provide, the government has to tax people, imprison criminals, and the like. The acts of coercion that a government can perform, then, can be classified into two categories: morally permissible acts of coercion and morally impermissible acts of coercion. Citizens (let us assume) do not have a right to defend themselves against permissible acts of coercion, and a fortiori outsiders do not have any right to assist them. If an outsider uses violence against the government in such a case, it violates the moral shield of that government, a shield that protects it from attempts to interfere with the permissible acts of coercion it performs.

So a humanitarian intervention, to be justified, must target impermissible acts of coercion. But of course, not every impermissible act of coercion generates an entitlement to use military force against the government that performs it. It is doubtful that even the individual victim has a right to resist by force just any act of impermissible coercion. (I do not address here what circumstances justify such resistance, the individual right to resist authority.) But it is certain, I believe, that relatively minor impermissible acts of coercion do not generate a right of outsiders to defend the victim. But why? Because military action is extremely costly, and so it must be confined to actions necessary to defend victims of *serious* acts of coercion. What the threshold is cannot be decided mechanically. We need a theory of just war that includes the requirement of proportionality, and I explore that below.

Intervention and state legitimacy

Some writers have proposed a different reason why outsiders may not use force to assist the victims of (most) impermissible governmental acts of coercion. They have suggested that the government has a *right to rule* that must be respected, even if some or many of the acts that the government performs in the exercise of that right to rule are morally impermissible. This is the large question of state legitimacy. In my previous writings I have suggested that the concept of legitimacy plays a crucial role in judging intervention.[6] On this view, humanitarian wars are impermissible against *legitimate* regimes precisely *because* those regimes are legitimate. Legitimate states have a moral shield against others, a right not to be attacked. On the other hand, for a humanitarian war to be permissible, the targeted regime must be *illegitimate*, and other conditions must obtain as well. On this view, illegitimacy is a necessary (though not sufficient) condition of the permissibility of humanitarian intervention. In a sense, this is correct: that an intervention is permissible against a regime entails, analytically, that that regime has lost its moral shield, that it no longer enjoys a right not to be interfered with, just as Attacker forfeits his right not to be attacked when he attacks Victim in the matrix discussed above. However, the facts that cause the collapse of that moral shield are impermissible acts of coercion against its citizens, not the property of being illegitimate. It is true that only intervention against illegitimate regimes is (sometimes) permissible, but not *because* it is illegitimate, as the statement wrongly suggests. Permissible intervention does not aim at restoring political legitimacy, but at ending or preventing impermissible violence against persons.

As indicated, all states perform acts of coercion, acts of violence, against their citizens in their territories. Some of those acts are morally justified and some are not. We may say, perhaps, that coercive acts of the state that are consistent with the moral rights of subjects are justified and coercive acts of the state that are inconsistent with those rights are unjustified. Any intervention to frustrate justified acts of coercion will be impermissible (even non-military interferences against such acts will be impermissible, let alone military ones). For a humanitarian intervention to even begin to be justified, then, it must be aimed at *unjustified* acts of state coercion. However, not all unjustified acts of coercion constitute *casus belli*. Governments perpetrate mild wrongs and serious wrongs. A humanitarian intervention is, in principle, justified only to end or prevent the most seriously wrong acts of coercion perpetrated by governments. This is so, not because states have a "right" to perform mildly wrong acts of coercion, but because war to redress those mild wrongs will often be

---

[6] Tesón, *Humanitarian Intervention*, especially chaps. 3 and 4. See also Andrew Altman and Christopher Heath Wellman, *A Liberal Theory of International Justice* (Oxford University Press, 2011), 78.

disproportionate. For this reason, whether or not governments have a "right to do wrong" is irrelevant for purposes of justifying humanitarian intervention. Intervention is impermissible against any act that is not seriously wrong *if*, as is almost always the case, the military intervention will impose significant costs. For the same reason, that a state is internally illegitimate (on whatever standard of legitimacy one chooses) is insufficient reason to intervene, as the prospective intervener must comply with the strictures of the proportionality principle as well.

Let us consider first states that are illegitimate, judged under some standard of substantive justice. These states perform unjustified acts of coercion. But here again, it will often be the case that a military intervention would be so costly in moral terms as to be disproportionate or counterproductive. When the military invasion is likely to cost significantly in terms of blood and treasure, it will be permitted *only* to end or prevent serious assaults on persons – seriously wrongful acts of state coercion, *because* only in those cases will the intervention be proportionate; only then will the costs of war be justified. Consider the case of a government that has rendered itself guilty of less extreme rights violations. A military junta, say, has taken power by undemocratic means, and has suspended constitutional guarantees – perhaps to prevent revolutionary activity. Let us assume that this undemocratic seizure of power violates the moral rights of the subjects, and (to avoid complications) that this junta has little support in the population. Now suppose that the democratic forces can secure the help of a powerful neighbor, and suppose further that the mere border-crossing by the foreign army will predictably cause the junta to surrender without a fight. It seems to me that this military intervention is morally justified, because the military invasion will *not* impose unacceptable costs (since the junta will surrender without resistance), *and* the violations of rights are relatively serious (although not egregious). The intervention, in other words, is proportionate. So the general proposition that only severe tyranny justifies humanitarian intervention will be true in most cases, but it is not strictly correct. The proposition has a hidden premise: that in less serious cases the intervention will impose unacceptable costs, as wars are prone to do. But if the military intervention, as in the example, is not costly, then the threshold of justification, in terms of the gravity of the cause, is lower. So the answer to the question: "Is it justified to intervene by force to restore democracy?" is that it depends. If the intervention will kill many innocents, destroy vast amounts of property, or will likely make things worse, the answer is no. If, on the contrary, the intervention will not have those dire consequences, then the answer may be yes. I hasten to add that the epistemic barriers faced by prospective interveners in calculating the likely costs of the war are so severe that perhaps the international norm should confine the permissibility of intervention to the really serious cases of tyranny.

Now consider legitimate states. I said that intervention against legitimate states is prohibited, but this is not strictly correct either. Suppose a state is considered legitimate, again, on some standard of substantive justice, such as general compliance with human rights. These states *also* perpetrate unjustified acts of coercion – usually on a minor scale, and usually less serious. *These* illegitimate acts of coercion, these violations of the moral rights of persons (say, incarceration of morally innocent people or systematic governmental acts of theft) are *not* deserving of protection. If someone could press a magical button and stop the rights violations without any collateral cost, then that "intervention" would be morally permissible. But because *military* intervention is extremely costly, it will never be allowed against the impermissible acts of coercion of otherwise (presumed) legitimate states. For one thing, these states have reasonable avenues of redress against rights violations. More than that: these states have valuable institutions that, on the whole, allow persons to pursue their personal projects, and, for that reason, violence against them, even if animated by a just cause such as ending illegitimate acts of coercion, is banned. But, again, the reason for not intervening is not that those morally impermissible acts of coercion are somehow "legitimate" (whatever that statement may mean).

We can see, then, that the concept of state legitimacy does not do any work in the justification of humanitarian intervention. Contrary to some suggestions,[7] states do not have any *rights-based* shield against foreign intervention directed at ending their wrongful acts of coercion. States do not have a *general* right to rule, that is, a right to rule *beyond* what the rights of the subjects (one could say, the social contract) allow.[8] All the work is done by the requirement of proportionality in war. War is justified *only* to end serious and systematic rights violations, that is, to protect persons against *attacks* by their own governments, because otherwise war in most cases would be disproportionate. If the rights violations are less severe, the principle of proportionality indicates less severe remedies. Because often war is *the most* severe remedy in terms of blood and treasure, it must be reserved to redress the most urgent situations. To see this, imagine yet another even less severe situation. Imagine a state that harasses political dissidents; for example, it closes newspapers that are critical of government, and it persecutes dissidents with phony charges of tax evasion and the like. Outsiders (say, liberal democracies) are perfectly authorized to put diplomatic pressure, even coercive pressure such as economic sanctions, on this regime to stop these rights violations, but are not authorized to invade – unless, as already indicated, the invasion itself will be costless (very unlikely in such scenario). The reason for the prohibition to invade is *not* (as conventional

---

[7] B. Van der Vossen, "The Asymmetry of Legitimacy," *Law and Philosophy* 31 (2012), 567–76; David Copp, "The Idea of a Legitimate State," *Philosophy & Public Affairs* 28, no. 1 (1999), 26–29; John Rawls, *The Law of Peoples* (Cambridge, Massachusetts: Harvard University Press, 1999).

[8] I realize that this is a contentious point, but I cannot fully justify it here. It is argued for in greater length in L. Lomasky and Fernando R. Tesón, *Justice at a Distance* (unpublished).

wisdom would have it) that sovereignty shields non-egregious governmental misdeeds. The reason is that a military intervention would be patently disproportionate.

Sovereignty and culture

Someone may object that in their path toward deposing bad regimes, interventions destroy political cultures. The principle of state sovereignty does not protect solely governments: it protects *cultures* as well. The problem with humanitarian intervention is that it violates sovereignty in this other sense. The idea is that there is something valuable in confining political processes to the citizens of the state, and that the principle of sovereignty protects precisely this collective autonomy.[9] Foreigners who use force to alter these processes are disrespecting the citizens of the target state.

Let us start with the idea that there is something within the state worth protecting against foreign intervention. However, if the government has turned against its own citizens, that is, perpetrates seriously wrong acts of coercion against them, what justification could there be for prohibiting the victims to secure foreign rescue? Some authors have advanced what I will call the "Popular Will argument." Intervention is banned because a substantial number, or a majority, of the population oppose the intervention. This opposition will likely translate into resistance, and it is this expectation of resistance that makes intervention wrong.

The Popular Will argument, however, is fatally flawed. To see why, let us first disaggregate the state where the violations occur. We have (roughly) three parties: the tyrant (joined by his henchmen and collaborators), his victims, and the bystanders. I concede at once that the intervener should not try to rescue victims from tyranny if they do not want to be rescued. But this principle identifies *the victims*, and the victims alone, as those whose consent matters. Others (collaborators and bystanders) are not entitled to veto the intervention on behalf of those who are victimized by the regime. Collaborators are accomplices in a crime, and bystanders, while they are not accomplices, do not have standing to resist attempts to rescue the victims. None of those groups has a valid communal interest in the tyrannical governance of their community. If they resist the intervention, they will be fighting an unjust war, a war *on behalf* of tyranny. Under any plausible theory of democracy, tyranny is not one of the things a majority can impose on a minority. While it is possible that, all things considered, the intervention predictably will have unacceptable costs, the reason to criticize the intervention will *not* be that those who resist the invader

---

[9] Michael Walzer, "The Moral Standing of States: A Response to Four Critics," *Philosophy & Public Affairs* 9, no. 3 (1980).

are protecting something valuable, but rather that the overall consequences of intervening are unacceptable.

However, the objection that foreign intervention violates state sovereignty has some force when the well-intentioned intervener (often unwittingly) significantly changes valuable social arrangements. When citizens of the state have cemented their social relations through cumulative processes over time, the resulting institutions and practices are prima facie worthy of respect by foreigners, provided those institutions and practices are morally justified. One can think of sovereignty as protecting valuable social structures from foreign interference. To this extent, and to this extent only, the sovereignty argument against intervention is plausible. Foreigners do not have the right to change non-oppressive political structures.

By the same token, cumulative historical processes do not deserve respect if they are oppressive. I am thinking here, not of oppressive regimes, but of social institutions and practices that originated from the bottom up, as it were, but are unacceptable from the standpoint of justice. For example, the historical subjugation of women in some cultures is not acceptable from the standpoint of justice, so the objection that a foreign intervention will alter *that* practice is unavailable to those who oppose the intervention. It does not follow, of course, that military intervention is justified *just* to reverse those oppressive social practices. But the critic of intervention cannot point to those oppressive practices as valuable elements of society that (he thinks) the intervention will upset. Sovereignty does not protect those.

Legitimate states, then, are morally protected from intervention, but not because they are legitimate (whatever the standard of legitimacy may be), but because a war against those states will always be disproportionate. However, the illegitimate acts of coercion performed by otherwise legitimate states are *not* protected against non-military forms of diplomacy. Legitimate social structures are themselves protected even in illegitimate states. Illegitimate states, meaning by that tyrannical states, are not protected, but this does not mean that intervention is always permissible against those states, all things considered. Also, if unaided revolution against a tyrant is justified, then aided revolution is also justified, provided that the other factors remain constant. If those factors do not remain constant, for example, if the foreign intervention predictably will greatly increase civilian casualties, then it may be unjustified under the doctrine of proportionality and the revolutionaries would have to fight alone.

Proportionality

This analysis leaves us with the following conclusions. Governments often perform unjustified acts of coercion. When these wrongful acts reach a high level of severity, we can say that the government has turned against its citizens by attacking them. No unjustified act of coercion is morally protected; the government's right to rule does not include a right to perform unjustified acts of coercion, however slight. Nonetheless, war is not permitted against milder unjustified acts but only against severe unjustified acts, those that amount to an attack against persons. The reason for this is that war is itself a serious act of violence that imposes serious moral costs on many people. Any intervention, therefore, must satisfy a proportionality test.

Assuming just cause in the sense described, the main reason to oppose a particular humanitarian war is that it is likely to be disproportionate. The cost of the intervention in terms of deaths (especially of innocents) may be unacceptable, or the intervention may be counterproductive in other ways – for example, it may give rise to evils (a new tyranny or anarchy) that are worse than the evil the intervention suppressed. For example, people have condemned the 2003 Iraq War, not because it was wrong to depose Saddam Hussein, but because the invasion initiated a complex and violent causal chain with terrible consequences (deaths of many innocents, widespread destruction). But suppose the coalition would have been able to depose Saddam with no adverse consequences – surgically, as it were. Surely the war would not have been so widely condemned. The general idea is that even when just cause is present, a military intervention may be impermissible because of its bad consequences. Just cause is a necessary but not sufficient justification for war. This is why we should be reluctant to encourage any war, even when it has a just cause and the warriors harbor genuinely noble purposes.

The idea of proportionality is highly complex, because it cannot be measured simply in terms of material costs and benefits. Thus, an intervener who wants to overthrow a tyrant cannot permissibly achieve that justified aim by rounding up and murdering innocents, even if that action would cause fewer deaths than allowing the tyrant to continue in power. Yet any war will bring about the deaths of innocent persons. Just-war scholars have replied to this objection by formulating the doctrine of double effect (DDE). The DDE distinguishes between *intended* killings and *merely foreseen* killings. It is morally wrong to deliberately target innocent persons. The commander who, in pursuit of a just cause, aims the guns at a school to kill children and in this way demoralize the enemy is guilty of murder, because he *wills* the deaths of the children. This immorality is not cured by the justice of the cause – deposing the tyrannical regime. But the commander who aims the guns at the enemy soldiers while merely *foreseeing* that this action may kill innocent children is on a different moral footing. The deaths of the children are not essential to his destruction of the enemy; he would spare the children if he could. Some authors say that in the first case the commander treats the children as *means* to his end of winning, whereas in the second case the commander does not treat the children as means. This intent-based distinction between the two cases is essential to the DDE.

The formulation of the doctrine varies considerably in the literature. As a first approximation, we can state the doctrine thus:

> An act with two effects, one good, one evil, may be performed
>
> 1) if the act is right (or not wrong),
> 2) if the good effect is intended, though the evil effect may be foreseen,
> 3) if the good effect does not come through the evil effect, and
> 4) if the good achieved by the good effect is significant enough to permit the evil of the evil effect to come to pass.[10]

Now let us adapt this formulation to the problem at hand, that is, the collateral deaths of non-combatants in an otherwise justified humanitarian intervention:

> An act of war aimed at saving persons that results in the deaths of innocents is permissible if, and only if:
>
> (1) The cause is in fact just (saving persons from unjustified attacks by their government). Killing in the legitimate defense of others is not wrong (i.e., third-party self-defense).
> (2) The good effect of saving persons is intended, although the evil effect of the deaths of innocent persons is merely foreseen.
> (3) The realization of the just cause thus defined does not come through the deaths of innocents.
> (4) The just cause is significant enough to permit the death of innocents to come to pass.

Most of the literature has focused on condition (2): the distinction between willed action and merely foreseen action. To it we now turn.

The distinction between intention and foresight

According to DDE scholars, the collateral deaths of innocents are not *intrinsic* to the just warrior's action, and that means that, in some important sense, the agent does not intend those deaths. In contrast, action aimed intentionally at an evil is *guided* by that evil.[11] Direct harmful agency is, therefore, more *disrespectful* than collateral harm, and therein lies the moral difference between both actions (or between both effects of the same action).[12] The commander who does not aim at innocents does not really wish to cause the deaths of

---

[10] R.G. Frey, "The Doctrine of Double Effect," in R.G. Frey and Christopher Heath Wellman (eds.), *A Companion to Applied Ethics* (Oxford: Blackwell, 2003), 464.

[11] Thomas Nagel, "Agent-Relative Morality," in P.A. Woodward (ed.), *The Doctrine of Double Effect: Philosophers Debate a Controversial Moral Principle* (Notre Dame, Indiana: Notre Dame University Press, 2001), 46.

[12] See W. Quinn, *Morality and Action* (Cambridge University Press, 1993), 192–193.

innocent persons; he would spare them if he could. The bad effect is nothing to his intent; his action is not guided by evil. The commander who aims at non-combatants wills their deaths; he does not want to spare them. Their deaths are essential to his intent; his action is guided by evil. The distinction, then, is plausible, and establishes the moral difference between direct and oblique harmful agency.

But it does not follow from the fact that there is a *moral difference* between direct harmful agency and oblique harmful agency that the latter is *morally permissible*. As Warren Quinn observed, the DDE raises the bar for the moral permissibility of killing; it does not lower the bar.[13] The doctrine does not justify collateral deaths in a military intervention, but merely says that collateral deaths are less bad than direct deaths. The critic may concede that a commander who directly kills civilians in order to demoralize the enemy is morally abject, while insisting that the commander who merely causes collateral deaths of civilians is still acting immorally – less immorally than the other one, to be sure, but still immorally. He agrees with the DDE's moral distinction of the two cases, but maintains that even the more benign case is objectionable. For the critic, the most reprehensible warrior is the unjust warrior who violates the DDE. Less blameworthy, but still bad (perhaps), is the unjust warrior who abides by the DDE. The second place (perhaps) goes to the just warrior who violates the DDE (I am unsure about how to rank the last two categories). And the least blameworthy is the just warrior who abides by the DDE. But for our critic, even this one, the least blameworthy of all, is acting unjustly because he performs an act of war that will predictably kill innocents, and this is *still* morally impermissible. We can see now why merely invoking the distinction in condition (2) of the DDE, namely, the distinction between direct harm and oblique harm, does not answer the objection. In order to respond, we must focus on condition (4): the requirement that the just cause (saving the victims of tyranny, genocide, and the like) be "significant enough" to allow for the moral cost represented by the deaths of non-combatants.

The role of the just cause in the Doctrine of Double Effect

As I said, the intervention must pursue the just cause of saving persons from unjustified attacks by their own governments. The just cause performs a crucial role in justifying oblique deaths of non-combatants in a just war. But this can only be done if condition (4) above is understood, not only as a quantitative proportionality test (a calculation of costs and benefits), but also as a *qualitative* evaluation of *how just* the just cause is, that is, how *urgent* it is to save the victims from these particular attacks.

---

[13] *Ibid.*, p. 188.

In order to see this, I start with a simple proportionality rule and amend it by stages to respond to the worries we have identified. The general idea of proportionality is that the good effect of the war (or of a particular act of war) must outweigh the bad effect under a suitable proportionality rule. According to Henry Sidgwick, the aim of the moral combatant must be to disable his enemy and force him into submission, "but not do him (1) any mischief which does not tend materially to that end, nor (2) any mischief of which the conduciveness to the end is slight in comparison to the amount of mischief."[14] Because Sidgwick thinks that the morality of killing in war is independent of the justice of the cause, this definition will be useful to our purposes only if suitably amended to include *jus ad bellum* considerations and in particular address the problem of collateral deaths.

So we amend Sidgwick's rule as follows:

> An act of war undertaken for a just cause that collaterally brings about the deaths of innocents will *not* be permissible if either (1) the act is not materially conducive to the realization of the just cause; or (2) the conduciveness to the just cause is slight in comparison to the number of collateral deaths.

This amendment introduces the concept of just cause as the morally justified war objective. But the amended version still does not capture the qualitative dimension of the concept of just cause. To be justified, a person who performs an act of war must have a grave reason to do so. The term "significant enough" in condition (4) of the DDE embodies the degree of moral urgency that animates the just intervener. The war must be *sufficiently* justified to compensate for the bad effect. This requirement is not quantitative but substantive. The more *compelling* the reason to fight is, the lower the threshold for justifying collateral deaths will be. I suggest, then, a further addition:

> An act of war undertaken for a just cause which collaterally brings about the deaths of innocents will *not* be permissible if (1) the act is not materially conducive to the realization of the just cause; or (2) the conduciveness to the just cause is slight in comparison to the degree of collateral harm; or (3) the cause is not *grave* enough to outweigh the collateral harm.

These three components of proportionality must be distinguished because the justification of war includes all of them. The act of war must be conducive to the realization of the good; the harm done (the bad effect) should be kept to a minimum and, at any rate, must be quantitatively proportionate to the good effect; and the reason to fight must itself be normatively compelling. Compliance with these three cumulative conditions justify war in general (that is, *starting* a war), and any particular act of war.

---

[14] Henry Sidgwick, *The Elements of Politics* (New York: Macmillan, 1908), 267.

We can now formulate an updated version of the doctrine adapted to humanitarian intervention. A humanitarian intervention will be justified if, and only if:

(1) The intervener does not directly intend the deaths of innocent persons. If he foresees those deaths, he must try to minimize them, even at some cost to himself. He must transfer some risk to himself.

(2) He has a just cause. Only the defense of persons is a just cause. More specifically: Only the act of stopping or preventing serious violence against persons is a just cause. This clause is strictly circumscribed by clauses 4 and 5 below.

(3) The intervention is materially conducive to the realization of the just cause. This rule condemns cases where the intensity of the intervention is unnecessary to the realization of the just cause.

(4) The degree to which the intervention is materially conducive to the realization of the just cause is great enough to compensate for the costs of the war, in particular collateral deaths. This rule establishes a requirement to weigh harms and benefits.

(5) The just cause mentioned in (2), saving persons, must be compelling enough, in a moral sense, to compensate for the costs of the war, in particular collateral harm. This condition recognizes that there are degrees of moral urgency, so that not all just causes will justify collateral harm. The more compelling the cause, the lower the threshold for collateral harm. (For example, stopping genocide is more compelling than restoring a deposed democratic government; therefore, the threshold for intervention will be higher in the latter case.)

I have subdivided the proportionality requirement into three distinct requirements. In particular, to the usual proportionality requirements discussed in the literature, I have added condition (5): the permissibility of the humanitarian intervention turns on whether the collateral harms that will inevitably occur are justified by the *moral urgency* of the cause. If the collateral harm is too great compared to how important it is to realize the good effect, the action will fail the test. Notice that, unlike the test established by condition (4), the test in condition (5) is qualitative, not quantitative. It takes into account what is at stake in winning. If the intervention is aimed at preventing genocide, then the threshold for collateral harm is lower. If the cause is still just but less morally urgent, for example, restoring constitutional government, then the threshold for justifying collateral deaths will be higher.

The justice of the cause informs all moral questions in the humanitarian intervention. Under condition (4) the collateral killings, say, of 50,000 civilians in order to gain a small military advantage is unjustified because it is *materially* disproportionate. But under condition (5), even a smaller number of collateral deaths may be unjustified if the cause of the intervention, while just, is not sufficiently compelling. The action will be *morally* disproportionate. There are degrees of moral urgency; and, correspondingly, there should be degrees of moral permissibility of bad things done in our way to the realization of a moral goal. The upshot is that, in order to justify an otherwise impermissible bad effect, it is not enough for the agent not to directly intend that bad effect. *Why* he causes the bad effect and how that effect measures (materially and morally) against the good one are decisive factors as well.

Here we must heed Sidgwick's warning that particular judgments about proportionality are extremely hard. In particular, the conditions laid down by the DDE are imprecise. The kinds of questions that a morally motivated intervener asks himself are very hard to answer: Is the just cause *compelling* enough to justify the destruction the intervention will cause? How much will the intervention contribute *causally* to the achievement of the good result? This is not surprising. Few things are more difficult and momentous for any leader who cares about human life and liberal values than the decision to go to war. If there is anything certain about war, it is that there is no mechanical procedure readily available to identify the right thing to do. That being said, we may hope to have identified the *kinds* of factors that responsible leaders and commanders should weigh in making these tough decisions.

5

All or nothing

Are there any "merely permissible" armed humanitarian interventions?

NED DOBOS AND C.A.J. COADY

After World War II, human-rights standards became international law, but the legitimacy of their enforcement would not be recognized for quite some time. If anything, the ban on foreign intervention to defend human rights was strengthened following the inception of the United Nations, which has as its foundation the "principle of the sovereign equality of all its Members." It was not until the 1990s that a new norm of international relations began to emerge. In his 1999 Annual Report, UN Secretary-General Kofi Annan made reference to the "developing international norm in favour of intervention to protect civilians."[1] The following year, Human Rights Watch applauded the "evolution in public morality" as a result of which "the international community seems more willing to deploy troops to halt massive slaughter."[2] The next round of punctuated equilibrium saw the right of intervention evolve into a duty. The International Commission on Intervention and State Sovereignty, formed under the auspices of the United Nations, formalized the transition in its 2001 report *The Responsibility to Protect*.

An increasingly common view among political philosophers is that, in fact, *all* justified humanitarian intervention is obligatory.[3] There is no such thing as "merely permissible": either there is a duty to intervene, or there is a duty *not* to intervene. Call this the "all-or-nothing view." In this chapter, we argue that even in the face of the most severe human-rights abuses, the citizens of

---

[1] Quoted in Nicholas J. Wheeler, *Saving Strangers: Humanitarian Intervention in International Society* (New York: Oxford University Press, 2000), 285.

[2] Human Rights Watch, *World Report 2000*, available at: www.hrw.org/wr2k/Front. htm#TopOfPage (accessed August 5, 2007).

[3] Kok-Chor Tan, "The Duty to Protect," in Terry Nardin and Melissa S. Williams (eds.), *NOMOS XLVII: Humanitarian Intervention* (New York and London: New York University Press, 2006), 85. See also Darrel Moellendorf, *Cosmopolitan Justice* (Boulder: Westview Press, 2002), 122–123; John Lango, "Is Armed Humanitarian Intervention to Stop Mass Killing Morally Obligatory," *Public Affairs Quarterly* 13, no. 3 (2001), 173–192. This view is also shared by both Michael Walzer and John Rawls. For a full exposition, see Ned Dobos, *Insurrection and Intervention: The Two Faces of Sovereignty* (Cambridge University Press, 2012), chap. 6.

even the most affluent countries do not always have an obligation to sustain the costs associated with carrying out an otherwise justified humanitarian intervention, whether unilaterally or as part of a multilateral effort. This becomes apparent once certain features of the duty to aid are fully appreciated. We also consider the possibility that humanitarian interventions, which are permissible but discretionary for citizens, are always either obligatory or prohibited for their government, depending on the circumstances. Despite appearances, this is neither paradoxical nor incoherent. Nevertheless, we will suggest that the all-or-nothing view cannot be salvaged regardless of whom we take its referent to be – the state, or its people.

I

There are oppressed and needy people everywhere. Severe deprivations and human-rights abuses are a permanent feature of the world in which we live. Some are suffering from malnutrition; some are even starving to death. Others lack access to basic medical supplies and are dying of easily preventable diseases. In some cases, the government of the victims is directly responsible for, or at least complicit in, their deprivation. In others, it is merely too negligent or incompetent to do anything about it. Some people have enough food and medical supplies, but do not enjoy physical security or any acceptable measure of civil and political freedom. For those of us fortunate enough to take the full complement of human rights for granted, standing idly by is not an option. We have a natural – which is to say a non-derived – duty to aid. On this point there is broad philosophical consensus, and it is not a proposition that we intend to challenge. However, the duty to aid is, in Kantian parlance, an *imperfect* one – or at least that is the *presumption*. It is indeterminate with respect to the kind and amount of aid, and the identity of the recipient.[4] Other things equal, no individual or group can rightfully demand that the performance of the duty be directed at them.[5]

But it is easy enough to think of cases where this latitude lapses. Recall Peter Singer's famous example of the drowning child.[6] All the passerby needs to do is to reach into the water. There is nobody else around, and the only cost he will sustain is that his brand new suit will be ruined. Clearly the passerby cannot defend his failure to act by insisting that he is free to choose how and when he

---

[4] Allen Buchanan, "Justice and Charity," *Ethics* 97, no. 3 (1987), 558.

[5] Henry Shue, "Mediating Duties," *Ethics* 98, no. 4 (July 1988). Some find the terminology of perfect/imperfect duties unacceptable and would prefer other frameworks for discussing the issues we raise. Our sense is that much the same case could be made in some alternative frameworks, such as that of prima facie/strict duties; but we have some reservations about them, particularly concerning their relative lack of specificity about the range of defeating conditions compared to the perfect/imperfect framework.

[6] Peter Singer, "Famine, Affluence, and Morality," *Philosophy & Public Affairs* 1, no. 3 (1972).

discharges his positive duties. The duty here is a *perfect* one. It *is* determinate with respect to the recipient of the aid and the form that it takes. In cases like this, the presumptive discretion that otherwise attends our positive duties is defeated by the agent's unique position. Usually when someone is in peril, there will be any number of potential rescuers. Often there will be no clear point at which the possibility of rescue is foreclosed. Sometimes it will not even be obvious what needs to be done and what would work. By contrast, in Singer's example the passerby can help the child; *only* he can help; there is a specific, easily identifiable thing that he needs to do and a time by which he needs to do it. Where this rare combination of features obtains, the presumptive discretion to choose whom one helps, and when and how one helps, gives way.

An agent's own prior actions and commitments also set limits to his presumptive discretion. If A is in some way responsible for B's dire need, he has lost the prerogative to fulfill his positive duty to aid by helping C instead of B. We might even say that, given the history between them, A helping B is not a case of aid, properly speaking; it is a case of compensatory justice. It is not the fulfillment of a positive duty, but the honoring of a negative one. However one describes it, the freedom that A might otherwise have to choose the object of his assistance has been overridden by his own past conduct. The same goes if A happened to make a commitment or promise to help B.

With these cursory remarks in the background, consider the following scenario. There is widespread malnutrition and starvation in country A, mass death caused by easily preventable diseases in country B, and civil war in country C. Suddenly in country D, armed paramilitaries (with the support of the government) initiate a campaign of ethnic cleansing against a detested minority group. Do the events in D simply give those of us looking on from affluent country X one more way of discharging our imperfect positive duty to aid? Or, does the ethnic cleansing cause the presumptive discretion to lapse and generate a *perfect* duty?

It depends. Is X in a unique position to put a stop to the ethnic cleansing? Did X causally contribute to the ethnic cleansing, say by arming or bankrolling its perpetrators? Did X make a commitment to the minority in D that it would protect them? Is there some other historical relationship between the two countries that is morally significant? An affirmative answer to any of these questions may suffice to put X under a perfect duty to direct its aid, resources, and energies to D. But otherwise, we see no reason to think that X is obliged to give the ethnic-cleansing victims priority over those suffering and dying elsewhere.

And this holds even if we concede that ethnic cleansing constitutes a humanitarian emergency that sets it apart morally from the more "routine" forms of violence and deprivation in A, B, and C. To see this, suppose that devoting a certain amount of our resources toward addressing the food shortage in country A will go a lot further than the same amount of resources used to intervene militarily in country D. The former option, in other words, delivers more bang for our humanitarian buck. This is not purely hypothetical. Military operations are hideously expensive. For every ten days of fighting in Iraq, the US taxpayer spent $5 billion – equivalent to what the United States delivers in foreign aid to Africa for a whole year. Linda Bilmes and economist Joseph Stiglitz estimate that when all the dust has settled, the Iraq War will have cost at least two trillion dollars; enough for the United States to meet its humanitarian commitments to the world's poorest countries for the next third of a century. Surely morality does not demand that we always address the most urgent humanitarian situation before all the others, regardless of whether or not it is the most efficient use of our limited humanitarian resources.

Our point here is not that a perfect duty, owed by the people of one country to the people of another, can *never* arise. Rather, it is that the occurrence of massacre or ethnic cleansing does not *necessarily* generate such a duty. It is conceivable that even in the face of "crimes that shock the moral conscience of humankind," paying for a humanitarian intervention will be our right, without being our duty, since we will retain the prerogative to discharge our aid obligations in some other way.

There is a second feature of positive duties that makes the all-or-nothing view untenable as a description of the moral requirements of citizens. Namely, all positive duties are subject to a high-cost qualification. They need not be fulfilled if this would involve making too great a personal sacrifice. The problem is that even with respect to the most affluent countries with all volunteer armed forces, there will often be some individual or group that can invoke this proviso in opposition to their country's involvement in a humanitarian war, reasonably complaining that the costs being imposed on them are too great.

In times past, wars could bankrupt societies. Today, at least in the advanced economies, Michael Ignatieff suggests that "no trade-off between guns and butter has to be made," that "war no longer faces society with painful choices."[7] For obvious reasons, this has ethicists worried. The chief concern is that disassociating war from the idea of economic sacrifice will gradually weaken the popular inhibition toward the use of military force. "Democracies may well remain peace loving as long as the risks of war remain real to their citizens."[8]

What Ignatieff fails to appreciate is that, while the economic cost to the *collective* might be negligible, the cost to many individuals within the collective can still be quite significant. Take the Iraq War for example. As mentioned, it is estimated to cost the American taxpayer at least two trillion dollars. Consider what this money *could* have been spent on, and what certain individuals will have to forego given their country's commitments in Iraq. Just one trillion dollars could have built eight million additional housing units, or hired another 15 million public-school teachers for one year, or paid for 120 million children to attend a year of the Head Start program, or bought health insurance for

[7] Michael Ignatieff, *Virtual War: Kosovo and Beyond* (New York: Metropolitan Books, 2000), 190.
[8] *Ibid.*, p. 179.

530 million children for a year, or provided 43 million students with four-year scholarships at public universities. The war crowded out, and will continue to crowd out, these other investments. In economic jargon, these are just some of the "opportunity costs" of the decision to "liberate" the Iraqi people.[9]

The reality, then, is that for some individuals within even the most affluent countries – particularly the disadvantaged who rely heavily on government support and services – the decision to wage war continues to force a choice between guns and butter, even if they are not aware of it. Can these opportunity costs make the high-cost proviso available to those forced to bear them?

Based on the intuition that it is obligatory for the passerby to save the drowning child, Peter Singer articulates the following principle of assistance:

> If it is in our power to prevent something bad from happening, without thereby sacrificing anything of comparable moral importance, we ought, morally, to do it.[10]

If this is a statement of what morality requires of us at a minimum, it looks too demanding. A life is clearly more important than a limb. Therefore, I am obliged to sacrifice not only my new suit, but also my arm if need be in order to rescue the drowning child. Indeed, I may be required to give up everything short of my own life to save the life of the child, since death is the ultimate loss to which nothing else compares. To say that such a sacrifice is not only praiseworthy, but *required* – that refusing to make it constitutes wrongdoing – is strongly counter-intuitive. While there is still disagreement among philosophers over where exactly the high-cost threshold should be drawn, common-sense morality seems to require only modest sacrifices for the sake of assisting others.

And it would be a mistake to think that this applies only to sacrifices of bodily integrity. Consider *Bob's Internet Banking*:

> Bob is sitting in his house doing some Internet banking. Unbeknownst to his neighbours (the Smiths), he can see and hear them through the open door on the veranda. He notices that they are discussing the state of their terminally sick child, Jimmy. They need a new and expensive treatment to cure Jimmy now. They live in a society that has no universal health coverage; they cannot afford the operation themselves, nor are they able to finance it or acquire the funds from relatives and friends. Bob understands that he can transfer the money for the operation with a click of his mouse (he already has the Smiths' bank account listed). Clicking over the money would save Jimmy, but most of Bob's savings for retirement would be gone. Bob decides not to click the mouse.[11]

If Bob can legitimately invoke the high-cost proviso to justify his refusal to save Jimmy – as he surely can – can the citizens of one country not also activate the

---

[9] *Ibid.*, p. xv.   [10] Singer, "Famine, Affluence, and Morality," 231.
[11] Taken from: Christian Barry and Gerhard Øverland, "How Much for a Child?" unpublished manuscript, 11.

proviso against involvement in a costly humanitarian operation abroad? After all, the aforementioned opportunity costs are far from modest.

Arguably, however, the language distorts the moral picture here. Unlike Bob or the pedestrian who gives up his arm to save the drowning child, the bearer of an opportunity cost does not actually lose anything. Rather, he is deprived of some future benefit. One might insist that only the imposition of losses, properly speaking, can bring the high-cost proviso into the moral equation. Is this right?

Imagine there is some third party that forces Bob to give up his retirement savings for Jimmy. In so far as Bob is being coerced into making a sacrifice that he has every right to refuse, this is plausibly an infringement of his rights. The high-cost proviso thus explains why Bob has no obligation to click the mouse, and it also explains (indirectly) why third parties are obliged *not* to impose the related cost on Bob without his consent. Now let us alter the scenario so that the cost imposed on Bob by the third party is an opportunity cost. Suppose there is some charity or community group that helps residents in the neighborhood who fall on hard times. Bob, faultlessly let us assume, has no retirement savings. The community group has a history of supporting residents in similar circumstances, so Bob is relying on the organization to support him in retirement. But when the community group learns of Jimmy's illness, it transfers all of its money to the Smiths. Bob is consequently left destitute. While Bob's situation is certainly unfortunate, it seems he cannot invoke the high-cost proviso to dispute or resist the committee's decision. From this, one might infer that the high-cost proviso is available only to those who lose something that they already have, not to those deprived of future benefits.

But that would be a generalization drawn too quickly. In this scenario, while the community group may have a history of being charitable toward people like Bob, we are given no reason to think that Bob has any legitimate moral claim to the group's assistance. He cannot rightfully demand it. But now suppose that the group is more like a co-op, and that Bob has paid into it throughout his life precisely to insure himself against post-retirement destitution (while Jimmy's family has no such association with the co-op). Our intuitions change: Now it seems that Bob does have a claim against the group, and he can say that the cost he is being asked to bear for the sake of saving Jimmy is too high. Whether the denial of a benefit – or the imposition of an opportunity cost – activates the high-cost proviso, then, seems to depend on whether the good you are being denied is in some sense *rightfully yours*.

The relevance to our present discussion is clear. Even if citizens do not have a rightful claim against the state to any *particular* form of welfare or assistance (at least not in the absence of legislation guaranteeing it), most would agree that every citizen does have a general claim to some minimal standard of welfare. If carrying out a humanitarian intervention will compromise a state's ability to meet this standard, those individuals whose welfare claims are unfulfilled can, we think, protest that the intervention imposes unreasonable burdens on them. In other words, our disadvantaged compatriots may well be able to invoke the high-cost proviso in opposition to an altruistic war, even if that war imposes only opportunity costs. To be sure, a government's decision to launch an expensive humanitarian intervention will seldom be the sole reason for its decision to withhold various kinds of social support and services. Nevertheless, as Bilmes and Stiglitz's figures show, an intervention can significantly contribute to the crowding out of domestic programs that remedy deprivation, poverty, and so on; and this is enough to sustain the point.

The characterization of modern war as "cost free" for citizens is often accompanied by the claim that it is, or can be, largely "risk-free" for military personnel. The idea is that advances in military technology have made it increasingly possible for soldiers to engage in combat without taking on the risks that were once inherent in it. Just look at NATO's war against Serbia: 11 weeks of bombing, without a single NATO casualty.[12]

There are several reasons to be wary of this. The first is that, far from setting the precedent for future interventions, the Serbian case is beginning to seem quite exceptional. Neither the Afghanistan War nor the Iraq War were humanitarian interventions, strictly speaking, though there were attempts to cast them as such when the flimsy nature of other justifications became challenged. Nonetheless, they illustrate the ways in which the risk-free story quickly loses its charm after an initial period of plausibility. Thousands of coalition troops have been killed; and the lives lost by Afghan and Iraqi civilians far exceed the casualties on the coalition side, which is not to mention the toll of enemy-combatant deaths. Admittedly, this does not imperil the lives of the invading forces directly, but the increased hostility it creates does.

A second consideration is that reducing the risk of *physical* injury does not necessarily minimize the risk of *psychological* damage. Even in circumstances of near perfect physical safety, in the course of a typical humanitarian intervention, a soldier can expect to witness killing and maiming.[13] He will often feel helpless to defend the people that he has been sent to rescue, and, for that matter, sometimes his comrades. On occasion, he may be called upon to clear or recover dead bodies. He must exercise restraint in the face of danger, but

---

[12] See Ignatieff, *Virtual War*. See also Paul Kahn, "The Paradox of Riskless Warfare," *Philosophy & Public Policy Quarterly* 22, no. 3 (2002), 2–8; Paul Kahn, "War and Sacrifice in Kosovo," in Verna V. Gehring and William A. Galston (eds.), *Philosophical Dimensions of Public Policy* (New Jersey: Transaction Publishers, 2003).

[13] As many as 85 percent of former peacekeepers reported that they witnessed shootings, and 47 percent had seen dead or wounded people. See I. Bramsen, A.J.E. Dirkzwager, and H.M. Van der Ploeg, "Predominant Personality Traits and Exposure to Trauma as Predictors of Post-traumatic Stress Symptoms: A Prospective Study of Former Peacekeepers," *American Journal of Psychiatry* 157, no. 7 (2000), 1115–19.

also resort to deadly force when necessary. These experiences almost invariably leave psychological scars. The natural resistance to killing one's own kind can unleash a psychological backlash resulting in depression, severe cases of post-traumatic stress disorder, and even suicide. In 1996, it was reported that the number of Vietnam veterans that had taken their own lives since the end of the war had tripled the number killed by enemy fire during the war.[14] Merely witnessing traumatic death – and even the *anticipation* of exposure to traumatic death – has been known to cause significant distress among military personnel.[15] Moreover, where the primary aim of a military operation is to protect civilians and keep the peace, soldiers are expected to exercise greater restraint than would usually be required, since this is crucial for effective peacekeeping.[16] Recent studies, however, suggest that this can cause anxiety and frustration among combat-trained soldiers, and lead to the development of mental disorders, such as chronic hostility, later in life.[17]

Thus, even where the risk of death or physical injury is negligible, as where force protection is taken to extremes, the soldier is often exposed to the kind of psychological damage that would render him incapable of living a flourishing life upon returning from duty. If participating in humanitarian intervention is potentially so costly for soldiers, are they not entitled to invoke the high-cost proviso?

The obvious response is that this proviso is not available to professional soldiers, since they have freely taken on a role where risking life and limb is part of the job description. They have, in other words, "contracted away" or relinquished their access to the proviso. But whether this is persuasive depends partly on what it is we think military personnel sign up for. According to Martin Cook:

> Military personnel live in a unique moral world. They exist to serve the state. The essence and moral core of their service is to defend that state through the management and application of violence in defence of the territorial integrity, political sovereignty, and vital national interests of the state … The military contract obliges military personnel to run grave risks and to engage in morally and personally difficult actions. They do these things on the basis of the implicit promise that the circumstances under which they

[14] See Dave Grossman and Bruce Siddle, "Psychological Effects of Combat," Killology Research Group, available at: www.killology.com/print/print_psychological.htm (accessed August 30, 2008).
[15] James E. McCarroll, Robert J. Ursano, Carol S. Fullerton, and Allan Lundy, "Traumatic Stress of a Wartime Mortuary: Anticipation of Exposure to Mass Death," *Journal of Nervous and Mental Disease* 181, no. 9 (September 1993).
[16] K. Allard, *Somalia Operations: Lessons Learned* (Washington, DC: National Defense University Press, 1995).
[17] Brett T. Litz, Lynda A. King, and Daniel W. King, "Warriors as Peacekeepers: Features of the Somalia Experience and PTSD," *Journal of Consulting and Clinical Psychology* 65, no. 6 (1997), 1008.

must act are grounded in political leadership's good-faith judgment that the defense of sovereignty and integrity of the nation (or, by careful extension, the nation's vital interests) require their action.[18]

The crucial point about Cook's thesis of the implicit contract is that members of the armed forces agree to fight and die for their country and its interests, not for the human rights of foreigners.[19] If this is accurate, then while professional soldiers may not invoke the high-cost proviso to resist deployment in a war of national self-defense, it remains available to them when it comes to armed humanitarian intervention. They have not contracted away their access to the proviso with respect to these kinds of missions.

Of course, one might dispute Cook's account of the implicit military contract. After all, on Cook's own showing, what the soldier implicitly consents to cannot be radically at odds with what it is reasonable for him to expect; and humanitarian intervention has by now become commonplace, at least among certain Western states. Some of the most recent engagements of the

---

[18] Martin L. Cook, *The Moral Warrior: Ethics and Service in the US Military* (Albany, New York: State University of New York Press, 2004), 123–24. See also Martin L. Cook, "Immaculate War: Constraints on Humanitarian Intervention," *Ethics & International Affairs* 14 (2000). The oath that recruits into the US military recite might be seen as lending support to Cook's account. The recruit solemnly swears "to support and defend the Constitution of the United States against all enemies, foreign and domestic." Michael L. Gross maintains that this limits one's deployment to missions necessary for the security of the United States. Thus, "without volunteers who consent specifically to humanitarian duties, states have no choice but to refuse their international obligations." Michael L. Gross, *Moral Dilemmas of Modern War: Torture, Assassination, and Blackmail in an Age of Asymmetric Conflict* (Cambridge University Press, 2010), 218. But the oath continues: "I will obey the orders of the President of the United States and the orders of the officers appointed over me, according to regulations and the Uniform Code of Military Justice. So help me God." The only reference to Cook's "circumstances under which they may act" is that the soldier is "required upon order to serve in combat or other hazardous operations." This is hardly restrictive as to circumstances of national defense or integrity of the nation, and offers little hope of some restrictive "implicit promise." This obviously complicates matters, but we will set aside the strict legal situation to pursue the underlying politico-moral problem.

[19] As Mickey Kaus puts it, "Is it fair to ask someone who volunteered to die for America to die for Father Aristide?" Kaus, "TRB from Washington: Somalia Syndrome," *The New Republic* (October 17, 1994), 61. Kaus does not endorse this view of the soldier–state contract. Here he is simply describing the position taken by fellow columnist Michael Kinsley. Thousands of active-duty troops involved in the recent Iraq war signed an online Appeal for Redress calling for the withdrawal from the country long before the war ended in 2011. Interviews with several of the signatories suggest that Cook's account of the soldier–state contract resonates with at least some members of the armed forces. "Lisa" of the US Air Force, having "joined up two weeks after [turning] 17 because [she] wanted to save American lives," now feels that "our troops have no reason for being there." "Sergeant Gary" signed up while still in junior high school on the pretence that Saddam "was a threat to America." The evidence to the contrary led Gary to sign the Appeal. See Marc Cooper, "About Face: Soldiers Call for Iraq Withdrawal," *The Nation* (December 16, 2006), available at: www.thenation.com/article/about-face-soldiers-call-iraq-withdrawal (accessed August 30, 2008).

Australian Defence Force, for example, include: Operation Astute, aimed at restoring peace in East Timor; Operation Anode, geared towards a similar end in the Solomon Islands; peacekeeping operations in Sudan; and, of course, the "rehabilitation and reconstruction" of Iraq. In light of this, the idea that the implicit contract of military personnel strictly excludes a commitment to serve in humanitarian operations starts to looks rather dubious.

A closer look at the official justifications provided for these missions, however, reveals that they invariably appeal to national self-interest *as well as* humanitarian concerns. Given this, those who sign up for the armed forces can arguably expect national self-interest to be somewhere in the mix whenever they are deployed. It may be unreasonable for them to expect that their deployment will be limited to missions where national self-interest is the sole motivation; but, at the same time, it seems they can expect not to be deployed in wars that are purely altruistic either. If so, there may be a limit to the sacrifice soldiers can be asked to make for interventions lacking a significant national-interest rationale.

There is, however, another possible line of response to Cook's argument: one that, rather than disputing his account of the *content* of the implicit contract, disputes the very *existence* of any contract that gives soldiers entitlements against their commanders and their state. A common view amongst some just-war theorists is that soldiers surrender their rights by enlisting. More accurately, soldiers are said to *exchange* their human rights – to life, liberty, etc. – for a different set of rights, what Michael Walzer calls "war rights." The list of war rights is a short one. It includes a liberty to do the things that combatants are meant to do, and a right to be treated as the POW conventions require if captured. The soldier loses his rights to life and physical safety, but thereby gains a right to compromise the safety and take the lives of others.[20] Contrary to Cook, Walzer claims, on the basis of this, that sending soldiers into battle is always consistent with their rights, whether it be for reasons of self-interest or otherwise: "I don't think it can ever be impermissible for an officer to send his soldiers into battle: that is what he is for and that is what they are for."[21]

If this is right, then soldiers do not have any access to the high-cost proviso, regardless of the nature of the mission. But Walzer's view seems far too strong, since it would imply that officers do not wrong their troops if they stupidly, callously, or negligently send them on futile and unnecessary missions where they will certainly be slaughtered. Walzer admits that such missions can occur and that officers are rightly criticized for them, but he cannot admit that these are violations of rights the troops have.[22] This is surely perverse. Treating the

[20] Michael Walzer, *Just and Unjust Wars* (New York: Basic Books, 1977), 136, 145.
[21] *Ibid.*, 20–21.
[22] See James M. Dubik, "Human Rights, Command Responsibility and Walzer's Just War Theory," *Philosophy & Public Affairs* 11, no. 4 (Autumn 1982).

consent of the soldier as sufficient to divest him of all his rights deviates radically from current thinking on the scope and limits of consent. In particular,
if we shift our focus from military to occupational ethics, employee rights are
usually treated as *inalienable*, as something that cannot be validly relinquished
through contract. Des Jardins and McCall, for instance, defend a conception of
workers' rights "as presumptive entitlements *not subject to bargaining within
the employment agreement*" (emphasis added).[23] If we want to maintain that the
soldier relinquishes his claim to the high-cost proviso by enlisting, it seems we
need some explanation for why soldiers can *validly* waive their rights if other
classes of employees cannot.

The explanation usually offered, or at least implied, is that soldiering is no
ordinary career. Military personnel do not sign a contract of employment; they
take a sacred oath to defend and preserve the state and the common life it is
supposed to serve. Perhaps this is so important a function that it explains why
soldiers can validly surrender their rights, including the right to invoke high
costs, even though other kinds of employees cannot. But notice that, again, this
would seem to leave soldiers with at least some recourse to the high-cost proviso when it comes to humanitarian operations that have nothing to do with
defending the state. This time, it is not because soldiers have implicitly contracted only to take risks for the state. Soldiers may well have consented to fight
for other purposes, too. But, on this line of argument, only the soldier's consent
to fight for the state can be presumed valid and binding in a way that restricts
access to the high-cost proviso. For anything else, further questions need to be
asked.

It appears that, even on very strong and contestable accounts of a professional soldier's function and derivative duties and rights, there remains room
for appeal to a high-cost proviso in relation to humanitarian intervention. One
cannot straightforwardly deny soldiers in humanitarian wars access to this
proviso on the same grounds that one might deny it to them in relation to wars
of national self-defense.

II

Even in cases of massacre or ethnic cleansing, then, the citizens of even
affluent countries will not always have an obligation to bear the costs associated with carrying out a military intervention. This becomes apparent once
we fully appreciate two facts about our positive duties: They are presumptively imperfect, and they are qualified by a high-cost proviso. Admittedly,

---

[23] Joseph R. Des Jardins and John J. McCall, "A Defence of Employee Rights," *Journal of
Business Ethics* 4 (1985), 367.

this conclusion is highly contingent. It holds for the world as we know it, not for the world as it might be. Certain developments in international institutions, as well as advances in military technology and pharmacology, have the potential to perfect our imperfect duties, and to make the high-cost proviso unavailable to both citizens generally and military personnel more specifically.

Suppose that one state – state X – plans to execute a humanitarian intervention in a troubled neighboring country, and to shoulder all of its associated costs. X may be asking too much of its constituents, especially if success depends on a long-term and expensive occupation, justifying them in declining to make this sacrifice. But what if state X, instead of acting unilaterally, makes the case for intervention to the United Nations or some other multilateral institution, which in turn arranges for the costs to be shared by a number of different states? The sacrifice asked of the citizens of X would be reduced to a fraction of what would be required to facilitate a unilateral action, and this might be a cost that the people of X *are* morally obliged to sustain.

Of course, the soldiers sent in to do the fighting might still be in a position to invoke the high-cost proviso, but there are things that a state can do to overcome this moral hurdle as well. Even something as simple as a shift in political rhetoric might go a long way toward rewriting the terms of the implicit moral contract of professional armed servicemen and women (if indeed there is such a contract). While today's soldier can expect to be deployed on an assortment of missions that do not neatly fit the mold of "defensive war," we have suggested that, given the way that military operations are justified publicly, he/she can arguably still expect national interest to be among the motives. Reducing or removing the explicit emphasis on national self-interest in cases where this is a secondary motive would gradually undermine the basis of this expectation. No longer would the professional soldier be in a position to sensibly and reasonably maintain that he/she has only "signed up" to fight and die for the national interest, and never purely for the national conscience.

Failing this, the state might look to recruit a special expeditionary force made up entirely of soldiers that volunteer specifically for humanitarian missions; and, again, the involvement of the international community is conducive to this end. A single state acting alone may not be able to recruit enough volunteers from within its own populace to do the job effectively. A multiplicity of states – perhaps acting under the banner of the United Nations – is less likely to run into this problem, given that it has a much larger pool of potential volunteers to draw from. This would also help meet the objection to interventions by single states (or even coalitions of such states) that such interventions run a high risk of being tainted by unworthy motives of self-interest, such as the gaining of economic or political assets in the target country. It is significant in this connection that an international UN volunteer, military force adaptable to such purposes has been proposed and strongly argued for by Sir Brian Urquhart and others for many years. Urquhart, a distinguished former soldier and a former Undersecretary-General of the United Nations, campaigned on this project for decades and carefully responded to various intellectual, political, and financial objections to it.

Hence, international institutions could one day make the high-cost proviso unavailable to both citizens and military personnel: by facilitating the recruitment of a special class of soldiers that unequivocally consent to fight for humanitarian purposes, and by distributing the economic costs of intervention in a way that ensures nobody is forced to bear a cost above the high-cost threshold.

In addition to this, international institutions could perfect our imperfect duties. Current arrangements do not quite achieve this. Suppose that state X is signed on to the UN Convention on the Prevention and Punishment of the Crime of Genocide. One might say that the people of X have thus surrendered the presumptive discretion not to respond to genocide where it is occurring. They do not have the option of committing their humanitarian resources elsewhere. This convention, however, does not simply cover mass killing, but any act "committed with intent to destroy, in whole or in part, a national, ethnical, racial or religious group." This encompasses imposing measures intended to prevent births within the group, forcibly transferring children from one group to another, and forced expulsion from territory as well. State X might also be signed on to the UN Covenant on Economic, Social, and Cultural Rights – which commits it to fighting poverty and securing healthcare and education – and a host of other international agreements. The fact that states have made so many commitments effectively takes us back to square one. State X may have signed on to prevent mass killing, but if it is also signed on to fight poverty, disease, ethnic cleansing, etc., in so far as it cannot possibly solve all of the world's problems, its people must retain the right to choose where to direct their limited humanitarian resources.

But things could change. Our imperfect obligations, via institutions, could be transformed into perfect ones. For every right, an international duty-bearer could be identified, and specific responsibilities could be allocated. That we have not yet devised a means to achieve this, Mark Evans laments, is one of our greatest moral failings collectively. What we need is a restructuring of the global order: the creation of some sort of authority that could "concretize, codify, and organize" our international moral responsibilities.[24]

---

[24] See Mark Evans, "Selectivity, Imperfect Obligations and the Character of Humanitarian Morality," in Alexander Moseley and Richard Norman (eds.), *Human Rights and Military Intervention* (Aldershot: Ashgate, 2002), 132–49. See also Henry Shue, "Mediating Duties."

Advances in military technology and pharmacology can also push the costs borne by soldiers beneath the high-cost threshold. We have suggested that, even where force-protection measures ensure that the risk to physical safety is negligible, as things stand, the prospect of severe psychological damage is very real. The latest remote weaponry is likely to offer some measure of protection to the mental health and well-being of professional soldiers, essentially by removing them from the battlefield.[25] As for those who cannot be insulated from the horrors of war, Pentagon chemists are busy seeking out ways to prevent the onset of combat-induced PTSD. One promising method involves the use of Propranolol (a beta-blocker) to prevent the formation of traumatic memories.[26]

Hence there are conceivable circumstances under which the occurrence of massacre or ethnic cleansing would always impose upon the citizens of some other particular country or countries a duty to sustain the costs associated with intervention. But for now, some interventions will remain merely permissible.

III

The all-or-nothing view, if taken as an account of the moral requirements of citizens, looks to be untenable. But might it nevertheless be accurate as a description of the moral responsibilities of governments? Returning to the scenario sketched in Section I (starvation in country A, mass death caused by easily preventable diseases in country B, civil war in country C, ethnic cleansing in D), suppose that the citizens of state X *do* have a duty to sustain the costs associated with carrying out a humanitarian intervention in country D. The taxpayers have a duty to finance it, and the professional military personnel have

---

[25] Of course, we should be careful not to overstate things. While remote warfare takes some of the common battlefield stressors out of the equation, it introduces others that military institutions have not yet learned to cope with. The remote warrior might operate his/her unmanned aircraft from 9 to 5, before going home to tend to his/her family responsibilities, household chores, etc. This can prove even more stressful than good old-fashioned deployment. As one operator explains, "when you are deployed, the mission is your only job. When you are at home, you still have the mission, but all the extras, plus the family." New stressors are introduced, but none of the pressures of ordinary civilian life disappear. Yet the cubicle warrior does not have access to the same kinds of psychological support systems that are made available to his/her battlefield counterparts. See P.W. Singer, *Wired for War: The Robotics Revolution and Conflict in the Twenty-first Century* (New York: The Penguin Press, 2009), 346.

[26] Against this, evidence suggests that our emotional response to a situation helps to bring its morally salient features to our attention. As Jessica Wolfendale points out, "drugs that significantly modified our emotional assessment of situations would thereby reduce our awareness of information relevant not only to moral decision-making but to practical risk-assessment." See Jessica Wolfendale, "Performance-Enhancing Technologies and Moral Responsibility in the Military," *The American Journal of Bioethics* 8, no. 2 (2008), 30.

an obligation to risk life and limb executing it. The duty is a perfect one – the victims of the ethnic cleansing in D, for whatever reason, have a right against the citizens of X that they intervene, and the high-cost proviso is not available to anybody whose interests are affected.

If I have a duty to bear a certain cost by way of rendering assistance, I cannot reasonably demand that the cost not be imposed on me by someone else if I am unable or unwilling to make the sacrifice without such interference. As Henry Shue explains, "what I give up in, say, time or money in fulfilling a positive right is not genuinely mine to retain if I truly have the duty to use that resource on behalf of someone else's right."[27] Thus if the people of one country are obliged to pay for an intervention into another, their government is permitted to use their resources – even against their will – to carry out the intervention.

But if the government is *merely* permitted in these circumstances, although it may, it *need not* fulfill the obligation of its people. This is unsatisfactory. The state is an agent empowered by its citizens to act in their name and on their behalf. Advancing the collective interests of its citizens is part of the state's purpose, but so too is discharging their legal and moral responsibilities to outsiders. Indeed, denying that the state has an obligation to act in these cir-cumstances seems to open a gaping moral loophole. The citizens are obliged to pay for the intervention, but the agent that has been entrusted with their col-lective resources has no duty to facilitate the fulfillment of this obligation. So it turns out that the citizens are able to evade their moral obligations simply by acting through an agent. The moral loophole can be exploited by empowering a government and letting it hold onto our money.

Now consider humanitarian intervention that is "merely permissible" from the point of view of the citizens – suppose the presumptive discretion that applies to their positive duties has not been rebutted. Let us imagine two such scenarios. In the first, the public is overwhelmingly against using public funds to pay for the intervention. Here the citizens have chosen to exercise their right not to intervene. Should the government proceed with the intervention regard-less, it forces its people to make a sacrifice that they have every right to refuse, and have refused – plausibly an infringement of their rights. In the second scen-ario, the citizens overwhelmingly support intervention. Here it is by *refusing* to intervene that the state might be said to infringe the rights of its people. The reason that humanitarian intervention is sometimes merely permissible even for citizens of affluent countries is that we enjoy a presumptive right to choose how and when we fulfill our positive obligations. But if a government need not cooperate with its people's choices regarding when and where they render assistance to the needy and oppressed, then the people do not have this discre-tion in any practically meaningful sense.

---

[27] Shue, "Mediating Duties," 690.

The upshot is this: Where intervention is merely permissible for citizens, depending on their collective preferences, intervention is either obligatory or prohibited for their government. In light of this, one might think the all-or-nothing view remains plausible as a description of the requirements of states, even if it does not hold true for citizens.

In a representative democracy, however, the state is not merely a delegate whose role is to transmit the instructions of its principals or authors. It is what Joel Feinberg refers to as a "free agent": "an expert hired to exercise his professional judgment on behalf of, and in the name of, his principal."[28] For a modern society, making each and every political decision through some process of collective deliberation or by referendum is impractical and overly burdensome for individuals. Thus we empower our representatives to make decisions for us, and we do not feel that the government must always consult with us and make whatever decision is most popular.

Why, then, does this not extend to decisions regarding the fulfillment of our positive duties? Is this decision not covered by the "free agency" invested in the government? Have we not, by electing our government, relinquished to it our presumptive discretion to choose where and when to render assistance? If so, then even where a proposed humanitarian intervention is overwhelmingly opposed, a government cannot be accused of infringing the rights of its citizens by proceeding. "Merely permissible" for the citizenry does not translate into "prohibited" for the state after all. By the same token, where a humanitarian intervention is strongly supported by the public – where the people have in some way communicated their preference to exercise their presumptive discretion in a particular way – the government need not cooperate. "Merely permissible" for the citizens does not translate, even via their clearly exercised discretion, into obligatory for the government.

Of course we can accept the basic arrangement of the representative democracy, while advocating certain reforms around the edges to facilitate greater popular participation. For instance, some would supplement a representative arrangement with a public veto function. The government need not consult with its people or execute their instructions on every occasion, but where a manifestly unpopular decision is made the citizenry – in whom political authority ultimately resides – can override it. At the very least, this public veto could be extended to cases where the decision involves a deviation from the core purposes of the state. A democratic government's mandate is to protect its citizens and promote their common good. In the pursuit of this objective, perhaps the government is not subject to any popular constraints whatsoever. But altruistically defending human rights abroad falls outside of this mandate, and a public veto in this connection seems an appropriate limit on the free-agency of government.

[28] Joel Feinberg, "Collective Responsibility," *Journal of Philosophy* 65 (1968), 675.

Even if we concede all this, however, we still do not arrive at the conclusion that humanitarian intervention is always either obligatory or prohibited for the state. It may be the case that it is either obligatory or prohibited when the preferences of the citizens are unequivocal (as in the clear-cut cases of "overwhelming support" or "overwhelming rejection" just considered). But many – perhaps most – cases will involve substantial or slim majorities, even divisions, large minorities, and so on. Here there is no exercise of a public veto either way; in which case, we see no reason to think the decision is not covered by the authority vested in a representative government.

Conclusion

If the all-or-nothing view is untenable as a claim about the moral requirements of citizens, as we have suggested, it cannot be salvaged as a position that holds for their governments. To be sure, the class of "merely permissible" interventions for governments is not necessarily identical to, or co-extensive with, the class of "merely permissible" interventions for their people, and may be significantly narrower. As argued in the previous section, an intervention that the citizens of a country are permitted but not obliged to finance may, in some cases, be obligatory or prohibited for their government, especially where the people's preferences are clearly communicated. Nevertheless the space reserved for the morally discretionary humanitarian intervention cannot be entirely closed off.

6

Judging armed humanitarian intervention

HELEN FROWE

Political commentators, and the general public, frequently express skepticism concerning the explanations given by states for engaging in "humanitarian interventions," often attributing to the interveners rather more self-interested reasons for action than those offered by the interveners themselves. Underlying this skepticism, and reflected in the philosophical literature, is a concern that an otherwise permissible instance of intervention might be rendered impermissible if the intervening state's motivations are not genuinely humanitarian.

In this chapter, I argue for what I call the *justification-based account* of humanitarian intervention, according to which the permissibility of humanitarian intervention is determined by two central criteria. The first is that there exists a sound justification for intervention – roughly, that there is a threatened or ongoing process of widespread and serious rights violations that can be averted only by military force and such force is proportionate. This criterion can be satisfied *ad bellum*.

The second criterion is that the actions of interveners are reasonably expected to aid. This criterion applies largely to the *in bello* behavior of the intervening state. I defend the priority of this criterion against Alex Bellamy's suggestion that the intentions of interveners are central to the permissibility of intervention. I suggest that both intentions-based and motives-based views wrongly prioritize the moral character of the intervener over the interests of the potential beneficiaries of intervention. This is not to deny that intentions or motives are ever relevant to permissibility, but to make the more limited claim that in situations in which one can act to avert significant suffering, imperfect intentions or motives do not render so acting impermissible.

A draft of this chapter was presented at the University of Kent Philosophy Department Seminar in October 2012. I am very grateful to the audience there for helpful comments. Special thanks to Christopher Monahan, Kristoffer Ahlstrom-Vij, Edward Kanterian, Julien Murzi, Julia Tanney, and Jon Williamson. Special thanks also to Don E. Scheid for helpful comments and suggestions, and to Andréas Lind for helpful conversations.

What is a humanitarian intervention?

Two broad ways of approaching the debate about how to identify humanitarian interventions have emerged from the literature. The first views the term "humanitarian intervention" as morally loaded, such that a use of force in a crisis must be legitimate (however we judge that) in order to count as a humanitarian intervention. On this view, a use of military force that fails to fulfill the relevant criteria for permissibility is not an illegitimate humanitarian intervention, but no humanitarian intervention at all. Bhikhu Parekh, for example, argues that an intervention in a crisis counts as humanitarian only if it is "wholly or primarily guided by the sentiment of humanity, compassion or fellow-feeling, and in that sense disinterested" and "is intended to address what is regarded as a violation of the minimum that is due to human beings."[1] For Parekh, these features are our criteria not only for judging the permissibility of humanitarian intervention, but for judging whether a use of force qualifies as a humanitarian intervention at all.

The second approach claims that the use of military force in a crisis can count as a humanitarian intervention, and yet still be illegitimate or impermissible. Private wars might be captured by this approach. If Bill Gates hires an army to curtail human rights abuses in Darfur, we might describe this as a humanitarian intervention, but deem it an illegitimate intervention – perhaps because we think that private individuals such as Gates should not be using military force to achieve even good ends. Alex Bellamy adopts an approach along these lines, asking "what it is that makes a particular intervention 'humanitarian' and therefore potentially legitimate."[2] On this view, whether a use of force is an example of humanitarian intervention is conceptually independent of whether it is morally permissible.

In this chapter, I assume that the second of these two approaches is correct: that whether a use of force is a humanitarian intervention is independent of whether it is permissible. My interest will be in how we judge this permissibility. I will focus on the moral, rather than legal, dimension of permissibility.

Judging permissibility

Motives versus outcomes

While accounts of the permissibility of intervention are often pluralist in that they allow that various factors might affect the legitimacy of an intervention, most identify one central factor as the primary criterion of permissibility.

---

[1] Bhikhu Parekh, "Rethinking Humanitarian Intervention," *International Political Science Review* 18, no. 1 (1997), 54–55.

[2] Alex J. Bellamy, "Motives, Outcomes, Intent and the Legitimacy of Humanitarian Intervention," *Journal of Military Ethics* 3, no. 3 (2004), 221.

Bellamy argues that much of the debate on intervention has focused on the division between those who identify motives as paramount, and those who identify outcomes as paramount.[3] As we have just seen, writers such as Parekh argue that it is motives that are crucial: interventions *just are* disinterested uses of force inspired by compassion and a desire to aid those in need.

Others reject this focus on motive. Michael Walzer, for example, claims that while an intervening state must "to some degree" share in the ends of the people whom it is supposed to be aiding, and ought not to behave in ways that thwart those ends, it is not crucial for permissibility that humanitarianism is the "chief consideration" of the intervening state.[4] Some scholars replace the focus on motive with a primarily outcome-based evaluation of intervention. One of the most prominent defenders of this view, Fernando Tesón, argues that, at least sometimes, we can judge interventions by their results – by whether they do in fact halt or mitigate humanitarian abuses. So, on this account, even if the United States' invasion of Iraq in 2003 was motivated by a dislike of Saddam Hussein and a desire to secure access to oil, it could still have turned out to be a legitimate humanitarian intervention if getting rid of Hussein secured some proportionate humanitarian good.

Bellamy argues that this dichotomy between motives and outcomes is mistaken. Proponents of the motives view often conflate motives with purposes. But, he thinks, motive and purpose can come apart. We can talk about what one is trying to do, without talking about why one is trying to do it. For example, one might use force for the humanitarian purpose of protecting some ethnic group abroad, while being motivated by a desire to increase one's political popularity with members of that group at home. Bellamy argues that because of this conflation, some writers are mistakenly adopted by the motives camp when they are in fact identifying purpose as the crucial factor in permissibility. He claims, for example, that Parekh "erroneously implies" that the writer Will Verwey "demands purity of motives," when Verwey's account stipulates only that the sole *purposes* of force should be humanitarian.[5]

Intentions

Bellamy argues that while purpose gives us a third category of evaluation, thus undermining the motives/outcomes dichotomy, those writers who make use of purpose in their work do so only vaguely, without explaining how one might judge what a state's purposes are. He suggests that we can better illuminate the debate if we substitute intention for purposes, perhaps not least because the criterion of right intention has an established place in traditional just-war

---

[3] *Ibid.*, 221.
[4] Michael Walzer, *Just and Unjust Wars* (New York: Basic Books, 1977), 104.
[5] Bellamy, "Motives, Outcomes, Intent," 222.

theory. Drawing upon the work of Augustine, Bellamy argues that right intention is the pivotal factor in determining the legitimacy of an intervention: we
must judge whether "the intervener *intended* to prevent or halt an injustice and
promote peace."[6]

Although we can never be entirely sure that we have correctly judged intentions, Bellamy argues that we can reliably assess them by:

(1) examining the state's given reasons for intervening, and comparing them
     with other possible explanations; and
(2) examining the way in which the state plans and executes its intervention.[7]

To achieve the latter, he combines Aquinas's modifications of the doctrine of
double effect with Walzer's notion of "double intent." Whereas Augustine held
that harms were permissible if they were foreseen but unintended, Aquinas
argued that, in addition, these harms must be outweighed by the good being
pursued. This revision – essentially a proportionality requirement – places
restrictions upon the means that may be employed by those seeking even a
good end: combatants cannot cause unlimited destruction provided that the
destruction is merely a foreseen side effect. This restriction enables the intentions-based account to acknowledge the importance of outcomes, but still hold
outcomes secondary to intent.[8]

According to Walzer's notion of "double intent," combatants do not count
as satisfying the requirement of discrimination just in case they cause only
foreseen but unintended harm to non-combatants.[9] Nor is it enough that the
harm done is proportionate to the good end. Rather, combatants must demonstrate a further "positive commitment" to protecting non-combatants, manifested by going out of their way to take measures that minimize the risks to
non-combatants, even (or especially) where this involves shouldering greater
risks themselves.[10] If a commander has two strategies that are equally likely to
achieve a military goal, but one will protect his troops and endanger non-combatants, while the other protects non-combatants but endangers his troops, he
is required to choose the strategy that protects the non-combatants. Bellamy
argues that by looking to see whether combatants engaged in a humanitarian

---

[6] *Ibid.*, 227.
[7] I will use Bellamy's terminology of "state intentions" here; but, for me, this is shorthand for
     the "intentions of the state's leaders."
[8] One might, for example, cause more harm than one averts (perhaps killing an attacker to
     avoid paralysis to oneself). The outcome of defending oneself is thus more harmful than not
     defending oneself. But the harm inflicted upon one's attacker as a side effect of saving one-
     self is unintended, and thus counts for less. The outcomes are not irrelevant – one cannot
     kill an attacker to save oneself a broken toe – but they are secondary to what is intended.
[9] Walzer, *Just and Unjust Wars*, 155–56.
[10] *Ibid.*, 156.

mission adhere to this requirement, we can judge whether their state is really acting with humanitarian intent.

Bellamy claims two main advantages of the intention-based view. First, he argues that our right to intervene in other states, ostensibly breaching their sovereignty, is a "limited right" that obtains when we need "to save strangers in dire need."[11] It is therefore "logically necessary that acts legitimized by the exception have a humanitarian intent: that is, the act must intend to do what the exception permits."[12] It is, he says, "the intent of the intervener, not the ostensible humanitarian outcome … that the limited norm of humanitarian intervention legitimises."[13] The second advantage is that the intentions-based approach reduces the likelihood of "the military means chosen by the intervener undermining the desired humanitarian ends."[14]

Ad bellum intentions

I think we should be skeptical both of Bellamy's methods of assessing intention and, partly as a result of this skepticism, the plausibility of using intentions to assess the permissibility of humanitarian interventions. Let us start with the *ad bellum* intentions.

State intentions

There is of course the general problem that arises in talking of a state's intentions, which Bellamy does not address – namely, that a state is an abstract entity that has no intentions at all. It is, presumably, the intentions of the leaders that are under scrutiny here. But there is no guarantee that the intentions of this group of people will converge. Imagine a British Cabinet considering intervening in Kosovo. The prime minister might generally dislike Serbs, and be glad of the opportunity to do some Serb-bombing. The defense minister might intend to use the intervention as a lengthy training exercise for the British armed forces, thinking it good practice for a proper war. Perhaps it is also a chance to test some new equipment or technology. The foreign minister might intend only to bring humanitarian aid. All favor the intervention, but their intentions differ significantly. Whose intentions matter? Assuming that the prime minister cannot act without the support of her Cabinet, all the intentions play a role in bringing the intervention about. It is not clear, then, how we can sensibly speak of *the* intention behind the intervention. I am not wholly skeptical of the role of intentions in determining permissibility when it comes to individual actions, but it is at least considerably harder to rely on them when assessing the permissibility of an action or series of actions initiated and steered by

[11] Bellamy, "Motives, Outcomes, Intent," 229.
[12] *Ibid.*, 229.   [13] *Ibid.*, 230.   [14] *Ibid.*, 230.

a group of people. This is not merely because of the difficulty of establishing intentions, which increases as one increases the number of relevant people. It is also because when we have multiple intentions, there is no clear way of ranking or reconciling those intentions, such that we can identify a single intention by which we can judge an action's permissibility.

Intentions and justifications

Moreover, a closer look at Bellamy's suggestions for establishing intention shows that intention is not as easy to establish as he believes. His first suggestion is that one might "analyze" a state's reasons for acting, where this is achieved in part by "comparing the justifications it gives with other possible explanations of its actions."[15] It is not made clear how Bellamy is conceiving of the relationship between intentions and justifications, but they seem to me to be different things, likely to elicit different commentaries.

For example, a state may say that it intends to mount an aerial bombing campaign in particular areas of the target state in order to disable certain parts of the state's infrastructure, followed by a ground offensive in which it aims to capture or kill certain groups or persons. It may say that its intention in so doing is to eliminate a threat to (a group of) civilians, and restore stability in the state. This is a description of the state's intentions, in terms of both what it intends to do, and what it intends to achieve by doing those things.

But it *is* purely descriptive. The justification of those actions, in contrast, will surely tell a different, normative story. Saying that one plans to eliminate a threat and restore stability is not enough to turn a description into a justification. The justification will have to include various other claims, such as that the threat in question constitutes a serious violation of important rights, that the proposed force is a proportionate means of halting that violation, that it is the most effective way to achieve it, and that alternative, non-military methods are not available. And none of these claims, which are the meat of any justification for military action, depends for their truth upon the intentions of the intervening state. It may be the case that the intervening state is merely seeking to assert its military power in the region, deterring potential aggressors. But this will not affect whether the proposed intervention is a proportionate means of halting the rights violations. Nor will it affect whether the threat posed to the potential beneficiaries is grave, whether the action is a last resort, and so on. An analysis of an offered justification, therefore, need not shed any light on intentions. What it will do is put forward reasons for intervening, the weight of which can be assessed independently of whether they are the reasons upon which the state's leaders are acting, and the soundness of which does not depend upon the leaders' intentions.

---

[15] *Ibid.*, 227.

Establishing intentions by comparison

The second component of analysis is comparative – Bellamy suggests that the proffered justification should be compared with other possible explanations. The idea is that if there exists an alternative possible explanation that would also explain the state's willingness to intervene, and this explanation has a goal of national interest rather than humanitarian beneficence, then it is reasonable to assume that it is the self-interested goal that the interveners intend to bring about: the comparison can tell us whether the state "is merely offering a pretext for action."[16] If so, Bellamy thinks that the intervention is "inspired by egoism rather than right intent and cannot, from this perspective, be justified."[17]

But this kind of comparative evaluation, which for Bellamy speaks not just to our assessment of the blameworthiness of the actors but also to the permissibility of their actions, is undesirable in at least two ways. If we cite intentions as crucial to the permissibility of purported humanitarian interventions, we surely want to base our judgments on the presence or absence of humanitarian intentions. But Bellamy's comparative evaluation makes the likelihood of finding in a state's favor contingent on factors other than whether it does in fact have humanitarian intentions.

Imagine that the proposed intervention is to take place in a country whose stability is regionally important, or that happens to be oil-rich, or where the dominant religion is hostile to the intervening state's dominant religion. Or perhaps the intervening state is due for an election, or has some new weapons it would like to test, or could use a war to assert their dominance in the region. Any of these facts could provide an alternative, prudentially based explanation of the intervention. Indeed, in almost any situation in which an intervention seems necessary, there are likely to be possible alternative explanations of using force that are self-serving rather than humanitarian in nature. The mere existence of these alternatives undermines, in Bellamy's view, the plausibility of the intervening state's acting for humanitarian reasons, irrespective of whether or not they are the reasons for which the state acts.

In addition, some of these features, such as being oil-rich, are pretty inescapable properties of some states, and thus these self-interested explanations will always be possible and perhaps always plausible when considering interventions in these states. On Bellamy's account, this seems to preclude its being permissible to intervene in such a state, no matter how dire the humanitarian situation. But we should not prohibit interventions that could rescue people from harm simply because a state that is prepared to intervene has various possible grounds for doing so, and its intentions may or may not be humanitarian. And, we should not make it harder to mount a case for intervening in

---

[16] *Ibid.*, 227.
[17] *Ibid.*, 227.

some states compared with others in virtue of that state's having certain natural properties.

What we need to know, if we favor the intention-based view, is not whether the state has sufficient alternative reasons for acting, but whether it is acting for humanitarian reasons. But how would one go about analyzing or judging which reasons are really operative at the *ad bellum* level? I contend that one cannot establish, simply by way of comparison, that an offered justification does not reflect the leaders' intentions. It seems to me that, setting aside the question of consent, all one can do to judge the permissibility of the intervention at the *ad bellum* level is to assess the soundness of the offered justification independently of whether or not the state might have other, prudential reasons to intervene. And, I suggest, if the reasons given would in fact justify intervention, it does not matter whether or not they reflect the leaders' intentions. I return to this second point below.

But in general, the whole direction of Bellamy's concern seems mistaken to me. Either people are in need of rescue from an actual or impeding catastrophe, or they are not. Whether they are or not is neither determined nor illuminated by examining the intentions of those who are well-placed to rescue them. If we care about their intentions, it should be only because of what they tell us about what the interveners are likely to do during the intervention: the kinds of strategies they are likely to adopt and so on. In Bellamy's account, the importance of rescuing the victims is completely overshadowed by his emphasis on the moral character of the interveners. When we think about the circumstances in which we might use force in another country, we must presumably begin by pointing to some kind of crisis that we think warrants intervention. But once this triggering condition is satisfied, Bellamy's attention shifts solely to facts about the intervening states.

Consider the Rwandan genocide of 1994. Imagine that State A, moved purely by the plight of the Tutsis, is willing to intervene to protect them. But State A is poor, with a fairly badly equipped army. Its intervention will halt the genocide, but their crude weaponry will cause much more collateral harm and take longer to secure the safety of the Tutsis, during which time some Tutsis will be killed. State B, in contrast, is rich and has a technologically advanced military that could quickly halt the genocide, with less collateral harm, saving many more Tutsi lives. But, State B's intention in intervening would be to give its troops some combat experience, and diminish the power of the Hutus in Rwanda, whom they've never liked much anyway. An account focusing on what motivates the intervention, or what the interveners intend, seems committed to the view that not only would it be *better* for State A to intervene, but that only State A is *permitted* to intervene. It is hard to reconcile that result with a concern for the welfare of the Tutsis.

We should notice that these considerations tell equally against the motives-based view that Bellamy is criticizing. Just as those governing a state may act with disparate intentions, so they may pursue the same goal as a result of disparate motives. The mere existence of a range of possible motivations, such as benevolence, greed, power, racial enmity, and so on, cannot tell us what in fact motivates an intervention. These possible alternative motives will be more readily available with respect to some troubled states rather than others, but that again does not, in itself, tell us what motivates an intervention. And focusing on the motives of interveners to the exclusion of the suffering of the victims misidentifies the primary object of moral concern. Bellamy is right, then, to reject motives as the ground of permissibility, but wrong to think that intentions can play that role instead.

Logical necessity

What of Bellamy's claim that intention is essential in justifying humanitarian intervention because it is logically necessary that a state have humanitarian intentions if its intervention is to qualify as an exception to the usual rules on breaching sovereignty? Well, logical necessity is surely too strong here: it is not part of the concept of a legal exception that one be intending to do what the exception permits. At best, the requirement of intention will be a contingent truth about this particular exception, if it turns out that those drafting the legislation, or those enacting it, have specified the exception in this way. But if things were so clear in the law, it is hard to see why there would be so much legal wrangling about the legitimacy of interventions. And, more importantly, there is no decisive reason to take this legal interpretation to be morally correct. Indeed, the currently prevalent view about sovereignty amongst moral philosophers is that a state's sovereignty is conditional upon its meeting and protecting its citizens' basic human rights. In the sorts of state in which we might consider intervening, the state (or its leader) has failed in this obligation, and thus has no sovereignty that would be violated by an intervention.[18]

In bello intentions

If we cannot reliably assess intentions, it is hard to see how they can help us to establish the permissibility of undertaking an intervention, at least if we want an account of permissibility that might be of some practical use, and could be used to guide legal deliberation. I have suggested that merely considering a state's given reasons for action does not reveal their intentions, and that relying

---

[18] See, for example, Michael J. Smith, "Humanitarian Intervention: An Overview of the Ethical Issues," *Ethics & International Affairs* 12, no. 1 (1998), 63–79; Larry May, "The Principle of Just Cause," in Larry May (ed.), *War: Essays in Political Philosophy* (Cambridge University Press, 2008).

upon a comparison with other possible justifications or intentions is unillu-
minating and undesirable.

But Bellamy thinks we can also evaluate intentions by looking at what a state
actually does in the course of an alleged intervention. This is, prima facie, more
promising (although it still will not help much with establishing permissibility
prior to an intervention, being largely grounded in the state's *in bello* behavior).
A state that claims to intend to rescue people from serious harm, only to bomb
the area where the alleged beneficiaries have taken refuge, clearly undermines
its claims regarding its humanitarian intentions.[19]

Distribution of risk

So, what is it about a state's actions, or the actions of its combatants, that we
should consider when trying to establish their intentions? Bellamy combines
Augustine's criterion of right intention with Walzer's double intent, which
requires combatants to actively minimize harm to non-combatants. When
combatants "take measures to ensure, as far as possible," that they do not harm
non-combatants, even when doing so exposes themselves to greater risk, we
can infer that their intentions really are humanitarian.[20] Thus, the strategies
employed by NATO in Kosovo revealed a lack of humanitarian intent, according to Bellamy, since "the selection of airpower alone rendered it almost impossible for it to halt the campaign of murder and ethnic cleansing."[21]

I think there are several problems with relying upon Walzer's criterion of
double intent. One difficulty concerns the appropriate distribution of risk
between combatants and non-combatants, especially in a war of humanitarian
intervention. Jeff McMahan has argued that it can be permissible for a rescuer
to shift the costs of rescue onto the beneficiary. Imagine that I can pull you out
of a river, saving your life, but in doing so I must break either your wrist or my
own. McMahan argues that, since it is you who will benefit from the rescue
mission, it is permissible for me to make you bear the costs of that mission by
breaking your wrist.[22] This seems to me to be correct. In addition, and germane
to our purposes here, it would be very odd to claim that, if I distribute the costs

---

[19] It seems especially hard to insist upon intentions as central if I am right about the problems
that attach to judging intentions *ad bellum*. If my objections are sound, Bellamy is left only
with judging intentions *in bello*. But now we have an even greater number of people whose
intentions must be considered. If we are to care about intentions when judging the permissibility of actions, surely our attention should fall primarily on the person or persons carrying out the action – in this case, the soldiers. The difficulties of identifying "the" intention of
the British Cabinet are only exacerbated when we try to identify "the" intention with which
the soldiers act.

[20] Bellamy, "Motives, Outcomes, Intent," 227.   [21] *Ibid.*, 227.

[22] See Jeff McMahan, "The Just Distribution of Harm Between Combatants and Non-
Combatants," *Philosophy & Public Affairs* 38, no. 4 (2010), 361.

of rescue in this way, my mission is no longer a humanitarian one – that I no longer count as having the intention or end of rescuing you. I surely do still have such a humanitarian end. If this is right, it is not clear why combatants should count as having humanitarian intent only if they are prepared to shoulder the costs of rescue themselves (in so far as doing so is compatible with the success of the mission). Perhaps they too can make the intended beneficiaries bear the costs of rescue without undermining their claim to be aiding those people.

A further problem is that Walzer's notion of double intent is meant to bolster the ordinary double effect distinction between intending and foreseeing, giving a more demanding account of what it means for combatants to adhere to the requirement of discrimination between combatants and non-combatants. And yet, as I have argued elsewhere, there is no reason why those engaged in terrorist attacks could not meet the requirements of double intent.[23]

Imagine that a terrorist needs to kill 50 civilians in order to deter enemy munitions workers from returning to their factory. He knows that the local hospital has an average population of 100 non-combatants during the day, and of 50 non-combatants during the night. He chooses to attack at night in order to avoid killing any more people than necessary to achieve his goal of terrorizing the munitions workers. Could not this meet the requirement of seeking to minimize harm to non-combatants, to the extent that doing so is compatible with the success of his mission? Perhaps attacking at night is more dangerous for him, and so in choosing this alternative, he even accepts greater costs to himself in order to minimize non-combatant deaths. If the terrorist bomber has no other way to stop production at the factory (perhaps the factory is underground, and cannot be directly attacked), he is choosing the least harmful means available to him. Of course, we can still point to the difference in the terrorist's intention compared to that of an ordinary combatant who kills non-combatants as a side effect. The terror bomber still intends to kill non-combatants – their deaths are part of his plan. But the extra requirement of minimizing harm was introduced by Walzer precisely because the distinction between intending and foreseeing harm does not seem able to support the difference in permissibility on its own.[24]

---

[23] Helen Frowe, *The Ethics of War and Peace: An Introduction* (London and New York: Routledge, 2011), 144.

[24] It is worth remembering here that Walzer himself does not endorse the intention-based view of humanitarian intervention. Rather, he argues that the intervening state needs to share the ends of the beneficiaries only to some extent: "It need not set itself to achieve those purposes, but it also cannot stand in the way of their achievement." *Just and Unjust Wars*, 104. This position seems closest to Nicholas Wheeler's suggestion that interveners' actions should not undermine humanitarian goals, and is weaker than my position that actions must be likely to promote humanitarian ends. See Nicholas J. Wheeler, *Saving Strangers: Humanitarian Intervention in International Society* (Oxford University Press, 2000).

As Bellamy indicates, Kosovo is probably the paradigmatic rejection of Walzer's double intent standard: NATO leaders opted for a form of intervention that minimized all risk to its own troops, exposing non-combatants to serious risks of harm. But I do not think this is enough to show that the intervention (1) lacked humanitarian intent, and (2) was therefore impermissible, for the reasons just given. The impermissibility arises not because the distribution of risk is incompatible with humanitarian intent – it is not – but because the means adopted were unlikely to promote humanitarian ends. This supports my view that it is what the state does, rather that its intentions, that grounds permissibility.

Parsing behavior

One of the difficulties in making sense of this debate lies in distinguishing the various components of behavior – motives, intentions, actions, ends, and outcomes. Bellamy seems confident that we can pull motives apart from intentions; and there is, of course, a ordinary sense in which we can talk of what you intend to do (rob a bank, for example) without talking about why you are trying to do it (which could be, for example, to fund your expensive lifestyle, because you want to get revenge on the bank for firing you, or because you need to pay off some debts you owe to a loan shark).

Along these lines, Bellamy claims that, for example, "Vietnam could have intervened with the *intention* of halting injustice and bringing peace to Cambodia and still have been primarily *motivated* by a desire to secure its borders, stem Chinese influence and remove the troublesome Pol Pot."[25] Presumably, he means that not only is it conceptually possible to pull the intention and motives apart, but that an intervention meeting this characterization would have been permissible.[26] But the distinction between intentions and motives now becomes rather woolly. I am not sure that an answer to the question of what your intentions are when you rob the bank will be complete if I say simply that you intend to rob the bank. A complete answer will say that you intend to steal some money to buy a fancy car, or to embarrass or impoverish the bank, or pay off the loan shark. And once we have this more complete story of your intentions, it becomes much harder to distinguish this from your motives. That you intend to get the money to buy a car seems to tie your intentions to a motive of greed. That you intend to embarrass or harm the bank ties your intentions to a motive of revenge. Our intentions and our motives (and indeed our ends) are often so intimately connected that I am not sure it really makes sense to insist upon the centrality of one, but deny the importance of the other.

---

[25] Bellamy, "Motives, Outcomes, Intent," 228–29.

[26] Bellamy describes as "questionable" the actual Vietnamese intervention because "the alleviation of human suffering [was not] the primary intention of the intervention." *Ibid.*, 228.

Similarly, if we are asked to identify Vietnam's intentions in Bellamy's suggested picture of their intervention in Cambodia, it is not clear that a full answer will stop at saying they intend to halt injustice. After all, on the picture he paints, halting injustice is a means to end. It is not an end in itself. Of course, in so far as one must intend the means to one's end, we can agree that the Vietnamese do intend to halt injustice. But that is not *all* they intend – one must intend one's ends as well. And in this case, the Vietnamese intend, ultimately and perhaps primarily, to secure goods for themselves.

This is problematic for Bellamy in two ways. The first is that if intentions are what matter, he needs to say something about the relevance of these non-humanitarian intentions to the permissibility of the intervention. We cannot take for granted that the intended means, and not the intended ends, are the source of the primary intentions. Second, positing these kinds of ends seems to me incompatible with Bellamy's reliance upon the doctrine of double effect. In his summary of this doctrine, Bellamy lists as a condition of an action's legitimacy that "the desired end must be good in itself."[27] In his picture of Vietnamese intervention in Cambodia, the halting of injustice is treated as a means to the desired end of securing Vietnamese borders, limiting Chinese influence, and getting rid of Pol Pot because of his "troublesomeness" (by which Bellamy presumably means to indicate his inconvenience for the Vietnamese, not his humanitarian abuse of his people). Are these desired ends good in themselves? It is hard to say; but as goods that serve the interests of Vietnam, they just do not seem like the right kind of ends to be counted in deliberations about whether to wage a war in Cambodia. By incorporating the doctrine of double effect into his account, Bellamy inadvertently commits himself not only to importance of intentions, but also of ends; and once he does that, it is hard to see how he can exclude the ends that motivate the intervention. But there is nothing obviously humanitarian about the ends he envisages the Vietnamese promoting in their intervention in Cambodia. Given this, it is hard to see how Bellamy can permit such an intervention after all, even if the Vietnamese would act in a way that would provide humanitarian relief.

The justification-based account

I think that rather than focusing on intentions or motives to determine permissibility of humanitarian intervention, we should look at justifications and actions. By "justifications," I mean that we should consider whether there are sufficient reasons to intervene in a given state. Roughly, this is going to mean that there are widespread serious rights violations occurring in the state (or a credible threat of such violations), and that the state's leaders are either unable or unwilling to prevent these violations, or are instrumental in their

---

[27] Bellamy, "Motives, Outcomes, Intent," 228.

perpetration. If military force is likely to be the only effective means of curtailing the violations, and is a proportionate response to those violations, I suggest that this provides sufficient reason to intervene in that state. I will take it as uncontroversial that these are the sorts of facts that justify intervention in what we can loosely call an "objective" sense, where this means that they are reasons that obtain independently of what any particular state might have in mind by intervening. They are certainly the sorts of facts that trigger debates about whether a particular state ought to intervene in another country.

Bellamy and I come apart because he wants permissibility to depend not on whether there *are* these reasons to act, but on whether they are the *intervening state's* reasons for acting. This seems to me a mistake. What matters is whether the relevant justifying reasons obtain: whether people are at risk of serious harm, and whether military force could avert this. Bellamy's emphasis on the rescuer, instead of those in need of rescue, displaces what ought to be of central concern in our account of intervention, namely, the peril of the potential beneficiaries. In calling my account the justification-based account, I mean to reassert the centrality of the potential harm in our account of permissible intervention.

The second feature of this account concerns what a state does in a rather basic sense: what kinds of weapons it uses, what kind of strategies it employs, where and how it engages the enemy, and so on. In this sense, I think Bellamy is right that we need to pay attention to the methods employed by a state's armed forces as they engage in interventions. But Bellamy thinks that we should study actions because they can reveal intentions, where it is the intentions that ground permissibility. I think we should study a state's actions because they themselves are a ground of permissibility. As long as actions are reasonably expected to aid, the agent's intentions need not be humanitarian in order for the action to be permissible. Note that I am distinguishing actions from outcomes here; when I talk of what a state does, I mean to indicate the courses of actions in which it engages considered in light of the likely or predicted outcomes. But I am not advocating a Tesón-style consequentialist account where permissibility turns on whether or not the actions do in fact prevent or curtail harm.

I suggest that when it comes to averting very serious harms, neither intentions nor motives determine the permissibility of an agent's actions. Imagine that I come over to your house to watch television. We watch my favorite show, *Crimewatch*, which makes an appeal for information regarding the whereabouts of a dangerous criminal who has murdered two people and is likely on the lookout for more victims. As luck would have it, only hours earlier, I rented an apartment to this man. In fact, he has just picked up the keys from me, and I gave him a lift over there; so I am pretty sure that I know exactly where he is. And, even more luckily, *Crimewatch* is offering a £10,000 reward for information leading to his arrest! I could not care less about his murdering people, as long as he pays his rent on time. But I am tempted by that £10,000 reward. I decide to call the hotline and tell them where he is in order to get the money.

Clearly, I am blameworthy for my indifference toward this man's victims, and toward the very real possibility that he will kill other people. It would speak much better of my character if I phoned the hotline out of a genuine concern that the man be brought to justice before he can harm anyone else. But my mercenary intentions do not render my phoning the hotline impermissible. On the contrary, morality requires me to call the hotline. Morality might also require me to call for the right reasons, but my failure to fulfill this second requirement does not undercut the first.

This seems to me to generally plausible when we think about opportunities to avert serious harm. I might rescue a drowning child because I intend to use my heroism in my campaign to be appointed to the local council, rather than because I intend to prevent harm to her and spare her parents the grief of having their child die. This speaks badly of my character. But it is still much better, and morally permissible, that I rescue the child rather than fail to do so.

There might be some cases in which my intention makes the difference between my acting permissibly and my acting impermissibly, of course. Throwing you a surprise party because I intend to give you a heart attack would render my throwing the party wrong, even if, as it turns out, you stubbornly fail to comply with my intentions and have a splendid time instead. But when it comes to actions that will avert very serious harm, I do not think it matters *for the purposes of determining permissibility* what my intentions are, provided that my actions can reasonably be expected to avert the harm. Similarly, while the intentions of a state's leaders are relevant to our judgments of their character, we should not take them to determine the permissibility of rescuing people from serious harm.

Of course, there is some sense in which we have to look at what a state is going to do in order to form a judgment about whether intervention is justified.[28] We cannot know whether war will be a proportionate response to some wrong unless we know what kind of tactics are going to be employed in the course of the war. Nor can we satisfy the requirement of a reasonable prospect of success – which means success by legitimate means – unless we know which means will be employed. So, there must be some description from the state of what it intends to do, in the way I described above – that, for example, it plans to launch an air offensive followed by a ground campaign and so on.

But this is familiar from our usual reasoning about *jus ad bellum* with respect to defensive wars. Here too we must have some idea of the proposed methods of warfare in order to judge proportionality and the prospect of success. But, as far as I am aware, nobody takes this to mean that intention is the pivotal factor in permissibility. And, as I suggested above, we should not care about the proposed strategy because it reveals the state's intentions in Bellamy's sense of

---

[28] Thanks to Christopher Monahan for pointing this out.

revealing whether they are genuinely humanitarian. The strategy *itself* is what is of concern: whether those methods are likely to promote humanitarian goals. This can be assessed independently of whether or not the state is acting with humanitarian intent.

Consent

It seems natural to think that it should be part of a justification for intervention that the intervention is consented to, or welcomed by, the intended beneficiaries. Those who advocate the inclusion of this sort of criterion will probably do so because of thoughts about self-determination. Such thoughts might include that it is important that states in periods of revolution or other transition are masters of their own fate, perhaps for reasons of national self-respect, or because this increases the chances of long-term stability. Or, we might think that if a population seems not to want outside interference, it would be morally wrong to force it upon them. Finally, we might think that foisting assistance upon those who do not want it is likely only to exacerbate the conflict.

But there are both practical and moral problems with including a consent-based criterion in our account of justification. The practical problems arise because it will be very hard to know what percentage of a population support foreign intervention in their country. We have no way of polling the intended beneficiaries to see whether there is general support for intervention. We might look to social media or news reports, or talk to refugees to try to get a sense of whether intervention is supported; but it will be hard to know whether the views expressed are representative. This unsystematic and informal surveying is unlikely to satisfy any reasonable standard of consent. It would also make it almost impossible to judge receptiveness to intervention in very repressive states, where citizens have limited access to the outside world, even though these might be just the sorts of states in which intervention is most warranted.

Because of these difficulties, there is a temptation to say that we can simply assume that the intended beneficiaries of the intervention consent to being rescued. After all, it is hard to imagine that people would not want to be rescued from serious harm, even if the rescue was to be enacted by a historical foe, or dented one's self-respect. Given this, when faced with an actual or looming humanitarian crisis, it is perhaps reasonable to assume that the people at risk welcome rescue, and that if they were able to more explicitly consent, they would do so.

But even if we could secure reliable information that intervention would be welcomed, or even if we can reasonably assume this to be the case, we must still consider what role this plays in our justification for intervening. We can see the difficulties most clearly by thinking about how the moral status of the intervention would be affected by a clear *lack* of consent. Imagine a state in which a humanitarian crisis is occurring, and yet all the signs indicate that less than 50 percent of the adult population supports foreign intervention. Would the fact that a majority of people do not want to be rescued undercut the rights of those who do want to be rescued to receive assistance? It is hard to see how this could be the case, since the right not to be the victim of serious unjust harm is so much more stringent than the right not to be made better off against one's will. And remember that this result reflects only the *adult* population's wishes. Any state will have a sizeable population of children whom we have a duty to aid even if their parents oppose the intervention. Even if the percentage of adults opposing the intervention were very high – an overwhelming majority – I am not sure that this could trump the right of the children to be rescued. Of course, if adult opposition were so strong that it seriously hampered the intervention's prospect of success, this could tell against the intervention. But here it would not be the lack of consent that undermined the case for intervention, but the diminished likelihood of success arising from the adults' opposition.

Given this, while the perceived attitude of the beneficiaries should feed into our considerations about the likelihood of success, and thus indirectly form part of our deliberations about the justification for intervention, we should not include consent as a separate component of justification for intervention.

Conclusion

There is still work to be done here developing the positive thesis that it is what a state does that matters, rather than its intentions or motives. But, at least, I hope to have shown that existing accounts that focus on intentions or motives are unsuccessful. This is in part because they face practical problems in establishing which intentions or motives are in play. But Bellamy's reliance on double effect and double intent also undermines his exclusive focus on intentions, and overlooks important questions surrounding the distribution of risk. I think the justification-based account is more attractive than Bellamy's because it is easier to establish at both the *ad bellum* and *in bello* level. Whether or not there is a looming or actual humanitarian crisis is something that is open to public scrutiny in the way that just causes for war should usually be.[29]

It is also possible, although I have not given an account of it here, to make informed judgments about what kinds of actions are likely to promote humanitarian goals. But my account also gives priority to the rescuing of people in dire need over the moral character of the interveners, something that gets lost in

---

[29] For a discussion of this idea, see George P. Fletcher and Jens David Ohlin, *Defending Humanity: When Force is Justified and Why* (New York and Oxford: Oxford University Press, 2008), 161.

the intentions-based account. Of course it would be better if we intervened in troubled states out of a genuine desire to aid. But intervening for self-interested reasons, but in a way that secures humanitarian goods, is better than not intervening at all.

7

Bombing the beneficiaries

The distribution of the costs of the responsibility to protect and humanitarian intervention

JAMES PATTISON

Introduction

In its 1999 intervention in Kosovo, NATO was criticized heavily for its reliance solely on bombing from high altitude. Although NATO did not suffer any casualties itself, several civilians were reportedly killed by NATO's sorties. One inference made was that NATO should have deployed ground troops and, in doing so, decreased harm to civilians by taking on greater costs itself. By relying on airpower alone, NATO – and the United States in particular – appeared to be too fearful of NATO soldiers coming home in body bags at the expense of innocent Kosovo Albanian and Serbian civilians. In other words, NATO placed all the human costs of the intervention on civilians.

NATO's 2011 intervention in Libya also largely relied on airpower. This reliance on airpower was similarly controversial. On the one hand, as in Kosovo, there were no reported NATO casualties. Anders Fogh Rasmussen, the Secretary-General of NATO, claimed that "[w]e have carried out this operation very carefully, without confirmed civilian casualties."[1] But, on the other hand, an investigation in 2011 by *The New York Times* of airstrike sites found that "at least 40 civilians, and perhaps more than 70, were killed by NATO at these sites."[2] Again, it seems that NATO transferred much of the human costs of the intervention to civilians.

In this chapter, I will defend what I call the "Restrictive View" for the conduct of armed humanitarian intervention. On this view, those conducting

An earlier version of this chapter was presented at the Euro-ISME conference at the UK Defence Academy in June 2012. I would like to thank the participants for their comments. I would also like to thank Gerhard Øverland and Don Scheid for their very helpful written comments on an earlier draft of the chapter.

[1] In C.J. Chivers and E. Schmitt, "In Strikes on Libya by NATO, an Unspoken Civilian Toll," *New York Times* (December 17, 2011), available at: www.nytimes.com/2011/12/18/world/africa/scores-of-unintended-casualties-in-nato-war-in-libya.html?pagewanted=all (accessed August 29, 2012).
[2] *Ibid.*

interventions and discharging the military intervention element of pillar three of the Responsibility to Protect (RtoP) are morally required to take on *greater* costs, rather than distributing these costs to morally innocent civilians, such as those whom they are trying to assist. (Note that I focus on human costs rather than the financial and other costs associated with humanitarian intervention.)

A few years ago, George R. Lucas Jr. presented a brief but cogent defense of the Restrictive View in his general account of the principles of *jus ad pacem*. He argued that armed humanitarian intervention is far closer to domestic law enforcement and peacekeeping, and as such entails greater restrictions than found in traditional accounts of *jus in bello*.[3] For Lucas, intervening soldiers are not entitled to remove themselves at all costs from harm and are not permitted to inflict collateral damage on non-military targets or personnel, but rather are required to incur some costs to themselves and to avoid the kind of acts they are intervening to prevent. Hence, interveners should not endorse policies that reallocate risk to non-combatants, such as force protection, but instead should incur considerable additional risk.

The Restrictive View has, however, been challenged recently by several leading just-war theorists. An alternative view, which I call the "Permissive View," seems to have become increasingly popular. On the Permissive View, those conducting armed humanitarian intervention are morally required to take on only some or a small amount of the costs of intervention, if any. Most notably, Jeff McMahan and Gerhard Øverland have recently argued that interveners can permissibly distribute much of the costs of intervention to the "beneficiaries" of the intervention, such as citizens who are freed from tyrannical rule.[4] Moreover, they claim that the beneficiaries of the intervention should bear the costs of armed humanitarian intervention and the discharging of the RtoP rather than innocent bystanders (who are not beneficiaries).[5]

---

[3] George R. Lucas, Jr., "From *Jus ad Bellum* to *Jus ad Pacem*: Re-thinking Just-war Criteria for the Use of Military Force for Humanitarian Ends," in Deen K. Chatterjee and Don E. Scheid (eds.), *Ethics and Foreign Intervention* (Cambridge University Press, 2003), 72–96.

[4] Jeff McMahan, "Humanitarian Intervention, Consent, and Proportionality," in N. Ann Davis, Richard Keshen, and Jeff McMahan (eds.), *Ethics and Humanity: Themes from the Philosophy of Jonathan Glover* (Oxford University Press, 2010), 44–72; Jeff McMahan, "The Just Distribution of Harm Between Combatants and Noncombatants," *Philosophy & Public Affairs* 38 (2010), 342–79; Gerhard Øverland, "High-Fliers: Who Should Bear the Risk of Humanitarian Intervention?" in Paolo Tripodi and Jessica Wolfendale (eds.), *New Wars and New Soldiers: Ethical Challenges in the Modern Military* (Farnham: Ashgate, 2011), 69–86.

In his comments on McMahan's "Humanitarian Intervention, Consent, and Proportionality," Jonathan Glover also shows sympathy for this view in his "Responses: A Summing Up," in Davis *et al.*, *Ethics and Humanity*.

[5] McMahan defines expected beneficiaries as those whose "overall risk of being harmed (which takes into account both the probability of their being harmed and the magnitude of the harms they might suffer) would be reduced by a war in their defense," even if "the war

It helps to distinguish between two claims made in defense of the Permissive View. The first is what I will call the "Rescuers Thesis." This asserts that the beneficiaries should be subject to greater costs than the rescuers. For instance, McMahan argues that when there exists a trade-off between harms to just combatants or non-combatant beneficiaries, the non-combatants' immunity is reduced by their status as beneficiaries.[6] The second is what I will call the "Bystanders Thesis." This asserts that the beneficiaries should be subject to greater costs than the bystanders. As we will see, McMahan thinks that, overall, these two considerations counterbalance the reasons in favor of the Restrictive View.

In what follows, I first present the prima facie case for the Restrictive View. I then reject the Rescuers Thesis and the Bystanders Thesis. I argue that these fail to show that there is a morally relevant distinction in this context between rescuers, beneficiaries, and bystanders and, as such, the Bystanders Thesis and the Rescuers Thesis do not repudiate the prima facie case for the Restrictive View. In the final section, I present three further, more applied reasons in favor of the Restrictive View.

Before beginning, it should be noted that (unless otherwise stated) my discussion of the costs to be borne by rescuers, beneficiaries, and bystanders is focused on cases where the rescuers, beneficiaries, and bystanders are morally innocent, that is, where they are not morally culpable for the situation where the need for rescue arises, that is, the humanitarian crisis. In practice, rescuers, beneficiaries, and bystanders may sometimes be culpable to some extent for creating the need for armed humanitarian intervention, such as when the beneficiaries previously repressed an ethnic group that then violently attacks them, thereby causing the humanitarian crisis. Overall, the distribution of the costs of intervention should also reflect the culpability of the rescuers, beneficiaries, and bystanders.[7]

It should also be noted that I am not concerned with the issue of the permissibility of intervening per se. The likely distribution of the costs of intervention does sometimes alter the permissibility of resorting to an intervention, but does not always determine it. For instance, an intervention (e.g., NATO's 1999 intervention in Kosovo) may be all-things-considered morally permissible,

---

would be fought in a way that would expose them to new and different risks." McMahan, "The Just Distribution of Harm," 359–60.

 I will also use to terms "beneficiaries," "bystanders," and "rescuers" to assist in the assessment of the philosophical issues. Of course, these labels simplify somewhat. I acknowledge that applying such labels to actual groups can lead to political problems associated with the stigmatization of particular groups.

[6] McMahan, "The Just Distribution of Harm," 373.

[7] I frame the chapter in terms of culpability for simplicity's sake, although I do not think that much turns on this. It seems to me that my defense of the Restrictive View could also be framed in terms of agent-responsibility (McMahan's measure of liability), that is, where the rescuers, beneficiaries, and bystanders are not agent-responsible for the crisis.

despite the highly problematic distribution of costs (e.g., the imposition of much of the costs onto the beneficiaries), because overall it does much more good than harm.[8] The distribution of the costs of intervention is a further, morally important issue in its own right and for other issues (e.g., it may determine the *degree* of justifiability of the intervention and which agent should undertake intervention), in addition to its import for the issue of permissibility.

The prima facie case for the Restrictive View

I will start by outlining the prima facie case for the Restrictive View. It should be made clear here that McMahan largely agrees with this case. He believes (mistakenly, I will argue) that it is counterbalanced by the Rescuers Thesis and the Bystanders Thesis.[9] As we will see, Øverland is less sympathetic to this prima facie case.

Doing and allowing

One reason why it might seem that interveners should accept costs and avoid harming bystanders and beneficiaries is the difference between "doing" and "allowing," which is sometimes framed in terms of "killing" and "letting die." In short, it is widely held that it is sometimes better that one avoids *doing* harm, even if this will lead to *allowing* greater harm. McMahan is very sympathetic to the import of this difference. He argues that if a combatant has a choice between "a course of action that will *allow* an innocent person to be killed and an alternative course that will prevent that person from being killed but will *kill* another innocent person as a side effect, he must not kill, even if the person he allows to be killed is himself."[10]

Although of some relevance, it should be noted that there are limitations to the significance of the difference between doing and allowing for the issue of the distribution of the costs of intervention. To start with, the import of this difference is generally not held to be absolute, so that it may still be acceptable for interveners to sometimes *do* harm.[11] It also does not straightforwardly follow from the difference between doing and allowing that rescuers should take

---

[8] I defend the weightiness of likely, relative effectiveness in the overall assessment of the permissibility of humanitarian intervention in James Pattison, *Humanitarian Intervention and the Responsibility to Protect* (Oxford University Press, 2010).

[9] More precisely, McMahan frames this the other way around. He thinks that "the effects of noncombatants' beneficiary status" is "offset by the combatants' professional duty and usually by the asymmetry between killing and letting die." McMahan, "The Just Distribution of Harm," 370.

[10] *Ibid.*, 370.

[11] See Pattison, *Humanitarian Intervention and the Responsibility to Protect*, 120. McMahan also rejects the view that the asymmetry between killing and letting die is of absolute moral significance. See Jeff McMahan, "Pacifism and Moral Theory," *Diametros*, 23 (2010), 3–20.

on greater costs. They can simply refrain from rescue that does harm. In other words, the difference between doing and allowing provides only a negative reason for why rescuers should not harm innocents. It only becomes relevant for the distribution of the costs of intervention when conjoined with a positive reason (e.g., a duty to rescue) that explains why interveners are required to *not* refrain from acting, but instead should intervene and, when doing so, avoid doing harm.

Role-based duties

So why are humanitarian interveners, and in particular intervening soldiers, required to take on greater costs? I suggest below that there is a duty to intervene, which may apply to states and other agents on occasion. Like the duty to rescue (e.g., in cases of a child drowning in a pond), the carrying out of this duty may require that *reasonable* costs be borne, even by those who have not consented to these costs (e.g., citizens, conscripts, and bystanders) (see pp. 123f). But I think volunteer soldiers can sometimes be required to take on *greater* costs. This is because some intervening soldiers have role-based duties to do so. That is, sometimes soldiers enter into a contractual bargain whereby, on the one hand, they accept greater risks as part of their role (including for cases of humanitarian intervention) and, on the other, they receive a set of benefits, such as a generous pension scheme, healthcare, and free higher education. When such a bargain is entered into freely and is fair, the soldiers are required to live up to the terms of their agreement and therefore accept greater risks. Similarly, McMahan argues that combatants have a professional duty to take risks because this is what "they have pledged to do and are paid to do" and are in this respect like other "professional defenders or rescuers," such as the police, firefighters, bodyguards, and lifeguards, who have role-based duties "to take risks and even on occasion to allow themselves to be harmed when that is necessary to fulfill the functions of their role."[12]

Accordingly, it may be reasonable to ask soldiers to accept greater risks than, for instance, civilians who are conscripted to undertake military intervention. To reiterate, even civilians and conscripts may be also required to accept some costs – namely, a certain level of *reasonable* costs that results from the duty to rescue. The point is that sometimes the contractual bargain agreed to by combatants means that they can be asked to take on *greater* costs.

Øverland is skeptical about this argument about role-based duties. He rejects an analogy between the police and intervening soldiers made by Lucas (Lucas claims that, like the police, intervening soldiers should accept greater costs and generally avoid the use of force if it will endanger civilians).[13] Øverland accepts

---

[12] McMahan, "The Just Distribution of Harm," 366–67.
[13] Øverland, "High-Fliers," 81.

that the police may be required to do things that involve a "background" of risk, such as looking for suspects, and that this risk is often higher than for other professionals. But, he argues, although in the long run police officers (like lifeguards and firefighters) may be exposed to an aggregated higher risk than those in other professions, when confronted with a particular situation where additional risks are involved, they have no duty to bear these risks. The same is true, Øverland seems to think, of intervening soldiers.

However, regardless of whether the police can be required to take on risks in particular situations, it seems that intervening soldiers can be required to do this. Indeed, this is what they are employed to do – to fight in occasional, risky wars. So, like the police, soldiers are exposed to an aggregated higher level of risk. But, unlike the police, for the armed forces, this is largely manifested in particular situations (i.e., wars and some training exercises). Moreover, even if one doubts that soldiers *generally* agree to risks in particular situations, *some* clearly do. Most notably, private contractors agree on a case-by-case basis to specific operations, consenting to the likely risks in the terms of their contractual bargain.[14] In addition, some regular soldiers agree to specific tours of duty and are paid additional danger money for risky operations.

Orders and duties

It might also be responded that, in practice, soldiers do not possess role-based duties of armed humanitarian intervention and therefore intervention when not risk-free is impermissible. For instance, it might be claimed that soldiers do not consent to perform interventions for humanitarian goals – such operations are beyond the terms of the soldier–state contract that focuses on defensive wars – and therefore they do not possess role-based duties to perform non-defensive operations.[15] However, as I have argued elsewhere, the claim that

---

[14] Øverland may be happy to admit that private contractors have role-based duties in risky interventions. At the end of his chapter, he asserts that we may have a duty to finance intervention "in the hope that willing soldiers will come forward ready to bear the necessary risk associated with a successful intervention. And if the intervening soldiers in this way have contracted to take on the additional risk, they would have a contract-based duty to do so." Øverland, "High-Fliers," 84–85. I consider the moral issues surrounding using contractors for such operations in James Pattison, "Just War Theory and the Privatization of Military Force," *Ethics & International Affairs* 22 (2008), 143–62; James Pattison, "Outsourcing the Responsibility to Protect: Humanitarian Intervention and Private Military and Security Companies," *International Theory* 2 (2010), 1–31; James Pattison, *The Morality of Private War: The Challenge of Private Military and Security Companies* (Oxford University Press, 2014); Deane-Peter Baker and James Pattison, "The Principled Case for Employing Private Military and Security Companies in Interventions for Human Rights Purposes," *Journal of Applied Philosophy* 29 (2012), 1–18.

[15] See Martin L. Cook, "'Immaculate War': Constraints on Humanitarian Intervention," in Anthony F. Lang Jr. (ed.), *Just Intervention* (Washington, DC: Georgetown University Press, 2003), 145–54.

soldiers do not consent to perform armed humanitarian interventions is erroneous, since such operations can now clearly be expected by soldiers when they enlist.[16] Moreover, it is worth noting, as an aside to the main issue of the just distribution of costs, that the case for the Restrictive View does not hang on the existence of such duties. Let me explain.

I have thus far focused on the duties of the *intervening soldiers*. But focusing on soldiers' duties alone misses an important point. Regardless of whether soldiers possess role-based duties to take on greater costs, interveners can sometimes justifiably *order* their soldiers to take on greater costs.[17] In fact, the leaders of the intervener (or the intervener as a collective) may have *duties* to order their soldiers to take on greater costs, even if it is the case that one holds that their soldiers do not have duties to do so (the soldiers may also not necessarily have duties to obey their leaders).

To see this, consider the following hypothetical example. The United States is planning to intervene in Angola in response to genocide. The intervening soldiers have no contractual, role-based duties (e.g., suppose that the United States reinstates the Draft and uses unjustly conscripted citizens). The President of the United States faces a choice whereby she can order ten American soldiers to likely death, thereby avoiding the collateral death of 1,000 Angolan citizens, or she can maintain very high levels of force protection, thereby avoiding any risk to American soldiers but leading to the unintentional collateral death of 1,000 Angolans. It seems to me that she should adopt the former option. Although she may herself have role-based duties to look after American soldiers, these are not of overwhelming weight. As such, they can be outweighed by the prospect of saving a much greater number of non-citizens' lives. Indeed, she may have a *duty* to do so, if we hold that there is a duty to save the greatest number[18] that is not outweighed by her associative duties and role-based duties as president. In fact, this is what I think lies at the heart of the frequent critique of political leaders for maintaining high levels of force protection. Such leaders give too much weight to the lives of their own soldiers at the expense of the lives of a greater number of non-citizens.

Thus, even if the soldiers do not possess role-based duties to accept greater costs when engaged in humanitarian intervention, their leaders may also have the right – and perhaps the duty – to order their soldiers to take on greater costs, as the Restrictive View asserts.

---

[16] See Baker and Pattison, "The Principled Case for Employing Private Military and Security Companies"; Pattison, *Humanitarian Intervention and the Responsibility to Protect*, 110–12. Also see McMahan, "Humanitarian Intervention," 69–70.

[17] This point is defended in much more detail in Baker and Pattison, "The Principled Case for Employing Private Military and Security Companies."

[18] On the duty to save the greatest number, see Nien-Hê Hsieh, Alan Strudler, and David Wasserman, "The Numbers Problem," *Philosophy & Public Affairs* 34 (2006), 352–72.

The Rescuers Thesis

I have claimed that, first, the difference between doing and allowing means that interveners should avoid doing harm (although this difference is limited in its relevance for how costs should be distributed) and, second, intervening soldiers often have contractual, role-based duties to take on greater costs. As such, there is a prima facie case for holding that intervening soldiers should take on greater costs than beneficiaries or bystanders. I have also claimed, third, that interveners may sometimes permissibly order their soldiers to take on greater costs.

Against this prima facie case, McMahan and Øverland claim that the beneficiaries of armed humanitarian intervention should take on much of the costs. For Øverland, this is because he appears to be skeptical about role-based duties (as we have seen), thinks that beneficiaries have reason to accept costs, and largely denies the duty to intervene (discussed below). For McMahan, this is because he thinks that rescuers and bystanders should not be required to bear the costs of intervention. He believes that this consideration ultimately balances out the points about doing and allowing and role-based duties.[19]

In this section and the next, I will argue that beneficiaries are *not* required to take on greater costs, in comparison with either rescuers or bystanders. As such, the prima facie case is not counterbalanced. More specifically, I will reject the Rescuers Thesis and the Bystanders Thesis in turn.

The Rescuers Thesis might seem to have some initial plausibility because those undertaking humanitarian intervention often have to perform risky operations that put their lives at risk in order to save the lives of others. To say that rescuers have a duty to rescue at significant cost to themselves seems to be overly demanding. In the case of a child drowning in a pond, we would not think that a passerby is morally required to significantly endanger his or her own life in order to save the drowning child. To be sure, it is widely held that a passerby has a duty to rescue and *is* required to take on *reasonable* costs. A rescuer may be required to get very wet and, in doing so, ruin his clothes and money in his wallet when saving the drowning child – this is a reasonable cost – but not to put his own life at notable risk – this is too demanding. I agree that rescuers are not required to take on high costs. But it does not follow from the general notion that *rescuers* cannot be required to take on high costs that *intervening soldiers* cannot be required to take on high costs. The intervening soldiers may have agreed to these costs, as we have seen.

McMahan and Øverland present a further argument, which runs as follows.[20] Those being rescued *benefit* compared to what would have happen without the

---

[19] McMahan, "The Just Distribution of Harm," 373.
[20] Øverland notes that this argument is conditional on intervening soldiers not having the duty to bear costs (about which, I have claimed, he is mistaken), "High-Fliers," 75.

intervention, so would agree to take on significant costs. This argument relies on a contrast between two options. In Option 1, there is no intervention and the would-be beneficiaries are left to their fate. In Option 2, there is intervention, but the beneficiaries take on significant costs. Since the beneficiaries would choose Option 2, they can be burdened with much of the costs of the military intervention. Thus, McMahan thinks that (when discounting the prima facie case discussed above) the beneficiaries should shoulder a *greater* amount of the costs than the rescuers. In his words:

> [I]t may not be wrong for combatants to fight in ways that involve a lower risk to themselves but expose noncombatants to new risks, provided that the noncombatants are nevertheless expected beneficiaries of the defensive action – that is, provided that the action's reduction of the risks they face from the original threat exceeds the risks to which the action itself exposes them.[21]

I agree that the victims have reason to accept significant costs compared *to what would have happened without the intervention*. But the options presented by the Rescuers Thesis are not the only available. There are in fact (at least) three options. In Option 1, there is no intervention and the would-be beneficiaries are left to their fate. In Option 2, there is intervention, but the beneficiaries take on significant costs. In Option 3, there is intervention, the would-be beneficiaries take on some costs, and the rescuers take on some costs. It seems clear that the would-be beneficiaries have reason to accept Option 3.[22]

What are the implications of this? The comparison between only Option 1 and Option 2 is valid only when considering highly non-ideal circumstances where rescuers would not accept Option 3 and will carry out *only* Option 1 or Option 2. Of course, this is often the experience of humanitarian intervention, where for political reasons (e.g., the domestic unpopularity of soldiers coming home in body bags) those undertaking humanitarian intervention do not want to accept costs. But we are not concerned with such highly non-ideal circumstances here. Rather, we are considering the most morally desirable distribution of the costs of the intervention and whether interveners should accept greater costs. And when our focus is on this issue, we need to consider all the options that are relevant to the distribution of the costs of the intervention. Since the would-be beneficiaries have reason to accept Option 3 and would reject Option 2 in favor of Option 3, they cannot be said to be "benefited" by Option 2. In other words, when we make a valid comparison for the issue at stake, it is clear that the would-be beneficiaries do not have reason to accept

---

[21] McMahan, "The Just Distribution of Harm," 359.

[22] Note that Option 3 is permissible since interveners can take on (1) at least the reasonable costs of the duty to rescue or (2) high costs if the intervening soldiers possess the relevant role-based duties.

significant costs. Accordingly, the Rescuers Thesis is largely premised on a problematic comparison.

The duty to intervene

One way, however, to maintain the Rescuers Thesis is to deny the duty to intervene. If one denies the duty to intervene, and humanitarian military intervention is at best supererogatory, then interveners do not have to a duty of rescue and do not have to accept even reasonable costs. They can therefore permissibly transfer *all* the costs to the beneficiaries.

But this seems to be an extreme position. After all, we tend to think that there are positive Samaritan duties of rescue and that these can apply at the international level, such as in cases of military intervention to assist those suffering in other states. To deny the duty to intervene in principle, one would have to, for instance, assert an unpalatably strong account of the moral import of state borders or communal bonds, reject international positive duties of rescue, or endorse pacifism. Each of these positions is widely regarded as untenable.[23]

Alternatively, one could accept that there is in principle a duty to intervene, but assert that in almost all actual cases the costs of intervention would be unreasonable for the intervening soldiers. They would be asked to bear too much in order to save the lives of foreigners, such as the risk of death and injury. Intervening soldiers can therefore transfer much of the costs to the beneficiaries of armed humanitarian intervention. This is, in essence, Øverland's view. He implies that humanitarian interventions are generally supererogatory for the intervening soldiers:

> Most interventions would seem to place a higher risk on the intervening
> soldiers than people in general are required to bear in order to save others
> from harm. The very idea that we could have a duty to intervene is therefore
> peculiar. After all, the risk would have to be imposed on some of us, namely
> our soldiers. If we do not think people have a duty to shoulder considerable
> risk to assist people with whom they have no special relationship, not even
> when the latter are in dire need, it is hard to think we can have a duty to
> intervene at all if such intervention will impose any substantial risk on the
> intervening soldiers.[24]

[23] See, for instance, Simon Caney, *Justice Beyond Borders: A Global Political Theory* (Oxford University Press, 2005) on state borders and communal bombs. See Allen Buchanan, "The Internal Legitimacy of Humanitarian Intervention," *Journal of Political Philosophy* 7, no. 1 (1999), 71–87, on positive duties. And on pacifism, see McMahan, "Pacifism and Moral Theory."

[24] Øverland, "High-Fliers," 78. Unlike Øverland, McMahan believes that humanitarian intervention is often a duty. He says "the reasons that favor humanitarian intervention actually rise to the level of obligation far more often than we intuitively recognize." McMahan, "Humanitarian Intervention," 63.

The problem, however, with Øverland's claims here are that, as we have seen, intervening soldiers may have role-based duties to undertake humanitarian intervention, and this means that even very risky actions can sometimes reasonably be required of them.[25]

The Bystanders Thesis

We have seen that the Rescuers Thesis is mistaken because it rests on a problematic comparison. We have also seen that rescuers are not required to take on high costs, but can be required to take on reasonable costs. Let us now consider the Bystanders Thesis. This, recall, claims that the beneficiaries should bear costs instead of bystanders. Like the Rescuers Thesis, the Bystanders Thesis depends on the claim that beneficiaries have a reason to accept costs, whereas bystanders do not. To that extent, McMahan presents the following example:

> Villain will cause Victim to lose a limb unless a third party, Defender, takes defensive action on Victim's behalf. Defender has two equally effective options, each of which will, however, have as an unavoidable side effect the breaking of an innocent person's arm. One option would break innocent Victim's arm while the other would break innocent Bystander's. It is clear that Defender ought to choose the option that will break Victim's arm. This option would involve harming Victim for his own sake; he would be better off overall for being defended even at the cost of a broken arm. But the second option would involve harming Bystander for the sake of another and would leave him worse off. If Defender breaks Victim's arm, Victim will have no grounds for complaint against Defender.[26]

In fact, McMahan thinks that bystanders should have "maximum immunity." This is because, he argues, they have no corresponding reasons to share in the costs of the rescue, since they are not liable, are not beneficiaries, and have no special duty to be sacrificed.[27]

However, like the Rescuers Thesis, the Bystanders Thesis largely rests on a problematic comparison, which runs as follows. In Option 1, there is no

---

[25] Cécile Fabre claims that soldiers do not have duties to perform humanitarian interventions (unless a specific volunteer army for that purpose is developed), because (1) in risky interventions, rescuers do not have duties to accept harm to themselves, and (2) in non-risky interventions, rescuers cannot be required to prepare to undertake intervention (which would be a transgression of individual autonomy), in Cécile Fabre, "Mandatory Rescue Killings," *Journal of Political Philosophy* 15 (2007), 363–84. For replies to these claims, see Baker and Pattison, "The Principled Case for Employing Private Military." See also David Lefkowitz, "On a Samaritan Duty of Humanitarian Intervention," in Tripodi and Wolfendale, *New Wars and New Soldiers*, 87–101.

[26] McMahan, "The Just Distribution of Harm," 361.

[27] *Ibid.*, 374. Øverland seems to agree that bystanders should enjoy maximum immunity, "High-Flier," 80.

intervention and the would-be beneficiaries are left to their fate. In Option 2, there is intervention and the beneficiaries take on significant costs. In Option 3, there is intervention, the bystanders take on some costs, and the beneficiaries take on some costs. It is suggested that since beneficiaries would rather be rescued than not, they have reason to accept the costs, whereas the bystanders do not. Hence, Option 2 is preferable, and Option 3 should not be chosen.

But this inference is mistaken. Beneficiaries also have reason to prefer Option 3 to Option 2, since they would be subject to less harm. So, if we are concerned with the reasons that apply to beneficiaries, Option 3 would be chosen. Of course, bystanders have reason to prefer Option 2 to Option 3. But why should the reasons that apply to bystanders outweigh the reasons that apply to the beneficiaries? Both sets of individuals would (we can assume) be morally innocent. Beneficiaries may benefit from the rescue, but they are already in a highly problematic position to start with, such as facing severe oppression. They have done nothing that means that they, rather than bystanders, should bear the costs. Status as a beneficiary is not a reason, then, to distribute costs to beneficiaries instead of bystanders. The fact that the situation of beneficiaries is improved by rescue is a morally irrelevant characteristic when it comes to the distribution of costs.

To be clear, I am not claiming that costs should be distributed to the bystanders *over* the beneficiaries because the former have had bad luck and so should not have to bear any further costs. This is a more controversial claim than I wish to present. My point, rather, is the more limited one that, when unavoidable, costs should be distributed fairly – by which I mean equally – between morally innocent beneficiaries and bystanders.

It is necessary to flesh out this claim a bit more. There is, I think, a universal duty to prevent human suffering. This translates into a duty to rescue in certain cases and for certain individuals. For instance, only certain actors may be able to perform the rescue effectively. However, since other actors possess the duty to prevent human suffering, they can be also asked to bear *reasonable* costs. Therefore, it is not only the rescuers that may be required to bear reasonable costs. Bystanders can as well. (Beneficiaries may also be required to bear reasonable costs in their rescue.)

Consider again the case of a child drowning in a pond. Suppose that there is a fit and capable swimmer who can save the child, but that saving the child would create a big splash that would ruin the clothes and the money in the wallet of an incapacitated bystander. Does the fact that the bystander would be subject to some costs mean that the capable swimmer should not act? After all, the bystander is innocent, but would be subject to some harm by the rescue. This seems mistaken. The bystander has, I think, a duty to prevent human suffering and can be required to take on *reasonable* (although not *high*) costs of another's performance of this duty. By saving the child, the rescuer is performing the bystander's duty as well as his or her own. The bystander is morally required to take on reasonable costs of the rescue if necessary.[28]

Moreover, it is worth noting, as an aside, that it is not clear that rescuers should *always* refrain from causing bystanders *high* costs. This is because the rescue may still be permissible because it will lead to highly beneficial consequences. For instance, the rescuer may be able to save 1,000 lives and, as a side effect, put a bystander at sizeable risk of serious harm. To reiterate, the bystander does not have a duty *herself* to take on high costs, but it does not follow from this that the rescuer should not place high costs on the bystander if this is necessary and will lead to highly beneficial consequences.

I have suggested, then, that bystanders can be required to bear *reasonable* costs and that rescuers may sometimes permissibly impose high costs on bystanders. But what of my claim that costs should be split *equally* between bystanders and beneficiaries? The point here does not relate to whether these costs are reasonable and, in particular, whether bystanders have duties to accept reasonable costs. It is a more general point about the distribution of costs, aside from the issue of the duties to accept costs, and again relates to how third parties may distribute costs. It runs as follows.

In forced-choice situations, if there is an unavoidable, large cost, this should be split equally between the bystander and beneficiary, even if the cost to the beneficiary and the bystander would be more than the costs that they have duties to bear. To see this, consider the following case.

> *Mine*: Bob has accidently stepped on a hidden mine, which is yet to go off. There are two ways to save him. In Option 1, although no one else would be hurt, Bob would be grievously injured in the rescue. As a result, Bob would no longer be able to live a flourishing life (e.g., he would be impoverished as the result of paying for the treatment of his severe injuries). In Option 2, when Bob would be rescued, he and five innocent bystanders would suffer the loss of an arm, but all would still be able to lead flourishing lives. In Option 3, Bob would not be rescued; he would be killed by the mine.

It does not seem to me that Option 1 should necessarily be chosen, which the Bystanders Thesis presupposes (since bystanders would not be hurt and Bob would benefit from the rescue compared to Option 3). The fact that Bob "benefits" here does not point to any morally relevant quality of Bob or action by Bob, such as his free choice or wrongdoing, that means that he should bear the costs of his rescue. It is morally arbitrary that he will benefit since it is arbitrary

---

[28] One way of defending the maximum immunity of bystanders is to invoke the difference between doing and allowing discussed above. However, this difference would also seem to apply to beneficiaries. That is, rescuers should also avoid doing harm to beneficiaries. Moreover, although the import of the difference between doing and allowing should be taken into account so that rescuers generally avoid doing harm, it is generally held that this difference is not of overwhelming magnitude and as such doing harm may still sometimes be morally permissible.

that he has stood on the mine in the first place. To that extent, being a beneficiary or a bystander is morally irrelevant.

Another way of putting this is that it does not seem that Bob, rather than anyone else, should necessarily bear *all* the costs of his brute bad luck. On the contrary, there is a strong case for holding that the costs of brute bad luck should be
shared in order to reduce their effects. This is in order to allow as many agents
as possible to lead flourishing lives. When one agent has to bear all of the costs
of brute bad luck, his opportunities to lead a flourishing life are likely to be
significantly reduced. But when the costs of brute bad luck are shared amongst
several agents, the costs borne by each agent will be lower and all the agents
may be able to lead flourishing lives, despite the costs.[29] The costs of brute bad
luck should be shared, where possible, *equally*, so that no particular agent will
suffer a greater harm to his or her chances than any other, thereby not undermining the equality of opportunity. Accordingly, there is a strong reason for
holding, contra the Bystanders Thesis, that costs should be distributed equally
between bystanders and beneficiaries, and that the status of being a beneficiary
is morally irrelevant.

In addition, it is worth noting that the Bystanders Thesis has highly counterintuitive implications. Most notably, in defensive wars citizens may be required
to bear *greater* costs than non-citizens on this position. In particular, this is
when citizens would be benefited by the defensive war because, for instance,
it fends off an unjust aggressor. They would be, in effect, "beneficiaries." In
fact, the Bystanders Thesis *could* potentially lead to the conclusion that *citizen beneficiaries* should be subject to greater costs than the (morally innocent)
non-citizen combatants who are fighting an unjust war of aggression against
the citizens' state. Consider a case, for instance, in which certain combatants
(e.g., some conscripts) are not morally responsible for their participation in
the war and, as such, are simply tools of their state's unjust aggression, whereas
the citizens of the defending state "benefit" from being defended. More clearly,
it follows from the Bystanders Thesis that morally innocent non-combatants
from the *unjust aggressor state* should be subject to lower costs than the morally
innocent non-combatants from the *just defending state*, given that the former
are in effect bystanders and the latter are beneficiaries.[30]

---

[29] It should be noted here that McMahan thinks that costs might permissibly be distributed by
bystanders if this will "significantly decrease the overall expected harm to the innocent," but
(in contrast to the position that I am defending here) not if the harms will simply be spread.
McMahan, "The Just Distribution of Harm," 362.

[30] To be sure, McMahan acknowledges this point. He says that, in such a case, "the view for
which I have argued implies that the just combatants ought to choose the course of action
that will involve killing a few of their own fellow citizens." McMahan, "The Just Distribution
of Harm," 364. He does think that special relationships might be relevant when the distribution of costs between just *defending soldiers* and *defending citizens* is at issue (*ibid.*, 372), but
this distribution is not what I am concerned with in this chapter.

One way to avoid this potentially counterintuitive implication is to invoke strong associative duties among citizens. If one holds such a position, the Bystanders Thesis' implication that citizen beneficiaries should bear the costs rather than non-citizens is outweighed by the duties to prefer citizens.[31] But the problem with relying on associative duties here is that they would need to be very strong to avoid the counterintuitive implications, whereby generally it is permissible for non-citizens to be distributed significant costs instead of citizens. But this seems far too permissive and is itself counterintuitive.[32] Indeed, McMahan avoids endorsing strong associative duties. He thinks that any special relationship between the civilians and combatants does not render it permissible to transfer the costs to the bystanders. He argues:

> Just as the state's duty to protect its citizens cannot make it permissible for its combatants to do what they would not be permitted to do in the absence of that duty, so the duty of just combatants to protect just civilians cannot make it permissible for them to cause more harm to innocent bystanders as a side effect than it would be permissible for the just civilians themselves to cause by acting in self-defense.[33]

Rather than asserting unpalatably strong associative duties, the much more intuitively plausible explanation as to why morally innocent citizens who are beneficiaries are not required to bear greater costs than non-citizens is simple. There is no morally relevant distinction between beneficiaries and bystanders.

The moral and political case for greater costs on interveners

Thus far, I have argued – against the Permissive View and in favor of the Restrictive Thesis – that those undertaking armed humanitarian intervention should take into account the difference between doing and allowing and may have role-based duties to accept greater costs than the potential beneficiaries of the intervention. The latter point presents a prima facie case for holding that interveners should take on greater costs. I have also rejected the Rescuers Thesis and the Bystanders Thesis that could potentially counterbalance this prima facie case. I want now to turn to consider some more practical considerations. I will start by considering – and rejecting – two arguments for holding that interveners should bear lower costs, before presenting two reasons in favor of the view that they should bear *greater* costs.

First, it might be argued that requiring of interveners that they bear costs is likely to discourage them from acting. If they know that they are likely to have to accept even reasonable costs, they may decide not to act. And, as McMahan

---

[31] McMahan notes this possibility, *ibid.*, 376.
[32] See Buchanan, "The Internal Legitimacy of Humanitarian Intervention"; Caney, *Justice Beyond Borders*; and McMahan, "The Just Distribution of Harm."
[33] McMahan, "The Just Distribution of Harm," 364.

and Øverland claim above, the would-be beneficiaries of intervention would prefer that the would-be interveners intervene than not. McMahan argues that, although this point about encouraging interveners does not provide a "basic moral reason" in favor of the Permissive View, it does provide "a reason to give some recognition to the distinction between beneficiaries and bystanders in law."[34] Yet, there is a notable countervailing danger with this position: if it is publicly asserted that interveners do not need to accept costs, they may in practice end up distributing *all* costs to the beneficiaries in cases where they would otherwise have shared the costs. Besides, when attempting to encourage humanitarian intervention, surely we should try to develop norms that encourage morally justifiable intervention whereby potential interveners both intervene *and* accept some costs. On a particular occasion, beneficiaries may grudgingly accept greater costs to themselves when interveners will not act otherwise. Yet we should strive for norms about armed humanitarian intervention where this is not the case.

Second, McMahan claims that humanitarian interveners may need to maintain higher levels of force protection in order to ensure that they can effectively achieve their aims.[35] However, in all post-World War II cases of humanitarian intervention,[36] the interveners have been militarily stronger than the opposing forces. It is unlikely, then, that this argument has any real-world applicability. The size and capability of the intervener means that they are likely to achieve the just cause without the need to preserve their soldiers' lives at all costs.[37]

On the other hand, there are three reasons to hold that interveners should accept greater costs. The first is because, simply, they are engaged in humanitarian intervention.[38] To that extent, Lucas claims there needs to be a consistency between the humanitarian ends of the intervention and the means used, since the justification of the military intervention rests on its achieving the promotion of human rights with minimal harm of the sort that it is trying to halt.[39] Øverland rejects such claims, arguing that "[t]he mere fact that you have ideals when entering into a rescue situation does not imply that you have to bear all the risk."[40] But this misses the point. Until recently, only defensive wars were conventionally and legally permitted by the governing rules of the international

---

[34] *Ibid.*, 366.   [35] *Ibid.*, 377.

[36] See the list of interventions in Pattison, *Humanitarian Intervention and the Responsibility to Protect*, 1–2.

[37] That said, if interveners were required to take on almost *all* costs in order to avoid *any* costs to innocent civilians, such instrumental reasons might be relevant. Sacrificing a large number of intervening soldiers to protect only a few civilians may be counter-productive. See *ibid.*, 109.

[38] Note that this reason is specific to humanitarian intervention and not to other types of war.

[39] Lucas, "From *Jus ad Bellum* to *Jus ad Pacem*," 77–78.

[40] Øverland, "High-Fliers," 83.

system. Armed humanitarian intervention has grown to be another generally accepted exception to the international prohibition on the use of force, but a circumscribed one, given the widespread fear of abuse of such interventions. To maintain the exception, interveners need to be *seen* to be intervening with significant care. If they cause significant harm to those whom they are supposedly trying to save, the skepticism surrounding armed humanitarian intervention may once again grow very large and the conventional and legal permission be foreclosed. To that extent, Lucas is right that the humanitarian purposes that sometimes permit overriding state sovereignty are compromised if the intervening forces harm innocent civilians.[41]

Second, and more straightforwardly, interveners that transfer costs onto the beneficiaries may soon lose the "hearts and minds" of those whom they are trying to assist. As a result, they may face greater internal opposition and find it more difficult to achieve their humanitarian purposes.[42]

Third, although perhaps indirectly, interveners may sometimes have been in part morally responsible for the humanitarian crisis. Since they were partly morally responsible for the situation, they should bear greater costs, and certainly more costs than the morally innocent beneficiaries of the intervention.[43] Consider, in this context, Western support for Saddam Hussein, the Rwandan Hutu government, and Muammar Gaddafi, whose states were later subject to humanitarian military interventions. (I refer here to French, British, and American intervention in northern Iraq in 1991 to create safe havens and to implement no-fly zones to protect thousands of endangered Kurds, rather than the 2003 war in Iraq.) Moreover, it might be claimed, *à la* Thomas Pogge, that the West is implicated in the imposition of an unjust global economic order that leads to severe humanitarian crises.[44] To be sure, the intervening soldiers may not be responsible and so may not have further additional duties to accept costs. Rather, the suggestion is that the interveners as a whole may be required to take on greater costs.

For these reasons, in addition to the prima facie case, the Restrictive View for the conduct of humanitarian intervention is correct. Those conducting armed humanitarian intervention are morally required to take on *greater* costs rather than transferring these costs to civilians.

[41] Lucas, "From *Jus ad Bellum* to *Jus ad Pacem*," 77.
[42] Øverland accepts this point, "High-Fliers," 84.
[43] Øverland also notes this possibility, *ibid.*, 77.
[44] See Thomas Pogge, "An Institutional Approach to Humanitarian Intervention," *Public Affairs Quarterly* 6 (1992), 89–103; and Thomas Pogge, *World Poverty and Human Rights*, 2nd edn. (Cambridge: Polity Press, 2008).

PART III

Ideas and reconsiderations

8

The costs of war

Justice, liability, and the Pottery Barn rule

By the time they were in Bush's office, Powell was on a roll.

"You are going to be the proud owner of 25 million people," he told the president. "You will own all their hopes, aspirations, and problems. You'll own it all." Privately, Powell and Armitrage called this the Pottery Barn rule: You break it, you own it.[1]

Recent years have seen a surge in philosophical writing and thinking about *jus post bellum* – justice after warfare's end.[2] Just as a war entered into for morally sufficient reasons (*jus ad bellum*) may be made wrongful if conducted badly (*jus in bello*), so may a war entered into and conducted well be made wrongful if ended poorly. If, for instance, the people whose interests are nominally the justification for the war are left to suffer indignity or injustice, we are right to think that the entire course of the war is best regarded as morally disreputable. The increased attention given to these ideas is due to facts both inside and outside the world of academia. We are right, of course, to think that the idea of *jus post bellum* is an important addition to the philosophical literature; the fact that it has become recognized as such, though, is largely attributable to the aftermath of the US invasion of Iraq, in which the importance of a good ending has been brought home to us in a particularly stark way.

This fact means, of course, that the philosophical debate about justice has not been the only debate to be found. Ideas of justice in warfare have been increasingly prevalent during the past decade of war. Colin Powell's invocation

Thanks to Lauren Jablonski and Patrick Taylor Smith for helpful comments in the drafting of this chapter.

[1] Bob Woodward, *Plan of Attack* (New York: Simon & Schuster, 2004), 150.
[2] See, for instance, Larry May, *After War Ends* (Cambridge University Press, 2012); Larry May and Andrew Forcehimes (eds.), *Morality, Jus Post Bellum, and International Law* (Cambridge University Press, 2012); Robert E. Williams and Dan Caldwell, "*Jus Post Bellum*: Just War Theory and the Principles of Just Peace," *International Studies Perspective* 7 (2006), 309–20; Gary J. Bass, "Jus Post Bellum," *Philosophy & Public Affairs* 32, no. 4 (2004), 384–412; and Brian Orend, "Jus Post Bellum," *Journal of Social Philosophy* 32 (2002), 117–37.

of the Pottery Barn rule has proven to be a resilient symbol of one particular vision of justice in the ending of war.[3] The idea is that the one who invades a country thereby obtains responsibility for that country: The one who breaks it, in other words, must be the one to fix it. On this vision, a country might – even if its cause and conduct were just – become an unjust aggressor after the fact, by refusing to provide adequate assistance after war.

The Pottery Barn rule has become part of the American political vocabulary.[4] It is worth asking whether this is a good thing; whether or not, that is, the rule describes valid moral principles. This chapter is an attempt to evaluate this rule and see if Colin Powell was on to something when he coined it.[5] My conclusion is that, yes, Powell was, indeed, saying something true – but that the rule has to be understood in a particular way for it to be both true and interesting. In particular, I will argue that the Pottery Barn rule is best understood as a piece of first-person moral guidance, useful for would-be interveners who are subject to the same cognitive errors and biases as the rest of us. It is not that we ought to hold interveners more responsible than others for the task of rebuilding a society after intervention; it is, instead, that we should not think ourselves licensed to intervene, unless we have both the means and the will to rebuild that society in the event that no other nation sees fit to help us in this task.

Before I make this case, I should mark out a few limits to what I intend to do here. The first thing to note is that I am not even attempting to write a full theory of *jus post bellum*. Much of *jus post bellum* deals with topics that are beyond the purview of this brief chapter – including topics such as war-crimes tribunals, reconciliation, and how a society might be reintegrated into the international community after atrocity.[6] My present topic is limited to the matter of how we ought to allocate the costs of rebuilding a society after war, and with whether or not justice requires the intervening state to be the one who bears these costs. I am, further, making the assumption that these costs are reducible to costs of money and manpower, such that it is in principle possible for a wide variety of states to bear these costs. It is possible that, as part of a fuller theory of *jus post bellum*, there might be some acts which only a belligerent party can even in principle perform; I will not here even attempt to work out what these actions

---

[3] It is worth noting that the actual business called "Pottery Barn" has no rule equivalent to the one cited by Powell, and it was rather annoyed by its selection as the representative holder of such a policy. See Helen Huntley, "Rule that isn't its Rule Upsets Pottery Barn," *St. Petersburg Times* (April 20, 2004).

[4] See William Safire, "Language: You Break it, You Own it, You Fix it," *New York Times* (October 14, 2004).

[5] There is some debate about whether the term was first coined by Powell or by Thomas Friedman. See *ibid.*

[6] See, on these issues, Larry May, *Justice After War* (Cambridge University Press, 2012); Jon Elster, *Closing the Books: Transitional Justice in Historical Perspective* (New York: Cambridge University Press, 2004); and Ruti G. Teitel, *Transitional Justice* (Oxford University Press, 2002).

would look like, and will instead focus only on the costs that could in principle be subject to allocation.[7] I am, finally, going to accept a widely (although certainly not universally) shared set of theoretical assumptions, including the idea both that there can exist a justified war, that some gross violations of human rights can give rise to a right to engage in warfare, and that the justification of warfare here entails the building of rights-respecting institutions after war.[8] Those who disagree with these assumptions are likely, of course, to disagree with what follows.

So: why should we think that the Pottery Barn rule is likely to be instructive? We should, I think, try to figure out what the rule means before we try to evaluate its usefulness. As a way of starting this, we might think that there are at least two different things that the rule might be taken to mean. One version of the rule argues that the agent who engages in a careless or unjustified action thereby acquires an obligation to absorb the losses felt by those who are injured as a result of this action. Another version of the rule argues that there are some activities so dangerous that anyone who engages in them acquires an obligation to compensate others who experience losses as a result of that activity. We can, borrowing from tort law, refer to these rules as the *fault-based* conception of the Pottery Barn rule, and the *strict liability* conception of the rule, respectively.[9] I will deal with each of these in turn.

The fault-based conception

Why should we think that the one who breaks a thing should buy it? Ordinarily, I suppose this is because we think that the one who has broken it has done something in such a way that she is guilty of having done something wrong; she has been careless, perhaps, or malicious, or otherwise has fallen below some threshold of care that she owes to others (including the owners of shops selling housewares). If this is right, then the reason that losses ought to be shifted from the one who first bears it to the one who acts is that the act is, in some way, deficient. We may not want to use the language of ethics to condemn the one who acts; it is possible, perhaps, to fall below a threshold of legal obligation, without

---

[7] I am not, in particular, going to examine the law of military occupation. This law, while it might be covered by some of the concerns I examine here, looks more particularly to forms of moral obligation that exist only during an ongoing form of military relationship, and so demands a specific attention I cannot here provide. I am grateful to Don Scheid for urging me to be more precise about these ideas.

[8] While the specific language used is controversial, the general pattern of argument found in the *2001 Report of the International Commission on Intervention and State Sovereignty* echoes these conclusions and provides one plausible way of understanding them. *The Report* is available at: www.responsibilitytoprotect.org.

[9] For philosophical discussions of fault and strict liability, see Arthur Ripstein, "Tort, The Division of Responsibility, and the Law of Tort," *Fordham Law Review* 72 (2004), 1811; and Jules Coleman, *Risks and Wrongs* (New York: Cambridge University Press, 1992).

also falling below a threshold of moral obligation. We do, however, think that some culpable action is required, and the agent's having deliberately acted in a way that makes her criticizable is a prerequisite for legitimate assignment of liability for the loss in question. To take this model from the literal Pottery Barn to the figurative: The agent who acts in a way that is insufficiently attentive to the duties she owes to others ought to bear the costs of the losses she has wrongly imposed on others. If this is our model for warfare, then the one who acts wrongly in initiating war should bear the costs she has created for others.

This is not implausible as a story, but there is one key fact we have to bear in mind: this all assumes that the war itself is unjust. If the decision to go to war is the source of our liability to pay the costs of fixing that society after the war, then, on the fault conception, that decision must have been made in a criticizable way. There are, I think, some things we ought to notice about this fact. The first is that this means that *jus post bellum* no longer forms an independent check on warfare. *Jus post bellum* means, after all, that there are some constraints on what a belligerent state can do after war, such that the conduct of a state after a just war can make that war retrospectively unjust. If the fault-based conception of liability is our analysis of the Pottery Barn rule, though, this means that it only has something to tell us about wars that were, at their outset unjust; it has nothing independent to tell us about how just wars ought to be conducted. This may or may not be a problem; the Pottery Barn rule, as I have said, is not the entirety of *jus post bellum*. It is, however, a reason to think that the rule is – as construed in its fault-based conception – not all that useful to us; it might give us guidance as to how to avoid making an unjust war worse, but it can hardly be thought to give us guidance about how to make wars *just*.

If we are to assume that this version of the Pottery Barn rule has something to tell us in a particular case, then, some argument must be given about why the war is unjust. Imagine, for the moment, that a potential intervener believes (not unreasonably) that the opposite is true. Imagine, in other words, that there is a potential intervention that is plausibly justified; perhaps the basic human rights of the inhabitants of a neighboring state are systematically violated, giving rise to some responsibility on the part of the potential intervener – and other legitimate states – to protect those inhabitants. Imagine, further, that the intervention actually does occur, and the one who intervenes bears the initial cost of the intervention itself, understood here to encompass both financial costs and the assumption of the risks involved in military action. Under these circumstances, should the intervening country think itself obligated to bear the remaining costs of rebuilding the country after the end of hostilities? The fault-based account of the Pottery Barn rule gives us no reason to think so. Indeed, it is plausible that the intervening society might be able to say, with some validity, that it has *already* borne a disproportionate share of the costs of defending the basic human rights of others. Unless there is some way to establish that the decision to intervene is wrongful, it seems that the one who acts to initiate a war is *less* obligated than others to bear the costs of justice after that war is ended.[10]

To bring this down to specifics: imagine that the basic human rights of individuals in Iraq were so badly protected that all countries prior to 2003 had a responsibility to do what they could to protect those rights. Imagine, further, that the situation was sufficiently grave – and the legal situation after United Nations Security Council Resolution 1441 sufficiently clear – to justify military intervention. (I take here no position about whether or not these two suppositions are plausible.) When the United States and its allies intervened in Iraq (2003), based upon what could the other states of the international community insist that the United States and its allies should bear responsibility for the rebuilding of governing capacity in Iraq? All states had a duty to do something – to bear some costs – to protect the inhabitants of Iraq. Most states did nothing.[11] Some, indeed, actively helped the Ba'ath party continue the abuses unchecked.[12] There is something morally unseemly about these states turning to the United States and saying, in effect: "You broke it, you bought it." The proper response to this refusal, I think, might be to insist that Iraq was broken, in the relevant sense, long before the United States began the invasion; the duty to fix Iraq was – and is – a collective one, and the United States is, if anything, less liable for the costs of its reconstruction than other states.

All the above relies, again, upon particular factual premises that may or may not hold true. My point here is not to defend the Iraq war, nor the way in which it was pursued. My point is simply this: on a fault-based conception of the Pottery Barn rule, the United States bears no more liability than any other state – if it can show that the invasion itself was justified. If the invasion was just, then the Pottery Barn rule gives us no guidance about how the costs of war ought to be allocated.

---

[10] Thus, Gary Bass is, on my view, wrong to think that George W. Bush acted unjustly in limiting the awarding of reconstruction contracts to nations that had assisted the intervention into Iraq. Bass thinks this decision was both politically tone-deaf and morally repugnant in that it marked the war as a simple search for economic advantage. On the contrary, I would argue that Bush could plausibly claim that coalition nations had already borne a disproportionate share of the costs of protecting the rights of Iraqi citizens, and were therefore entitled to have the benefits of economic trade with Iraq as a way of bringing their net contribution closer to what justice would require. Bass's point about tone-deafness, of course, persists. Bass, "Jus Post Bellum," 408.

[11] I am ignoring the admittedly important issue of whether or not the United Nations had effectively removed from member states the ability to independently seek to change Iraqi policy. I believe that the answer is no; many states, even if they did not believe that force was justified, had some discretionary space within which they could act against Iraqi human-rights abuses, through soft power, if through nothing else.

[12] France, in particular, seems to have played a role in helping Saddam Hussein evade United Nations' restrictions. See Craig Whitlock and Glenn Frankel, "Many Helped Iraq Evade UN Sanctions on Weapons," *The Washington Post* (October 8, 2004).

Very well, then: could we just assume, for the moment, that the war was not justified? Imagine, then, the opposite of the rosy scenario discussed above. Imagine that the situation, while undoubtedly grave, was not grave enough to warrant military intervention. Imagine, further, that while all legitimate countries had the collective obligation to do *something* about human-rights abuses in Iraq, military invasion was an illegitimate response to these abuses. Under these circumstances, the United States and its allies acted unjustly in invading Iraq. Does this set of circumstances give us any reason to think that the Pottery Barn rule now provides us with practical guidance?

The answer is, I think, no – once the deep perversity of the rule's guidance is made clear. Before the invasion, the international community as a whole had some collective duty to bear the costs of protecting the rights of the Iraqi people. It is clear, from the factual situation described, that the costs did not include military adventurism. But the burden was real enough; all states had a duty to expend their time and treasure in seeking a better world for the Iraqi people. To think that this shared burden disappears in the face of an unjustified American invasion is to allow the wrongful acts of others to absolve us from our own moral duties. It is to give us reason to hope for an unjustified intervention, so that the costs of our duties are transferred from us to a wrongful party. This seems counterintuitive, to say the least. If I have the obligation to pay my fair share for the upkeep of some shared property – say, a local park – I do not lose my obligations when someone else carelessly or maliciously damages that park. The one who damages the park might have a duty, as we will shortly see, to repair her *specific* damages. But the idea that the park is now hers and hers alone is without any plausible justification. We cannot allow the wrongs of others to allow us to escape the duties we have.

We might, at this point, shift gears a bit; perhaps we have been too literal in our reading of the Pottery Barn rule. It might be the case that we have been reading the concept of "buying" a thing as equivalent with bearing the entirety of the costs of reconstructing a particular place. We might want, instead, to shift away from this, to looking at a more restrictive conception of the obligations that we "purchase" through wrongful action. Following on the park example above, we might want to look at the obligation to reverse the *specific* damages done by our intervention. One who negligently drives her truck onto a park has not thereby acquired some ongoing obligation to keep that park green and pleasant; she has, though, certainly acquired the obligation to fix the damage to the grass caused by her own negligent action. Similarly, even if all legitimate countries had some obligation to assist the people of Iraq, the obligation to fix the specific damages caused by one's own unjust intervention might fall upon the United States specifically. This is to keep the idea that the Pottery Barn rule is a fault-based rule, but to alter the sort of damages that might emerge from that rule. We have, before, assumed that the duties purchased by the United States were what the people of Iraq had the right to expect – which is to say, a government that protected their basic human rights. We might, instead, assume that what the United States has acquired is a duty to make the situation in Iraq no worse than it was before it entered. The United States has not, on this analysis, become the sole country with an obligation to make Iraq a functioning rights-respecting country; all countries continue to have that general obligation. But the United States has a particular obligation as well; it, unlike other countries, has the obligation to reverse the specific damages made during the course of its invasion, so as to make the country no less rights-respecting (no more dangerous, no more anarchic) than it was prior to that invasion.[13]

On this construal, the Pottery Barn rule is entirely right – but it is also largely uninteresting. What it tells us is only that one who unjustly causes a specific damage to another party acquires the duty to reverse those damages. The costs of doing so are hers, and hers alone. The rule, though, gives us no information that we do not already have. We are, I think, generally aware of the fact that we should not do wrong to others and think that the losses we thereby create should be borne by our victims (or by the world as a whole). It is, of course, never a bad thing to be reminded of these facts; the physician's *primum non nocere* is a good thing to have in one's head, whether one is a physician or not. But the Pottery Barn rule is, or should be, more than this. It should tell us something more general about how interveners should think of their duties and those of third parties. It should give us some information about the ethics of war that is not obvious. The fault-based conception, though, fails at these tasks. In particular, it tells us nothing about how the costs of doing justice after war should be allocated between an intervener and the world community as a whole. The rule here says only that an aggressor in an unjust war should clearly bear the costs of repairing the damage the aggressor has done – a fact which leaves up for grabs the remainder of the work to be done to transform a non-rights-respective regime into something better. If the Pottery Barn rule is to tell us something about the costs of war more generally, it cannot do so on the fault-based conception described here.

All this should give us some reason to think that the fault-based conception of the Pottery Barn rule is not the best way to understand this rule. If it meant simply what the fault-based conception seems to imply, then the rule is true, but largely useless – a pithy restatement of moral truths we already knew. We should, therefore, see if something more meaningful can emerge from the Pottery Barn rule interpreted as a principle of strict liability.

---

[13] The difference between these two measures of what is owed by the United States corresponds somewhat to the difference between restitution damages and expectation damages in contract law. The former is a measure of damages that looks to what the claimant had prior to entering into the contract; the latter is a measure of damages that look to what the claimant was entitled to under the contract's terms. The traditional case used to explain these matters is *Hawkins* v. *McGee*, 84 N.H. 113, 146 A. 641 (N.H. 1929), the so-called "hairy hand" case.

Strict liability

Strict liability in law entails holding someone responsible for the costs of an act without showing that the agent has done something wrong in the commission of that act. Fault-based liability relies upon the existence of some standard of action; one who acts in disregard of this standard – who fails to live up to it – is justly held liable in virtue of this fact. Fault-based liability is thus susceptible to being excused, if it is possible to show that one's action was not actually made in disregard of the appropriate standard. If I break a dish in a housewares store, but only because someone else frightened me with an unreasonably loud scream, I might not have to pay for that dish. Strict liability, in contrast, assesses liability for losses based simply upon the fact that I have entered into a particular course of action. The mere fact that I have engaged in that particular course of action is enough to cause losses that emerge from that action to be shifted onto me. I am, accordingly, given no opportunity to excuse myself with reference to the quality of the choice I have made to act in a particular way. If I am strictly liable for the actions of my pet lion, for example, then I will be liable for your damages when he escapes and runs amuck in your housewares store; the fact that I was not negligent in designing my lion's enclosure is not, legally speaking, relevant – I am liable for your damages, simply in virtue of my activity of lion-keeping.[14]

Strict liability is imposed in civil law in a variety of areas, including some parts of product liability, and in the allocation of damages that emerge from ultra-hazardous activities (including, in most places, the keeping of lions). Strict liability will shift all losses that emerge from these activities to the one who undertakes the activity. The justification for this pattern of cost allocation tends to look at what pattern of incentives and penalties will be produced by this form of liability. In particular, strict liability is often justified by appealing to certain facts about the activity in question, based upon which we might think that we would have an oversupply of the activity if it were dealt with by a system of fault-based liability – and a need to ensure the highest standards of care when that activity is undertaken. Take the case of lion-keeping, once again. Were lion-keepers able to avoid paying for the losses created by their lions by citing the care with which they enclosed their lions, we would likely find it cheaper to keep lions. If we have decided that circumstances make it such that we want to have fewer lion-keepers – without banning lion-keeping entirely – we might want to insist that lion-keepers bear the costs of their lions, strictly. In this way, we hope to accomplish two goals: first, we want to have less of the activity; and, second, we give incentives to those who engage in the activity to

[14] The keeping of wild animals is traditionally dealt with by strict liability. See *Restatement of Torts, 2d*, at §507a.

do the activity well. A lion-keeper who knows he will be liable for anything his lion does, after all, is likely to invest in a very secure enclosure indeed.[15]

The question we can now ask is the following: Is entering into war an activity to which strict liability ought to be attached? We might think this question is answered simply in virtue of the idea of an ultra-hazardous activity; war is nothing, after all, if not hazardous. This is not quite enough of an answer, though. What counts as an ultra-hazardous activity makes reference to the norms and practices of a particular place. Something that is ultra-hazardous in one part of the world might be rather normal in another; keeping lions in a park in Africa is presumably a different matter from keeping them in Manhattan. We have, instead, reason to examine whether the pattern of justification for the imposition of strict liability applies to the case of entering into war. Do we have reason to think that there might be an oversupply of war, as it were, that might be limited if initiators were forced to bear the costs of their activity?

The answer depends, of course, on a mix of empirical and normative factors; but it seems plausible to me that these answers might eventually answer the question in the affirmative. We might, indeed, have a temptation to engage too often in warfare, if certain assumptions about human psychology are true. These temptations might be somewhat reduced, if not eliminated, if we were forced to bear all the costs that emerged from our actions – if, indeed, we were forced to bear the entirety of the costs of creating a just society in the target of our military attentions. If this is right, then the two goals of strict liability – having there be less of the activity in question, and incentivizing right conduct during the activity – might be sufficient to justify the imposition of strict liability upon those who engage in war. Put simply, if we had to bear all the costs of rebuilding after war ourselves, we might engage in warfare less often, and do it better when we did.

Why, though, should we think that we face an oversupply of military actions? Answering this question fully requires a theory of what justice in war would entail, which is beyond the scope of this chapter. We might, though, deal with this question indirectly, by looking at some psychological factors that seem to bias decision-makers in favor of warfare, even when warfare might not be the preferred option. If these factors are plausible, then we might have reason to think that we do, indeed, face an oversupply of war, even before we develop a theory sufficient to understand what an ideal supply would look like.

The first factor I would address is the simple fact that our interpretation of practices and norms found in other societies is subject to enormous bias. This is hardly a novel insight. It is important to notice, though, that this fact is likely to infect our decision to go to war as much as any other decision. We are likely

---

[15] For the canonical discussion of this pattern of justification, see Guido Calabresi and Douglas Melamed, "Property Rules, Liability Rules, and Inalienability: One View of the Cathedral," *Harvard Law Review* 85 (1972), 1089–28.

to find practices of those nations culturally similar to ourselves as more justifiable than the practices of nations more dissimilar; we are likely to find our
allies' sins more forgivable than those of our enemies. Kishore Mahbubani has
argued that Western democracies are more willing to countenance deviations
from human rights undertaken by leaders of Western powers than similar
deviations performed by leaders with Asian faces.[16] We should combine this
sad truth with the simple fact that there are rarely – if ever – any interventions
that are made with unmixed motives; we are unlikely to find any pure cases of
interventions undertaken for humanitarian motives. Interventions are generally made for reasons of state, in whole or in part.[17] If this is right, then we face
a tremendous temptation to find moral concerns as a useful cover, sufficient to
convince others – and, sometimes, ourselves – that our cause is just. We face a
standing temptation to dress up our self-interest in the robes of altruism; the
fact that we are already tempted to misunderstand and dislike the practices of
others makes this temptation that much more severe.

All of this, I believe, applies with equal force to military interventions undertaken for humanitarian reasons and to military interventions undertaken for
reasons of self-defense. In the first instance, we should note that the two are
rarely all that distinct; any particular military action is often given a wide number of public justifications, including ideas associated with humanitarianism
and those associated with self-defense and reasons of state.[18] This means that
we should be hesitant before thinking that armed humanitarian interventions
are a distinct category of military actions; we ought to think of humanitarianism as property attaching to *justifications* for a given military action, rather
than as a property of the *actions themselves*. All recent military actions undertaken by the United States, I would argue, have been justified with a mix of
justifications – certainly those provided for the actions in Iraq, Afghanistan,
and Kosovo have been justified through both humanitarian and non-humanitarian motives. It is worth remembering that even the intervention in Kosovo –
the high-water mark for armed humanitarianism – was justified in part with
reference to European stability and the illegality of Serbian aggression.[19] We
have no reason to think that some imagined purity of heart protects us from
the risks of our own biases and bad judgments; we are unlikely to ever be all
that pure. Even if we were, of course, it is hard to see how such moral purity
would protect us from the risks of biases and moral error. Imagine a perfectly

---

[16] Kishore Mahbubani, *Can Asians Think? Understanding the Divide Between East and West* (Hanover: Steerforth, 2001).
[17] For my discussion of these issues, see Michael Blake, "Collateral Benefit," *Social Philosophy & Policy* 23 (2006), 218–30.
[18] Arthur Applbaum discusses this fact and its relation to Iraq in his article: "Forcing a People to be Free," *Philosophy & Public Affairs* 35, no. 4 (2007), 359.
[19] See William Glaberson, "Conflict in the Balkans: The Law," *New York Times* (March 27, 1999).

humanitarian intervener, unwilling to take any action not ultimately justified through humanitarian means; why should we think that such an intervener is free from the biases in interpretation and evaluation that all human agents experience? Purity of heart gives us no reason to expect clarity of vision.

If all this is correct, then it might, indeed, be thought that we have a risk of an oversupply of warfare. If we were forced to bear all the costs of war, though, we would have some incentive to avoid the impact of this temptation. We would have, I think, some incentive to at least make sure that we were truly confident in our judgment, that the cause was truly rightful, prior to engaging in war. We would also, I suspect, have more incentive to maintain a solid plan for the reconstruction of the society after war. Being forced to bear the costs of reconstruction, after all, tends to focus the attention on that reconstruction. It is, at the very least, plausible that strict liability here would ensure that we had less of the activity, and that it was done better in the cases in which it was performed.

The second factor I want to address looks to our natural tendency to privilege the present over the future. This tendency is sometimes rational; few of us think that the proper discount rate, social or individual, should be zero. But it can be irrational to ignore the future in favor of the present, and this irrationality is often pronounced in cases where emotions are heightened. Warfare, after all, is rarely entered into – by politicians, soldiers, or citizens – without emotion and passion being stirred up. There is a persistent worry that this emotion, which is often focused on the pursuit of battlefield victory, will dissipate once this victory is achieved. The result can be that we privilege the immediate result, the first destruction of the enemy's capability, without developing an adequate plan for what is to be done after that victory. Two recent examples come immediately to mind. US President George W. Bush's declaration of "Mission Accomplished" in May 2003 encouraged the thought that the point of the invasion of Iraq was simply the destruction of the Ba'ath party, rather than the reconstruction of a civil and political society for the Iraqi people.[20] In the earlier Gulf War (Operation Desert Storm, 1991), the elder Bush, US President George H.W. Bush, called upon the Kurdish population in Iraq to "take matters into their own hands" against Saddam Hussein; when the United States left, having accomplished the goal of defending Kuwait's territorial integrity, thousands of Kurds were slaughtered.[21] In both cases, the long-term viability of a rights-protecting government was not made a high priority. Indeed, George H.W. Bush made it entirely clear that the problem of the Kurds was one he felt should not be the focus of American military attention, with the exception of a brief and unsuccessful program called Operation Provide Comfort.[22]

---

[20] See Peter Baker, "The Image Bush Just Can't Escape," *The Washington Post* (May 4, 2007).

[21] Haroon Siddiqui, "Hapless Kurds Double-crossed Again," *Toronto Star* (April 4, 1991).

[22] Peter Stothard, "Allies Search for Face-saving Exit from Kurd Haven," *The Times* (June 19, 1991).

These cases indicate that the moral rights of others, so important in the justification of war, can be too easily abandoned after the emotion of war's beginning has faded. The insistence upon paying the costs of war, up to and including the creation of something respecting these rights, might go some way toward giving the initiator of a war some incentive to plan it through to a justifiable completion.

This argument looks to the second half of the justification of strict liability: we want those who propose to do these extraordinary acts (war) to do them in an extraordinary way. We want them to plan fully and carefully for how they will deal with the new risks they create. This seems to be a plausible vision for how we might think of the notion of strict liability attaching to warfare. Military action creates particular risks for particular people; those who have helped the invasion succeed, for example, have been placed in jeopardy through their cooperation with the invading force.[23] These individuals might have a claim under any plausible account of liability for warfare, of course, but strict liability has the advantage of bringing home to the intervener that these individuals are entitled to protection *by the intervener*. Interveners cannot focus on the early stages of the war, and think that their actions then excuse them of obligations during the later stages. Indeed, the strict liability rule would be justified in virtue of its insistence that the entire course of the war – from beginning to end – is to be dealt with by the one who proposes to initiate it.

There is much to be attracted to in this vision of strict liability. All the costs that emerge from a war – including the costs that are ordinarily justly ascribed to the world community as a whole – might be pressed against the one who makes war. This might, I think, plausibly be thought to reduce the amount of war we have; and it might make the war's planning more coherent. We might, in other words, have fewer wars and better ones. There is, however, something deeply perverse here as well; it is the same problem that we dealt with above. Simply put, this rule of liability lets third parties escape from their moral duties simply in virtue of someone else's actions. Whether the invasion is rightful or not makes no difference, on the rule imagined here; other parties are able to insist that the one who begins the war must pay for its just completion. This seems to put third parties in a very odd position, morally speaking. They might have very strong duties to rescue the inhabitants of some non-rights-respecting society. They no longer have these duties, though, once an aggressor – rightly or wrongly – begins a campaign of military force against that society. The one who breaks the country, on this rule, bears all the costs of reconstruction. Third parties are put in a position in which they have reason to hope for others to initiate military force, whether that force is justifiable or not.

This is a serious difficulty. I think it tells us something about how the Pottery Barn rule ought to be understood. It is, I think, somewhat perverse for third

---

[23] I am grateful to Patrick Taylor Smith for discussion of these ideas.

parties to cite the rule as a way of dispelling duties they would otherwise have had. It is, though, less perverse for it to be accepted from the first person, as a rule that the leadership of countries ought to accept, prior to resorting to the use of military force. We ought to treat the Pottery Barn rule as a rule of thumb: Do not enter into an invasion intended to transform another society, unless you are able to commit to doing all the work required to transform that society – and doing it all yourself. In other words, we ought to reason *as if* we were the only society that would ever be able to provide resources, manpower, and the will to act. Reasoning in this way is, I think, a plausible way of weeding out interventions undertaken for insufficient reason, or interventions whose conclusions suffer from unclear objectives and insufficient funds. We should ask, in other words, whether we are willing and able to do it all ourselves. Where we are not, we should not even begin the project.

There are several reasons to adopt this principle. The first, and most powerful, is the reason I have been defending above: We are subject to several biases that make the invocation of war too attractive, and a concern for its conclusions too remote, in our thinking.[24] We ought to force ourselves to imagine that the costs are our own, before we commit to the course of action. A further reason, which I have not emphasized in what has gone before, is that sometimes halfway measures are worse than no measures at all. The Kurds were not only not helped by the American invasion of Iraq in 1991; they were actively harmed, by being induced to place themselves in harm's way, under the expectation of protection that never came. I mentioned, previously, that we did not need special moral insight to think that we should avoid actively harming people with our military interventions. The Pottery Barn rule, as I construe it in this section, might be one way of insisting that we keep this simple moral fact in view; we should not act unless we are able to bear the costs of acting so as to bring about a morally justified state of affairs after warfare ends. The final reason is that planning for the worst case is often very nearly the same as planning for the actual case. In a global society in which each state is able to effectively avoid its obligations to foreign citizens, assuming that the one who acts will not be able

---

[24] One possible worry here is whether we are unduly attracted to armed humanitarian intervention; we might think that we have an *undersupply* of humanitarian warfare, rather than an oversupply, in a world as unjust as our own. I believe this is a possibility, but I do not believe we can so easily cordon off armed humanitarian intervention from other forms of intervention. As I have argued, we may have to accept that humanitarianism is one possible justification for warfare, and that this justification is rarely if ever found by itself. This means that we are not able to ask about the supply of humanitarian warfare in isolation; we are forced to ask about the supply of warfare more generally. If this is true, then it seems we would be hard-pressed to think that we have an oversupply of warfare *simpliciter*, and we are likely right to adopt the Pottery Barn rule as a way of ensuring that we are not likely to engage in ill-conceived interventions – whether or not those interventions are justified with reference to humanitarian norms. I am grateful to Don Scheid for urging me to consider these issues.

to rely upon the moral agency of other states is simply a smart thing to do. Even if others have a moral duty to aid, it is only rarely going to be true that they will regard this fact as a sufficient reason for action.

The Pottery Barn rule, on this construal, is thus a rule of action from the first person. Other states cannot rely on it to shirk their moral duties, if those exist. A state that proposes to intervene, however, should subject its own plans to the rule. Can we truly commit to the plan of action we have laid out? Are we prepared to bear the costs of doing justice ourselves? Have we determined what course of action is likely to lead to a justified outcome, and have we limited the costs of getting to that outcome? If we are unable to answer these questions in a satisfactory way, we should not begin the plan of military intervention. The rule is a rule for state leaders, and for those who advise them; it is, accordingly, somewhat appropriate that it was US Secretary of State Colin Powell – rather than, say, French President Jacques Chirac – who first pressed it against President George W. Bush.

There is, of course, something odd even on this version of the Pottery Barn rule. It is a rule intended to counteract our biases in evaluating the morality of intervention; it is, accordingly, a rule that tends to press in favor of a bias against intervention. Accordingly, there might be some cases in which there is a good case to be made for intervention, but the Pottery Barn rule tells us not to do it. (Perhaps we have a just cause and pursue it justly, but would need the financial help of others in order to make the society in question truly rights-respecting.) Is this a problem with the Pottery Barn rule? I do not think so – so long as its role is understood in the right way. The rule is intended to guide the decisions of states in the long run, given the standard biases and cognitive errors made by humans, including humans who run states. If it is true that these biases and errors are, indeed, likely to lead to too many interventions, if we consider each potential intervention as an individual case, then we have reason to restrict the sorts of reasons we can employ in defending warfare. Larry May uses the concept of *meionexia* to explore similar ideas: Under some very common circumstances, it is virtuous for a state to do less than that state might be morally permitted to do.[25] I am not here concerned primarily with virtues, but I believe the best interpretation of the Pottery Barn rule is markedly similar to May's analysis. Only by doing less than we might – and refusing to intervene in all except the most obvious cases – will we arrive at the right quantity of warfare, and ensure the best practices during warfare's pursuit.

The Pottery Barn rule, then, contains a surprising amount of wisdom. It is, in the end, an odd sort of a rule; it tells us to reason from false premises – to imagine that other states have no duties to the state we propose to invade, that we are responsible for these duties once the invasion has begun. These false premises, though, are likely to lead to better results than case-by-case analyses

---

[25] May, *After War Ends*, 7.

beginning with true premises. The rule, further, gives guidance to individual agents about whether or not they should engage in warfare; it gives us no right to think that we lose our own duties when other parties choose to engage in warfare and we do not. The rule is, in sum, more complex than it might at first appear – but it is not a bad rule to have in political discourse, and recent history suggests we are right to keep it in mind going forward.

9

Armed humanitarian intervention and the problem of abuse after Libya

LUKE GLANVILLE

> Antient and modern History indeed informs us, that Avarice and
> Ambition do frequently lay hold on such Excuses; but the Use that wicked
> Men make of a Thing, does not always hinder it from being just in itself.
>
> (Hugo Grotius, *The Rights of War and Peace*, 1625)

> We are aware that any altruistic concept may be abused by the powerful.
> We know this from experience. Although they might seek to legitimize
> interventions that have little or nothing to do with – in this case – the four
> major crimes, the misuse of a concept does not invalidate it.
>
> (Heraldo Muñoz, Chilean Ambassador to the United Nations, 2009)

Introduction

The idea of armed humanitarian intervention has long been attended with
warnings that it will be abused by powerful states seeking to justify wars fought
not for humanitarian purposes but for self-interest. This problem of abuse has
received renewed attention in the wake of NATO's recent intervention in Libya.
Critics charge that NATO misappropriated a UN Security Council resolution
authorizing limited use of force to protect civilians and that it instead waged an
expansive military campaign in pursuit of self-interested objectives of regime
change and the establishment of favorable diplomatic and trade relations. As it
has in the past, such apparent abuse has led some critics to reject the idea of a
right of humanitarian military intervention in any form.

This chapter represents an attempt to find a way through this problem of
abuse. I cautiously advance an argument that the problem is not as fatal to the
idea of humanitarian intervention as some suggest. As Hugo Grotius argued,
just because a principle can be misused does not necessarily make the principle itself unjust.[1] After outlining how the problem of abuse has evolved as the

---

[1] Hugo Grotius, *The Rights of War and Peace*, 3 vols., edited by Richard Tuck (Indianapolis:
Liberty Fund, 2005), vol. II (Bk. II, chap. XXV, "War Undertaken for Others," sec. viii, para.
4), 1162.

idea of humanitarian intervention has itself evolved over time, I consider three reasons that might be offered for why we should embrace the idea of military intervention for the protection of populations in spite of its persistent abuse. First, when states employ humanitarian arguments in an attempt to legitimize unjust interventions, their arguments restrain their actions. Second, appeals to humanitarian principles do not automatically provide legitimacy that an intervention would otherwise not enjoy; duplicitous justifications are commonly rejected and abusive interventions condemned. And third, it is doubtful that the availability of humanitarian justifications generates abusive interventions that would otherwise not occur. While I suggest that the first of these reasons is unsatisfactory, I endorse the second and third. However, I also note that they offer "sorry comfort" to those who are victims of unjust wars waged in the name of humanitarianism, or justifiable humanitarian wars waged unjustly, and I recognize that the long and continuing history of abusive interventionism understandably gives many states deep and abiding reasons for seeking to restrain any weakening of the presumption against the resort to force. I conclude by briefly contemplating what options, if any, might be available to the society of states for further limiting the problem of abuse without abandoning the idea of armed humanitarian intervention altogether.

The evolving problem of abuse

For as long as arguments have been advanced for a right of military intervention to protect populations from atrocities, these arguments have been abused by states seeking to justify self-interested and non-humanitarian uses of force. Theorists have been confronted with this problem of abuse for over 2,000 years. In the fourth century BC, for example, Mencius, a Confucian scholar and political advisor in the multi-state system of ancient China, argued that a benevolent ruler was justified in waging "punitive war" against a tyrannical ruler in order to punish him and to rescue the oppressed population. Mencius recalled with approval an earlier king who "punished the rulers and comforted the people, like a fall of timely rain, and the people greatly rejoiced," and he argued that a benevolent ruler could claim the moral authority to undertake such wars of rectification in his own day.[2] As has been repeated so often in history, the large states of Qi and Chu adopted this argument to justify self-interested attacks on the small state of Song. Qi and Chu spread propaganda casting the king of Song as "unprincipled" and "unrighteous." One indictment against the Song began, "I have heard it said that it is the duty of a king who aspires to the praise of the world to punish tyrants, suppress disorders, remove the unprincipled and attack the unrighteous." It then proceeded to catalogue the iniquities of the

---

[2] *Mencius*, revised edition, translated by D.C. Lau (London: Penguin, 2004), i.B.11. See also i.A.5, ii.B.8, and vii.B.4.

king of Song and concluded by advising the king of Qi: "If your majesty does not slay him, your reputation will suffer." Historians suggest that it is doubtful that the king of Song committed the various atrocities for which he was accused. Rather, Qi and Chu developed these false accusations as part of their attempt to justify what was in reality a war of self-aggrandizement waged by the powerful against the weak.[3]

The perception that arguments for humanitarian intervention will inevitably be abused has long led some theologians, jurists, and philosophers to insist that there should be no such right of intervention. The argument made by Grotius for a right of sovereigns to wage war to punish those who "exercise such Tyrannies over Subjects, as no good Man living can approve of," for example, was met with stern rebukes by other early modern European theorists.[4] German scholar Samuel Pufendorf argued it was "contrary to the natural *Equality* of Mankind, for a Man to force himself upon the World for a *Judge*, and *Decider of Controversies*. Not to say what dangerous Abuses this Liberty might be perverted to, and that any Man might make War upon any Man upon such a Pretence."[5] Swiss jurist Emer de Vattel charged Grotius with articulating a dangerous doctrine: "Could it escape Grotius, that, notwithstanding all the precautions added by him in the following paragraphs, his opinion opens a door to all the ravages of enthusiasm and fanaticism, and furnishes ambition with numberless pretexts?"[6] A common refrain of those arguing against a right of humanitarian intervention from the early modern period through to the present day has been that consolidation of such a right will facilitate abuse and lead to a proliferation of unjust wars fought for self-interest.

Arguments about the problem of abuse became particularly prominent from the early 1990s onwards as skeptical states and commentators sought to restrain the emergence of a right of humanitarian intervention in international discourse and interstate relations. We can identify several phases through which this supposed problem of abuse has evolved. Initially, as the UN Security Council demonstrated an increasing willingness to involve itself in sovereign affairs and authorize Chapter VII interventions to protect populations, critics expressed a fear that Council deliberations on internal conflicts and human-rights crises would be manipulated by powerful states seeking to

---

[3] Arthur Waley, *Three Ways of Thought in Ancient China* (London: George Allen & Unwin, 1939), 137–43.

[4] Grotius, *The Rights of War and Peace*, Bk. II, chap. XXV, sec. viii, para. 2, 1161.

[5] Samuel Pufendorf, *The Law of Nature and Nations*, translated by Basil Kennett (London: 1729), Bk. VIII, chap. VI, sec. 14.

[6] Emer de Vattel, *The Law of Nations*, edited by Béla Kapossy and Richard Whatmore (Indianapolis: Liberty Fund, 2008), Bk. II, chap. I, sec. 7, 265. It is worth noting, however, that while Pufendorf and Vattel rejected the right to punish tyranny, they did offer formulations of a right to use force to rescue victims of tyranny, and they drew on Grotius to make their arguments.

advance their own interests. In 1992, for example, the Zimbabwean foreign minister warned the Security Council that "great care has to be taken to see that these domestic conflicts are not used as a pretext for the intervention of the big powers in the legitimate domestic affairs of small states or that human-rights issues are not used for totally different purposes of destabilizing other governments."[7] In the wake of NATO's controversial intervention in Kosovo in 1999, it became clear to critics that the greater danger was not that power-ful states would manipulate the deliberations of the Security Council, but that they would simply bypass the Council and intervene "unilaterally" in the affairs of states. The Russian ambassador to the United Nations lamented that NATO's attempts to arrogate to itself the authority to decide when and where to intervene and to disregard the basic norms and principles of international law created a "dangerous precedent that could cause acute destabilization and chaos on the regional and global level."[8] The Chinese foreign minister warned that deviation from the principles of sovereign equality and non-interference in internal affairs "would lead to the rule of hegemonism ... new gunboat dip-lomacy would wreak havoc, the sovereignty and independence by virtue of which some small countries protect themselves would be jeopardized, and international peace and stability would be seriously endangered."[9] This fear was seemingly realized when a coalition of states led by the United States and the United Kingdom invaded Iraq in 2003. Despite the various arguments offered by the coalition, there was widespread agreement that this was a war fought without UN Security Council authorization and without just cause. The seemingly disingenuous efforts by the coalition to belatedly justify the inva-sion on humanitarian grounds confirmed for many that the right of humani-tarian intervention would inevitably be abused by states seeking a pretext for unjust wars.

The concept of armed humanitarian intervention was now in disrepute. Thomas Weiss suggested that the sun had set on the idea at least for the moment.[10] Nevertheless, some degree of consensus began to rapidly emerge around a new and related concept, the "Responsibility to Protect" (RtoP). The original authors of the RtoP concept, the International Commission on Intervention and State Sovereignty (2001), had insisted that intervention for the protection of populations was most appropriately authorized by the UN Security Council, but the Commission also sought to establish procedures that could allow the use of force even if the Council refused to act. They further outlined criteria that should guide decision-making on intervention, based on

---

[7] UN Document, S/PV.3046 (January 31, 1992), 131.
[8] The Russian representative in UN Document S/PV.3988 (March 24, 1999), 3.
[9] UN Document, A/54/PV.8 (September 22, 1999), 16.
[10] Thomas G. Weiss, "The Sunset of Humanitarian Intervention? The Responsibility to Protect in a Unipolar Era," *Security Dialogue* 35, no. 2 (2004), 135–53.

traditional just-war criteria, just as numerous scholars and states had done in the 1990s.[11] The backlash against the Iraq War and the fear that such abusive interventionism could become the norm ensured that many states would refuse to consent to any agreement providing legitimacy for unauthorized intervention. However, at the UN World Summit in 2005, the society of states did agree to endorse the permissibility of Chapter VII collective action to protect populations so long as such action was authorized by the Security Council. Moreover, while they did not articulate guidelines for Council deliberations, they did offer a fairly clear statement of the range of situations in which the Council might legitimately authorize collective action. The society of states was prepared to act through the Council, they declared, "should peaceful means be inadequate and national authorities manifestly fail to protect their populations from genocide, war crimes, ethnic cleansing, and crimes against humanity."[12]

Over the next five years, and in fits and starts, the agreement reached at the 2005 Summit was consolidated. While states continued to warn about the dangers that the right of intervention could be abused, almost all of them came to accept that the Security Council had a role to play in authorizing Chapter VII military actions to protect populations where necessary. The problem of abuse was perceived to be mitigated by the development of consensus among states that military intervention required the authority of the Security Council and by the agreement that such intervention only be authorized as a last resort and only in response to the occurrence of the specific crimes delineated at the Summit. Indeed, states that had once been skeptical of military intervention in any form now warned against inaction by the Council as much as they warned against action outside of the Council. In a landmark 2009 General Assembly debate on RtoP, for example, India declared that RtoP "should in no way provide a pretext for humanitarian intervention or unilateral action," but recognized that collective action through the Council could be necessary as a last resort if peaceful mechanisms had failed, and even lamented that the society of states had "in the past failed in its duty to respond to mass atrocities."[13]

Numerous states expressed reservations about the Council's role in authorizing coercive measures against states, but their emphasis tended to be on the need for the Council to act consistently, impartially, and effectively rather than a need to prevent the Council from being overactive. They demanded Council reform, clarification of decision-making criteria, and agreement to restrain the exercise of veto, not only to prevent the abusive misapplication of RtoP, but also to ensure that the Council would exercise its authority, where appropriate,

---

[11] International Commission on Intervention and State Sovereignty (ICISS), *The Responsibility to Protect: Report of the International Commission on Intervention and State Sovereignty* (Ottawa: International Development Research Centre, 2001), XII–XIII.

[12] *2005 World Summit Outcome*, UN General Assembly Resolution, UN Document A/60/1 (October 24, 2005), para. 139.

[13] UN Document, A/63/PV.99 (July 24, 2009), 2

to ensure the protection of populations. Singapore, for example, asserted that the concept needed to be applied "without political bias or hidden agendas," but also lamented the failure to halt the Rwandan genocide and declared that the Council must "commit to exercising fully that grave responsibility" to protect populations from atrocities. Chile embraced the "responsibility to protect" as the "balanced formula" that Latin American states had been look-ing for, between abusive unilateral intervention and lamentable international inaction.[14] The increasing clarity and consensus about who could authorize intervention and the kinds of situations in which such intervention could be authorized meant that the problem of abuse was now less pressing for many states than it had been in previous years. This clarity and consensus meant that if a state did resort to force without Council authority and with seemingly non-humanitarian objectives, such as Russia was widely perceived to have done in invading Georgia in 2008, any appeals that the state might make to RtoP or the right of humanitarian intervention could be readily rejected and the inter-vention condemned.[15] The mere invocation of a right of intervention was not enough to confer legitimacy on an intervention. Abuse could be readily recog-nized for what it was and rightly denounced.

The problem of abuse, however, has seemingly re-emerged in the wake of NATO's intervention in Libya in 2011, and this time with a new twist. For many, the Libyan intervention has demonstrated that the requirement that the resort to force be authorized by the UN Security Council is not sufficient to ensure that the right of intervention will not be abused by powerful states in pursuit of their own ideological and self-interested objectives. The danger, critics now suggest, is that intervening states will take a mandate conferred by the Council regarding the use of force to protect populations from atrocities and they will use it to pursue rather different objectives of regime change and Western-style democratization. Such concerns have been repeatedly expressed by states criti-cizing NATO's intervention.

Six months after NATO's action in Libya had begun, for example, Russia and China vetoed a draft resolution condemning violence against civilians by the Syrian government, and Russia made clear that its decision was prompted by what it believed to be NATO's ongoing misrepresentation and abuse of the Security Council's Resolution 1973 on Libya. "The situation in Syria," the Russian representative insisted, "cannot be considered in the Council sepa-rately from the Libyan experience." He firmly rejected the notion that NATO's implementation of the Libyan resolution should be taken as a model for future implementation of RtoP and warned against repeating the model in Syria. The Russian representative then catalogued the lamentable ways in which NATO

---

[14] UN Document, A/63/PV.98 (July 24, 2009), 6–8, 12.
[15] Alex J. Bellamy, "The Responsibility to Protect–Five Years On," *Ethics & International Affairs* 24, no. 2 (2010), 150–53.

had abused its mandate such that "a Security Council resolution turned into its opposite":

> The demand for a quick ceasefire turned into a full-fledged civil war, the humanitarian, social, economic, and military consequences of which transcend Libyan borders. The situation in connection with the no-fly zone has morphed into the bombing of oil refineries, television stations, and other civilian sites. The arms embargo has morphed into a naval blockade in western Libya, including a blockade of humanitarian goods. Today the tragedy of Benghazi has spread to other western Libyan towns – Sirte and Bani Walid. These types of models should be excluded from global practices once and for all.[16]

China has similarly made clear its rejection of "any arbitrary interpretation of the Council's resolutions or of any actions going beyond those mandated by the Council."[17] And Syria, not surprisingly, has been even more critical, warning not only that powerful states will misapply Council resolutions, but that they will foment and exacerbate crises and concoct arguments to mislead the Council into adopting these resolutions in the first place. The Syrian representative charged that Western states tried to do this in Iraq, they succeeded in doing it in Libya, and now they were attempting to do it again in Syria. Western states simply cannot be trusted:

> Some speakers have said that they would not move towards military intervention in Syria and that a decision of the Council would not necessarily lead to military intervention. That is all well and good, but can anyone assure us that what was done to Libya, Somalia, Iraq, the former Yugoslavia and Kosovo will not be repeated in the case of Syria?[18]

When Russia and China again vetoed a resolution condemning the Syrian government in early 2012, the Syrian representative expressed his appreciation to them for defending "the inadmissibility of intervention in the internal affairs of countries, of waging wars against countries to gain exclusive control of their geographic location and their lucrative natural resources, and of resolving the economic problems of the Western Powers at the expense of the peoples of developing nations."[19] The problem of abuse is firmly back on the agenda of states deliberating the concept of humanitarian intervention.

Embracing humanitarian intervention despite its abuse

At the conclusion to his argument justifying wars "made for the Defense of another's Subjects" in *The Rights of War and Peace* (1625), Grotius acknowledged

---

16 UN Document, S/PV.6627 (October 4, 2011), 4.
17 UN Document, S/PV.6528 (May 4, 2011), 10.
18 UN Document, S/PV.6710 (January 31, 2012), 31.
19 UN Document, S/PV.6711 (February 4, 2012), 12.

that such arguments had and would continue to be abused by "wicked Men" before offering a tantalizing response:

> Antient and modern History indeed informs us, that Avarice and Ambition do frequently lay hold on such Excuses; but the Use that wicked Men make of a Thing, does not always hinder it from being just in itself. *Pirates sail on the Seas, and Thieves wear Swords, as well as others.*[20]

Almost four centuries later, the Chilean Ambassador to the United Nations, Heraldo Muñoz, offered a strikingly similar response to the problem of abuse:

> We are aware that any altruistic concept may be abused by the powerful. We know this from experience. Although they might seek to legitimize interventions that have little or nothing to do with – in this case – the four major crimes, the misuse of a concept does not invalidate it. Selective application of RtoP is evidently a risk; yet no principle has withstood the test of application in a perfect or flawless manner and, in any event, principles lose credibility precisely when they are applied in a self-serving or partisan way.[21]

The mere fact that a right is open to abuse is not reason enough to reject it. The right to self-defense, for example, has repeatedly been misappropriated by states seeking to justify wars of aggression throughout history, but only the strictest of pacifists deny that this right should be a fundamental attribute of statehood. Yet, it is notable that neither Grotius nor Muñoz suggests that the problem of abuse can *never* render an idea unjust. Grotius only asserts that the fact of abuse does not "always" demonstrate the injustice of an idea. Presumably, to offer an extreme scenario, if an idea only facilitates abusive acts of injustice and never encourages principled acts of justice, we might then conclude that the idea itself should be rejected. Muñoz expresses the caveat in socio-political rather than moral terms. If an idea is repeatedly applied in a self-serving way, he suggests, it will simply "lose credibility."

How then should we think about the particular idea of armed humanitarian intervention? I here consider three possible reasons for why we ought to embrace the idea despite the problem of abuse. I reject the first as unsatisfactory but endorse the second and third.

Humanitarian arguments demand humanitarian actions

One reason that has been suggested for why we might embrace the idea of humanitarian intervention despite the problem of abuse is that the adoption of humanitarian arguments by intervening states restrains the scope of action available to them such that they will need to act in ways that can be plausibly

---

[20] Emphasis in original. Grotius, *The Rights of War and Peace*, Bk. II, chap. XXV, sec. viii, para. 4, 1162.
[21] UN Document, A/63/PV.98 (July 24, 2009), 12.

justified as humanitarian. This argument is offered by Nicholas Wheeler in his landmark study, *Saving Strangers*. Wheeler responds to the realist argument that states will abuse humanitarian rationales for military intervention by claiming that this underestimates the extent to which actors become "entangled in their justifications." "Governments that justify intervention in humanitarian terms," he suggests, "establish a benchmark against which we can judge their subsequent actions." Drawing on the work of Quentin Skinner, he claims that "actors who accept the 'need to legitimate' will be limited to actions that can plausibly be defended in terms of the legitimating reasons that are claimed to have motivated the action." This, he says, even applies to powerful states. "Even the powerful do not want to be exposed as hypocrites, and, once a state has legitimated an intervention as humanitarian, its subsequent actions will be constrained by the need to avoid acting in ways that undermine a positive humanitarian outcome."[22]

This is an appealing argument, but I think it is overstated and insufficiently borne out by the available evidence. There are certainly grounds for thinking that the use of humanitarian arguments does restrain some states in some circumstances. While NATO was criticized by some for conducting a duplicitous intervention in Libya, for example, its humanitarian justifications coincided with a careful effort to ensure minimal loss of life through the course of its mission. NATO conducted an air campaign of "unparalleled precision, which, although not perfect, greatly minimized collateral damage."[23] Over seven months, NATO flew more than 26,000 air sorties, almost 10,000 of them involving missile strikes, leading to the deaths of between 40 and 70 civilians.[24] While any civilian deaths are, of course, to be lamented, this was a remarkably small number of casualties given the scope of the mission. The evidence suggests that NATO sought to conduct its military intervention in a humanitarian manner. However, I do not think that this example demonstrates the veracity of Wheeler's claim, since I reject the assertions of skeptical states and commentators that humanitarian objectives were not central to NATO's mission.

What about Russia's intervention in Georgia in 2008? This supposed humanitarian intervention was widely criticized as a war fought for ulterior motives. Did the use of humanitarian arguments restrain Russia? It may well be the case that Russia was more restrained in its actions than it otherwise would have been because it had justified the intervention as a legitimate response to genocide

[22] Nicholas J. Wheeler, *Saving Strangers: Humanitarian Intervention in International Society* (Oxford University Press, 2000), 39, 40, 296.

[23] Ivo H. Daalder and James G. Stavridis, "NATO's Victory in Libya: The Right Way to Run an Intervention," *Foreign Affairs* 91, no. 2 (2012), 3.

[24] Nick Hopkins and Richard Norton-Taylor, "NATO Winds Down Libyan War Effort after 26,000 Air Missions," *The Guardian* (October 20, 2011); C.J. Chivers and Eric Schmitt, "In Strikes on Libya by NATO, an Unspoken Civilian Toll," *New York Times* (December 17, 2011).

and did not want to be exposed as being hypocritical. Nevertheless, it is difficult to conclude that Russia took sufficient care to avoid "acting in ways that undermine a positive humanitarian outcome," as Wheeler suggests they should have. An independent international fact-finding mission established by the Council of the European Union concluded that, while Georgian forces had indeed violated international law in attacking civilians and Russian peacekeepers, so too had Russia in intervening in August 2008. Georgia had not committed genocide in South Ossetia as Russia claimed, and Russia's military campaign, which reached not only into this region but also Abkhazia and Georgia proper, was a disproportionate response to Georgia's actions.[25] Russia's initial assertion that Georgia's genocidal forces had killed 2,000 civilians in South Ossetia would later be revised down to 162. Meanwhile, Russia's intervention itself contributed to substantial loss of civilian lives. About 850 people, including civilians, policeman, and servicemen, died in the five days of fighting. More than 100,000 civilians fled their homes. And when the war concluded, the political conflict remained unresolved. Russia's humanitarian case is further undermined by its apparent use of cluster munitions, which represent a particular threat to civilians because of their indiscriminate effects.[26]

An even more damning story can be told with respect to the 2003 invasion of Iraq. Again it may well be, as Wheeler predicts, that the US-led coalition was more restrained in its prosecution of the war and its aftermath than it would have been had it not invoked the language of humanitarian intervention. Nevertheless, we cannot conclude that this ideational entrapment led the coalition to take sufficient care in its treatment of civilians. In a well-known piece criticizing the assertion that the war was a humanitarian intervention, executive director of Human Rights Watch, Ken Roth, argued that "a dominant humanitarian motive is important because it affects numerous decisions made in the course of an intervention and its aftermath that can determine its success in saving people from harm." Humanitarianism, Roth insisted, "was at best a subsidiary motive for the invasion of Iraq" and this "affected the way the invasion was carried out, to the detriment of the Iraqi people."[27] He catalogued the

[25] "Report of the Independent International Fact-Finding Mission on the Conflict in Georgia" (September 2009) (www.ceiig.ch/pdf/IIFFMCG_Volume_I.pdf, 24, 28–29).

[26] *Ibid.*, 21, 5, 28.

[27] Ken Roth, "War in Iraq: Not a Humanitarian Intervention," *Human Rights Watch World Report 2004*, available at: www.hrw.org/legacy/wr2k4/3.htm.
   Wheeler and Morris reply that the humanitarian motives of the coalition should not be so quickly discounted, but they nevertheless agree that the war failed the test of a humanitarian intervention and that the coalition failed to discharge its responsibility to provide security for civilians in the aftermath of the war. Nicholas J. Wheeler and Justin Morris, "Justifying the Iraq War as a Humanitarian Intervention: The Cure is Worse Than the Disease," in Ramesh Thakur and Waheguru Pal Singh Sidhu (eds.), *The Iraq Crisis and World Order: Structural, Institutional and Normative Challenges* (Tokyo: United Nations University Press, 2006), 444–63.

failures of the coalition, as occupying power, to discharge its responsibility to fill the security vacuum and protect civilians, including a failure to deploy sufficient troops, particularly troops trained in policing, to prevent violence and disorder, especially since the occupying authorities had disbanded the entire Iraqi army and police force. He also catalogued the failures of coalition forces to comply with international human rights and humanitarian law. He recognized that they took great care to avoid harming civilians when attacking fixed, pre-selected targets, but suggested that their methods in attempting to bomb mobile targets, such as individual leaders, "bordered on indiscriminate" such that "Significant civilian casualties were the predictable result." Further, army troops regularly used cluster munitions in populated areas, causing substantial casualties. "Such disregard for civilian life," he concluded, "is incompatible with a genuinely humanitarian intervention."[28] This fierce condemnation of the coalition's conduct, moreover, was offered before the infamous revelations of widespread abuse of prisoners in Abu Ghraib and elsewhere.

I do not think that the claim that humanitarian arguments lead to humanitarian actions is satisfactory. It does not give us sufficient reason to embrace the idea of humanitarian intervention despite its abuse. The invocation of humanitarian arguments may frequently restrain states to some degree, but it in no way ensures that they will satisfactorily strive for humanitarian outcomes.

Abuse can be labeled for what it is and rejected

A more promising reason for accepting the permissibility of armed humanitarian intervention despite its persistent abuse is that abuse can be labeled for what it is and rejected. As Alex Bellamy has recently suggested with respect to Russia's military action in Georgia, the concept of RtoP might provide language that powerful, self-interested states can adopt in seeking to legitimize abusive interventionism, but the appeal to this concept does not automatically legitimize the intervention.[29] To expand upon Grotius' argument, the mere right to sail on the sea does not legitimize piracy, and neither does the right to bear arms legitimize armed robbery. Likewise, the right of military intervention for the protection of populations does not automatically legitimize its abuse. Rather, the misapplication of humanitarian arguments can be rejected, and illegitimate interventions can be condemned. This may seem an obvious point, but it is worth making. Russia's attempt to legitimize its invasion of Georgia as an appropriate response to genocide in accordance with RtoP was widely condemned.[30] The invocation of humanitarian arguments did not enable Russia to "get away with" their illegitimate intervention any more than they would

---

[28] Roth, "War in Iraq."   [29] Bellamy, "The Responsibility to Protect," 150–53.
[30] See "Report of the Independent International Fact-Finding Mission on the Conflict in Georgia."

have had they not invoked these arguments. The belated attempt by the United States and its coalition partners to justify its invasion of Iraq as a humanitarian intervention was similarly rejected by a significant proportion of international society and, to the extent that these arguments were rejected, the coalition drew little benefit from invoking them.[31] To be sure, neither Russia nor the US-led coalition was punished in any material sense for its illegitimate intervention, but neither would they have been if they had not invoked humanitarian ideas.

Humanitarian justifications are rightly understood as part of the politics of legitimation in international discussions about the use of force. Their invocations are not automatically accepted. Rather, they are subject to deliberation and debate. If they are perceived to be disingenuous and hypocritical, or simply naive and imprudent, the society of states can reject them. The emergence of international consensus on RtoP has seen the bounds of legitimate intervention become increasingly well-defined in recent years. As noted earlier, the 2005 Summit agreement clearly asserts that intervention must be authorized by the UN Security Council and in response to the manifest failure of a state to protect its population from four crimes that are well defined in international law. In subsequent debates within the Council and the UN General Assembly, states have repeatedly emphasized the restraint on the resort to force implied by these Summit provisions. The ability of a state or coalition of states to justify an intervention that falls outside of these bounds, therefore, is tightly circumscribed.

There will, nevertheless, commonly be ambiguous cases in which the question of abuse is fiercely debated and no clear consensus emerges in the society of states. This again is part of the politics of legitimation. The intervention in Libya is such an example. Allegations that NATO abused its mandate to protect civilians and instead pursued a self-interested war aimed at regime change are countered with claims that the only way to ensure the protection of civilians was to make certain that Muammar Gaddafi's regime was overthrown, given that Gaddafi had declared his intention to "cleanse Libya house by house" of the "rats" and "cockroaches" who protested against his rule.[32] To the extent that skeptical states have perceived that the intervention was conducted in a manner that violated international laws and norms, the intervening states have been condemned. They are not immune from condemnation simply because they appealed to the language of humanitarianism.

At the same time, neither are skeptical states immune from condemnation if they themselves are perceived to excessively overstate the problem of abuse and prevent seemingly legitimate action aimed at protecting populations. The backlash over Russia's and China's exercise of their veto powers to deny the passage of draft resolutions condemning violence by the Assad regime and

[31] See the discussion in Wheeler and Morris, "Justifying the Iraq War." See also Alex J. Bellamy, "Responsibility to Protect or Trojan Horse? The Crisis in Darfur and Humanitarian Intervention after Iraq," *Ethics & International Affairs* 19, no. 2 (2005), 31–54.
[32] "Libya Protests: Defiant Gaddafi Refuses to Quit," *BBC News* (February 22, 2011).

supporting plans for a peaceful transition of power in Syria is such an example. As discussed earlier, Russia in particular has drawn parallels between the international response to Libya and the proposed responses to Syria and defended its use of the veto at least partly on the grounds that a resolution condemning human-rights abuses could again be misappropriated by states seeking a pretext for intervention. It is widely perceived that Russia and China have overstated the danger of abuse and stood in the way of necessary international action aimed at ensuring the protection of civilians. In early 2012, 12 days after the second draft resolution on Syria was vetoed in the Security Council by the two states, the General Assembly adopted a resolution which condemned the human-rights violations perpetrated by Syrian authorities with an overwhelming majority of 137 to 12, with 17 abstentions.[33] Russia and China were fiercely condemned for what was perceived to be their "shameful" intransigence in the face of human suffering. In response to the second veto on Syria, the British Ambassador to the United Nations declared, "The United Kingdom is appalled by the decision of Russia and China to veto an otherwise consensus resolution," and the US Ambassador pronounced, "The United States is disgusted that a couple of members of this Council continue to prevent us from fulfilling our sole purpose here," accusing the two states of holding the Council hostage while standing behind "empty arguments and individual interests."[34] US Secretary of State, Hillary Clinton, was even more scathing. "It's quite distressing to see two permanent members of the Security Council using their veto while people are being murdered – women, children, brave young men – houses are being destroyed," she declared. "It is just despicable, and I ask whose side are they on? They are clearly not on the side of the Syrian people."[35]

Allegations and denials of abuse, then, are subject to international deliberation and argument and interventions are only legitimized to the extent that they are accepted by the society of states. As Chile suggested in 2009, by debating interventions according to the agreed terms of RtoP, the society of states is able to seek a balance between abusive interventionism and lamentable inaction,[36] and where states are perceived to act in ways that are inconsistent with RtoP, they can be rightly condemned for doing so.

Humanitarian ideas do not facilitate abusive interventions that would otherwise not occur

A similarly persuasive reason for not rejecting the idea of armed humanitarian intervention is that it is doubtful that the idea facilitates abusive interventions

---

[33] UN General Assembly Res., GA/11207/Rev.1 (February 16, 2012).
[34] UN Document, S/PV.6711 (February 4, 2012), 5, 6.
[35] "Syria: Hillary Clinton Calls Russia and China 'Despicable' for Opposing UN Resolution," *The Telegraph (UK)* (February 27, 2012).
[36] UN Document, A/63/PV.98 (July 24, 2009), 12.

that would otherwise not occur. One indicator supporting this claim is that the emergence of the right of humanitarian intervention since the end of the Cold War has not been accompanied by an increase in instances of war between states. Indeed, interstate war, defined as armed conflict between states inflicting at least 1,000 battle or battle-related deaths in a given year, has been on the decline since the end of World War II, even as the number of states has itself increased almost four-fold.[37] It has continued to decline even as the idea of humanitarian intervention has gained increased acceptance over the last two decades. This trend led Mary Kaldor to speculate in 1999 that "the barbarity of war between states may have become a thing of the past."[38] In 2009, John Mueller stated the case more firmly, concluding: "We may be reaching a point where war … ceases, or nearly ceases, to exist, a remarkable development that has attracted little notice."[39] At least when we measure wars according to the threshold of 1,000 deaths, the rise of the idea of humanitarian intervention does not appear to have facilitated an increase in states resorting to war. Indeed, a tentative argument can be made that the emergence of the right of armed humanitarian intervention is actually playing a role in the decline of aggressive war. Ryan Goodman cautiously suggests that the emerging imperative to justify the use of force on humanitarian grounds can actually facilitate conditions of peace between otherwise aggressive states and their prospective targets. Appealing to the sociological consequences of being required to justify war in a particular way, he argues that "framing the resort to force as a pursuit of humanitarian objectives, or adding humanitarian issues to an ongoing military effort, can reshape domestic political arrangements and the character of interstate relations that lead to war."[40] According to this argument, the expansion of the permissibility of armed humanitarian intervention actually restrains aggressive war.

Despite the promising trends, however, it remains that states do continue to abuse the idea of humanitarian intervention. In response to this reality, I would suggest that, in those instances where states have been judged to have abused the principle of humanitarian intervention to justify the resort to military force, it seems likely that they would have resorted to force even if humanitarian arguments were not available. The fact that Russia did not attempt to gain Security Council authorization for its intervention in Georgia indicates that it never seriously anticipated that its humanitarian justifications would be accepted by the society of states. Russia likely offered humanitarian arguments in an attempt to lighten the socio-political costs of violating international law, but the circumstances of the case suggest it is doubtful that Russia would have

---

[37] John Mueller, "War Has Almost Ceased to Exist: An Assessment," *Political Science Quarterly* 124, no. 2 (2009), 297–321.

[38] *Ibid.*, 303.   [39] *Ibid.*, 298.

[40] Ryan Goodman, "Humanitarian Intervention and Pretexts for War," *American Journal of International Law* 100 (2006), 110.

refrained from intervening if these arguments were unavailable. Likewise, the fact that humanitarian arguments featured only belatedly and secondarily in the case for war against Iraq made by the US-led coalition indicates that, while the coalition may have hoped that these arguments would make the war more acceptable to some, it would most likely have waged the war even if there was no humanitarian norm that they could appeal to. To be sure, these counterfactual assertions cannot be proven. Nevertheless, it seems difficult to argue that, in either instance, the existence of ideas of humanitarian intervention facilitated military action that would otherwise not have occurred.

What about the intervention in Libya? It seems clear that NATO would not have initiated the intervention and therefore would not have completed its campaign of regime change in the absence of humanitarian arguments that could legitimize its actions. In this instance, then, the idea of humanitarian intervention did facilitate the resort to force. I can only respond that I believe that the action in Libya actually was from beginning to end a laudable example of armed humanitarian intervention. In contrast to those who have criticized the conduct of the mission, I contend that this was not an example of abusive interventionism, since the protection of civilians actually required the overthrow of the tyrannical regime. In this instance, therefore, humanitarian ideas facilitated humanitarian actions, not abuse. Nevertheless, it is understandable that some would view this case as deeply troubling. Even if this particular instance of intervention did not amount to abuse, it has established a precedent in which a Security Council mandate for the use of force to protect civilians might be stretched and perhaps twisted to other purposes. The evidence suggests that the idea of armed humanitarian intervention has not in recent years facilitated abusive interventions that would otherwise have not occurred. It is to be hoped that the renewed caution against manipulation of Council authority witnessed in the wake of Libya will ensure that this trend continues.

Conclusion – a sorry comfort?

The reasons that I have offered for accepting the idea of armed humanitarian intervention despite its persistent abuse of course provide little comfort to those that have been or will be subject to abusive intervention. The mere fact that duplicitous humanitarian justifications can be rejected and condemned does not help those who are the victims of unjustified military action. And while my assertion that the availability of humanitarian justifications does not necessarily generate abusive interventions that would otherwise not occur appears to be supported by recent evidence, it is understandable that those non-Western political communities that have endured centuries of oppressive and humiliating interventionism, in the name of humanitarianism and civilization and at the hands of powerful Western states, will be skeptical of any suggestion that the problem of abuse is not as terrible as they think it is.

The fact that the idea of humanitarian intervention is persistently abused by powerful states pursuing ulterior objectives, and often at substantial cost to civilian lives, is of course a very real problem, and it has not been my intention to try to reason this problem away. Rather, my claim is that the idea of humanitarian intervention is not itself the problem and its persistent abuse should not lead us to abandon the idea. To clarify this claim a little, I finally turn to Immanuel Kant.

In his classic essay, *Perpetual Peace* (1795), Kant attributed the label of "sorry comforter" not only to Grotius, who had argued in favor of intervention for the defense of innocents, but also Pufendorf and Vattel, who had warned against the danger of abuse. These three theorists, he argued, are "sorry comforters" because they "are still dutifully quoted in *justification* of military aggression, although their philosophically or diplomatically formulated codes do not and cannot have the slightest *legal* force, since states as such are not subject to a common external constraint." Despite each of these thinkers offering clear principles on the use of military force, he suggested, "there is no instance of a state ever having been moved to desist from its purpose by arguments supported by the testimonies of such notable men."[41] The problem, as Kant understood it, was not the particular articulations of principles about the resort to force by any of these theorists, but the fact that these principles were unenforceable. Today, international legal principles about the conditions in which military force may be used are much more clearly established, positivized in the UN Charter and in international customary law, and institutionalized in the UN system. This has been accompanied by a corresponding decline in instances of war between states. And yet we are still confronted, at least to some degree, with the problem that Kant observed: While principles and ideas for the legitimate resort to war do matter, they sometimes fail to restrain powerful states intent on pursuing their self-interests.

The solution to this problem is not to reject the idea of armed humanitarian intervention and reassert the almost unconditional principle of non-intervention that was embraced during the Cold War. After all, as states increasingly acknowledge, the failure of the society of states to intervene when confronted with compelling cases of mass atrocities is no less pressing a problem than is abusive interventionism.[42] Rather, the solution, as Kant recognized, is to strengthen the mechanisms for the enforcement of international laws and

---

[41] Immanuel Kant, "Perpetual Peace: A Philosophical Sketch," in *Political Writings*, edited by Hans Reiss (Cambridge University Press, 1970), 103.

[42] As Hersch Lauterpacht once suggested in another context, "exaggeration and abuse ought not to determine the fate of an otherwise beneficent idea … We would rather err in pursuit of a good life for all than glory in the secure infallibility of moral indifference." Hersch Lauterpacht, "Kelsen's Pure Science of Law," in Elihu Lauterpacht (ed.), *International Law: Being the Collected Papers of Hersch Lauterpacht* (Cambridge University Press, 1975), vol. 5, part 1, 428.

norms.[43] Kant asserted that the "only one rational way" in which the restraint of war could be assured was through the formation of an "*international state*" or a "*world republic*," but he acknowledged that such a global order was "not the will of the nations." Neither is it today. In the absence of such will, Kant recommended a "general agreement between nations," a "pacific federation" of states which "may check the current of man's inclination to defy the law and antagonize his fellows, although there will always be a risk of it bursting forth anew."[44] This is arguably what we find today, that is, general agreement and a federation of states, realized through positive international law and the United Nations, that largely checks the inclination of states to wage self-interested war but which cannot prevent such war from occasionally "bursting forth anew." International agreement on the conditions for the legitimate use of force does restrain states to a large degree, but the lack of enforcement mechanisms means that they cannot be fully restrained. Abusive interventionism can be condemned, and there are socio-political costs that attend such condemnation, but where it is the powerful that conduct these interventions, as was the case in the actions in Iraq and Georgia, they can rarely be punished.

Many states and commentators suggest that an alternative solution to the problem of abuse is to develop agreement on criteria to guide the Security Council in its deliberations on how to respond to mass atrocities, so that the Council will act more consistently, impartially, and effectively. Proposed criteria commonly include suggestions that the use of force be authorized, proportionate, and undertaken only as a last resort, with reasonable prospects of success, and in response to the four crimes delineated in the 2005 Summit agreement.[45] Of course, any efforts to further clarify and strengthen the consensus on the bounds of legitimate intervention are to be welcomed. However, it is not at all clear that agreement on criteria is the cure-all that observers are hoping for. The Summit agreement already spells out fairly clearly the scope of legitimate action to protect civilians, and Council deliberations on the use of force already proceed along the lines suggested by proponents of criteria. Further agreement on criteria will not guarantee agreement on the nature of a crisis or the appropriate response in any particular instance. Even well established criteria can be subject to misappropriation and used as a pretext to intervention by self-interested actors.[46]

---

[43] That is not to say that Kant himself was necessarily in favor of a right of armed humanitarian intervention. For some discussion, see Antonio Franceschet, "Kant, International Law, and the Problem of Humanitarian Intervention," *Journal of International Political Theory* 6, no. 1 (2010), 1–22.

[44] Kant, "Perpetual Peace," 104–5.

[45] A recent example can be found in the Brazilian proposal, "Responsibility while Protecting," UN Document, A/66/551-S/2011/701 (November 11, 2011).

[46] For discussion, see Alex J. Bellamy, "The Responsibility to Protect and the Problem of Military Intervention," *International Affairs* 84, no. 4 (2008), 625–30.

In the absence of a "world republic" or something like it that has the ability to enforce principles on the resort to force, the problem of abusive interventionism will never be completely resolved. This is obviously far from ideal. However, I do not think that the idea of armed humanitarian intervention is to blame. Ideas matter. But we cannot blame ideas for everything. There surely comes a point (once we have reached substantial agreement on and sufficiently clarified the bounds of ideas) where we must lay the blame, not upon the ideas, but upon the pirates, the thieves, and the states that abuse them.

10

The responsibility to protect and the problem of regime change

ALEX J. BELLAMY

The use of attack helicopters by the UN mission in Côte d'Ivoire (UNOCI) to oust Laurent Gbagbo from power in April 2011 and NATO's decision to interpret Security Council Resolution 1973, passed a few weeks earlier, in such a way as to permit the use of airpower and other forms of assistance to aid the National Transitional Council of Libya in overthrowing the Gaddafi regime provoked a strong and negative response from some quarters in international society. Several states argued that, as a matter of principle, the protection of populations from genocide, war crimes, ethnic cleansing, and crimes against humanity (hereafter "genocide and mass atrocities") should never entail "regime change." Three members of the emerging "BRICS" (Brazil, Russia, India, China, South Africa) group – all of whom had moved over the past few years toward an accommodation with RtoP – spoke out strongly against the actions in Côte d'Ivoire and Libya. China, a permanent member of the UN Security Council, argued: "There must be no attempt at regime change or involvement in civil war by any party under the guise of protecting civilians."[1] Brazil concurred:

> The protection of civilians is a humanitarian imperative. It is a distinct concept that must not be confused or conflated with threats to international peace and security, as described in the Charter, or with the responsibility to protect. We must avoid excessively broad interpretations of the protection of civilians, which could … create the perception that it is being used as a smokescreen for intervention or regime change.[2]

And South Africa noted that: "international actors and external organizations … should nonetheless comply with the provisions of the United Nations Charter, fully respect the will, sovereignty and territorial integrity of the country concerned, and refrain from the advancing political agendas that go beyond the protection of civilian mandates, including regime change."[3] The expression of these sentiments led some analysts to argue that the UN Security Council's failure to reach consensus on a timely and decisive response to the crisis in Syria

---

[1] These quotations are from UN document S/PV.6531 (May 10, 2011).
[2] *Ibid.*   [3] *Ibid.*

was caused, to some extent, by the global discord generated by intervention in Libya.[4]

The insistence that the protection of populations from genocide and mass atrocities must never entail regime change poses the thorny question of what international society should do when states massacre large sections of their own population. How, except by regime change, might Cambodia have been saved from the Khmer Rouge? Uganda from Idi Amin? Or the Tutsis from the government-backed *Interehamwe* genocidaires? This chapter examines the relationship between RtoP and regime change. It argues that although regime change should never be allowed as the legitimating primary goal of armed humanitarian intervention, regime change is sometimes necessary as a means for the protection of populations terrorized by their own government. That is, regime change is sometimes necessary to bring about the protection of a population. Obviously, the relation the other way around, with protection activities used as a means to bring about regime change, is hardly plausible.[5] Much hinges, I argue, on this causal chain. As such, the chapter proposes five tests that may help guard against the abuse of protection arguments for self-interested purposes while permitting regime change for protection purposes in rare and exceptional cases.

First, though, we need to define what is meant by "regime change" and clarify its normative content, as this is a politically charged and highly contested term. As used here, "regime change" refers to the changing of a government by unconstitutional means. This may involve complete change – as when the government of a whole country is changed (e.g., Libya 2011) – or partial change – as when a government remains in office but loses authority over a particular region, which may or may not subsequently achieve formal independence (e.g., Indonesia/East Timor, 1999–2000). As such, it is important to resist a priori assumptions about the normative quality of particular regime changes. Some, such as the sometimes violent changing of colonial regimes and the ending of regimes founded on racial discrimination, have been welcomed and legitimized by international society; others, such as the ousting of the genocidal Khmer Rouge regime, exposed gaps between legality, legitimacy, and morality; and a third category of regime changes, including the unconstitutional removal of the Arbenz and Allende governments in Guatemala and Chile respectively, were widely condemned and failed most tests of legitimacy. Given this history, unless one adopts a rigid absolutist morality, which holds that governments are entitled to do whatever they like to their own population, we cannot plausibly condemn regime change a priori. Instead, judgments about the normative quality of changes to regimes must be based on the circumstances at hand.

---

[4] For example, see Jess Gifkins, "Syria and the Responsibility to Protect," *Global Responsibility to Protect* 4, no. 4 (2012).
[5] Thanks to Don Scheid for suggesting this way of formulating the argument.

It is important to clarify two other definitional points. The term "regime change" does not identify the agents or processes of change. Agents of change may be foreign states, domestic armed groups, popular uprisings, elements within a governing elite, or some combination of these. As I will show in the following section, regime change as a response to government-perpetrated genocide and mass atrocities is caused most often by domestic actors. Foreign-induced regime change in such circumstances is relatively rare. In relation to the process of regime change, armed conflict – predominantly civil war – is often a key driver. Other "change" processes include negotiated settlements (which may involve the exiling of members of the ruling elite), the ousting of a leader by civilian members of the ruling elite, military coups, the natural death of the leader, and popular uprisings/protests.

The chapter proceeds in three parts. First, I clarify the empirical dimensions of the debate. Second, I examine in more detail the grounds for insisting that RtoP must never entail regime change and argue that, while these are compelling reasons for wariness about the use of force for protection purposes found in accounts of sovereignty that rest on self-determination, they do not constitute a convincing case against regime change in all circumstances. Third, I propose a series of checks designed to ensure that regime change may be used in extreme situations as a pathway to protection while guarding against the abuse of protection as a pathway to regime change.

Historical contours

The question of the relationship between RtoP and regime change is, in part, an empirical one. Debates are infused with assumptions about the possibility or impossibility of achieving RtoP's goals of protecting populations from genocide and mass atrocities with or without regime change and a deeply held belief in some quarters that RtoP has been used to legitimize military interventions motivated by selfish political considerations. Because these empirical assumptions are often used to validate moral arguments, this section offers a brief examination of the data. Looking at the period 1945–2011, it considers how episodes of genocide and mass killing perpetrated by states against sections of their own populations have ended.

I compiled a dataset of cases in which states committed genocide and mass atrocities (defined as episodes where states intentionally killed *at least* 5,000 non-combatants) against sections of their own populations and tracked how those episodes ended. The results offer little comfort to those who eschew the possibility of regime change in such cases in part because they believe in the possibility of protecting populations by other means (see Figure 10.1).

Of the 60 identified cases that started and ended between 1945 and 2011, a little over half (31 cases) had ended only when the perpetrators themselves decided to terminate or reduce the killing, usually because they had

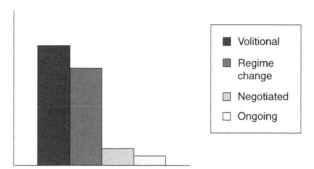

Figure 10.1 State-based mass atrocity endings (1945–2011)

accomplished their goals or revised them in such a way as to make genocide and mass atrocities unnecessary. External pressure played a role in influencing local elites in a small number of these cases, most notably US diplomatic pressure on the Pinochet regime in Chile and the imposition of a no-fly zone over southern Iraq. But in all of these cases, the decision to terminate mass atrocities was essentially voluntary – there were no physical restraints placed on the perpetrators' capacity to continue killing. By comparison, there were only four cases in which states were persuaded to cease killing by international diplomacy or other means short of regime change – Angola, Guatemala, the Philippines, and Indonesia (East Timor). In each of these cases, states negotiated agreements in contexts where atrocities had been committed in the course of protracted civil wars and only after local armed resistance had prevented them accomplishing their goals by violent means. The ending of atrocities in the remaining 25 cases involved some degree of regime change. Of these 25, a little over two-thirds (17 cases) involved complete regime change, while the remainder (8 cases) involved partial regime change.

It would seem, therefore, that historically speaking, responding in a "timely and decisive" fashion, as required by the RtoP principle to bring an end to genocide or mass atrocities perpetrated by a state against sections of its own population, has tended to involve some degree of regime change. Since 1945, the principal alternative to regime change has been that the perpetrators have been allowed to determine for themselves when to stop the killing. Negotiated settlements are possible, but they are rare (accounting for only 6 percent of the whole) and seem to require that victim groups have the capacity to mount armed opposition sufficiently strong to prevent the perpetrators from accomplishing their goals.

We should avoid the temptation, however, of regarding regime change as synonymous with external armed intervention. The dataset presented here identified five modes of regime change, only one of which is foreign armed

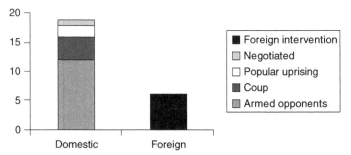

Figure 10.2 Source of regime change endings (1945–2011)

intervention. The others are domestic armed opposition, coups, popular upris-
ings/revolutions, and negotiated regime changes (Figure 10.2).

A little over three-quarters of all the mass-atrocity endings produced by
regime change were achieved by principally domestic opponents through one
of these four mechanisms. Less than a quarter ended with regime change forced
by external intervention. Thus, while regime change of one form or another is
a critical mechanism for ending mass atrocities perpetrated by states against
their own populations, it is three times more likely to be produced by domestic
forces than international ones.[6]

This section suggests that in the vast majority of cases, episodes in which a
state perpetrates genocide and mass atrocities against sections of its own population tend to end either because the perpetrators themselves decide to stop the
killing – usually because they are satisfied that they have accomplished their
goals – or because the government is removed from power – usually by domestic opponents.

There is little reason to think that a determined state perpetrator can be persuaded to change course by diplomacy or other non-forcible measures. Mass
atrocities are not normally a state's first course of action. More often than not,
governments choose not to resort to deliberately killing civilians, even when
they stand to gain and have the means to do so.[7] Massacring civilians is usually entered into reluctantly and only after alternative strategies have been

---

[6] For similar results, using different data, see Alex de Waal and Bridget Conley-Zilkic,
"Reflections on How Genocidal Violence is Brought to an End," *Report for the Social Sciences
Research Council* (December 22, 2006), available at: http://howgenocidesend.ssrc.org/de_
Waal (accessed August 9, 2012).

[7] The tendency to use atrocities as a last resort is widely recognized in the literature. See
Alexander Downes, *Targeting Civilians in War* (Ithaca, New York: Cornell University Press,
2008); Benjamin Valentino, *Final Solutions: Mass Killing and Genocide in the Twentieth
Century* (Ithaca, New York: Cornell University Press, 2004); Daniel Chirot and Clark
McCauley, *Why Not Kill Them All? The Logic and Prevention of Political Mass Murder*
(Princeton University Press, 2006).

contemplated and found wanting. Massacres are inhibited by a combination of fears about the potential for retribution against one's own population, an interest in maintaining rules governing conflict in order to limit damage to the underlying social order, the potential for third-party intervention or punishment, and ideologies or moral codes that prohibit such killing.[8] As a result, governments perpetrate mass atrocities usually only when they believe the stakes to be very high and in the perceived absence of alternative remedies. In such situations, they often anticipate that their actions will draw international opprobrium and attract other costs but calculate that these are worth paying to achieve their goal. International responses that fall short of physical coercion are unlikely to have much effect on this calculus in the short term, though dramatic forms of economic coercion may, and regular sanctions may, have some longer-term impacts.

The dilemma of protecting populations from their own murderous governments without promoting regime change cannot, therefore, be avoided by wishing up alternative, non-forcible responses likely to persuade determined perpetrators to stand down their arms. When prevention fails, the historical record seems to suggest that international society has limited options and that either victory for the perpetrators or some form of regime change – usually at the hands of armed local resistance – is often unavoidable.

Despite this history, as I noted in the introduction, since the NATO-led intervention in Libya, a significant number of states have begun to argue that the protection of populations from genocide and mass atrocities must *never* entail regime change. The next section considers their foundations in more detail.

Sovereignty, self-determination, and human rights

The chief principled objection to regime change as an action aimed at protecting populations from genocide and mass atrocities is that it is a violation of state sovereignty. There are at least two critical dimensions here. The first is the value of sovereignty as a principle of international order. This objection is based on a logic that is now well-known: In a world characterized by a plurality of radically different communities, international society is made possible by rules that permit communities to pursue their own conceptions of the good without infringing on others' right to do likewise.[9] Sitting at the heart of this system of rules of co-existence are the principle of sovereign equality, the prohibition on the use of force in international affairs (Article 2(4) of the UN Charter), and the principle of non-interference in the domestic affairs of states (Article 2(7)

---

[8] Fears of intervention and retribution are identified by Downes, *Targeting Civilians*; and by Valentino, *Final Solutions*.

[9] Andrew Linklater, *The Transformation of Political Community* (Cambridge: Polity, 1998), 59.

of the UN Charter). The interests of international peace and the potential for international cooperation are best served by maintaining these rules; their erosion would increase international insecurity and hinder cooperation.

This line of thinking is a well-known part of the debate about armed humanitarian intervention that preceded RtoP. It is consistent with:

(1) A pluralist conception of world politics as a society of independent units (states) bound together by constitutive and regulatory rules which guide their mutual relations but do not place demands on their internal characteristics;

(2) a rule-utilitarian view which holds that the greatest good is served by the preservation of international order;[10]

(3) legal-positivist arguments about the necessity of protecting sovereign equality, without which powerful states would receive "an almost unlimited right to overthrow [other] governments";[11] and

(4) basic communitarian assumptions about the irreconcilable diversity of the values and goals of different communities.

However, this argument speaks more to general problems of armed humanitarian intervention than to the relationship between RtoP and regime change per se. As agreed by Heads of State and Government in the Outcome Document of the 2005 UN Summit, RtoP requires that the use of force or other forms of coercion to protect populations from genocide and mass atrocities be authorized by the UN Security Council.[12] It is partly for this reason that the UN Secretary-General, Ban Ki-moon, repeatedly argued that the principle does not alter, or seek to alter, existing international law but that it is embedded within the law. Thus, any use of force conducted under the auspices of RtoP would need to be consistent with existing legal rules. To that end, it should be recalled that the UN Security Council expressly authorized the use of force in both Côte d'Ivoire and Libya. Thus, this first line of critique is not compelling because RtoP does not purport to change the rules of co-existence found in the UN Charter. Instead, RtoP pursues its goals by working within this normative framework. That explains why Heads of State and Government were prepared to endorse the principle, but also why it remains hostage to the vicissitudes of world politics.

The challenge posed by Côte d'Ivoire and Libya was not constitutional in nature. Critique of regime change in both cases related not to the interveners' authority to act, but to the widely held perception that they exceeded their

---

[10] Louis Henkin, *How Nations Behave: Law and Foreign Policy*, 2nd edn. (New York: Columbia University Press, 1979), 145.

[11] Oscar Schachter, "The Legality of Pro-Democratic Invasion," *American Journal of International Law* 78 (1984), 649.

[12] *2005 World Summit Outcome Document* (UN General Assembly), A/60/1 (para. 139).

mandate: that the interveners turned a mandate to use force to protect civilians from mass atrocities into a license to change a regime. This brings us to the problem of abuse. The poster-child for this issue is the historical fact that Adolf Hitler insisted that the 1939 invasion of Czechoslovakia was inspired by a desire to protect Czechoslovak citizens whose "life and liberty" were threatened by their own government.[13] Traditionally, the general ban on the use of force found in the UN Charter has been held up as the primary barrier against such abuse.[14] However, critics maintain that RtoP allows interveners to pursue self-interested regime-change agendas while outwardly complying with the rules. As one of RtoP's key champions, Gareth Evans, put it when reflecting on the aftermath of Libya: The BRICS are concerned that if they "give an inch" on the adoption of enforcement measures for protection purposes, the West and the UN itself might "take a mile."[15] The response to this problem has been to insist, a priori, that action in the name of RtoP absolutely never result in regime change.

The historical record does not match the fear of abuse. As I observed earlier, foreign armed intervention in response to genocide and mass atrocities remains extremely rare. Armed intervention authorized by the Security Council for human protection is still more rare – the 2011 intervention in Libya being the first of its kind. Nor have there been many obvious cases of "abuse" since 1945. The most commonly discussed cases are the 1983 US intervention in Grenada, the 1994 French intervention in Rwanda, and the 2003 US-led invasion of Iraq. But the intervention in Grenada was justified more in terms of defending democracy than humanitarian considerations; although the French intervention in Rwanda was not primarily motivated by humanitarian concerns, the intervention did have a positive humanitarian effect in the short term; and the US-led intervention in Iraq was primarily justified by reference to the problem of weapons of mass destruction (indeed, this was the whole basis of the war's legal justification).[16] The problem, then, would seem to boil down to the political question of ensuring that those who act on the authorization of Security Council mandates remain accountable to the Council itself.

---

[13] Ian Brownlie, *International Law and the Use of Force by States* (Oxford: Clarendon Press, 1974), 217–21.

[14] Simon Chesterman, *Just War or Just Peace? Humanitarian Intervention and International Law* (Oxford University Press, 2001), 231.

[15] Gareth Evans, "Responding to Mass Atrocity Crimes: The Responsibility to Protect After Libya," Lecture to the Royal Institute of International Affairs, London (October 6, 2011).

[16] On Grenada, see Karin von Hippel, *Democracy by Force: US Military Intervention in the Post-Cold War World* (Cambridge University Press, 2000), 27–53; on Rwanda, see Nicholas J. Wheeler, *Saving Strangers: Humanitarian Intervention in International Society* (Oxford University Press, 2000); and on Iraq, see Alex J. Bellamy, "International Law and the War with Iraq," *Melbourne Journal of International Law* 4, no. 2 (2003).

The seemingly deeper objection to regime change derives from the principle of self-determination. A long strain of political and moral philosophy and action holds that political communities enjoy a "common life" and should be free to determine their own system of governance. This right is grounded in each individual's basic human right to select his or her own mode of living.[17] This account holds that there is a "fit" between the nation and the state, and that it should be assumed that the latter enable the former to develop and protect its own values and ideas about how its members ought to live.[18] According to Michael Walzer:

> justice is relative to social meanings: there are an infinite number of possible lives, shaped by an infinite number of possible cultures, religions, political arrangements, geographic conditions and so on. A given society is just if its substantive life is lived in a certain way – that is, in a way faithful to the shared understandings of its members.[19]

Sovereignty protects this right to self-determination because it entails a presumption against external interference in people's domestic affairs. At its heart, it holds that people might choose to live and be governed in many different ways and that outsiders have no right to impose their particular way of life on others. Ultimately, it is for peoples themselves to select their form of government by whatever means, including violence.

This view has several prominent adherents. Immanuel Kant argued that states ought to scrupulously obey sovereignty's rule of non-interference in each other's domestic affairs. One of the core principles of his *Perpetual Peace* was that "no state shall violently interfere with the constitution and administration of another." This, he argued, was a basic principle of international order derived from the individual duty to respect one another's autonomy. Another liberal thinker, John Stuart Mill, insisted along similar lines that foreign governments should play no part in the overthrowing of tyrannical regimes, as this should be the responsibility of peoples themselves.[20] Where there is insufficient domestic support for the overthrow of a tyrannical regime, foreign intervention is unlikely to succeed and has the effect only of imposing an alien form of government.

The argument that this national right to self-determination translates to states and creates a powerful moral basis for the rule of non-interference has been widely voiced in international society since 1945. It was aired by

---

[17] Michael Walzer, *Just and Unjust Wars* (New York: Basic Books, 1977), 57.

[18] *Ibid.*, 87. Also see Michael Walzer, *Thick and Thin: Moral Argument at Home and Abroad* (New Haven: Yale University Press, 1994).

[19] Michael Walzer, *Spheres of Justice: A Defence of Pluralism and Equality* (Oxford: Basil Blackwood, 1983), 312–13.

[20] John Stuart Mill, "A Few Words on Non-Intervention" [*Fraser's Magazine*, December 1859], in *Essays on Politics and Culture by John Stuart Mill*, edited by Gertrude Himmelfarb (Garden City, New York: Doubleday Anchor Books, 1963).

several "small" or "new" states during negotiations about the UN Charter.[21] Chief among the concerns of Latin American states was that the new world organization should contain rules protecting the sovereign right of a state to determine its own form of government. In 1960, the General Assembly issued its Declaration on the Granting of Independence to Colonial Countries and Peoples which proclaimed that: "all peoples have the right to self-determination; by virtue of that right they freely determine their political status and freely pursue their economic, social and cultural development." The United Nations' subsequent resolutions on self-determination all used this wording and in 1975 the International Court of Justice (ICJ) recognized the statement as the "basis for the process of decolonization."[22] The insistence that all peoples have a right to self-determination including a right to "freely determine their political status" was also incorporated into the General Assembly's International Covenants on Human Rights in 1966.

For many post-colonial leaders and theorists, there was a direct relationship between a people's right to freely determine its political status and the non-interference rule. After all, there could be no effective right of self-determination if powerful states felt entitled to interfere in the affairs of the weak. As such, the General Assembly's 1970 Declaration on Principles of International Law Concerning Friendly Relations stated categorically that: "No state or group of states has the right to intervene, directly or indirectly, for any reason whatever, in the internal or external affairs of any other state."

In this account of sovereignty, there is an implicit direct link between an individual's human right to determine his or her own way of life and form of government free of foreign and colonial interference and the rule of non-interference. Simply put, peoples have a right to determine their own destiny. Opening the door to foreign interference in the name of humanitarian principles would only pave the way to colonial or hegemonic domination. This colonizing logic was perhaps best exemplified in the work of the Neo-Scholastic friar, Francesco de Vitoria. Writing in the sixteenth century, Vitoria had argued against the colonial acquisition of lands in the Americas on the grounds that native peoples had legitimate political institutions which exerted legitimate authority over their lands. However, he also accepted that the Spanish had a right to travel and trade in the New World and could use force to protect their rights and, more importantly, had a right to use force to overthrow despotic (cannibalistic) kings. It was this latter right – armed humanitarian intervention of sorts – that was seized upon as justification for the colonization of the Americas and destruction of native peoples.[23]

[21] Chesterman, *Just War or Just Peace?*, 49.
[22] Malcolm N. Shaw, *International Law*, 5th edn. (Cambridge University Press, 2003), 227.
[23] See Antony Anghie, *Imperialism, Sovereignty and the Making of International Law* (Cambridge University Press, 2005).

Commitment to this view of sovereignty as resting on the principle of self-determination remains widespread and steadfast in contemporary international society. This thinking clearly underpinned the global movement against colonialism and helped animate the often bitter and violent struggles waged to end foreign domination. As I mentioned earlier, it is a position endorsed by a majority of states in the General Assembly (especially a majority of members in the G-77 and Non-Aligned Movement), by many international lawyers, and by a large academic literature.

This conception of sovereignty, as derived from self-determination predicated on human rights, should not be confused with the "absolutist" view that sovereigns are entitled to act however they please, a view championed by nineteenth-century German scholars such as Hegel, Fichte, Ihering, Treitschke, and Heller and closely associated with nationalism. For the German absolutists, sovereignty implied not just the absence of a superior authority, but also *plenitudo potestatis* – competence to the full reach of its material power. Ihering maintained that sovereigns were limited only by their own will, while Treitschke argued that it was legitimate for a state to do anything at all to satisfy its interests and that these interests took priority over contractual obligations.[24] As a nineteenth-century French jurist, Fauchille, put it, "to say a person is sovereign, not merely means to say that it does not recognize any authority above its own, but that it may issue orders at its own discretion, that it may do freely and without limitation all that it considers fit to do."[25] The two sets of ideas (sovereignty as self-determination and absolutism) part company because the former welcomes the view that states are obliged to conduct their international relations with due respect for international legal rules (chiefly the rule of non-interference) and cannot dismiss human-rights concerns per se because it is itself predicated on a human-rights claim – the right to autonomy and self-determination.

The self-determinationist account can provide grounds for some limited support for foreign interference when regimes obviously deny self-determination to their peoples. It is perhaps not surprising, therefore, that it was at the behest of the UN General Assembly that the Security Council imposed a raft of mandatory enforcement measures on the governments of South Rhodesia and South Africa, including authorizing the use of force by the United Kingdom against the former. In both cases, the existence of racist-minority governments exposed an obvious disconnect between the regime and the people. For similar reasons, it is sometimes suggested that advocates of the self-determinationist position would not oppose armed intervention in situations where a government committed genocide and mass atrocities against sections of its own

---

[24] Heinrich von Treitschke, *Politik* (Leipzig: Insel, 1899), vol. II, 100.
[25] Paul Fauchille, *Traité de Droit International Public* (Paris: Librairie Arthur Rousseau, 1921), 428.

population. Certainly, advocates of this position tend to not dispute the legal and moral right of the Security Council to authorize collective intervention in such situations.

That might explain why states such as South Africa, Nigeria, and Togo supported Resolution 1973 that authorized the use of force in Libya, while India, China, and Russia decided to not block the resolution, in a context where mass atrocities were imminently threatened and in which the regime in question had clearly lost the support of a large section of the people (including its own Permanent Representative to the United Nations, who defected early on). However, there were a series of exceptional circumstances in the Libya case that made Resolution 1973 possible. Typically, while they may admit a theoretical right to militarily intervene against murderous states, political leaders have tended to be wary of supporting the use of force in particular cases, especially in the absence of other extenuating considerations. As a result, the 2011 intervention in Libya remains the only instance of armed intervention against a state guilty of committing genocide and other mass atrocities against its own population to be authorized by the UN Security Council.

The view that sovereignty rests on the principle of self-determination, itself widely considered an inviolable human right, lies at the core of international concern about the potential relationship between RtoP and regime change. The fear is that once ground is given to enable the legitimate removal of regimes in the name of human protection, the hard-won independence of peoples in the post-colonial world and their culturally specific ways of life will become conditional upon the judgments of a small number of powerful states. The historical record suggests that although in *theory* they might accept foreign military intervention in cases where states abuse their own populations on a massive scale, on the grounds that such states could not plausibly claim to be representative of the popular will, in *practice* adherents to the self-determinationist account of sovereignty are predisposed toward protecting sovereigns. In close cases, the self-determinationists are certainly inclined to give the state in question the benefit of the doubt. But the predisposition in favor of sovereignty has been shaken by the commission of genocide and mass atrocities by states against the populations they are assumed to represent.[26] Nevertheless, even as this predisposition to favor sovereignty has been shaken, there remains a wariness about the prospect of regime change and deep suspicion about the motives of those charged with executing protection mandates, often to a degree in excess of concerns about the targeted populations themselves.

This poses a particular challenge to RtoP because, as I mentioned at the outset, its rise to prominence was based on an alignment between the principle and existing international laws and norms. Partly as a result, from the very outset, the language of RtoP – and its predecessor, "sovereignty as responsibility" – has

---

[26] Thanks to Don Scheid for suggesting this formulation.

been suffused with the idea that it is an "ally to sovereignty," a means of helping
states realize their full sovereign potential through the discharge of responsibilities that are as inherent to sovereignty as the rule of non-interference.[27]

There are, of course, a number of problems with these views. Most significantly, the assumption that states facilitate the autonomy and self-determination of their populations – upon which the whole argument is predicated – is
often proved to be false. Over the course of the past two centuries, people
have been far more likely to be massacred by their own governments than by
either non-state actors or foreign governments. An additional problem, which
stems in part from this empirical observation, is that it does not at all follow that self-determination should necessarily give rise either to a determined
commitment to non-interference or wariness toward international human-
protection activism. We may, instead, go back to first principles and focus on
the autonomy of individuals as the only irreducible ontological feature. From
this stance, the right of self-determination makes sense only if one accepts the
view that individuals have rights to autonomy and participation in government. If that proposition is denied, then it becomes very difficult to mount a
moral case in defense of self-determination as a right enjoyed by nations or
states.

Once this relationship between individual and collective rights is recognized,
it is a short leap to the view that sovereignty should be understood as an instrumental value and not as an end in itself. That is because sovereignty ultimately
resides in the people who confer authority upon the state to act in their name.
As such, state sovereignty derives it moral value from the state's capacity to protect the autonomy of its citizens and facilitate their participation in government.
From here, it is an equally short leap to the view that when states fail in their
duty to protect the "basic rights" of their citizens – those thought necessary for
their autonomy and participation in government, the "right to life" being chief
among them – they lose their moral standing and forfeit sovereign rights.[28]
There are a variety of ways of arriving at this conclusion. Simon Caney draws
on Kant's concept of the rational individual to insist that all individuals have
certain pre-political rights.[29] Others use St. Augustine's insistence that force be
used to defend public order to argue that military intervention to end injustice

[27] E.g., Francis M. Deng, Sadikiel Kimaro, Terrence Lyons, Donald Rothchild, and William
Zartman, *Sovereignty as Responsibility: Conflict Management in Africa* (Washington, DC:
The Brookings Institution, 1996).
[28] Fernando Tesón, "The Liberal Case for Humanitarian Intervention," in J.L. Holzgrefe and
Robert O. Keohane (eds.), *Humanitarian Intervention: Ethical, Legal and Political Dilemmas*
(Cambridge University Press, 2003), 93. On the idea of "basic rights" see Henry Shue, *Basic
Rights: Subsistence, Affluence and US Foreign Policy*, 2nd edn. (Princeton University Press,
1996).
[29] Simon Caney, "Human Rights and the Rights of States: Terry Nardin on Non-Intervention,"
International Political Science Review 18, no. 1 (1997), 34.

was "among the rights and duties of states until and unless supplanted by superior government."[30] Alternatively, historical accounts show that in both theory and practice, sovereign rights have always been associated with responsibilities of one form or another.[31] Whichever path one takes, the basic proposition is that state sovereignty is rooted in the popular sovereignty of the people, which is in turn grounded in individual human rights. Sovereignty is conferred upon the state by the people and can be revoked by the people when the sovereign fails to protect their core rights. The point was perhaps made most eloquently by Thomas Jefferson in America's Declaration of Independence (1776).

Although this thinking lends itself more obviously to support for domestic rebellion against despotic regimes than to foreign humanitarian intervention, it shows that commitment to the principle of self-determination can just as easily provide moral support for regime change as it can for non-interference. These theoretical points notwithstanding, however, it is the vision of self-determination as being tightly wedded to non-interference that tends to prevail in world politics. The challenge for the next, and final, section is to examine whether there is room for accommodation between these two accounts of self-determination and, through that, between RtoP and the antipathy of a large part of international society towards regime change.

Toward responsible protection

This section presents a way of thinking about the relationship between RtoP and regime change that accommodates the two key points raised in the previous sections: first, that the most common way of stopping governments that choose to massacre sections of their own population before their objectives are met is through regime change and, second, that a large section of international society is concerned that the forcible changing of regimes could undermine the principle of self-determination and rules of international co-existence.

A useful place to start is with the common ground identified thus far. The most significant is the shared belief that – whether for the purposes of maintaining order or protecting people – international society is entitled to take collective action, including the use of force, to promote common goals and that the UN Security Council is empowered with the authority to mandate such action. What concerned critics about the NATO-led intervention in Libya was not the question of whether the alliance had authority to act or whether the Security Council was entitled to issue such a mandate, but whether NATO was authorized to remove the regime. The various moral approaches to the

---

[30] Paul Ramsey, *The Just War: Force and Political Responsibility* (Lanham: Rowman & Littlefield, 2002), 20, 35–36.

[31] Luke Glanville, "The Antecedents of 'Sovereignty as Responsibility'," *European Journal of International Relations* 17, no. 2 (2011), 233–55.

question of sovereignty and self-determination surveyed in the previous section seem to accept the view that, in theory at least if not always in practice,
there are situations in which collective action, including the use of force, could
be legitimate to achieve common purposes. Where the approaches differed was
in their presumptions in relation to regime change, whether in favor of the
sovereign state or the sovereignty of the people, and their degree of wariness
about the motives and intentions of foreign interveners. What is clear, however,
is that there is little basis in the arguments reviewed thus far for insisting, a
priori, that regime change must never be used as a means of protecting populations. We have also, however, found little reason to support the argument at the
other extreme – that regime change by foreign military intervention needs no
special authorization. What we are left with is the argument I broached in the
introduction – that in some circumstances regime change may be necessary for
human-protection purposes, but that human protection must never be used as
a vehicle for advancing regime change. This poses the question of how to disen-
tangle the two in practice?

An appropriate starting point is the question of international authority. I
want to argue that the UN Security Council can legitimately authorize forcible
regime change, or measures that effect regime change. The self-determinationist position, which is related to communitarianism, holds that conceptions
of the good are constituted within political communities, but also that political communities may agree upon rules of co-existence to govern relations
between them. The cornerstone of these rules in contemporary international
society is the UN Charter, which confers upon the Security Council primary
responsibility for international peace and security and authority to employ any
means it deems to be necessary for this purpose. The Charter's drafters intentionally left it for the Council alone to determine what constituted a threat to
international peace and security and placed no restrictions on the measures
it might call upon in the service of peace.[32] The Council's authority therefore
derives from the voluntary granting of authority by member states themselves.
Two of the UN Charter's less quoted articles make precisely this point. Article
24(1) stresses the conferral of authority from states to the Security Council: "In
order to ensure prompt and effective action by the United Nations, its Members
confer on the Security Council primary responsibility for the maintenance of
international peace and security, and agree that in carrying out its duties under
this responsibility the Security Council acts on their behalf." In Article 25,
states bind themselves to the Council's decisions through their unconditional
commitment to "accept and carry out the decisions of the Security Council in
accordance with the present Charter." Through accession to the Charter, therefore, member states confer authority on the Security Council and recognize

---

[32] On this, see the excellent discussion in Edward C. Luck, *UN Security Council: Practice and
Promise* (London: Routledge, 2006), 9–15.

that it acts in the common good. As such, when the Council authorizes the use of force and/or regime change for protection purposes, it does so on the basis of the authority conferred upon it by states and acts to protect the common good and in support of commonly held values. Irrespective of which account of sovereignty is held, therefore, there is little disputing the notion that the Security Council is entitled by the authority vested in it by sovereign states to employ whatever measure it deems necessary, including regime change, in the interests of international peace and security. This rules out the case for the a priori banning of regime change for human-protection purposes, as well as the notion that states enjoy a right unilaterally to change unfriendly regimes.

This brings us to the more difficult argument about the presumption in favor of the state. I noted earlier that while self-determinationists might agree in theory to the possibility of UN-authorized regime change in situations where the state commits genocide or mass atrocities against sections of its population, they have been reluctant to do so in practice. Especially egregious in this regard was international society's near unanimity of condemnation of Vietnam for its ousting of the genocidal Pol Pot regime in Cambodia, whose short reign of terror accounted for a quarter of that country's population in a three-and-a-half-year period.[33]

I suggested earlier that the presumption in favor of the state is prefaced on a deeply held – if not always well-founded – suspicion about the motives or intentions of would-be interveners. That is, international society is often prepared to grant state perpetrators the benefit of the doubt because many of its members fear that some powerful states would exploit any relaxation of the principle of non-interference for their own self-interested purposes, resulting in the weakening of rules considered essential to sovereign equality.

This takes us back to a long-standing debate about the importance of humanitarian motives in shaping the legitimacy of armed intervention.[34] By focusing on motives, this created an impossibly high barrier to intervention because, in practice, states always act out of mixed motives, especially in decisions about whether to go to war. Only the imprudent statesperson would commit forces to "wars of choice" for a singular reason and without compelling national interests. As a result, scholars who focused on motives found that there had been no genuinely humanitarian interventions, as all had some degree of self-interest. This type of analysis supports the skeptics' view that states use humanitarian justifications to excuse the self-interested use of force. The problem with this line of argument, however, is that it misconstrues the Christian just-war tradition's attention to the moral significance of *intentions* as synonymous with the

[33] Wheeler, *Saving Strangers*, 90–91; Chesterman, *Just War or Just Peace?*, 80.

[34] Wil Verwey, "Humanitarian Intervention in the 1990s and Beyond: An International Law Perspective," in J.N. Pierterse (ed.), *World Orders in the Making: Humanitarian Intervention and Beyond* (London: Macmillan, 1998).

more modern attraction to *motives*. There are, though, important differences between motives and intentions.

Motives are the reasons why an actor chooses to behave the way she does, and intentions relate to what she intends to achieve. Motives are talked about in the plural because they are seldom, if ever, singular. For just-war thinking and many derivative ethics of war, therefore, it is the actor's *intentions* that are of critical importance. According to just-war thinking, individuals must wage war for the common good, not for self-aggrandizement or out of hatred for the enemy. This principle, often ignored or downplayed in more recent accounts of the ethics of war, is absolutely critical to the just-war tradition's basic defense of killing in war. As is well known, the tradition starts from the proposition that killing in itself is wrong but sometimes necessary for the preservation of order or to right a greater wrong. When soldiers fight, they must do so with the intention of serving the common good.

How might we judge whether those proposing to use force for the purpose of protecting populations from genocide and mass atrocities are acting in good faith and with humanitarian intent? Understanding another's intent is a notoriously difficult business, but somewhat less difficult than understanding his motives, because there is a stronger connection between inward intentions and outward actions. Here, I propose five checks. Whenever all five are satisfied, I think it would be very difficult indeed to believe that an intervention was about anything other than saving populations from genocide and mass atrocities. As such, the checks provide a way of guarding against abuse and the weakening of self-determination and non-interference principles while allowing international society the flexibility it sometimes needs to stop the perpetrators of genocide and mass atrocities in their tracks.

First, any armed intervention must have a mandate from the Security Council. As well as being necessary from the point of view of international authority (see above), the insistence on a Security Council mandate adds additional political checks. Although the Council is an imperfect institution, especially from the perspective of dialogic ethics, it nonetheless imposes a strong and useful procedural check by demanding that it is not sufficient for a state simply to convince itself, or its like-minded friends, of the justice of its cause when intervening. Insisting on Security Council approval demands that would-be interveners persuade their peers – including the permanent five members – to accept the case for action.

Second, states that champion armed intervention should demonstrate their humanitarian intent by acknowledging – through their words and deeds – a duty to prevent genocide and mass atrocities and respond in the most effective ways possible. This requirement is potentially controversial, as states typically are not well disposed to accepting that they owe positive duties toward strangers. When it comes to the question of acting to protect foreigners from harm, states – and many political theorists – tend to be more comfortable with the language of negative rights than positive duties. However, when international society recognizes – as it has – "failures" in relation to genocides in Rwanda and Srebrenica, it acknowledges that inaction was wrong and thereby implies a duty to act in such cases. Properly understood, rights always entail corresponding duties. Rights without duties are hollow, and since it is broadly understood that there is at least a thin layer of universal rights (including, presumably, the right to not be massacred), it follows that there must be some universal duties. Because it would be unrealistic to expect every individual to take action to realize the fundamental rights of every other individual, duties are mediated by political institutions.[35] This is not to say that there is a duty to intervene militarily whenever genocide and mass atrocities are perpetrated, but that actors should do whatever they can at a reasonable cost and without inflaming the situation further to protect endangered populations. Recognizing a right but not a duty to protect opens the door to the abuse that is so feared by those who cling to the presumption in favor of the state, because it allows states to act on their own self-interest without burdening themselves with duties. States that accept a duty to protect will not only advocate intervention when it suits other interests, they will also dedicate resources to preventing mass-atrocity crimes in the first place and to protecting civilians even when it is not politically convenient for them to do so.

The third test relates to the use of humanitarian justifications and their relationship to the known facts of the case. The simplest test of a state's intention is to compare what they say they are doing with what is known about the case. Do actors justify their behavior in humanitarian terms, and is there a pressing humanitarian situation to respond to? For example, most proponents of RtoP, this author included, quickly dismissed attempts to argue that the US invasion of Iraq in 2003 was a legitimate humanitarian intervention. We did so on two grounds. First, the United States did not primarily justify its actions in these terms, nor did its pre-2003 policy of maintaining harsh general sanctions on Iraq evince much concern for the civilian population in that country. Second, at the time of the intervention, there was no immediate humanitarian crisis caused by genocide and mass atrocities precipitated by the Iraqi government. Most governments and analysts applied similar logic to Russia's attempt to justify its 2008 invasion of Georgia on humanitarian grounds, finding that there was no evidence to support claims that the Georgian government was perpetrating mass atrocities.

The fourth test is the calibration of means and ends. Would-be interveners should select strategies that allow them to prevail without undermining humanitarian outcomes and violating individual human rights.[36] This requires

[35] Henry Shue, "Mediating Duties," *Ethics* 98, no. 4 (1988), 698.
[36] Tom J. Farer, "The Ethics of Intervention in Self-Determination Struggles," in Deen K. Chatterjee and Don E. Scheid (eds.), *Ethics and Foreign Intervention* (Cambridge University Press, 2003), 143.

more than simply abiding by the laws of war. First, above and beyond the requirements of law, intervening militaries should pay attention to the principle of "due care" in the selection of targets and weapons. When the purported purpose of an intervention is to save civilian lives, failure to exhibit due care casts serious doubts on the humanitarian intentions of the interveners and therefore on the legitimacy of the operation. Second, within the boundaries of what they have been mandated to do by the Security Council, interveners should choose strategies calculated to achieve the best humanitarian outcome in the shortest amount of time and with the least danger to civilians.

This requirement raises difficult questions about the relative value of force protection and civilian protection. On this question, Michael Walzer offered the compelling argument that soldiers should be prepared to accept additional risks if doing so reduced the risks faced by civilians.[37] There are, however, limits to how much additional risk can be accepted by military personnel. As a rule of thumb, we might say that soldiers should be prepared to accept additional risk so long as it does not jeopardize their chances of prevailing. After all, when states intervene to end genocide and mass atrocities, the purpose is best served by rapid victory. However, few things are likely to damage the humanitarian credentials of a military operation more than the perception that it is increasing the overall risk to civilians.

Fifth, states that intervene in the affairs of others ought to recognize a duty to help the country rebuild afterwards, with a focus on re-establishing its self-determination. This is somewhat related to the idea of *jus post bellum* – the notion that the ethics of war includes a commitment to building peace afterwards – but is particularly important in this setting as further surety of a state's intention to fulfill humanitarian goals. One concern might be that a demonstrative commitment to peacebuilding could give rise to a new form of imperialism through the imposition of certain institutions or modes of governance. With this in mind, perhaps the best broad vision of what is required ethically is Michael Barnett's notion of "republican peacebuilding" – peacebuilding focused on supporting a people's capacity to govern itself.[38] Institutional checks on this potential problem might include a requirement that peacebuilding activities be channeled through the UN's Security Council or, better still, the UN Peacebuilding Commission, which focuses on building partnerships with the state concerned.

Armed interventions aimed at halting genocide and mass atrocities that satisfy these five conditions – (1) Security Council authorization, (2) recognition of humanitarian duties, (3) an obvious connection between justifications and known facts, (4) the calibration of ends and means, and (5) evident commitment

---

[37] Walzer, *Just and Unjust Wars*, 156.
[38] Michael N. Barnett, "Building a Republican Peace: Stabilizing States After War," *International Security* 30, no. 4 (2006), 87–112.

to long-term peacebuilding – are pursued primarily with humanitarian intent. In such circumstances, the causal flow between protection and regime change flows in the right direction, such that regime change is a contribution to the pursuit of protection from genocide and mass atrocities. It would be difficult, indeed, to think of a situation in which these five tests were satisfied but where the causal chain flowed in the opposite direction (protection used as a vehicle for regime change). What is more, the tests present substantial hurdles that will be difficult to jump in practice. Not only should this provide reassurance to those still wary about the potentially negative impact of protection-induced regime change on the principle of self-determination, it will also ensure that the instances of protection-induced regime change remain, as they have to date, rare.

Conclusion

This chapter has examined the fraught relationship between RtoP and regime change and especially the argument that international military action aimed at protecting populations from genocide and mass atrocities must never entail regime change. I argued that while states were right to be wary about the capacity for humanitarian justifications to be used in support of self-interested military action, the proposed a priori prohibition was misplaced for two principal reasons. First, historical experience clearly demonstrates the necessity of regime change in ending episodes of genocide and mass atrocities perpetrated by states against sections of their own population. Second, accounts of sovereignty as being derived from self-determination that underpin the main arguments in favor of the prohibition do not lend strong support to the idea of an absolute a priori ban.

From this, I suggested that opposition to regime change as an occasional pathway to protection outcomes was primarily based on a presumption in favor of the state which admitted a theoretical right of collective action against state perpetrators of genocide and mass atrocities but which remained deeply wary about the practice of collective action. Underlying this wariness is a concern that powerful states might abuse the theoretical right by reversing the logic of the relationship between RtoP and regime change such that the former becomes a vehicle for the latter.

Recognizing those concerns, I proposed five tests that ought to be fulfilled when force is employed against a state for RtoP purposes:

(1) Security Council authorization;
(2) recognition of humanitarian duties;
(3) an obvious connection between justifications and known facts;
(4) the calibration of ends and means; and
(5) evident commitment to long-term peacebuilding.

These tests create significant obstacles for would-be interveners and significantly reduce the potential for abuse to the point where it becomes difficult
to conceive scenarios in which the conditions might be fulfilled by an abusive
intervener. Their satisfaction would provide proof that regime change induced
by external action arose from genuine humanitarian intentions and was necessary to protect populations from genocide and mass atrocities. As a result,
although externally induced regime change will remain a rare and exceptional
pathway to the protection of populations from genocide and mass atrocities, it
is a pathway that may nevertheless be occasionally considered without fear of
abuse or concern about the erosion of sovereignty and self-determination.

11

Law, ethics, and the responsibility to protect

MICHAEL W. DOYLE

The events in Libya in 2011 and Syria in 2012 have severely tested the balance between emerging global norms and the pushback they have generated, a contest between global and local, with outcomes as yet unclear.

Some established great powers, particularly Russia and China, suffered "buyer's remorse" for the global principle of "responsibility to protect" peoples from massacres, when that responsibility was seen as authorizing regime change in countries such as Libya. This remorse occurred just a few short years after they and the entire rest of the United Nations member states unanimously endorsed the principle at the World Summit in 2005 and reaffirmed it in 2009.

The international community has answered the most fundamental sovereign questions of who rules and what rules in evolving ways. In the nineteenth century, European states, the United States, and just a few other powerful states such as Japan constructed high walls about their sovereign domestic jurisdiction. No foreign interference was allowed. Governments treated their subjects poorly or well according solely to local whims, laws, or constitutions. Other political societies, in Africa, East and South Asia, or Latin America, had very low sovereign walls. The great powers ruled them as colonies or intervened at will to impose foreign rules and foreign interests, whether it was protecting foreigners, or collecting debts, or enforcing Christian morality.

Two of the great global-governance achievements of the twentieth century revolutionized those norms. The first was the principle of sovereign equality – self-determination for all peoples, East and West, North and South. The second was the articulation of human rights – rights that should be accorded to all human beings.

Much of this was moot in the Cold War, when the United States and the Soviet Union repeatedly and unilaterally intervened to protect their interests and promote their ideologies throughout the world. But in the 1990s, sparked by both the opportunities emerging for global cooperation at the end of the

I particularly want to thank Olena Jennings, Eliav Lieblich, and Stefanie Pleschinger for their assistance, Don Scheid for valuable editorial suggestions, and Yasmine Ergas, Larry Johnson, Edward Luck, Matt Waxman, Thomas Weiss, the members of the Columbia Law School international seminar, and the participants of the Justice and/or Peace Conference at the Goethe University, Frankfurt, for advice.

Cold War and the failures to protect peoples from genocide and violations of basic human rights in Rwanda and the Balkans – and specifically the failure of the United Nations to protect Kosovars from war crimes and ethnic cleansing – humanitarian activists proposed a new doctrine called "Responsibility to Protect" ("R2P" by the activists and, in self-conscious distinction, "RtoP" by the United Nations). RtoP was designed to fill a doctrinal governance gap between legal sovereignty and ethical humanity.

A global commission chaired by Gareth Evans, former Australian foreign minister, and Mohamed Sahnoun, former Algerian foreign minister, proposed that the international community widen the legitimate grounds for international protection to include protecting the most basic human rights. In 2005, the UN General Assembly narrowed those protections to genocide, war crimes, crimes against humanity (slaughter of innocents during peace), and ethnic cleansing; and at the same time, restricted the enforcement of these principles to the UN Security Council in order to preclude nineteenth-century or Cold War-style unilateral interventions. In other words, they created a new global-governance norm: both a substantive license to protect more and a procedural leash tied to Security Council approval.

Articulated as part of the Outcome Document[1] that expressed the consensus of the United Nations' 192 members at the 2005 Summit, RtoP's core commitments in two key paragraphs are worth quoting:

> **Responsibility to protect populations from genocide, war crimes, ethnic cleansing and crimes against humanity**
>
> **138**. Each individual State has the responsibility to protect its populations from genocide, war crimes, ethnic cleansing and crimes against humanity. This responsibility entails the prevention of such crimes, including their incitement, through appropriate and necessary means. We accept that responsibility and will act in accordance with it …
>
> **139**. The international community, through the United Nations, also has the responsibility to use appropriate diplomatic, humanitarian and other peaceful means, in accordance with Chapters VI and VIII of the Charter, to help to protect populations from genocide, war crimes, ethnic cleansing and crimes against humanity. In this context, we are prepared to take collective action, in a timely and decisive manner, through the Security Council, in accordance with the Charter, including Chapter VII, on a case-by-case basis and in cooperation with relevant regional organizations as appropriate, should peaceful means be inadequate and national authorities are manifestly failing to protect their populations from genocide, war crimes, ethnic cleansing and crimes against humanity.

The paragraphs appear revolutionary. They seem to (but do not) overturn established international law that has been designed to maintain national

---

[1] UN General Assembly, A60/1.

jurisdiction free from external intervention. International moral philosophy has long incorporated humanitarian intervention, for which RtoP is the current incarnation. In practice, the policy doctrine of RtoP is significant, but it is likely to remain much less than revolutionary. For, straightforward as the paragraphs appear, both their significance and the will to implement them are far from clear.

In this chapter, I propose to examine the roots of RtoP in international law and international ethics. RtoP is in tension with established Charter law on the use of force, but it may be beginning to change the law. It is, on the other hand, deeply familiar to Liberal international ethics. But, controversially, I argue that even the Realist and Marxist traditions include commitments to human respect that make humanitarian concerns far from foreign. I then explore how RtoP evolved out of the crisis in Kosovo and discuss its policy significance today in the controversial case of Libya.

My conclusion is that RtoP has contributed to the increasing pluralism, contested and contestable, of the normative architecture of world politics, and thus has produced confusion. But, this confusion may reduce as RtoP norms are accumulated in customary law and reshape the discourse of international ethics. In any case, where the alternative to pluralism is a clarity that either abandons vulnerable populations or imposes unrealistic expectations of enforced human rights, this kind of confusion is a step forward, a resource for responsible policy and the best we are likely to get if we continue to care about both vulnerable populations and national sovereignty.

International law

International law remains highly protective of the domestic jurisdiction of states. UN Charter Article 2(7) specifies that "nothing contained in the present Charter shall authorize the United Nations to intervene in matters which are essentially within the domestic jurisdiction of any state." The exception is "enforcement measures under Chapter VII," which in turn are formally limited in Article 39 to measures the Security Council finds appropriate "in order to maintain or restore international peace and security." Domestic abuses generally do not – in black-letter Charter law – qualify as "international" threats. The "Outcome Document" articulating RtoP is a General Assembly resolution; and, as such, it is a recommendation (UN Charter, Article 10), not a binding international-law obligation on the Security Council. And, while the Security Council established tribunals for the former Yugoslavia and Rwanda in order to punish genocide and war crimes (authorized by reference to international peace and security), the Security Council is neither a global legislature nor a global court. It does not set general legal precedents; it addresses specific cases according to its discretion.

It is thus not surprising that UN General Assembly President, Miguel d'Escoto Brockmann, began his "Concept note" on responsibility to protect, written to introduce the General Assembly reconsideration of RtoP in the summer of 2009, with the observation that "None of the documents [including the 'Outcome Document' and Security Council Resolution 1674, recognizing RtoP] can be considered as a binding source of international law in terms of Article 38 of the Statute of the International Court of Justice which lists the classic sources of international law."[2]

RtoP is not a treaty, Article 38's primary source of law. It might be argued that RtoP is emerging customary international law, another Article 38 source of law. Unlike treaty law, customary law is established by a pattern of general state practice when practice is motivated by a sense of its legal obligation ("*opinio juris*"). But a General Assembly resolution does not per se qualify as *opinio juris* (voting can be purely political) and state or Security Council practice, though significant, is not yet extensive. But, as I will discuss later, RtoP could indeed evolve into customary law, if Security Council practice confirms, and states express, a continuing "responsibility" to act.[3]

But the picture was not as straightforward as the General Assembly president suggested. Genocide, even if inflicted solely domestically, is outlawed by the Genocide Convention, a treaty so widely endorsed that it is regarded as fundamental international law, binding on all. It requires states to "prevent and punish" genocide (Article 1). It leaves interpretation of genocide to the International Court of Justice (Article 9) and invites states to enforce protection through the United Nations (Article 8). Thus, for genocide, RtoP was well-established, internationally enforceable law, even if the specific role proposed for the Security Council seemed to go beyond Article 39 of the Charter. Equally powerful obligations clashed.

Most importantly, the Security Council has claimed a very wide discretion in practice. It is a legal body, authorized by the UN Charter to make binding resolutions (Articles 25 and 48) on matters of "international peace and security" (Chapter VII). But it also is a political body, authorized to decide based on its own judgment of what constitutes "threats to the peace, breaches of the peace and acts of aggression" (Article 39). The Security Council has a long record of

---

[2] Article 38 cites treaties, custom, general principles of law, and (without *stare decisis*) previous court decisions and the opinions of scholars. Miguel D'Escoto Brockmann, *Concept Note on Responsibility to Protect Populations from Genocide, War Crimes, Ethnic Cleansing and Crimes Against Humanity* (UN: Office of the President of the General Assembly, July 2009).

[3] Lori F. Damrosch, Louis Henkin, Sean D. Murphy, and Hans Smit, *International Law* (St. Paul: West Group, 2001), 451–66, 990–1004. For RtoP's grounding in human-rights discourse, see D. Gierycz, *Responsibility to Protect: A Legal and Human Rights Based Perspective* (Oslo: NUPI, 2008).

wide discretion, acting on the basis of Chapter VII against perceived "threats to the peace" that did not constitute international attacks. For instance, the Council imposed obligatory sanctions on Rhodesia (1966) and South Africa (1977), citing with regard to the obligatory arms embargo imposed on South Africa – in effect an arms blockade – South Africa's "massive violence" against its own population, its "military build-up," and its past record of "persistent acts of aggression" against its neighboring states.[4] Drawing up a list just three years into the expansion of Council activity that characterized the post-Cold War period, Lori Damrosch has identified a wide range of other triggers for successful Chapter VII determinations of threats against the peace, including genocide, ethnic cleansing, and war crimes (former Republic of Yugoslavia, Iraq, Liberia); interference with the delivery of humanitarian supplies (former Republic of Yugoslavia, Iraq, Somalia); violations of ceasefires (former Republic of Yugoslavia, Liberia, Cambodia); collapse of civil order (Liberia, Somalia); and coups against democratic governments (Haiti).[5]

Its judgment thus has had wide scope, constrained (arguably) only by the law of the Charter and *jus cogens* norms (such as those against genocide). Many states, especially in the South, as I will discuss below, have come to view the Security Council as acting far beyond the parameters of "international peace and security." Many legal scholars would share Yoram Dinstein's[6] interpretation of the International Court of Justice's ruling in the *Lockerbie Case*: The Security Council has wide discretion but this jurisdiction may not be infinite. It could not legally, manifestly violate the Charter or authorize genocide. Whether acting irrespective of a credible reading of the Charter's authorization in Article 39 to maintain "international" peace is the disputed question raised by President d'Escoto Brockmann and a few states allied with him at the 2009 plenary General Assembly consideration of RtoP.

Other tensions in international law revolve about the role of the Security Council as enforcer, the International Criminal Court (ICC), and regional law. Domestically inflicted war crimes (now including ethnic cleansing) and crimes against humanity in non-international, civil-war conflicts are parts of international law outlawed by custom and treaties, including the Rome Statute defining the jurisdiction of the International Criminal Court. But they are not clearly within the jurisdiction of the Security Council for its own coercive enforcement, which is limited in Article 39 to "international peace and security." The ICC has residual jurisdiction for certain types of grave crimes when states party to the court do not prosecute those crimes domestically. But major

---

[4] UN Security Council Resolution 418, S/RES/418 (November 4, 1977).

[5] Lori F. Damrosch (ed.), *Enforcing Restraint: Collective Intervention in Internal Conflicts* (New York: Council on Foreign Relations Press, 1993), 10–14.

[6] Yoram Dinstein, *War, Aggression, and Self-Defence*, 4th edn. (Cambridge University Press, 2005), 324.

powers, including the United States, China, India, and Russia, are not parties to the treaty that establishes the ICC.

Thus, the strict legality of RtoP as a new basis for Security Council action supplementing global "international" peace and security has not yet been established formally. The Security Council may have the legal authority, and states can exercise their obligation to prevent and punish genocide through the United Nations.[7] But the Security Council, so far, has neither the authority nor the legal obligation to prevent or stop the RtoP harms unless it determines that international peace and security is threatened. Given the supremacy of the Charter over all treaties (Article 103), a Charter revision would be needed to do this. Short of that, RtoP will remain legally contested.

Nonetheless, the contestation in international law is narrow compared to the contestation in international ethics, where the most basic premises of obligation are up for dispute in the policy and philosophic literature.

International ethics

Principles of non-intervention and intervention have been justified in various ways.[8] Intervention is dictatorial interference in the political independence and territorial integrity of a sovereign state. The principles underlying this prohibition have been justified by scholars, by politicians, and by citizens – all of whom have sought to provide good ethical reasons why one should abide by the conventional principles of non-intervention and good reasons why one should, on some occasions, override or disregard them.[9]

International ethics has long rested on broad foundations in political theory. The classic tripartite division has separated Realists, Socialists, and Liberals, the great doctrines that divided the West, and were transferred to much of the

---

[7] Common Article 1 of the Geneva Convention imposes obligations, but they are less distinct. It requires that all states "undertake to respect and ensure respect for the present Convention." Laurence Boisson de Chazournes and Luigi Condorelli, "Common Article 1 for the Geneva Conventions Revisited: Protecting Collective Interests," *International Review of the Red Cross*, 857 (March 31, 2000), 67–87.

[8] For a valuable survey and introduction, see J.L. Holzgrefe, "The Humanitarian Intervention Debate," in J.L. Holzgrefe and Robert Keohane (eds.), *Humanitarian Intervention: Ethical, Legal, and Political Dimensions* (Cambridge University Press, 2003), 15–52; Michael Walzer, *Just and Unjust Wars* (New York: Basic Books, 1977). For the recent policy debate, see Thomas G. Weiss, *Humanitarian Intervention* (Cambridge: Polity Press, 2007).

[9] Insightful study of the historical context on the doctrine of non-intervention can be found in J. Vincent, *Nonintervention and International Order* (Princeton University Press, 1974); G. Graham, "The Justice of Intervention," *Review of International Studies* 13 (1987), 133–46; Fernando R. Tesón, *Humanitarian Intervention: An Inquiry Into Law and Morality* (New York: Transnational Publishers, 1997); F.K. Abiew, *The Evolution of the Doctrine and Practice of Humanitarian Intervention* (The Hague: Kluwer Law International, 1999); S. Garrett, *Doing Good and Doing Well: An Examination of Humanitarian Intervention* (Westport: Praeger, 1999).

rest of the world after World War II. They posit differing and consequential views on the actors in international politics, their interests, values, environment, and capacities. In doing so, they provide contingent justification for non-intervention but also permit intervention, though for differing reasons.

The *Realist* school has seen state interests as the essential determinant of public policy and the international system as a "state of war" in which state security is relative, inherently under threat and therefore primary. When to or not to intervene was already a key theme of the founding Western text on what is later called Realism, Thucydides's *History of the Peloponnesian War*. States should intervene when it is in their interest and should not when it is not – unconstrained in either case by international law or ethics. The simplest, "hardest," and most skeptical version of this proposition is an argument often erroneously taken to be Thucydides's own view. Instead, it is a view Thucydides attributes to two Athenian generals, Cleomedes and Tisias, in command of the blockade of Melos where the generals declare "the strong do what they will and the weak what they must."[10] All the men of the rebellious island were executed and the women and children enslaved in order to deter future resistance to Athenian imperial expansion.

Even though destroying Melos may have seemed the right thing to do in the view of the two Athenian generals, there is good reason for us to believe that this was not necessarily Thucydides's own view.[11] His own, a "softer" Realist view on intervention, was more evident in an earlier debate on the fate of Mytilene, a subordinate ally of Athens. There, a group of rebels against the Athenian empire sought to establish a self-determining, independent state. When they did so, they came up against the might of Athens.[12]

In the Athenian Assembly, Cleon, a hard-liner, lines up against Diodotus, a "soft-liner" (literally, in Greek, "soft speaker"), and they debate the fate of the Mytileneans. What form of punishment, Cleon asks, is the correct fate for those who rebel against the alliance and law of Athens? He says the punishment must fit the crime: They seek to destroy Athens' power, on which its security, indeed, survival rests. The rebels must be killed – men, women, and children – in order to teach a lesson to all others who might be tempted to imitate them. Diodotus corrects Cleon's demands for punishment and responds as the better (Thucydidean) Realist. Diodotus says that thinking about international politics as a matter of right and wrong confuses politics with a court of law. International politics should cover no more than the prudent calculation of long-run security. He warns that although the Athenians may intimidate subject cities in the short run by slaughters, they will stir up resistance elsewhere in the empire or with potential allies. Thus, Diodotus argues for a

[10] Thucydides, *History of the Peloponnesian War*, Bk V (Melian Dialogue).
[11] R.W. Connor, *Thucydides* (Princeton University Press, 1984).
[12] Thucydides, *History of the Peloponnesian War*, Bk III.

softer course. In fact, the softer course is not too soft – it involves the execution of about 1,000 Mytilenean rebels. But he advocates sparing the rest of the
island in hopes of a future of imperial reconciliation, imperial stability, and
reputational gains.[13]

Socialism, a second foundational theory of world politics (one more prevalent before the collapse of the Soviet Union), tends to regard international
politics, particularly international law, as a mere reflection of the much more
fundamental class interests that truly govern international society. International
society, according to Socialists, is akin to international civil war, where capital-
ists line up against workers, both domestically and internationally. State borders among nations are semi-fictions and not the fundamental dividing blocks
of world politics. Nonetheless, national borders can and have played a progressive role in history. Marx himself saw reasons to support the development
of the working class within a national framework. For that development to be
successful, one had to appreciate the value of national sovereignty and therefore the value of national defense. So he usually condemns aggressive wars as
he sees them occurring in his own times.[14]

When Marx considers a doctrine that should guide Socialists in their own
choices for world politics, he wants to remind them that even though they have
a duty to advance to the greatest extent that they can the processes of Socialism
on a worldwide front, this does not include a duty to crusade for Socialism. He
warns that the liberation of the working class can be achieved only by the working class. One cannot create revolutions for others by prematurely attempting
to put a working-class or union movement in political power. Socialist cru-
sades would create the grounds for an enormous amount of suffering, a great
deal of instability, and the defeat of that particular working class at the hands
of social forces (i.e., capitalist and others) that it has not yet historically been
able to master. Therefore, Socialists of the Second International, the pre-1914
Marxists and the post-1914 social democrats, often lined up in favor of the
principle of non-intervention, except when they saw war as distinctly advancing progressive forces or suppressing reactionary ones.[15]

Leninism and Stalinism absorbed class interests into the Soviet state.
Once the Soviet Union acquired great power of its own after World War II,
interventionism became a practice that turned into doctrine: the Brezhnev
Doctrine. Following the forcible "Stalinization" of East European states after

[13] For a discussion of Realist skepticism, see Marshall Cohen, "Moral Skepticism and
    International Relations," in Charles R. Beitz, Lawrence A. Alexander, and Thomas Scanlon
    (eds.), *International Ethics* (Princeton University Press, 1985), 3–50. For Thucydidean eth-
    ics, see Michael W. Doyle, *Ways of War and Peace* (New York: W.W. Norton, 1997), 81–92.
[14] Walzer, *Just and Unjust Wars*, 64–66.
[15] A. Gilbert, "Marx on Internationalism and War," *Philosophy and Public Affairs* 7, no. 4
    (1978), 353–54. See Doyle, *Ways of War and Peace*, in the conclusion to Part III and the
    sources cited there for the Socialist war crisis of August 1914.

1948 and then the interventions in Germany in 1953, Hungary in 1956, and Czechoslovakia in 1968, Leonid Brezhnev declared that the Soviet Union stood in a particularly privileged position as the guardian of the collective interest of the working class worldwide and particularly, of course, within the Soviet bloc.[16] The Communist Party of the Soviet Union thus claimed to act in the name of the worldwide working class in intervening against governments that it claimed were about to "betray" the interests of the working class.

Liberalism was the third major claimant on twentieth-century political allegiances and the one that engaged most deeply with the ethics of non-intervention and intervention. Like the other two, it engaged with nationalism in the form of self-determination as a principle to be balanced with universal human rights and national security.

Non-intervention has been an especially important principle for liberal statesmen and moralists with a commitment to universal human rights. On the one hand, Liberals have provided some of the strongest reasons to abide by a strict form of the non-intervention doctrine. It was only within secure borders that peoples could govern themselves as free citizens. On the other hand, those same principles of universal human dignity have provided justifications for overriding or disregarding the principle of non-intervention.

Like many other liberals, John Stuart Mill, in his classic discussion of non-intervention,[17] dismissed (without much attention) Realist arguments in favor of intervention to promote national power, prestige, or profits. However prevalent those motives have been in history, they lack moral significance, as for that matter would justifications associated with intervening to promote an idea or ideology.

The most important direct consideration for the liberals was that non-intervention reflected and protected human dignity (or rights, though Mill disliked the word). Non-intervention could enable citizens to determine their own way of life without outside interference. If democratic rights and liberal freedoms were to mean something, they had to be worked out among those who shared them and were making them through their own participation.

For Mill, as for a later group of liberals often called **communitarians**, intervention undermined the authenticity of domestic struggles for liberty. A free government achieved by means of intervention would not be authentic or self-determining but determined by others and not one that local citizens had themselves defined through their own actions.

Mill provided a second powerful direct argument for non-intervention, one focusing on likely consequences, when he explained in his famous 1859 essay,

---

[16] For a general background on the bloc, see Z.K. Brzezinski, *The Soviet Bloc* (Cambridge, Massachusetts: Harvard University Press, 1967).

[17] John Stuart Mill, "A Few Words on Non-Intervention" [*Fraser's Magazine*, December 1859], in *Essays on Politics and Culture by John Stuart Mill*, edited by Gertrude Himmelfarb (Garden City, New York: Doubleday Anchor Books, 1963).

"Nonintervention," that it would be a great mistake to export freedom to a foreign people that was not in a position to win it on its own. A people given freedom by a foreign intervention would not, he argued, be able to hold on to it. It is only by winning and holding on to freedom through local effort that one acquired a true sense of its value. Moreover, it was only by winning freedom that one acquired the political capacities to defend it adequately against threats both at home and abroad. The struggle mobilized citizens into what could become a national army and mobilized as well a capacity and willingness to tax themselves for public purposes.

If, on the other hand, liberal government were to be introduced into a foreign society, in the "knapsack," so to speak, of a conquering liberal army, the local liberals placed in power would find themselves immediately in a difficult situation. Not having been able to win political power on their own, they would have few domestic supporters and many non-liberal domestic enemies. They then would wind up doing one of three things:

> *Either* (1) begin to rule as did previous governments, that is to repress their opposition. The intervention would have done no good; it simply would have created another oppressive government.
>
> *Or* (2) simply collapse in an ensuing civil war. Intervention, therefore, would have produced not freedom and progress, but a civil war with all its attendant violence.
>
> *Or* (3) the interveners would have continually to send in foreign support. Rather than having set up a free government, one that reflected the participation of the citizens of the state, the intervention would have set up a puppet government, one that would reflect the wills and interests of the intervening, the truly sovereign state.

Liberal communitarian arguments supporting intervention fall into various camps. J.S. Mill argued that there were good reasons to override or disregard what should be the usual prohibition against intervention. One is when a civil war becomes so protracted by military stalemate that the suffering of the non-combatant population overwhelms the value of letting local forces settle the outcome. Another is counter-intervening against a previous intervention or assisting the secession of a subordinate and less powerful national community from a larger and dominant one.[18] When communitarian Liberals see a pattern of massacres or of genocide, the institutionalization of slavery – violations that "shock the conscience of mankind" as Michael Walzer puts it[19] – one has grounds to question whether there is any national connection between the

---

[18] It is also worth noting that Mill advocated (based on very problematic readings of indigenous cultures) a benign, tutelary imperialism that almost all modern communitarians would reject. See Michael W. Doyle, "A Few Words on Mill, Walzer and Nonintervention," *Ethics & International Affairs* 23, no. 4 (Winter 2009), 349–69.

[19] Walzer, *Just and Unjust Wars*, chap. 6.

population and the state that is so brutally oppressing it. Under those circumstances, outsiders may intervene.

But the intervener should have a morally defensible motive and share the purpose of ending the slaughter and establishing a self-determining people. Furthermore, interveners should act only as a "last resort," after exploring peaceful resolution. They should then act only when it is clear that they will save more lives than the intervention itself will inevitably wind up costing, and then with minimum necessary force. It makes no moral sense to rescue a village and start a third world war or destroy a village in order to save it. Walzer has suggested that, as a modern example, the Indian invasion of East Pakistan in 1971, designed to save the people of what became Bangladesh from the massacre that was being inflicted upon them by their own government (headquartered in West Pakistan), is a case of legitimate humanitarian intervention. It allowed the people of East Pakistan to survive and form their own state, Bangladesh.

Other Liberals, strong **cosmopolitans**, hold that the rights of cosmopolitan freedom are valuable for all people. Any violation of them should be resisted wherever it occurs, provided that we can do so without causing more harm than we seek to avoid. [20] The cosmopolitans are radically skeptical of the principle of non-intervention, almost as much as are the Realists.

Articulating just such a flat, confident moral universe, right-wing cosmopolitans hold that a morally adequate recognition of equal human freedom requires freedom from torture, free speech, privacy rights, and private property. It also demands democratic elections and an independent judiciary and a right of emigration. The entire package goes together, as Hadley Arkes has eloquently argued.[21]

Equally cosmopolitan but at the other end of the Liberal political spectrum is the left cosmopolitan view. David Luban argues powerfully that we can make clear judgments about basic rights, but his basic rights are different.[22] Basic rights include both subsistence rights – that is, rights to food and shelter and clothing – and security rights – that is, rights to be free from arbitrary killing,

---

[20] The best discussion of the practical applications of the proportionality issue that I have seen is R. Ullman, "Human Rights and Economic Power: *The United States vs. Idi Amin*," *Foreign Affairs* 56, no. 3 (April 1978), 529–43. The author explains how carefully targeting sanctions on the government and bypassing the people could have put pressure on the murderous Amin government.

[21] Hadley Arkes, *First Things: An Inquiry into the First Principles of Morals and Justice* (Princeton University Press, 1986). Transformed in a political and expediential way, these views relate to those adopted by the Reagan administration in its defense of global "freedom fighters." See a valuable discussion of this by Charles Beitz, "The Reagan Doctrine in Nicaragua," in Steven Luper-Foy (ed.), *Problems of International Justice* (Boulder: Westview Press, 1988), 182–95.

[22] David Luban, "Just War and Human Rights," *Philosophy & Public Affairs* 9, no. 2 (Winter 1980), 160–81, building on arguments in Henry Shue, *Basic Rights: Subsistence, Affluence and US Foreign Policy*, 2nd edn. (Princeton University Press, 1996).

from torture, and from assault. We all have a duty to protect these socially basic rights. They are the rights held by humanity and claimable by all against all human beings.

In international politics, this means that states that fail to protect those rights do not have the right to be free from intervention. The most complete form of non-intervention thus is claimable only by states that do not violate basic rights. Moreover, all states have a duty to protect and to intervene, if an intervention is necessary, in order to provide subsistence needs held by all human beings. Both these considerations are subject to standard proportionality: We should never do something that would cause more harm than it saves. One implication of this principle is that if 500 individuals were to die of torture in country X this year, and we could prevent this militarily or otherwise at a cost of 499 lives or less, then intervention would be the right thing to do; and we would have a duty to do it. In another implication, if the only way that Haitians could provide subsistence for themselves is by sailing a boat to Florida, the United States has no right to stop them.

It is worth noting that both cosmopolitans and communitarians ascribe to the principles of "last resort" and proportionality, such that in practical terms the more interventionist cosmopolitans are likely to endorse intervention only in the more extreme cases – that is, where the communitarians would also be willing to override or disregard national community. An important exchange between Michael Walzer and David Luban highlighted significant differences in their judgments on when to intervene in the civil war in Nicaragua.[23] Luban favored an early intervention to stop the ongoing victimization of the Nicaraguan opposition. Walzer favored non-intervention and, in retrospect, noted that the opposition was eventually able to win power on its own and, in the process of so doing, transform itself into a much more representative movement. Luban, in reply, highlighted the loss of life that the extra time involved.

The evolution of the RtoP doctrine

Humanitarian intervention is differentially rooted in international ethics – central and fundamental to Liberalism, marginal and instrumental to Realism, and relevant but tangential to Marxism. It is conflicted in international law – required to stop genocide, but rejected by Charter law. Its recent evolution as the international norm of RtoP both reflects those tensions and helps to reconcile them. It builds on, but narrows, the liberal tradition in ways that expand international legitimacy and address the many skeptics of humanitarian intervention.

The Kosovo crisis was a watershed event in the reformulation of doctrine of intervention. When the United Nations did not protect the Kosovars, NATO did. US President Bill Clinton, echoing earlier promises by British Prime

[23] Luban, "Just War and Human Rights," and Walzer, "The Moral Standing of States," in Beitz et al., International Ethics, 195–237.

Minister Tony Blair, announced a "Clinton Doctrine" of humanitarian protection to the assembled KFOR troops (UN Kosovo Force) on June 22, 1999, following their successful, though belated, occupation of Kosovo.

UN Secretary-General, Kofi Annan, three months later also endorsed the principle of humanitarian intervention, but highlighted a problem: the imperative of "halting gross and systematic violations of human rights" had clashed with "dangerous precedents for future interventions without a clear criterion to decide who might invoke these precedents, and in what circumstances."[24] Both the Blair–Clinton doctrine and the Annan equivocation alarmed developing states of the "South" who feared that humanitarian concern might be used as a pretext for imperial intervention.[25] The G-77 (132 states of the "South") condemned "the so-called right of humanitarian intervention" in paragraph 69 of their Ministerial Declaration of September 24, 1999, three months after the NATO intervention.[26]

The Kosovo Commission was then commissioned to write an objective, international, and non-governmental report to assess the intervention. It famously concluded that the intervention was "illegal but legitimate." It was not legally defensive, and it lacked the needed Security Council approval under Article 39; but it was a legitimate humanitarian rescue in the eyes of the commission of notables. In making this judgment, they defined what they saw as relevant "threshold principles" for a genuine "humanitarian intervention":

> The first is severe violations of international human rights or humanitarian law on a sustained basis. The second is the subjection of a civilian society to great suffering and risk due to the "failure" of their state, which entails the breakdown of governance at the level of the territorial sovereign state.[27]

The principles still were noticeably broad ("international human rights or humanitarian law"); and they allowed for action if the Security Council would not act, albeit as a last resort. The Commission did not assuage the concerns of the South.

In an effort to include more viewpoints from the global South (and more representation from former government officials), Canada supported a new and more ambitious commission, one co-chaired by Mohamed Sahnoun and Gareth

---

[24] Kofi Annan, "Reflections on Intervention," Ditchley Park, United Kingdom (June 26, 1998), in Annan, Kofi, *The Question of Intervention: Statements by the Secretary-General of the United Nations Kofi Annan* (New York: United Nations, Department of Public Information, 1999), 4.

[25] Alex J. Bellamy, "Kosovo and the Advent of Sovereignty as Responsibility," *Journal of Intervention and Statebuilding* 3, no. 2 (2009), 163–84.

[26] See discussion in Ian Brownlie, *Principles of Public International Law*, 6th edn. (Oxford University Press, 2003), 712.

[27] Independent International Commission on Kosovo, *The Kosovo Report* (Oxford University Press, 2000), available at: http://reliefweb.int/sites/reliefweb.int/files/resources/F62789D9FCC56FB3C1256C1700303E3B-thekosovoreport.htm.

Evans. The International Commission on Intervention and State Sovereignty (ICISS) reframed the debate as "Responsibility to Protect" rather than "right" to intervene, and by dint of numerous meetings at the regional level around the world built a multilateral coalition. They identified a threefold responsibility: to prevent, to react, and to rebuild. Compared to the Kosovo Report, they narrowed the triggers for action to the threat of, or presence of, "large-scale loss of life" whether by action or inaction of states and "large-scale ethnic cleansing." Building on classic just-war doctrine underlying humanitarian intervention, they specified "right intention," "just cause," "proportionality," and "right authority" as further qualifiers on when international force could be used if states failed to meet their responsibility to protect their own populations. "Right authority," furthermore, was the UN Security Council. "No better or more appropriate" authority could be found; but, at the same time, it was not the last word. In "shocking situations," "concerned states … may not rule out other measures" if the Security Council does not act. And "the SC should take note." The ICISS had narrowed the triggers and the authority, but in 2001 much of the global South was still alarmed. Secretary-General Annan personally welcomed the report, but no UN premise would host its formal New York presentation in 2001. The Commission unveiled its report in a hotel across the street from the UN buildings.

This record reveals the significance of the 2005 World Summit Outcome Document paragraphs (quoted in the introduction to the chapter) that won the unanimous assent of the member states. Paragraphs 138–9 reflected four additional years of assiduous lobbying and doctrinal adjustment. They further narrowed the triggers for RtoP from "international human rights" or "large-scale killings" (the elements raised by the Kosovo and ICISS commissions) to four specific elements: "genocide, war crimes, ethnic cleansing and crimes against humanity." To emphasize the point, these four specific elements are repeated *five* times in the original two paragraphs! In addition, the assembled states removed the ambiguity in authorization found in the earlier reports and clearly restricted "right authority" to use coercive means to the Security Council when it contemplates: "collective action, in a timely and decisive manner, through the Security Council, in accordance with the Charter, including Chapter VII, on a case-by-case basis." The United Nations reaffirms the importance of state responsibility and the triad of prevention, reaction, and rebuilding and, importantly, that RtoP is a "responsibility" – though only undertaken on a "case-by-case," hence discretionary, basis.

Libya

The UN-authorized and NATO-led intervention in Libya in March 2011 was the doctrine's most important test case. In classic UN Security Council language, Resolution 1973 of March 17, 2011, authorized UN member states to "take all necessary measures … to protect civilians and civilian populated areas" in Libya, including by establishing a no-fly zone and enforcing an arms embargo against Colonel Muammar Gaddafi's regime.[28]

The resolution thus gave teeth to the much-heralded Responsibility to Protect, for this was only the third time since the doctrine of the Responsibility to Protect was adopted in 2005 that the Security Council had invoked it to enforce the protection of civilians. The first case was to authorize an arms embargo over the Sudan in 2005. The second case occurred only weeks before, when the Security Council's first resolution targeted Gaddafi's crackdown against Libya's rebellion by calling for financial sanctions and an arms embargo. Resolution 1973, however, marked the first Security Council approval of military force in the name of the Responsibility to Protect.

Humanitarian rescue seems to offer the best justification for the intervention. Gaddafi and his sons were reported to have made threats of merciless expulsion and extermination against the rebels, their supporters, and perhaps the entire city of Benghazi.

On March 28, US President Barack Obama spoke in increasing order of importance of:

(1) The threat to regional stability in Egypt and Tunisia and the need to stand with the popular forces in the region.
(2) Gaddafi's record of "extreme violence," launching jets and helicopters against civilians, cutting off of water for tens of thousands in various towns, including Misrata, shelling cities and towns, unleashing gunships on the people, and raiding homes and hospitals. (When the Gaddafi regime's record of arbitrary arrests, torture, and the ordering of rapes was added in, all these led to the ICC arrest warrants.)
(3) But most important was the threat of worse to come: the looming slaughter in Benghazi that could "not wait one more day."[29]

The key to the indictment had to be threats, because much violence was to be averted. Post-war surveys by Red Cross and other humanitarian agencies found a total of fewer than 3,500 accountable deaths – in the "hundreds" in major cities, not thousands. Yet the National Transitional Council claimed

---

[28] UN Security Council Resolution 1973, S/Res/1973 (March 17, 2011); UN Security Council Resolution 1970, S/Res/1970 (February 26, 2011).
  In late March, I addressed the Libya issue at www.foreignaffairs.com/articles/67666/michael-w-doyle/the-folly-of-protection.
[29] The US president warned that Gaddafi bore down on the "700,000" people of Benghazi – helpfully noted to be the "size of Charlotte." The US administration also reported that Gaddafi's subordinates threatened "no mercy" and vowed to hunt the rebels down, apartment by apartment, like "rats." *United States Activities in Libya* (Wahsington, DC: White House, 2011), 2–5.

30,000–50,000.[30] The numbers were unclear, but this is not unusual in civil conflicts. Combatants have more to do than count bodies. Still, the Libyan conflict is closer to Kosovo than to Bosnia and Croatia, not to speak of Rwanda. It was the *threat* of ethnic cleansing and massacres that seems to have justified the action, not the numbers already killed.[31]

Should President Obama have waited until the death numbers were generated before acting? Moreover, how could one not take Gaddafi's threat seriously? He had killed civilians publicly in large numbers before. Protection is better than regret. But Obama's and NATO's judgment was, and will be, challenged.

The intervention in Libya joined *legality* (Security Council approval) to *legitimacy* (the cause of protecting civilians). But, as described above, it still strained against the letter-of-the-law role that the Charter assigns the Security Council and risked going beyond (as it did) the protection of civilians. It also remained ethically problematic unless it succeeded in resolving the crisis without further large loss of life and left behind a viable, legitimate, and rights-respecting Libyan polity. All these provoked concerns and made the intervention problematic.

One problem was a likely stalemate. Gaddafi probably would have been able to conquer the rebel capital of Benghazi with his air force, artillery, and armor in the lead; but commencement of the allied intervention destroyed the air force and protected the civilian population from large-scale attacks. On the other hand, it was not clear that the rebels could conquer the country even if Gaddafi's air force was neutralized, unless they were aided by international arms or forces on the ground – aid not authorized by Resolution 1973, which authorized only the protection of civilians. President Obama hoped economic sanctions would undermine Gaddafi's regime, but Gaddafi had too much loose cash and gold for sanctions to truly bite anytime soon.

This led to unpalatable alternatives: If Gaddafi stopped victimizing civilians and retained power while the rebels maintained their own territory, would partition provide a workable solution? If Gaddafi and the rebels could not achieve political agreement, could the international community see itself as legitimately, ethically, holding the ring and watching the casualties mount, while the two sides battled it out with small arms? Or should the interveners brush aside the restrictions of the Security Council resolution, aid the rebels, and topple Gaddafi?

Obviously, the third was chosen. Qatar provided funds, possibly arms; the United Kingdom and perhaps France added "trainers" on the ground for the rebels; and others (Americans?) served as bombing spotters and air coordinators. The air campaign went after targets – headquarters, communications,

---

[30] See Rod Nordland, "Libya Counts More Martyrs than Bodies," *New York Times*, (September 16, 2011), A1.

[31] In Former Yugoslavia, 130–140,000 were killed by 1995, before protection was fully provided. The 10,000 margin of error 15 years after the end of the conflict is standard.

troop and arms depots – remote from areas actually directly inflicting harm on civilians.

This was all arguably necessary to end the crisis. But it also undermined the "Immaculate Intervention" contemplated by RtoP, and thereby discredited the legal authorization of RtoP, which was limited to protecting civilians.

Another problem was the endgame in Libya itself. Could the transitional authorities establish a legitimate and rights-respecting regime? It would have been a sad outcome if the new regime simply replicated Gaddafi's style of oppression. The immediate aftermath of the intervention offered a mixed picture. African minorities and Berber minorities in the far south and west of Libya were victimized by local authorities, and the militias in control of Benghazi were reluctant to cede power. Tripoli appeared to function best, and the national elections seemed to offer a step toward stability and legitimacy. From the beginning, the National Transition Council rejected the heavy UN "footprint" (on the East Timor model) that UN official Ian Martin planned; Libya, for better or worse, was in the hands of Libyans.[32]

An assessment of the Libyan intervention highlights wider implications. On the one hand, RtoP and the Libya precedent have "solved" the genocide problem. By that I do not mean that future genocides have been prevented, but that the new standards preclude the trap of a genocide threshold for protection. In 2003, Darfurians suffered while the International Commission of Inquiry on Darfur to the UN researched. Months of interviewing produced an accurate conclusion that Darfur did not then constitute "genocide." Darfur slaughters lacked the intention to kill on the basis of race or ethnicity or religion – some of the standards required by the Genocide Convention. And then nothing happened, despite a documented record of crimes against humanity and war crimes. Employing the genocide standard for humanitarian intervention, Michael Walzer concluded that Libya was not a "humanitarian emergency" – not like the 800,000 deaths of Rwanda that would justify anyone to step in and stop.[33]

Now we have a new more credible standard for international protection. It is more restrictive than Security Council practice of intervention in the 1990s, when anything that could garner the right votes qualified, and more restrictive than the "human-rights abuses" set by the Kosovo Commission or the indefinite "large-scale deaths" of the ICISS, but less restrictive than Chapter VII of the Charter ("international" threats), or the genocide standard of the Genocide Convention. RtoP includes genocide, ethnic cleansing, crimes against humanity, and war crimes. But, procedurally and unlike customary law, Kosovo,

---

[32] Nicolas Pelham, "Is Libya Cracking Up?" *The New York Review of Books* (June 21, 2012), 66–69.

[33] Michael Walzer, "The Case Against Our Attack on Libya," *The New Republic* (March 20, 2011).

and ICISS, RtoP avoids unilateral exploitation by the requirement of Security Council multilateral authorization. This is a reasonable combination of substantive license and procedural leash.

The other hand of the assessment is that Libya has wounded RtoP. To gain approval for their intervention in Libya, Western nations secured a resolution that passed with ten votes in favor, and no vetoes. But the legitimacy, in the sense of wide support, was not fulsome. There were five abstentions from the not insignificant countries of Brazil, China, Germany, India, and Russia. Brazil, Germany, and India are seeking permanent membership on the Security Council. So is South Africa; and, though it voted for SC Resolution 1973 while on the Council, it opposed what it saw as regime change in the intervention. The Arab League supported, but only the United Arab Emirates and Qatar provided any assistance. The African Union condemned Gaddafi's violence, but it also condemned the air strikes. Most importantly, the dissenters on the Security Council felt that they had been hoodwinked – sold a protection intervention that turned into a regime-change intervention.

And the costs of that were soon visible in Syria[34] where, burned once, neither Russia nor China were prepared to abstain on resolutions presented by the United States and the Europeans to sanction the Assad regime. Both, in fact, vetoed resolutions, the vetoes carefully negotiated in advance to limit their impacts.[35]

The Arab League then imposed sanctions on Syria, as did the Europeans and the United States. The Security Council agreed to monitor a putative ceasefire and a mediation under the leadership of former Secretary-General Kofi Annan. But the ceasefire lacked credibility in 2012, in part because Russia and China prevented the Security Council from threatening more severe UN-authorized measures should Assad fail to comply. Syria was a much more problematic intervention in any case. But it was unfortunate as casualties mounted in 2012 that the multilateral authority and legitimacy of RtoP no longer seemed available.

The international community has thus developed a new global norm, RtoP; and that is a large step toward more protective human-rights-based global governance. We have evolved beyond multilateral neglect and beyond unilateral imperialism. But we have not quite achieved a consensus on:

[34] "RtoP Discussion" at International Press Institute (June 28, 2011). One prominent Security Council member remarked: "Libya will give RtoP a bad name, resistance to sanctions in Syria is a product of Libya experience in which NATO has run away with RtoP and is imposing regime change."

[35] Neil MacFarquhar, "With Rare Double UN Veto on Syria, Russia and China Try to Shield Friend" (October 5, 2011), available at: www.nytimes.com/2011/10/06/world/middleeast/with-united-nations-veto-russia-and-china-help-syria.html?.

(1) When to invoke it. When does the gravity of the crimes rise to a level warranting intervention?
(2) How to manage it. How can one preserve multilateral principles of impartial administration when enforcement must be delegated to the militarily competent – usually NATO?
(3) How to assist former victims (e.g., the Libyan people) to become an effective and humane government – and thereby avoid another cycle of repression and war.

We need to find answers to these questions soon. Failing to learn these lessons could make innocent Syrians and others in the future bear the costs of the learning exercise that the international community should already have begun in order to make RtoP genuinely responsive and responsible.

Implications for law and ethics

The UN Charter is a "living constitution," and the UN members are nothing if not lively in their fluid commitments. So RtoP continues to evolve. The Security Council reaffirmed RtoP in SC Resolution 1674 (2006) and operationally made the protection of civilians in ongoing peace operations an important commitment. (Protecting civilians during an established and authorized peacekeeping operation is not, however, the same as legislating intervention whenever a government harms or threatens to harm its own nationals.) The Secretary-General presented a valuable report, "Implementing the Responsibility to Protect" (January 12, 2009, A/63/677), outlining all that the United Nations could and should do to help prevent and rebuild with the consent of the affected state. The report, by emphasizing prevention and rebuilding, thereby further distanced RtoP from a focus on coercive intervention.

In the summer of 2009, as noted above, the General Assembly considered the Secretary-General's report, and RtoP more generally, at a special meeting organized by General Assembly president and strong RtoP critic, Miguel d'Escoto Brockmann (former Sandinista commandant and Nicaraguan foreign minister). Highlighted by an invitation to Professor Noam Chomsky to address the General Assembly, the session in D'Escoto Brockmann's plan was designed to roast the doctrine.

Instead, a considerable majority of states – developing and developed – reaffirmed their commitment. But many also warned of abuses that might follow from it. Egyptian Ambassador Maged Abdelaziz, on behalf of the 118 member states of the Non-Aligned Movement, while condemning the four crimes covered by RtoP, expressed concern that the doctrine could be abused by opening up the possibility of unilateral intervention or extending its triggers beyond the four elements, attempting thus to legitimize "intervention in the internal affairs of states." Only a handful (Venezuela, Cuba, North Korea, and a few others) acknowledged sufficient "buyer's remorse" to outright reject the commitment made in 2005. Most Southern states shared the concerns their Non-Aligned Movement expressed and with China, for example, averred: "The concept of 'RtoP' applies only to the four international crimes of 'genocide, war crimes, ethnic cleansing, and crimes against humanity.' No state should expand on the concept or make arbitrary interpretations." Not authorizing an intervention in Myanmar during the Cyclone Kargis emergency implicitly excluded health, climate, and other natural disasters as appropriate triggers for RtoP. Thus, when it came to a consensus endorsement of the Secretary-General's report, the best that could be achieved was a tepid "takes note," rather than a more full-throated "approves" or "endorses."[36]

From the standpoint of international law, the commitment to RtoP was not legislative – not equivalent to either a Charter amendment of Chapter VII or an international treaty. But it was part of a twofold process bending the meaning of "international threats to the peace" as defined by the Council under Chapter VII.

First, while far from settled, RtoP is beginning to build the record of general practice supplementing the sense of obligation that builds customary international law. The RtoP norm does not quite qualify as *opinio juris vel necessitatis* – acting on the basis of legal obligation – but the repeated use of "responsibility" is approaching the normative commitment that evidences obligation.[37]

Second, it is important to recognize that the vast majority of states in 2009 were explicitly and implicitly endorsing the RtoP elements of genocide, war crimes, crimes against humanity, and ethnic cleansing as legitimate causes for the Security Council (when necessary) to authorize coercive force.

They were proposing a "license" and "leash": attempting to both broaden standards and narrow practice. Since General Assembly resolutions are not binding or measures that could amend the UN Charter, states, in effect, were trying to redefine and broaden the standard that does authorize force: Chapter VII's "international peace and security" language. At the same time, these same states were also denying the Security Council the discretion it had exercised so

---

[36] A. Maged Abdelaziz, "Statement by the Permanent Representative of Egypt on behalf of the Non-Aligned Movement" (New York: Permanent Mission of the Arab Republic of Egypt, 2009). Liu Zhenmin, "Statement by Ambassador Liu Zhenmin at the Plenary Session of GA Debate on Responsibility to Protect" (New York: Permanent Mission of China, 2009). U.K.Z.M., "Statement of the Deputy Permanent Representative of the Union of Myanmar to the United Nations on Agenda Item 44 and 107" (New York: Permanent Mission of Myanmar, 2009). Dept. of Public Information, "Delegates Weigh Legal Merits of RtoP Concept," GA/10850 (July 28, 2009), available at: un.org/News/Press/docs/2009/ga10850. doc.htm.

[37] The standards are from *North Sea Continental Shelf Case* (International Court of Justice, 1969).

often in the 1990s to auto-interpret "international peace and security" seemingly without restraint or credible attention to "international." Will this new assertion of an authoritative interpretive role by the General Assembly create a lasting precedent?[38]

RtoP could not claim clear legality, but it could claim "legitimacy" after the 2005 Summit Outcome. In this light, it is worth recalling that Security Council action during the Rwandan genocide was in part stymied by claims from Rwanda and its few supporters on the Council that the crisis was a domestic issue, not one subject to international authority.[39] Ironically, the increasing power of the norm is reflected in the way in which the United States invoked humanitarian concerns generally and Russia invoked RtoP explicitly to try to justify their interventions in Iraq (2003) and Georgia (2008). But the experience of Libya and Syria may prove decisive in strengthening or weakening the doctrine.

This has implications for international ethics. Realists will need to acknowledge that RtoP is becoming part of what constitutes the conventional standards of stabilizing behavior – standards that should be overridden only when significant security interests are at stake. Socialists, while challenging borders in the name of class solidarity, will also need to acknowledge that there is a new floor and standard for acceptable national policy that legally bars a state from intervention.

Clearly, RtoP is most consequential for Liberals. On its face it defines and limits what are acceptable communitarian standards from an international point of view. The principle of sovereignty can protect states from a wide and poorly defined set of interferences, but no longer from proportional, Security Council-endorsed actions to prevent or stop the four harms outlined in the RtoP doctrine. It also operates against the cosmopolitan conception of utilitarian calculus, where every harm counts the same and the sum of harms (including preventable starvation, for example) rather than the kind of harms (e.g., RtoP's four harms) counts the most.

We should not assume that it will resolve the most important issue of political will – getting states to take these principles seriously, abide by them, and

---

[38] The Charter has been informally amended before, as when states chose to define SC abstentions not to have the effect of permanent-member vetoes despite Article 27's provision that substantive decisions of the Security Council have the "affirming" and "concurring votes" of the five permanent members. This process of deliberation and interpretation is well covered in Ian Johnstone, *The Power of Deliberation* (Oxford University Press, 2011).

[39] See the important personal account by the former Czech permanent representative to the United Nations, and then Security Council member, Karel Kovanda, in "The Czech Republic on the UN Security Council," *Journal of Genocide Studies and Prevention* (2010).

be willing, where justified, to enforce them.[40] Nor does RtoP resolve debates in moral philosophy. Much of the value of ethical thinking is that it constantly questions received standards in the name of security, solidarity, and human welfare. And RtoP should not be immune from this critique.

[40] At a special, unofficial meeting, a "retreat of the Security Council" at Pocantico Hills, New York, in May 2001, all the permanent representatives of the 15 members were prepared to acknowledge that RtoP was a legitimate cause of action for Security Council enforcement, but none was prepared to publicly issue a statement that it constituted a general responsibility to act. The case-by-case language of paragraphs 138 and 139 reaffirmed in 2005 this reluctance.

12

Responsibility to protect and the language of crimes
Collective action and individual culpability

JENNIFER M. WELSH

The debate surrounding the legitimacy of armed humanitarian intervention often constructs a duel between those committed to the protection of individual rights and those concerned with preserving the rights of sovereign entities to non-interference. This framing, however, obscures the fact that there are *three* sets of ethical and legal norms that collide in situations of mass human suffering: the inviolability of state sovereignty (and the associated norm of territorial integrity); the right of individuals to be free of gross violations of their rights (particularly the right to life); and the just-war injunction against the use of force, except as a last resort. The latter principle, which arises from a sober recognition of the human suffering, physical destruction, and political and social instability that frequently accompanies the use of military force, is often forgotten in the heated exchanges between proponents of individual rights and the guardians of sovereign rights. Yet the imperative of last resort has become central to contemporary efforts to forge a consensus around the implementation of the principle of the Responsibility to Protect (RtoP),[1] particularly in the wake of 2011 military action in Libya, which many countries in the global South viewed as an illegitimate extension of the mandate of civilian protection to the more contested objective of overthrowing the Gaddafi regime.[2] A Brazilian government initiative, *Responsibility while Protecting*, is aimed at reinterpreting RtoP – and enhancing the consensus around it – by emphasizing the international community's *non-military* options for exercising the norm, limiting the recourse to force to instances in which diplomatic and other means

[1] As suggested elsewhere in this volume, it is important to distinguish between the broader principle of Responsibility to Protect and the specific practice of armed humanitarian intervention. The former can encompass a wide range of responses to humanitarian crises, including negotiation, sanctions, or other non-military tools. In addition, it involves a broad array of actors (states, international organizations, and non-governmental organizations) and not just those with the capacity to use military force. Finally, while armed humanitarian intervention is primarily reactive, RtoP places strong emphasis on the prevention of humanitarian crises.
[2] See, for example, statements by Permanent Representatives Viotti (Brazil), Churkin (Russia), and Sangqu (South Africa) in the Security Council in the months following the authorization of the military action in Libya. UN document, S/PV.6531 (May 10, 2011).

have been exhausted, and strengthening the accountability of those who act militarily on behalf of the Council.[3]

The most common approach to overcoming the tension among the three norms outlined above is to insist that interventions for humanitarian purposes must be limited to extreme emergencies – what Michael Walzer memorably referred to as actions that "shock the moral conscience of mankind."[4] Conscious of the historical record, in which states have used the cover of humanitarianism to dominate their neighbors or pursue other strategic ends, Walzer reserves the practice of humanitarian intervention for situations of massacre and enslavement. Interventions aimed at redressing the suppression of political rights, or the denial of democracy, are unlikely to generate support as *humanitarian* crises, which justify infringements of sovereignty or the prohibition on the use of force. It is only in extreme cases, when governments turn savagely upon their own people, that we must, in Walzer's words, "doubt the very existence of a political community" and therefore suspend the principle of non-intervention.[5]

The strategy of focusing on conscience-shocking situations was also adopted by the International Commission on Intervention and State Sovereignty (ICISS), whose 2001 report marked a critical stage in the development of the principle of RtoP. Like Walzer, the Commissioners' starting point is the norm of non-intervention, which they insist should be the default position of the international community. It is only in grave and rare circumstances, they argue, that it is legitimate to depart from this important ordering principle of international society. Thus, in its discussion of the threshold for justifying military action, the Commission insists that "there must be serious and irreparable harm occurring to human beings, or imminently likely to occur." More specifically, the report refers to "large-scale loss of life" (with or without genocidal intent) or "large-scale ethnic cleansing."[6]

Despite this attempt to specify the threshold for intervention, the ICISS report left unresolved the precise circumstances which the label of RtoP was intended to cover. Did it encompass only intentional killing, or also, for example, widespread human-rights violations short of violent death or deaths that occurred during what the Commissioners referred to as "overwhelming natural or environmental catastrophes"?[7] In 2005, at the UN World Summit,

---

[3] In November 2011, the Brazilian Permanent Representative sent an official letter to the Secretary-General with an annex entitled "Responsibility while Protecting: Elements for the Development and Promotion of a Concept," UN document, A/66/551-S/2011/701 (November 11, 2011).

[4] Michael Walzer, *Just and Unjust Wars*, 3rd edn. (New York: Basic Books, 2000), 107.

[5] *Ibid.*, 101.

[6] *The Responsibility to Protect*, Report of the International Commission on Intervention and State Sovereignty (Ottawa: International Development Research Centre, 2001), xii.

[7] *Ibid.*, 33, para. 4.20.

heads of state and government took a further step toward clarifying the scope of RtoP, by confining it to four specific crimes: genocide, crimes against humanity, ethnic cleansing, and war crimes.[8] Article 138 of the Outcome Document acknowledges the responsibility of individual sovereign states to protect their own populations from these atrocity crimes, and to prevent both their commission and incitement. The subsequent paragraph, Article 139, endows the international community (working through the United Nations) with a remedial responsibility to take collective action, "on a case-by-case basis," using diplomatic, humanitarian and – if necessary – forceful means in situations where national authorities "are manifestly failing to protect their populations" from such crimes.

This chapter assesses the impact of the 2005 move to frame RtoP in criminal terms. The first section argues that while the narrowing of the scope of RtoP to four particular crimes was designed to forge a greater consensus around the extraordinary situations that might justify the use of force, contestation has lingered over the trigger point for activating international action. In the second section, I demonstrate that the framing of RtoP in the language of crimes has significant implications for the broader approach to conflict prevention and resolution that has traditionally been used by international institutions such as the United Nations. In particular, the imperative to protect individuals from criminal acts has compromised another imperative that for a generation defined UN diplomacy and peacekeeping: to treat both sides as equal. Drawing on the cases of Libya and Syria, I focus on two particular practices that flow from this relinquishing of impartiality: (1) the tendency to employ a "rational actor" framework, which creates fixed categories of perpetrators and victims; and (2) the increased use of the threat of criminal justice as a tool of preventive diplomacy. In the final section, I posit a tension between the idea of responsibility to protect as a *collective* responsibility – held and operationalized by the international community as a whole – and the need within most criminal frameworks for a centralized authority to both threaten and deliver justice.

Greater precision, but continuing contestation

It is commonplace within International Relations literature, both rationalist and constructivist, to see institutionalization and legalization as important steps toward facilitating compliance with norms. According to this view, the specificity provided by the World Summit Outcome Document should have dampened contestation around the scope of RtoP and brought states' expectations

---

[8] *2005 World Summit Outcome*, UN General Assembly Resolution, UN document A/60/1 (October 24, 2005), paras. 138 and 139.

about appropriate behavior into greater alignment.[9] During the difficult negotiations over the text for the 2005 document, states concerned about creating
a pretext for widespread intervention succeeded in forging agreement around
a conception of RtoP that was limited to the four crimes outlined above.[10] This
list was similar to those crimes which had been identified in both the 1998
Rome Statue and the 2001 Constitutive Act of the African Union, and therefore
reflected definitions which states had already accepted as legitimate.

In particular, the formulation in Articles 138 and 139 of the Outcome
Document was designed to add greater precision to the original ICISS notion
of "large scale." This narrower reading of RtoP quickly became the settled interpretation within the United Nations system. For example, after Cyclone Nargis
wreaked its devastation in Myanmar in 2008, and some commentators – such
as former French Foreign Minister Bernard Kouchner – tried to claim that the
government's slow provision of humanitarian assistance constituted a crime
against humanity, China (supported by some other Asian countries) strongly
opposed any attempt to coerce Myanmar into accepting humanitarian assistance from other countries.[11] These states also insisted that RtoP, as defined in
2005, was not applicable to natural disasters – a view that was shared by many
high-level officials within the United Nations, including Secretary-General Ban
Ki-moon, who worried about stretching the concept beyond operational utility
and damaging the fragile consensus on the principle that had been achieved
at the World Summit.[12] As one of RtoP's most passionate advocates, ICISS
Co-Chair Gareth Evans, has argued:

> to use the responsibility to protect too broadly, in non-mass-atrocity
> contexts, is to dilute to the point of uselessness its role as a mobilizer of
> instinctive, universal action in cases of conscience-shocking killing, eth-
> nic cleansing, and other such crimes against humanity ... if R2P is about

[9] Martha Finnemore and Kathryn Sikkink, "International Norm Dynamic and Political
     Change," *International Organization* 52, no. 4 (1998), 887–917; Ann Florini, "The Evolution
     of International Norms," *International Studies Quarterly* 40, no. 3 (1996), 363–89; Kenneth
     W. Abbott, Robert O. Keohane, Andrew Moravcsik, Anne-Marie Slaughter, and Duncan
     Snidal, "The Concept of Legalization," *International Organization* 54, no. 3 (2000), 401–19.
[10] For an overview of diplomacy leading to endorsement of RtoP, see Alex J. Bellamy, *Global
     Politics and the Responsibility to Protect: From Words to Deeds* (London and New York:
     Routledge, 2011), 21–25.
[11] M. Bernard Kouchner, "Burma," *Le Monde* (May 20, 2008). For the views of two ICISS
     Commissioners on this case, see Ramesh Thakur, "Should the UN Invoke the 'Responsibility
     to Protect'?" *Globe and Mail* (May 8, 2008); and Gareth Evans, "Facing Up to Our
     Responsibilities," *Guardian* (May 12, 2008).
[12] *Implementing the Responsibility to Protect*, Report of the Secretary-General, UN document,
     A/63/677 (January 2009), para. 10b. For further discussion of the issue of "stretching" RtoP,
     see Joanna Harrington, "R2P and Natural Disasters," in Andy W. Knight and Frazer Egerton
     (eds.), *The Routledge Handbook of the Responsibility to Protect* (New York: Routledge, 2012),
     141–51.

protecting everybody from everything, it will end up protecting nobody from anything.[13]

Proponents of a limited scope for RtoP insist that a narrower meaning does not detract from the gravity of the acts that the principle is designed to address. Three of the four crimes specified in the Outcome Document (genocide, crimes against humanity, and war crimes) form part of a unique and distinct category in international law, known as "international crimes." Unlike transnational crimes, which arise from the various international conventions concluded by states to control criminal activities that have trans-boundary effects (such as counterfeiting, money laundering, drug or arms trafficking, or the financing of terrorism), international crimes encompass acts which threaten values considered vital to the international community as a whole. These *extraordinary* crimes transform those who commit them into what Mark Drumbl calls "enem[ies] of all humankind."[14] Consequently, there is both a universal interest in repressing them and mechanisms for holding perpetrators of such crimes accountable at the international level.[15] Indeed, because crimes represent socially stigmatized behavior, not mere wrongdoing, they incorporate society's (in this case, *international society's*) norms and beliefs about appropriate behavior and arguably create a stronger imperative to respond.

But while the Outcome Document did provide greater precision around RtoP's meaning, and restricted its application to the most egregious wrongdoings in international society, the employment of crimes language has not ended the debate over the threshold that should activate coercive action. There are two reasons for this continuing contestation.

First, as Don Hubert and Ariela Blätter have argued, there has, to date, been surprisingly little effort to articulate in more detail what these four crimes entail so that debates about RtoP can move beyond more general notions of humanitarian crisis. Drawing on international legal standards, they contend that the four RtoP crimes outlined in the Outcome Document are not all of equal importance or relevance, and that the legal category of crimes against humanity represents the best characterization of the kind of large-scale and systematic targeting of individuals that the principle of RtoP was designed to address.[16] First,

---

[13] Gareth Evans, *The Responsibility to Protect: Ending Mass Atrocity Crimes Once and For All* (Washington, DC: Brookings, 2008), 64–65.

[14] Mark Drumbl, *Atrocity, Punishment and International Law* (Cambridge University Press, 2007), 4.

[15] Antonio Cassese, *International Criminal Law*, 2nd edn. (Oxford University Press, 2008), 11–12. The fourth international crime, aggression, is not encompassed by the principle of RtoP.

[16] Don Hubert and Ariela Blätter, "The Responsibility to Protect as International Crimes Prevention," *Global Responsibility to Protect* 4 (2012), 33–66. Their efforts to specify the scope of RtoP are similar to those taken by the International Criminal Court to determine

unlike war crimes – which require the specific context of armed conflict – crimes against humanity can be committed in both war and peacetime (including situations of government-sponsored violence against a rebelling population). Second, whereas war crimes can include random acts committed by a single soldier or member of a rebel group, crimes against humanity are more widespread and demand some evidence of an organizational policy. Third, while crimes against humanity encompass instances of genocide, they do not need to satisfy the latter's demanding requirement of proof of discriminatory intent. Thus, for example, the acts committed by Janjaweed militia against civilians in Darfur, while not initially found to constitute genocide, did satisfy the requirements of crimes against humanity.[17] Furthermore, whereas genocide refers particularly to racial, religious, or ethnic groups, crimes against humanity can be committed against any population. Finally, while the term "ethnic cleansing" is prominent in popular discourse, it has an ambiguous status in international law and is usually subsumed under other crimes.[18] Crimes against humanity, by contrast, are firmly established as a category in international jurisprudence and have led to systematic efforts to establish what would serve as evidence of such crimes.

However, even if we were to agree that the threshold for justifying coercive international action is the commission or threat of crimes against humanity, this would not ensure that states and other actors would begin to consistently act on the precepts of RtoP. This brings us to the second factor: the common tendency for norms to generate contestation over their meaning *as they are used*.[19] Contestation over the scope of a norm can persist beyond its early genesis into the post-legalized, implementation phase, particularly as new circumstances and crises (different from those surrounding the norm's birth) arise.[20]

In the case of RtoP, contestation has continued not only over how to respond, but also, at a more substantive level, over what situations should be identified, to use Evans' phrase, as "countries of R2P concern": cases where atrocity crimes are occurring or imminent, or where circumstances might deteriorate

levels of "gravity" when considering the crimes under its jurisdiction which it will seek to prosecute.

[17] See *Report of the International Commission of Inquiry on Darfur to the United Nations Secretary-General* (Geneva; January 25, 2005).

[18] For a discussion of ethnic cleansing's status, see David Scheffer, "Atrocity Crimes Framing the Responsibility to Protect," *Case Western Reserve Journal of International Law* 40, no. 1 (2008), 128–29.

[19] Antje Weiner, "Enacting Meaning-in-Use: Qualitative Research on Norms and International Relations," *Review of International Studies* 35, no. 1 (2009), 175–93.

[20] Weiner suggests that contestation is conditioned by both changes in practice and situations of crisis, which can reduce the "social feedback" necessary to interpret a norm and therefore heighten the possibility for different meanings to emerge. See *The Invisible Constitution of World Politics* (Cambridge University Press, 2008), 6.

to produce crisis in the medium term.[21] So, for example, in the spring of 2009, at the height of the Sri Lankan government's military assault against the Tamil Tigers, advocates of RtoP engaged in a lengthy debate as to whether the approximately 150,000 civilians caught up in the fighting in the jungle area near Mutulivu were being subjected to atrocity crimes.[22] On the one hand, actors like the NGO, Global Centre for the Responsibility to Protect, called on the Security Council to place the situation on its agenda and act upon its responsibility to protect civilians in Sri Lanka by dispatching an envoy to the region and considering the imposition of sanctions.[23] This view was supported by some UN member states, who also asserted that the crisis should be characterized in RtoP terms. Others, however, insisted that the Sri Lankan government was engaged in an existential battle with terrorists that had threatened all its citizens for decades, and that its actions were therefore both necessary and proportionate. They also argued that it was unclear whether the alleged "victims" of the aerial bombardment (or the later occupants of displacement camps) were all innocent civilians. One of the original ICISS Commissioners, Ramesh Thakur, accused Western states of hypocrisy in their critique of Sri Lankan officials and calls for a ceasefire, given the intense focus that they had given to counter-terrorism in their foreign policy, post-9/11. "Given the Tigers' nature and record," he wrote, "it was not unreasonable for the government to acquire the capacity and demonstrate the determination to defeat the Tigers as part of its responsibility to protect."[24] In the end, Sri Lankan diplomacy was successful in making its case and preventing the crisis from being considered by the Security Council under the banner of RtoP.

Such substantive disagreement is exacerbated by the fact that it is frequently the Council – a political rather than legal body – that is tasked with making assessments about the nature or likelihood of atrocity crimes in particular situations. In order to do so, it often relies upon fact-finding missions or commissions of inquiry to establish the "facts." However, these bodies cannot always deliver definitive or timely assessments that enable the Council to respond decisively to escalating crises. In the case of Syria, for example, the initial report

---

[21] Evans, *Responsibility to Protect*, 71.

[22] The civilians were prevented from leaving by the Tamil Tigers (Liberation Tigers of Tamil Eelam, LTTE), who effectively used them as human shields. They subsequently became the victims of government bombing and mortar fire aimed at the LTTE and were denied access to humanitarian assistance from international NGOs working in the country. Once the government captured the area, the civilians were transferred to government-run camps where they endured harsh conditions and had minimal access to medical support.

[23] "Open Letter from the Global Centre for the Responsibility to Protect to the UN Security Council" (April 15, 2009). The letter was signed by, among others, the former UN Coordinator for Humanitarian Affairs, Jan Egeland, and the former Special Advisor on the Prevention of Genocide, Juan Méndez.

[24] Ramesh Thakur, "West Shouldn't Fault Sir Lankan Government Tactics," *Daily Yomiuri* (June 12, 2009).

of the Independent International Commission of Inquiry on the Syrian Arab
Republic could not definitively establish responsibility for the May 2012 massacre at Houla, in which over 100 people (half of them children) were killed.
While media reports at the time tended to blame the incident on local militia operating with, or under the orders of, Syrian government security forces,
the Commission outlined two other sets of potential perpetrators which it
could not yet rule out: anti-government forces trying to escalate the conflict
and to punish those not supporting the rebellion, and foreign fighters with an
unknown affiliation.[25] For its part, the Syrian government claimed that it had
been defending itself at Houla from "terrorist" attacks and that large numbers
of its own soldiers had been killed. Two months later, in its final report, the
Commission concluded that the Houla massacre had indeed been committed
by Syrian government forces and militia, backed by state officials at the highest
levels, and that the killings met the requirements of the war crime of murder.[26]
But by then, the moment for decisive political action had passed; the Security
Council was hopelessly deadlocked over how to respond to the escalating crisis, a draft resolution on tougher measures against the Assad regime having
been vetoed by both China and Russia in July 2012.

Examples like these highlight a key weakness in relying on a criminalized
conception of RtoP. The problem, alluded to by David Luban and Henry Shue
in their discussion of torture, is the tendency to equate the narrowness and precision of criminal categories with the defining features of the wrong in question.
As a result of this "forensic fallacy," they write, concepts of right and wrong are
weakened; the criminal law definition, "cramped and narrowed," becomes *the*
de facto policy definition as well.[27] But though it might appear more rigorous
to limit the discussion and implementation of RtoP to four crimes, the criminal definition of the acts associated with this important principle cannot be
authoritative for all purposes. With respect to the Security Council, it will usually be the case – as it was in Libya in March of 2011 – that diplomats must pass
judgment on the necessity and legitimacy of action to forestall atrocities *without* firm knowledge that crimes are being committed.[28] In such time-sensitive

---

[25] *Oral Update of the Independent International Commission of Inquiry on the Syrian Arab
Republic*, UN document, A/HRC/20/CRP.1 (June 26, 2012). The Commission was not able
to visit the site of the killings before issuing this update, and therefore it relied on interviews
with witnesses, information provided by governmental and non-governmental sources,
and satellite imagery.

[26] *Report of the Independent International Commission of Inquiry on the Syrian Arab Republic*,
UN document, A/HRC/21/50 (August 15, 2012).

[27] David Luban and Henry Shue, "Mental Torture: A Critique of Erasures in US Law," *The
Georgetown Law Journal* 100 (2012), 850–55.

[28] In Resolution 1970, the Security Council referred the situation in Libya to the International
Criminal Court, and requested the Chief Prosecutor to determine whether war crimes and
crimes against humanity had been committed. See UN document, S/Res/1970 (February
26, 2011). The Prosecutor did not come back to the Council until May, at which point he

situations, despite the invocation of legal discourse, political and moral considerations will predominate.

The implications of criminalization

Framing RtoP in the language of crimes also has implications for the broader approach to conflict prevention and resolution employed by the United Nations, an institution at the center of efforts to implement the principle. The United Nations remains, at its core, a state-based organization, founded on the recognition of sovereign equality and a desire to eradicate conflict between states. Although Chapter VII of the Charter empowers the Security Council with the right to identify those who threaten the peace, and to mobilize the efforts of member states to respond to affronts to international order, in reality the Council has operationalized this "finger-pointing" power in only a handful of cases.[29] Instead, through the creative interpretation of Chapter VI and the practice of peacekeeping, the United Nations since 1945 has tended to eschew notions of blame and punishment in favor of impartiality, minimal use of force, and host-state consent for its activities. Indeed, these three principles have become a kind of "holy trinity" that defines the United Nations' posture with respect to both interstate and intrastate conflict. This is why Security Council Resolution 1973, which authorized the use of force against Libya, *without its consent*, in the pursuit of humanitarian objectives, was such a path-breaking moment for the United Nations' commitment to civilian protection.[30]

However, if the United Nations in general, and the Security Council in particular, is to act on its responsibility to protect populations from *crimes*, its state-based perspective and commitment to treat both sides as equal may not always be appropriate or possible to maintain. Crimes are most often understood as acts committed *by* perpetrators *against* victims. This has two implications. First, it involves a move away from states or regimes, toward *individuals* who are plotting or preparing to carry out attacks, and toward *individuals* who need protecting. Second, the actions required to change the incentives of the former (for example, through targeted sanctions or threats of prosecution), and to decrease the vulnerability of the latter (for example, though no-fly

---

indicated that on the basis of evidence gathered, he planned to seek arrest warrants for Colonel Gaddafi, his son Saif al-Islam, and the regime's intelligence chief Abdullah al-Sanussi. See *Security Council Press Release*, UN document, SC/10241 (May 4, 2011).

[29] The most prominent examples include the UN responses to the North Korean invasion of South Korea in 1950, and the Iraqi invasion of Kuwait in 1990.

[30] Alex J. Bellamy, "Libya and the Responsibility to Protect: The Exception and the Norm," *Ethics & International Affairs* 25, no. 3 (Fall 2011), 263–70. As Bellamy notes, while the Security Council authorized "all necessary means" to protect civilians in other instances, such as Haiti, Bosnia, the Congo, and Sudan, in all of these cases there were pre-existing peacekeeping missions operating with the consent of the host state.

zones or the provision of arms), will invariably involve choosing sides. And
with this choice will come a narrowing of opportunities for political settlement
and charges of bias against the United Nations. In some of the United Nations'
more recent peacekeeping efforts, where there have been alleged crimes against
humanity, the meaning of impartiality has been stretched almost to breaking
point. This can be demonstrated, for example, by the United Nations' helicop-
ter strikes against hardware close to the palace of the former President of Côte
d'Ivoire, Laurent Gbagbo, following the stand-off over disputed election results
in 2011[31] – a response which was seen by some member states of the United
Nations as decidedly partial. Diplomatic representatives from China and India,
for example, insisted that UN peacekeepers had inappropriately crossed a
line, becoming parties to the conflict rather than abiding by the principle of
impartiality.[32]

The application of a crimes lens has also encouraged two practices that have
the potential to complicate – or in some cases undermine – both the protection
of populations and the pursuit of justice for crimes committed.

The limits of a "rational actor" framework

The first is the tendency to employ a "rational actor" framework, with fixed
categories of perpetrators and victims, when designing strategies for responding to or preventing RtoP crimes. Perpetrators are approached as shrewd cal-
culators of costs and benefits, who can be denied the means to commit their
crimes or deterred through sanctions or threats of punishment. Victims, on
the other hand, are viewed as weak, vulnerable, and in need of both protection
and deliberate assistance from third parties to "tilt the balance" in their favor.
But the use of these labels inhibits outsiders' appreciation of the fluid identities
of actors within a conflict situation. Today's victims can quickly morph into
tomorrow's perpetrators – particularly if they are supplied with material and
financial support from the outside. This was vividly illustrated during the latter
phases of the conflict in Libya, when rebel fighters committed atrocities against
Gaddafi loyalists, captured soldiers, and foreign nationals suspected of fighting

---

[31] In December 2010, the Security Council passed a resolution declaring Gbagbo's opponent,
Alassane Ouattara, winner of the election and called on all parties to accept this result. UN
document, SC/Res/1962 (December 20, 2010). A few months later, as the situation deteri-
orated, it unanimously passed a resolution condemning Gbagbo's refusal to negotiate and
authorizing "all necessary means" to protect civilians. UN document, SC/Res/1975 (March
30, 2011).

[32] Their views, along with those of other Council members, can be found in the debate surrounding the passage of Resolution 1975. See UN document, S/PV.6508 (March 30, 2011).
For further discussion of the controversy created by the UN's action in Côte d'Ivoire, see
Alex J. Bellamy and Paul D. Williams, "The New Politics of Protection? Côte d'Ivoire, Libya,
and the Responsibility to Protect," *International Affairs* 87, no. 4 (2011), 825–50.

on behalf of Gaddafi as mercenaries.[33] The general label of "perpetrator" also simplifies the very different motives and standing of those who resort to mass violence. As Drumbl has shown, atrocity situations usually involve at least three different categories of perpetrator: so-called conflict entrepreneurs (who are the commanders of violence); intermediaries (who receive orders but also exercise some authority over others); and actual killers ("ordinary" people who are conforming to perceived social expectations or, in some cases, committing crimes under duress).[34] This suggests that, at a minimum, the rational-actor framework needs refinement if it is to generate effective strategies to persuade and punish perpetrators.

More broadly, as hinted above, the very notion of perpetrator may forestall efforts to negotiate political solutions to conflicts that provide the context (or in some cases, the impetus) for atrocity crimes. To put it another way, if the goal is the civilian protection, then – in theory – actions that bring violence and violations of international humanitarian law to an end should be welcomed, even if they accommodate particular individuals as part of the post-conflict settlement. This was precisely the argument forwarded by some African states, most notably South Africa, as the NATO-bombing campaign in Libya continued. Once Gaddafi no longer posed an immediate threat to civilians, they contended, the skies should have fallen silent and the negotiations on a political transition should have begun.[35] Russian diplomats at the United Nations have leveled a similar kind of charge over the crisis in Syria, criticizing the language of blame and confrontation that they believe underpins the strategy of Western members of the Council. In the Russian view (which is also heavily influenced by geostrategic factors), the international community must pursue even-handed dialogue that does not treat one of the parties as a criminal outlaw, but rather criticizes both parties for the use of violence and accommodates both as part of any political settlement.[36]

But these cases raise the question of whether the prevention of, or response to, atrocity crimes can ever employ "true" mediation, which is guided by impartiality. If RtoP is about crimes, can international actors adopt a stance whereby any outcome, as long as agreed to by negotiating parties, is acceptable? Some scholars of mediation contend that while mediation should treat *parties*

---

[33] See *The Battle for Libya: Killings, Disappearances and Torture*, Report of Amnesty International (September 13, 2011).

[34] Drumbl, *Atrocity*, 25–35.

[35] The views of South African diplomats can be found in the May 2011 debate on the Protection of Civilians, during which the crisis in Libya was discussed. See UN document, S/PV.6531 (May 10, 2011). South Africa also expressed concern about the UN's move away from imparitiality during the 2011 crisis in Côte d'Ivoire. See Thabo Mbeki, "What the World got Wrong in Côte D'Ivoire," *Foreign Policy* (April 29, 2011), available at: www.foreign-policy.com/articles/2011/04/29/What_the_world_got_wrong_in_cote_d_ivoire (accessed November 26, 2012).

[36] Russian views were expressed during the Council debate surrounding the vetoed resolution of July 2012. See UN document, S/PV.6810 (July 19, 2012).

even-handedly, it cannot be impartial with respect to underlining international *norms*. The latter must be upheld vigorously and consistently.[37] This would suggest, however, that mediation efforts in cases involving the threat or commission of mass-atrocity crimes would have difficulty offering political "side deals" to particular individuals with liability for criminal acts. Yet, it is precisely such deals that many believe are essential to the resolution of conflict.[38]

The false promise of deterrence?

The second effect of applying a crimes lens has been the increased use of criminal-justice mechanisms, particularly the threat of prosecution, as a tool of coercive diplomacy in situations where atrocity crimes have been committed or are imminent. In the case of Libya, for example, the Security Council's referral of the crisis to the International Criminal Court (in Resolution 1970) was explicitly designed to try to pressure Gaddafi into changing his behavior and to encourage defections from his regime. The fact that in the run-up to the vote on the resolution Council members debated whether to refer, or merely to *threaten* to refer, illustrates that the prospect of prosecution was viewed primarily as part of a package of threats to dissuade, as opposed to a mechanism of justice.

In many respects, this practice has been actively encouraged by institutions such as the United Nations and the International Criminal Court (ICC). In his 2009 report on the responsibility to protect, Secretary-General Ban Ki-moon refers to the role of the International Criminal Court and UN-assisted tribunals as tools of dissuasion and deterrence.[39] Similarly, the UN Office of Legal Affairs, which participated in the drafting of the 1998 Rome Statute, observed that "[e]ffective deterrence is a primary objective of those working to establish the International Criminal Court."[40]

Assessing the effectiveness of threats of prosecution in deterring atrocity crimes is a difficult task which is beyond the scope of this chapter.[41] However, it is worth noting that even those involved in prosecution and the prevention of

---

[37] Eileen Babbitt, "Mediation and the Prevention of Mass Atrocities," in Monica Serrano and Tom Weiss (eds.), *The International Politics of Human Rights: Rallying to the R2P Cause?* (Paterson: Routledge, 2014).

[38] This view is expressed most clearly by Jack Snyder and Leslie Vinjamuri in "Trials and Errors: Principle and Pragmatism in Strategies of International Justice," *International Security* 28, no. 3 (2003/2004), 5–44.

[39] *Implementing the Responsibility to Protect*, para. 18.

[40] Martin Mennecke, "Punishing Genocidaires: A Deterrent Effect or Not?" *Human Rights Review* 8, no. 4 (2007), 319. The preamble to the Rome Statute also speaks of the importance of ending impunity so that future crimes can be prevented. See UN document, A/CONF.183/9 (July 17, 1998).

[41] For one attempt at such an assessment, see Dan Saxon, "The International Criminal Court and the Prevention of Crimes," paper presented to the Workshop on the Responsibility to Prevent, Oxford Institute for Ethics, Law and Armed Conflict (December 9, 2011).

genocide doubt some of the expansive claims made about the impact of criminal justice.[42] What we *do* know is that deterrence is a process involving subjective assessments, and that threats of criminal justice will only be effective if potential perpetrators both fear prosecution (because of its severity) and believe that prosecution is a real possibility. Indeed, some researchers have found that the latter has a stronger deterrent effect than the former.[43] As former international criminal prosecutor Dan Saxon argues, this result highlights "the simplistic nature of suggestions that the mere existence of institutions such as the ICC will deter the commission of crimes. The ICC will have a strong deterrent effect only when it can demonstrate to potential perpetrators that the court has the consistent ability to hold individuals accountable for their actions."[44] In order for it to do so, political as well as legal preconditions must be in place – most notably a willingness on the part of states to promptly execute arrest warrants.

The case of Libya illustrates the limits and consequences of deterrence in practice. First, and most obviously, referral to the International Criminal Court did not deter high-level members of the Gaddafi regime from continuing their attacks or planning their intended assault on Benghazi. (Though there is anecdotal evidence that threats of prosecution may have played a role in some decisions to defect and in prompting Colonel Gaddafi to consult lawyers in London about his options.) In addition, the Council's resolution was not accompanied by clear signals that exile or asylum would not be tolerated – thereby leaving the impression that indictment and prosecution would not necessarily be pursued. At the same time, however, the threat of prosecution (and subsequent indictment) may well have foreclosed other avenues for resolving the conflict through negotiation – arguably prolonging the suffering of civilians.

These effects reflected a tension at the heart of the Security Council's approach – one that is linked to the trend away from impartiality. On the one hand, as part of its coercive diplomacy, it imposed targeted sanctions (such as asset freezes and travel bans) on particular members of the Gaddafi regime. These sanctions were made conditional; "better behavior" (i.e., meeting the demands of the Council) could have led to the lifting of such measures. On the other hand, referrals and indictments are inherently unconditional; they cannot be retracted. Therefore, once employed, there is no room for give and take. The fact that the Security Council combined both of these measures, simultaneously, reveals an uncertainty (or even a confusion) over whether it really

---

[42] Juan Méndez, then the Special Advisor on the Prevention of Genocide to the United Nations Secretary-General, observed in 2004 that the idea that criminal punishment plays a role in the prevention of crimes was "an act of faith." See Mennecke, "Punishing Genocidaires," 319.

[43] See Andrew von Hirsch, Anthony E. Bottoms, Elizabeth Burney, and Per-Olof H. Wikstrom, *Criminal Deterrence and Sentence Severity: An Analysis of Recent Research* (Oxford: Hart Publishing, 1999), 5, 46.

[44] Saxon, "The International Criminal Court."

wants to deal with perpetrators – by involving them in a political settlement – or whether it believes their behavior is unchangeable and that they should be handed over for criminal prosecution.[45] Given that most of the contexts in which RtoP crimes occur are political conflicts (that have been militarized),[46] the question of whether and how to address criminal behavior will continue to confront those charged with operationalizing RtoP.

There is one final problematic aspect of efforts to deter perpetrators with Security Council referrals: the potential to erode the standing and legitimacy of the International Criminal Court itself. The Rome Statute envisages that most states will themselves prosecute international crimes, as signatories of the treaty, thereby avoiding the need for justice to be meted out by the International Criminal Court. Council referrals are therefore to be exceptional measures, relevant only in those cases where the country in question has not ratified the statute (as was the case in Libya in 2011). They were not intended to become part of the ordinary "toolkit" of international diplomacy, as they effectively run against the spirit of the treaty creating the International Criminal Court, which sought to create a consensual mode of accountability. Moreover, as Louise Arbour has argued, Council referral will appear to many as a profoundly unprincipled act, given that three permanent members of the Council are not parties to the Rome Statute and are therefore shielded from the possibility of ICC investigation.[47]

Conclusion

This chapter has argued that formulating RtoP in the language of crimes – while significant in helping to achieve the 2005 consensus and in clarifying the scope of the norm – has not ended debates about when international action is justified to address atrocities or how international actors should respond. It has also suggested that the criminal framework has problematic implications for the institutions tasked with operationalizing the norm, most notably the United Nations.

The adoption of a criminal framework also serves to individualize what is, at heart, a collective responsibility. The 2005 World Summit Outcome Document endows the international *community* with the responsibility to

[45] Leslie Vinjamuri, "Deterrence, Democracy, and the Pursuit of International Justice During Comflict," *Ethics & International Affairs* 24, no. 2 (2010), 191–211.

[46] A database of instances of mass atrocities (from 1945) compiled by Alex Bellamy shows that approximately two-thirds of episodes occurred in the context of armed conflict. See Alex J. Bellamy, "Mass Atrocities and Armed Conflict: Links, Distinctions, and Implications for the Responsibility to Prevent," *Policy Analysis Brief* (The Stanley Foundation, February 2011).

[47] Louise Arbour, "Address to the Stanley Foundation Conference on the Responsibility to Protect," New York (January 18).

protect populations. But as with many collective responsibilities, there is a need to further specify, or "distribute," the responsibility to protect to a more specific agent if it is to be meaningfully implemented.[48] I have argued elsewhere that while Article 139 of the Outcome Document distributes RtoP broadly to the United Nations, and to the Security Council, for the responses involving military force, the decentralized and politicized nature of the Council means that the effective exercise of that responsibility is frequently found wanting.[49] These problems of fragmented authority are compounded when the range of actors is broadened to include institutions of justice, such as the International Criminal Court, which are often tasked with carrying out aspects of the strategy to prevent or address "crimes" but which are also frequently undermined in their efforts by wavering Council commitment. Ultimately, even in collective bodies such as the Security Council, the international community rarely speaks with one, clear voice. The collective is fractured by narrower political considerations, differential capacities, or special relationships with the parties or individuals at the heart of the actual (or impending) crisis. The individuals committing or preparing to commit crimes against humanity know how to exploit these divisions, to the great cost of innocent victims.

---

[48] For more discussion of why and how collective responsibilities should be allocated, see David Miller, "Distributing Responsibilities," *Journal of Political Philosophy* 9, no. 4 (2001), 453–71; James Pattison, *Humanitarian Intervention and the Responsibility to Protect* (Oxford University Press, 2010).

[49] Jennifer M. Welsh, "Who Should Act? Collective Responsibility and the Responsibility to Protect," in Knight and Egerton, *Routledge Handbook*, 103–14.

13

Post-intervention

Permissions and prohibitions

BRIAN OREND

Almost always, with any kind of armed conflict, disproportionate attention gets showered on two major issues: (1) when (if ever) one should resort to war (*jus ad bellum*); and (2) how one should best fight that war, after it has begun (*jus in bello*).[1] But a war, of course, has not only a beginning, and a middle, but also an end. What should one do at the end of armed conflict? How should nations conduct themselves during the termination phase of war (*jus post bellum*)?[2]

Armed humanitarian intervention (AHI) is a kind of armed conflict, wherein the use of force is deemed necessary to protect innocent lives from severe violence, and/or slavery, and/or genocide, at the hands of a brutal, rights-violating regime. AHI is somewhat unique as a form of armed conflict because: (1) it involves moving forcefully into another country which has not committed *international* aggression; and (2) it is motivated, in the main, by the *moral objective* of saving lives (as opposed to various non-moral objectives, such as gaining control over natural resources).[3] Thus, we profit to examine not only the conditions under which AHI is permissible, and how best to fight an AHI, after that original decision has been made, but further how best to bring an AHI to a successful end, to the benefit of as many people as possible. This is the main subject of this chapter: post-intervention justice.

The method for this chapter will be as follows. First, we will examine different models of post-war justice in general. We will apply such models to real-world historical cases, to gain insight into exactly how they work, and the kinds of judgment to which they give rise. We will then look at armed humanitarian

---

[1] For perhaps the best treatment of such, see Michael Walzer, *Just and Unjust Wars*, 4th edn. (New York: Basic Books, 2006). See also Brian Orend, *The Morality of War* (Peterborough, Ontario: Broadview Press, 2006).

[2] An issue I first examined, inspired by Immanuel Kant, in Brian Orend, *War and International Justice: A Kantian Perspective* (Waterloo, Ontario: Wilfrid Laurier University Press, 2000), 217–67.

[3] Nicholas J. Wheeler, *Saving Strangers: Humanitarian Intervention in International Society* (Oxford University Press, 2000); Simon Chesterman, *Just War or Just Peace? Humanitarian Intervention and International Law* (Oxford University Press, 2001).

intervention as a particular kind of war, and see to what extent we can use the general models of post-war justice to guide our understanding. Here, too, we shall look at historical cases, ranging from Rwanda to Iraq to Libya. The culmination will be a substantial sense of the basic principles which ought to be operative in any post-AHI situation.

Post-war justice in general

There is, perhaps surprisingly, very little international law regulating things in this regard, unlike for *jus ad bellum* (governed, notably, by the UN Charter) and for *jus in bello* (regulated, famously, by the Hague and Geneva Conventions). The post-war preference, historically, has been for "the winner to enjoy the spoils of war," that is, for the war winner to impose whatever terms of peace it prefers upon the loser.[4] Generally, one of two approaches tends to be followed in this regard: retribution or rehabilitation. Let us examine each of these policies – their nature, strengths, and weaknesses – with illustrative application to recent, and ongoing, case studies. The result, hopefully, will be a much fuller sense of the deep choices nations confront in the aftermath of war in general.

The retribution *model of post-war policy*

According to the *retribution model*, the basic aspects of a decent post-war peace are as follows. (Crucially, they assume that "the good side" – that is, the countries with international law, *jus ad bellum*, and human rights on their side, at the start of the conflict – won, and that the aggressive side lost. This does not always happen, of course, as a matter of fact. But these are abstract models as to what states *ideally try to achieve* in the post-war period.)[5] The desired elements are:

- *Public peace treaty*. While it does not need to be particular in detail, the basic elements of a peace agreement should be written down, and publicly proclaimed, so that: everyone's expectations are clear, everyone knows the war is over, and everyone has an idea of what the general framework of the new post-war era will be. (Sometimes, by contrast – for example, back in medieval

---

[4] Michael Reisman and Chris T. Antoniou (eds.), *The Laws of War* (New York: Vintage, 1994); A. Roberts and R. Guelff (eds.), *Documentation on the Laws of War*, 3rd edn. (Oxford University Press, 2000); Gary D. Solis, *The Law of Armed Conflict: International Humanitarian Law in War* (Cambridge University Press, 2010).

[5] In practice, it thus becomes an issue of trying, as best one can, to realize these ideal terms in a more complex, and often suboptimal, real-world setting. For more on the real versus the ideal, see John Rawls, *The Law of Peoples* (Cambridge, Massachusetts: Harvard University Press, 1999).

Europe – the most crucial parts of a peace treaty were deliberately kept secret from the public.)[6]

- *Exchange of prisoners of war (POWs).* At war's end, all sides need to exchange all the POWs from the armed conflict.
- *Apology from the aggressor.* The aggressor in war, like the criminal in domestic society, needs to admit fault and guilt for causing the war by committing aggression. (And *aggression*, in international law, is the unjustified first use of armed force across an international border, thus violating the rights of political sovereignty and territorial integrity which all recognized countries enjoy.)[7] This may seem quaint and elemental, yet, in practice, it can be quite controversial. For example, Germany has offered many, and profuse, official apologies for World War II, and especially for the Holocaust. (Germany to this day still pays an annual reparations fee to Israel for the latter.) By contrast, Japan has been nowhere near as forthcoming with a meaningful, official apology for World War II (perhaps as a result of suffering the atomic bombings of Hiroshima and Nagasaki?). This reticence enrages China, in particular, which suffered mightily from Japanese aggression and expansion in the 1930s.[8]
- *War crimes trials for those responsible.* The world's first post-war international war crimes trials were held after World War II, in 1945–1946, in both Nuremberg and Tokyo. The vast majority of those tried were soldiers and officers charged with *jus in bello* violations, like torturing prisoners of war and targeting civilians. But a handful of senior Nazis were also charged with the *jus ad bellum* violation of "committing crimes against peace," that is, of launching an aggressive war.
- In 1998, the international community passed the *Treaty of Rome*, creating the world's first *permanent* international war-crimes tribunal. Situated mainly at The Hague, in Holland, its ambitious mandate is to prosecute *all* war crimes, committed by *all* sides in *all* wars, and to do so using lawyers and judges from countries which were *not* part of the war in question (unlike in Nuremberg and Tokyo). Recently, this new court has heard many cases from the Bosnian civil war and from various African wars. It has even put on trial former heads-of-state, and not just ordinary soldiers: Slobodan Milosevic of Serbia (until his death in 2006), and Jean Kambanda, the former prime minister of Rwanda during the 1994 genocide (about which, more below).[9]

---

[6] In modern times, US President Kennedy's settlement offer to end the Cuban Missile Crisis in 1962 contained secret aspects: notably his private pledge to remove American missiles from Turkey, so long as the Russians removed theirs from Cuba. See S. Stern, *The Week The World Stood Still* (Stanford University Press, 2005).

[7] See Reisman and Antoniou, *The Laws of War*; Roberts and Guelff, *Documentation*; Solis, *The Law of Armed Conflict*.

[8] John Keegan, *The Second World War* (New York: Vintage, 1990).

[9] Joseph E. Persico, *Nuremburg: Infamy on Trial* (New York: Penguin, 1995); Timothy P. Maga, *Judgment at Tokyo: The Japanese War Crimes Trials* (Lexington, Kentucky: University

- *Aggressor to give up any gains.* The thinking here is that the aggressor, as the wrongdoer, cannot be rewarded for its aggression and be allowed to keep any gains it may have won for itself during its aggression. For instance, during its initial campaign in 1992–1994, the Serb side of the Bosnian civil war initially conquered 70 percent of Bosnia, way beyond the area traditionally occupied by ethnic Serbs. More dramatically, during the Blitzkrieg of 1939–1940, Hitler's Germany conquered Austria, Czechoslovakia, France, Poland, and the Scandinavian countries. This principle requires that, at war's end, the aggressor relinquish all such unjust gains.[10]
- *Aggressor must be demilitarized to avoid a repeat.* Since the aggressor broke international trust, so to speak, by committing aggression, it *cannot* be trusted *not* to commit aggression again (at least in the short term, and in the absence of a change in government there). The international community is entitled to some added security. The tools the aggressor has to commit aggression must thus be taken away from it, in a process known as "demilitarization." This is to say that, often, defeated aggressors lose many of their military assets and weapons capabilities, and have "caps" placed on their ability to rebuild their armed forces over time.
- *Aggressor must suffer further losses.* What makes this model one of *retribution* is the conviction that it is *not enough* for the defeated aggressor merely to give up what it wrongly took, plus some weapons. *The aggressor must be made worse off than it was prior to the war.* Why? The defenders of this model suggest several reasons. First, it is thought that justice itself demands retribution of this nature – the aggressor must be made to feel the wrongness, and sting, of the war that it unjustly began. Second, consider an analogy to an individual criminal: In domestic society, when a thief has stolen a diamond ring, we do not just make him give the ring back and take away his thieving tools; we also make him pay a fine, or send him to jail, to impress upon him the wrongness of his conduct. And this ties into the third reason: By punishing the aggressor, we hope *to deter or prevent* future aggression, both by him (so to speak) and by any others who might be having similar ideas.
- But what will make the aggressor worse off? Demilitarization, sure. But two further things are frequently employed: *reparations payments* to the victims of the aggressor, plus *economic sanctions* slapped onto the aggressor as a whole. These are the post-war equivalent of fines, so to speak, on all of the aggressive society. Reparations payments are due, in the first instance, to the countries victimized and hurt by the aggressor's aggression and then, second, to the broader international community. The reparations payments are *backward-looking* in that sense, whereas the sanctions are more

Press of Kentucky, 2001); William A. Schabas, *An Introduction to the International Criminal Court* (Cambridge University Press, 2001).

[10] David Reiff, *Slaughterhouse: Bosnia and The Failure of the West* (New York: Touchstone, 1995); Keegan, *Second World War.*

forward-looking in the sense that they are designed to hurt and curb the aggressor's future economic growth opportunities, at least for a period of time (a sort of probation), and especially in connection with any goods and services which might enable the aggressor to commit aggression again.[11] (Defined, *sanctions* are a tool of foreign policy, signaling a move away from *positive* incentives, and mutually beneficial deal-making, and toward *negative* incentives: threats, non-cooperation, punishment, deliberately taking actions one believes will thwart the interests of the other country. Sanctions can vary in level, intensity, and effect. "Targeted sanctions" are when the measures of punishment, non-cooperation, and interest-thwarting are focused upon hurting *only* the elite decision-makers in the target country. "Sweeping sanctions" are those measures of punishment and non-cooperation which either deliberately target, or at least directly affect, *the majority* in the target country.)[12]

Two examples of the retribution model

Two of the most obvious, and infamous, historical examples of the retribution model in action concern the settlements of World War I and the Persian Gulf War.

The *Treaty of Versailles* ended World War I (1914–1918); and it is widely deemed to be a controversial failure, which contributed to the conditions sparking World War II (1939–1945). World War I was a disaster for perhaps all belligerents except the United States. It cost much more, and lasted much longer, than anyone had predicted; and, indeed, the war only came to an end, with victory for the Allied side, when the United States intervened in 1917. Because of all the cost and misery, the European powers were determined to punish Germany for invading Belgium and starting the war. So Germany was extensively demilitarized, had all its war gains taken away, and, furthermore, lost some valuable territory of its own as one aspect of punishment. Crushing reparations payments were levied upon Germany, and they would have lasted into the 1980s had the peace terms stuck. But they did not, because essentially these fines bankrupted Germany within only a few years, causing massive economic dislocation, hardship, and, eventually, civil unrest. The victorious powers also tried to force elections upon Germany; but the result was that the people there came to associate democracy with the economic problems, and they began to turn to radical, non-democratic parties promising simple solutions in a time of complex crisis. Hitler was thus able to come to power: He stopped all reparations payments, he cancelled all elections and named himself dictator, he rebuilt the German war machine (growing the economy, in the

---

[11]   Brian Orend, "Justice After War," *Ethics & International Affairs* 16, no. 1 (2002), 43–56.
[12]   Brian Orend, *Introduction to International Studies* (Oxford University Press, 2012), chap. 4.

short term), and he promised to get back all the lost lands. He did, or tried to, thus starting World War II.[13]

The *1991 Treaty ending the Persian Gulf War* was similarly punitive and also paved the way for a second war. The treaty called upon Saddam Hussein's Iraq to give up any claims on Kuwait (which it had invaded in 1990), officially apologize for its aggression, and surrender all prisoners of war. Saddam was left in power, however, and no attempt was made either to change his regime or to bring anyone to trial on war-crimes charges. But Iraq *was* to be extensively demilitarized. It lost many weapons, and had strict caps put on any rebuilding of its military. Iraq had "no-fly zones" imposed on it, both in the north (to protect the Kurds in Iraq from Saddam) and in the south (to protect the Shi'ites).

Saddam also had to agree to a rigorous, UN-sponsored weapons-inspections process. This process lasted from 1991 to 1998; and it found and destroyed many tons of illegal weapons, including chemical and biological agents. After Saddam kicked out the inspectors in 1998, this issue grew into a major factor in favor of war in 2003, as the Americans suspected Saddam still had *weapons of mass destruction* (WMDs) and, moreover, was plotting to give some to Al Qaeda to enable another 9/11-style terrorist strike on the United States.

Finally, and financially, Iraq had to pay reparations to Kuwait for the aggressive 1990 invasion and, moreover, had to suffer continuing, sweeping sanctions on its economy, especially on its ability to sell oil. These sanctions devastated Iraqi civilians but did very little to hurt Saddam. There is, in fact, evidence that the sanctions *only cemented Saddam's grip* on Iraq, as increasingly impoverished citizens grew more and more dependent on favors from Saddam's government in order to survive.[14]

The rehabilitation *model of post-war policy*

There is no sharp split, as if in-kind, between the retribution and rehabilitation models. They share commitment to the following aspects of a decent post-war settlement: the need for a public peace treaty, official apologies, exchange of POWs, trials for war criminals, some demilitarization, and the aggressor must give up any unjust gains.

Where the models differ is over three major issues. First, the rehabilitation model *rejects sweeping sanctions*, especially on grounds that they have been shown, historically, to harm civilians. Second, the rehabilitation model *rejects*

---

[13] Manfred F. Boemeke, Gerald D. Feldman, and Elisabeth Glaser (eds.), *The Treaty of Versailles: A Reassessment After 75 Years* (Publication of the German Historical Institute, 2006); Margaret Macmillian, *Paris 1919: Six Months That Changed the World* (New York: Random House, 2003).

[14] Wolfgang F. Danspeckgruber and Charles Tripp (eds.), *The Iraqi Aggression Against Kuwait: Strategic Lessons and Implications for Europe* (Boulder: Westview Press, 1996); Geoffrey L. Simons, *The Scourging of Iraq: Sanctions, Law and Natural Justice*, 2nd edn. (London and New York: Macmillan/St. Martins, 1998).

compensation payments, for the same reason. In fact, the model favors *investing in* a defeated aggressor, to help it rebuild and to help smooth over the wounds of war. Finally, the rehabilitation model *favors forcing regime change*, whereas the retribution model views that as too risky and costly. That it may be, but those who favor the rehabilitative model suggest that it can be worth it over the long term, leading to the creation of a new, better, non-aggressive, and even progressive, member of the international community. To those who scoff that such deep-rooted transformation simply cannot be done, supporters of the rehabilitative model reply that, not only *can* it be done, it *has* been done. The two leading examples are West Germany and Japan after World War II.[15]

Reconstructing Germany and Japan

World War II's settlement, in 1945, was not contained in a detailed, legalistic peace treaty. This was, partly, because Germany and Japan were so thoroughly crushed and had so little leverage. But World War II's settlement was sweeping and profound, with immense effects on world history. It was worked out, essentially, between the United States and USSR at meetings in Tehran and Yalta, but with participation from Britain, France, China, and other of the "lesser" Allies. Both Britain and France kept control over their colonies, but everyone knew that powerful forces of anti-colonialism – abetted by the exhaustion of Britain and France – would soon cause those old empires to crumble. As for the new empires, it was understood that the Soviet Union would hold sway in Eastern Europe, ostensibly to serve as a barrier between itself and Germany, preventing another Nazi-style invasion. (It also, however, provided for the export and spread of communism the other way.) The United States, by contrast, would get Hawaii, a number of Pacific Islands, and total sway over the reconstruction of Japan. As for Germany, it was agreed that the United States, Britain, France, and Russia would split it into Western and Eastern halves. (Ditto for the German capital of Berlin, which otherwise was within the Eastern, Soviet territory.) Within this Soviet sphere, police-state communism came to dominate as readily as it did in Russia. But within the West, there was a concerted effort to establish genuine free-market, rights-respecting democracies. In Japan, the same experiment was undertaken; but there the US military, under the firm leadership of Douglas MacArthur, held more direct control, and for longer, than it did in West Germany.[16]

---

[15] Orend, *Morality of War*, 190–220.

[16] Material for this section on post-war reconstruction in Germany and Japan draws upon Leon V. Segal, *Fighting to the Finish: The Politics of War Termination in America and Japan* (Ithaca, New York: Cornell University Press, 1989); Howard B. Schonberger, *Aftermath of War: Americans and The Remaking of Japan, 1945–1952* (Kent, Ohio: Kent State University Press, 1989); James Dobbins and Rollie Lal, *America's Role in Nation-Building: From Germany to Iraq* (Washington, DC: RAND, 2003); Eugene Davidson, *The Death and Life of Germany: An Account of the American Occupation* (St. Louis: University of Missouri Press, 1999).

The Allies, working with nationals in both countries – more so in Germany than Japan, perhaps – first undertook a purging process, which in Germany came to be known as "de-nazi-fication." All signs, symbols, buildings, literature, and things directly associated with the Nazis were destroyed utterly. The Nazi Party itself was abolished and declared illegal. Surviving ex-Nazis – though not all of them – were put on trial, put in jail, or otherwise punished and prohibited from political participation. The militaries of both Germany and Japan were utterly disbanded; and for years, the Allied military became *the* military, and the direct ruler, of both Germany and Japan.

After the negative purging process, the Allies in both countries established written constitutions or "Basic Law." These constitutions, after the period of direct military rule ended, provided for bills and charters of human rights, eventual democratic elections, and, above all, the checks and balances so prominently featured in the American system. Since government had grown so huge and tyrannical in both Germany and Japan in the 1930s, it had to be shrunk down and then broken into pieces, with each piece only authorized to handle its own business. Independent judiciaries and completely reconstituted police forces were an important part of this, and they went a long way to re-establishing the *impersonal* rule of law over the *personal* whims of former fascists. The executive branches, much more so than in the American system, were made more accountable to, and closely tied to, the legislative branch. The goal, of course, was to ensure that the executive could not grow into another dictator. By design, there were to be no strong presidents. So Germany and Japan became true *parliamentary* democracies, more in the European than American style.

Western-style liberal democracy was not the only change forcibly implemented. The education systems of both Germany and Japan were overhauled, since they had played huge propaganda roles for both regimes, and the content of their curricula had been filled with racism, ultra-nationalism, and distorted ignorance of the outside world. Western experts redesigned these systems to impart the concrete skills needed to participate in reconstruction, and to stress a more objective content favoring the basic cognitive functions ("the three Rs"), as well as critical thinking and especially science and technology. The curricula were radically stripped of political content, though, of course, some lessons on the new social institutions and their principles were required.

The Americans quickly saw that their sweeping legal, constitutional, social, and educational reforms would lack stability unless they could stimulate the German and Japanese economies. The people had to have their vital needs met, as well as a sense of hope that, concretely, the future would get better. Otherwise, they might revolt, and the reforms would fail. Instead of making the (World War I) mistake of *sucking money out* of these ruined countries through mandatory reparations payments, the Americans were the ones *who poured money into* Germany and Japan. The United States shunned the retribution paradigm and embraced the rehabilitative one. It was a staggering sum of money, too, channeled through the so-called "Marshall Plan."[17] Money was needed to buy essentials, as well as to clear away all the rubble and ruined infrastructure. It was also just needed to circulate, to get the Germans and Japanese used to free-market trading. Jobs were plentiful, as entire systems of infrastructure – transportation, water, sewage, electricity, agriculture, finance – had to be rebuilt. Since jobs paid wages, thanks to the Marshall Plan, the people's lives improved and the free-market system deepened. But it was not just the money. American management experts poured into Germany and Japan, showing them the very latest, and most efficient, means of production. Within 30 years, Germany and Japan had not only rebounded economically, they had the two strongest economies in the world after the United States itself, based especially on quality, high-tech manufacturing, such as automobiles.

The post-war reconstructions of Germany and Japan easily count as the most impressive post-war rehabilitations in modern history, rivaled perhaps only by the United States' rebuilding of its own South after the Civil War (1861–1865).[18] Germany and Japan, today, have massive free-market economies, and politically remain peaceful, stable, and decent democracies. They are both very good citizens on the global stage. In addition, these countries are by no means "clones" (much less colonies) of the United States. They each have gone their own way, adding local color, and pursuing political paths quite distinct from those that most interest the United States – consider especially Germany's formative role in the European Union. So we have clear evidence that even massive and forcible post-war changes need *not* threaten "a nation's character" or what makes it unique and special to its people. But such success *did* come at a huge cost in terms of time and treasure: it cost trillions of dollars, it took trillions of "man-hours" in work and expertise, it took decades of real time, it took the cooperation of most of the German and Japanese people; and, above all, it took the will of the United States to see it through. It was American money, American security, American know-how, American patience, and American generosity which brought it all into being.

Rehabilitation's principles

Based on these best-case practices, supporters of rehabilitation have devised their own list of desirable elements during the post-war period. These can simply be listed here, as they were explained above in connection with Germany and Japan. The occupying war winner, during post-war reconstruction, ought to:

[17] Charles L. Mee, *The Marshall Plan* (New York: HarperCollins, 1987).
[18] James M. McPherson, *Battle Cry of Freedom: The Civil War Era* (Oxford University Press, 2003); David H. Donald, Jean Harvey Baker, and Michael F. Holt, *Civil War and Reconstruction* (New York: W.W. Norton, 2000).

POST-INTERVENTION: PERMISSIONS AND PROHIBITIONS   233

- Adhere diligently to the (*jus in bello*) laws of war during the regime take-down and occupation.
- Purge much of the old regime, and prosecute its war criminals.
- Disarm and demilitarize the society.

But then:

- Provide effective military and police security for the whole country.
- Work with a cross-section of locals on a new, rights-respecting constitution that features checks and balances.
- Allow other, non-state associations, or "civil society," to flourish.
- Forego compensation and economic sanctions in favor of investing in and rebuilding the economy.
- If necessary, revamp educational curricula to purge past propaganda and cement new values.
- Ensure that the benefits of the new order will be: (1) concrete; and (2) widely, not narrowly, distributed.
- Follow an orderly, not-too-hasty exit strategy when the new regime can stand on its own two feet.[19]

Application to Afghanistan and Iraq

Let us examine the ongoing, high-profile cases of Afghanistan and Iraq. And let us do this not only to see the rehabilitation model in contemporary action (so to speak) but, moreover, because Iraq can, arguably, be seen as a recent armed humanitarian intervention. (It was, admittedly, not packaged as such – rather, it was packaged as a pre-emptive form of self-defense; but it could be argued that the 2003 Iraq attack was an act, and *much better seen as an act of AHI*.)[20] Afghanistan has been in a period of post-war reconstruction since early 2002; Iraq since mid 2003. (These dates refer to when the regime fell in each society, as a result of American invasion, leading then to US military *occupation* (i.e., when country X's military controls the affairs of another country Y).)[21] It seems true that the international community, as led by the United States, has – more or less – been trying to implement the above, ten-step "rehabilitation recipe"

---

[19] Dobbins and Lal, *America's Role in Nation-Building*; J. Dobbins and S. Jones (eds.), *The United Nations' Role in Nation-Building* (Washington, DC: RAND, 2007); Orend, *Morality of War*.

[20] In fact, one could argue that, in the United States, the 2003 Iraq War was justified and pack-aged to the people as an act of pre-emptive self-defense (especially in light of 9/11, which had just happened two years before) whereas in other Allied countries, notably the United Kingdom, much stronger emphasis was placed on Saddam's tyranny and the need to rescue the Iraqi people from such. For the American case, see Bob Woodward, *Plan of Attack* (New York: Random House, 2004). For the British, see Tony Blair, *A Journey: My Political Life* (New York: Knopf, 2010).

[21] Eric Carlton, *Occupation* (London: Routledge, 1995).

in each instance. It has been a very difficult process, in both countries, and has seen a mixture of both successes and failures.

Successes

The major post-war successes, in both nations, have been the replacement of aggressive, rogue regimes with new governments. The old regimes have been purged; and these new governments enjoy democratic legitimacy – through multiple elections, in both countries – and are based on written, public constitutions crafted by locals. The civil societies – compared to what it was under Saddam, or the Taliban – have blossomed. The gains in terms of personal freedom, in both societies, have been huge. Also, in Afghanistan anyway, the gains in terms of gender equality have been very substantial with, for example, the international community (including Canada) building and staffing many new schools for girls and women.[22]

The problem, though, is that the evidence suggests that it is *not* things like individual liberty and gender equality that matter most when it comes to the success and durability of post-war reconstruction. The historical data suggest, rather, that the most important things are physical security (i.e., personal safety) and economic growth. Jim Dobbins, probably the leading scholar on the issue, has distilled all this data into one crystal-clear rule-of-thumb regarding post-war success: *the war-winning occupier, and the new local regime, have about ten years to form an effective partnership and to devote themselves in particular to making the average person in that society feel better off – more secure and more prosperous, especially – than they were prior to the outbreak of the war.* If they do this, post-war reconstruction will probably succeed. If not, there will be failure, and a serious risk of backsliding into armed conflict.[23] Using this rule of thumb, we note that the approximate deadline for achieving this in Afghanistan would be 2012, and in Iraq, 2013. Now, the US occupation of Iraq has been declared officially over (as of December 2011), but the reality is that a number of US troops remain indefinitely to help train the new Iraqi army and to protect Iraqi oil infrastructure.[24] And, in Afghanistan, NATO troops have committed to being there until 2014. So, will physical security and economic improvement be achieved in the time remaining?

---

[22] Matteo Tondini, *Statebuilding and Justice Reform: Post-Conflict Reconstruction in Afghanistan* (London and New York: Routledge, 2010); US Government Accountability Office, *Afghanistan Reconstruction: Despite Some Progress, Deteriorating Security and Other Obstacles Continue to Threaten Achievement of U.S. Goals* (Washington, DC: Bibliogov, 2011); Mokhtar Lamani and Bessma Momani (eds.), *From Desolation to Reconstruction: Iraq's Troubled Journey* (Waterloo, Ontario: CIGI, 2010).

[23] Dobbins and Lal, *America's Role in Nation-Building*; Dobbins and Jones, *The United Nations' Role in Nation-Building*.

[24] This was widely reported in December 2011 by the Associated Press, along with the following figures: the Iraq War lasted nine years (2003–2011), costing over 800 billion US dollars, and involving 4,500 US military dead and 32,000 US military wounded.

Challenges
The two most important challenges are security and the economy.

Security   While the capital of Afghanistan, Kabul, *is* quite secure, the same *cannot* be said for the rest of the nation; there is a deep urban–rural split in this regard. Afghanistan is a highly weaponized society, with nearly all men owning guns and with local tribal leaders protecting their families' farms (and crops) with their own armed militias. The Taliban is making a comeback in rural areas by clamping down on these local tribal "war lords," and promising a return to the very strict (religious) law-and-order state they feel they achieved when in power. So, would the *average* Afghans feel they are more secure now than back when the Taliban were in power? Maybe not, and this is one reason why US President Barack Obama ordered a new surge of US troops into Afghanistan. He did this to: bring security, turn the tide against a resurgent Taliban, and deal more effectively with the border area – keenly focused on ensuring radical Islamic extremists do not use it to rebuild and, potentially, strike the United States once more.[25]

Things were so bad, security-wise, in Iraq during 2005–2006, that experts spoke openly of there being a civil war among the three main groups: Kurd, Sunni, and Shi'ite. At the time, President George W. Bush ordered a big surge of more US troops into Iraq; and, as led by General David Petraeus, they succeeded beyond anyone's expectations in cutting down group-on-group violence and in keeping the peace. (This success is what inspired Obama to order the same for Afghanistan.) But is it enough? Dobbins would remind us that more security now than in 2006 is not the same thing as more security than back when Saddam was in power in 2003. Saddam was a brutal tyrant, but he did keep law and order. So would the average Iraqis say they feel safer and more secure than before the war? It is hard to say, and might depend on which group one is speaking to: the Kurds and Shi'ites might well say yes, whereas those of Saddam's own Sunni ethnicity might say no. While there have been clear gains since 2006, all the groups are concerned as to what might happen once the United States pulls out entirely.[26]

Economy   Would the average Afghani and Iraqi say they are more prosperous than prior to the wars in their countries? Thankfully, the Americans did not implement the retribution model in either case and, instead, have sent investment flowing into both countries. Iraq probably has a better shot here, as it

---

[25] US Government, *Afghanistan Reconstruction* (Washington, DC: Bibliogov, 2011); Dov S. Zakheim, *A Vulcan's Tale: How the Bush Administration Mismanaged the Reconstruction of Afghanistan* (Washington, DC: Brookings Institute, 2011).

[26] US Special Inspector General, *Hard Lessons: The Iraq Reconstruction Experience* (Washington, DC: US Independent Agencies and Commissions, 2009).

at least has lots of oil and gas, as well as a large, reasonably educated work-force. Yet huge challenges remain. The near-constant war since 1979, plus the effects of the economic sanctions from 1991 to 2003, devastated Iraq's basic infrastructure and well-being. Hence, much rebuilding needs to be done. Unemployment remains a terrible problem. One solution would seem to be to pay the unemployed to perform all the rebuilding, but the costs would be enor-mous – in the dozens of billions, or more – and the Americans have been reluc-tant to pay the bill all on their own. Other countries, for their part, reply that it was the United States' war, and so the United States needs to pay the price.[27]

Afghanistan is one of the world's poorest countries, where two-thirds of the population lives on the equivalent of two US dollars per day. The same propor-tion of the population is thought to be functionally illiterate, and unemploy-ment is also thought to afflict half the workforce. Afghanistan faces the same issues of ruined infrastructure, and the brutal consequences which constant warfare has inflicted on the economy. (These consequences can be condensed as follows: *would you open a business in a war zone?*) Afghanistan's economy is a toxic mixture of war and drugs. Poppies grow well there, and farmers can earn much more growing them than legal crops like wheat or corn. It is estimated that one-third of Afghanistan's economy comes from poppy production and from the heroin and opium trade which comes out of it. Transforming Afghanistan's economy from one of war and drugs to a peaceful and legal economy rooted in broad-based, healthy economic growth is proving terribly difficult. It is deeply unclear whether true success will happen on this front, but at least here the Americans can count on international support, as all of NATO is involved. The United Kingdom, for example, is thinking of buying Afghanistan's poppies and using them for medical-grade opiates in Western hospitals (e.g., for pain-killers). Canada and Germany are heavily involved in building and running schools for Afghan children. Even Russia, in 2010, signed an agreement to help cooperate in stopping the narcotics trade, as much of Afghanistan's drugs wind up on the streets of Moscow (as the closest big city).[28]

It is therefore clear that, if post-war reconstruction "succeeds" in Iraq and Afghanistan, it will not be anywhere near the same degree of success achieved in Japan and Germany in the 1945–1955 period. This does not necessarily mean that these recent cases have been "failures," as this comparison is to the very best cases. It is hard to beat, or match, the very best. What these complex, mixed, imperfect, contemporary cases *do* mean – for the Middle East, and the rest of the world – is, as yet, deeply unclear.[29]

---

[27] Lamani and Momani, *From Desolation to Reconstruction*.

[28] Zakheim, *Vulcan's Tale*.

[29] Jeff Bridoux, *American Foreign Policy and Post-War Reconstruction: Comparing Japan and Iraq* (London and New York: Routledge, 2012).

Transition to armed humanitarian intervention

We have already defined "armed humanitarian intervention" (AHI). Because Iraq in 2003 could be interpreted as a case of AHI, all the post-war measures implemented in Iraq are thus highly relevant for a discussion of post-intervention justice. Recent AHI discussion, of course, is dominated by the so-called "Responsibility to Protect" (or RtoP) doctrine. A quick, impressionistic history is in order.

The emergence of RtoP: from Rwanda to Libya

The issue concerns when, if ever, states may intervene with armed force in the internal crises of another country. Typically, this is referred to as an armed humanitarian intervention or a military intervention for humanitarian purposes. It is feared, by supporters of RtoP, that the status quo of international law shows too much respect to state sovereignty and, as such, is mainly concerned only with wars *between* countries. But, when it comes to civil wars, and/or to so-called "mass-atrocity crimes" within a state (defined below), when, if ever, may other countries intervene with armed force?

The governments of several middle-power countries, such as Australia and Canada, came to believe in the mid 1990s that it is not enough – not a satisfying answer – to reply, as international law does: "whenever the United Nations' Security Council (UNSC) says so."[30] This is so because the UN Security Council can sometimes fail completely in this regard. The most searing recent example of this – in which Canada played an important part – was the 1994 near-genocide in Rwanda, in Africa. (*Genocide* is when an entire group, or people, becomes targeted for murder at the hands of another, as for instance the European Jews at the hands of Nazi Germany during the Holocaust. The term "genocide" literally means "the killing of a whole people.")[31]

Rwanda, during its colonial days under the rule of Belgium, was dominated by a minority group, the Tutsis. The majority group, the Hutus, resented being dominated and, when independence from Belgium came in 1959, the Hutus turned the tables and took control. Relations between the groups were always tense, and at times broke out into armed conflict between the Hutu-dominated Rwandan Army and the Tutsi-dominated rebel force, the Rwandan Patriotic Front (RPF). In 1993, after several years of fighting, a peace accord and power-sharing arrangement were achieved. Before these agreements could be implemented, Hutu extremists formed private *militias* – small, non-state, private

---

[30] See Reisman and Antoniou, *The Laws of War*; Roberts and Guelff, *Documentation*; Solis, *The Law of Armed Conflict*.

[31] Adam Jones, *Genocide: A Comprehensive Introduction* (London and New York: Routledge, 2010).

military groups – to carry out an audacious and murderous plan: not only to destroy the peace accords, but to eliminate the Tutsis and even any moderate Hutus who supported peace with the Tutsis. They truly had genocide on their minds: to destroy the Tutsi people.

These Hutu extremists seized power in a coup in early 1994, killing the moderate Hutu leadership. While the United Nations did have a peacekeeping force already in Rwanda, as soon as some of its (Belgian) members were killed in the coup's early days, the UN Security Council ordered a complete withdrawal – in spite of the pleas of the peacekeeping unit's own commanding officer, Canada's Roméo Dallaire. He knew what was going to happen and presented the United Nations with evidence of a genocidal plot. The United Nations ignored him; and all Western troops left the country, taking their own nationals with them. They even closed their embassies. The Hutu extremists had free reign to execute their horrible plan; and, by April, they had killed about 800,000 people, both Tutsi and Hutu. Most were butchered brutally with machetes, or shot at point-blank range with small guns. *Fully one-third of all Tutsis on earth were murdered.* France, alone amongst Western countries, re-intervened late in June and helped re-establish some sanity (though some say France allowed the perpetrators to leave the country as well). Then – then! – the UN Security Council voted to return "peacekeeping" forces back to Rwanda.[32]

In 2000, Canada – feeling its peacekeepers in Rwanda were betrayed by the UN Security Council – convened the International Commission on Intervention and State Sovereignty (ICISS) to try to better guide the Security Council regarding when it ought to authorize armed humanitarian interventions. The RtoP doctrine outlined in the ICISS report, *The Responsibility to Protect*, asserts that:

(1) All states have the responsibility to protect their own people from such "mass-atrocity crimes," specifically: genocide, war crimes, crimes against humanity, and ethnic cleansing. (We defined *genocide* above. A *war crime* is a violation of the *jus ad bellum* and *jus in bello* laws of war. A *crime against humanity* includes war crimes and also such things as violating basic human rights. Finally, *ethnic cleansing* is when a group is being driven out of their home territory to make way for another group to come in and occupy that territory.)

(2) If a state *fails* in this responsibility, then other states have *the duty to step in*:
    (a) in the first instance, to aid and enable the state's capacity, if that is the

---

[32] Gérard Prunier, *Rwanda: History of a Genocide* (New York: Columbia University Press, 1995); Michael N. Barnett, *Eyewitness to a Genocide: The UN and Rwanda* (Ithaca, New York: Cornell University Press, 2003); Linda Melvern, *A People Betrayed: The Role of the West in Rwanda's Genocide* (New York: Zed Books, 2000); Roméo Dallaire, *Shake Hands with the Devil: The Failure of Humanity in Rwanda* (New York: Carroll & Graf Publishers/ Random House, 2004).

issue; or (b) to intervene with armed force, if the issue is (rather) the state itself turning murderously against its own people.[33]

Though RtoP is *only* considered a new *norm* (or rule, or expectation), and *not* international law, some experts have argued that it is well on its way to becoming the latter. After all, in 2005, the UN General Assembly hosted a World Summit on this subject and issued its unanimous *Outcome Document*, which clearly endorsed RtoP. More to the point, the UN Security Council itself has endorsed the RtoP in principle, on at least two occasions: once in 2006 following the World Summit; and, more to the point, in 2011 when it authorized an armed humanitarian intervention in Libya.

Fighting broke out in Libya in late 2010 as part of the Arab Spring uprising.[34] The fighting eventually coalesced into two groups: those supportive of existing dictator Muammar Gaddafi, and those devoted to his overthrow. When Gaddafi's army turned violently against not only the rebel groups but unarmed civilians, and even whole towns were deemed to be "enemies," NATO – as initially led by France and Italy, which have historical ties to Libya – sought authorization from the Security Council to intervene with armed force. In March 2011, the Council gave its approval – citing the RtoP doctrine as rationale. From March to October 2011, NATO forces provided aid to the rebels, and performed on their own many direct strikes – especially air strikes – against Gaddafi's forces. Canada and the United States were also robust participants in this action, which ended when Gaddafi was killed in October. The NATO mandate ended in November 2011, and Libya began a period of transition.[35]

What does RtoP say about post-intervention justice?

At least the RtoP document does address, explicitly, the issue of post-intervention reconstruction. Indeed, there is a whole mini-chapter entitled "The Responsibility to Rebuild." Now, it only spans four pages and 21 generally phrased paragraphs (several of which are long, direct quotations from *other* UN documents), but at least this forward-looking effort goes beyond the standard obsessions with issues of when to start an intervention, and how to conduct oneself during an intervention.

It is fair to say that, to the extent to which there is a coherent doctrine in the RtoP regarding post-intervention justice, it is that of rehabilitation. The document

---

[33] The International Commission on Intervention and State Sovereignty, *Report: The Responsibility to Protect* (Ottawa: International Development Research Centre, 2001).

[34] Lin Noueihed and Alex Warren, *The Battle for the Arab Spring: Revolution, Counter-revolution and the Making of a New Era* (New Haven and London: Yale University Press, 2012).

[35] Alex J. Bellamy, *Responsibility to Protect* (London: Polity, 2009); Gareth Evans and Mohamed Sahnoun (co-chairs), *The Responsibility to Protect*, Report of the International Commission on Intervention and State Sovereignty [ICISS] (Ottawa: International

intones: "Responsibility to protect implies the responsibility not just to prevent and react but to follow-through and re-build."[36] The document goes on to list the following as desirable aspects of post-intervention activity:

- "disarmament"
- "repairing infrastructure"
- "commitment of sufficient funds"
- "close co-operation with local people"
- "building a durable peace"
- "promoting good governance, economic growth and sustainable development."[37]

It is fair to say, given previous discussion, that these are familiar elements. There is also considerable attention paid to the need to repatriate those people driven out of the country by the aggressive activities of the former regime, and/or by the fighting needed during the intervention to defeat the regime. It also expresses the need to reconstitute the existing armed forces, and police forces, into new, more responsible ones with new leadership not complicit in the crimes of the old regime.[38]

Drawing it all together

I would argue that the best model for guiding decision-makers post-intervention is that of rehabilitation, and I am pleased to claim general support in this regard from the official RtoP doctrine. I stress this, even though I realize that recent difficulties (especially in Iraq and Afghanistan) with the rehabilitation model may naturally incline countries, in the future, towards options they may feel are less burdensome in the short term – whether such an option is an ultra-minimal version of the rehabilitation model (as with the "in-and-out" experience in Libya)[39] or, worse, a reversion to the retribution model. Historically, there probably is a pendulum swing between these models, depending on the last previous experience and its perceived success or failure. But, for the reasons above, I side with rehabilitation in general and urge others

Development Research Centre, December 2001); Nikolas Gvosdev, "R2P: Sovereignty and Intervention After Libya," *World Politics Review* (June 28, 2011).

[36] *The Responsibility to Protect*, ICISS Report, 39.

[37] *Ibid.*, 39–42.   [38] *Ibid.*

[39] This term is owing to Michael Walzer. The "in-and-out" model of AHI is precisely that: get in, overthrow the murderous regime, and then get out as soon as that objective has been achieved. It appeals in many ways – simplicity, closure – but, as others, including the RtoP report, have noted, it can leave the locals with insufficient help to realistically rebuild and prevent their backsliding into either another tyranny or a renewed round of fighting. See Walzer, *Just and Unjust Wars*, 4th edn. (New York: Basic Books, 2006) 82fn; Orend, *Morality of War*, 90–104.

to do the same. Thus, for me, the basic elements of a just post-intervention policy are:

- AHI is justified, initially, by the norms of RtoP and the need to save innocents from slaughter and slavery at the hands of their own regime. Once the decision for military action has been made, one ought to adhere diligently to the (*jus in bello*) laws of war during the regime take-down and occupation.
- Purge much of the old regime, and prosecute its war criminals.
- Disarm and demilitarize the society.

But then:

- Provide effective military and police security for the whole country. Over time, there will need to be a rebuilding, retraining, and re-professionalization of such forces.
- Allow for, and aid, the repatriation of any former citizens or permanent residents who were either displaced by the old regime, and/or by the fighting needed to topple the old regime.
- Work with a cross-section of locals on a new, rights-respecting constitution that features checks and balances.
- Allow other, non-state associations or "civil society" to flourish.
- Forego compensation and economic sanctions in favor of investing in and rebuilding the economy.
- If necessary, revamp educational curricula to purge past propaganda and cement new values.
- Ensure that the benefits of the new order will be: (1) concrete; and (2) widely, not narrowly, distributed.
- Follow an orderly, not-too-hasty exit strategy when the new regime can stand on its own two feet.
- Pay particular attention to the need for the average citizen to feel more secure and more prosperous within ten years after the fall of the old regime. Draw upon as much help from the international community as you can to achieve this.

These are only general elements, and obviously they require tailoring to the specific needs of the particular intervention in question. Yet, they remain 12 very substantial and concrete requirements, clearly advancing beyond the bulk of the literature on this vital but underdeveloped subject. One final thing, returning to perhaps our very first point of post-war justice: *all 12 of these elements must be carried out in a public way, with maximal transparency and inclusiveness.*[40]

---

[40] Kant himself – probably the first *jus post bellum* thinker – would have stressed transparency and inclusiveness. Immanuel Kant, *Perpetual Peace And Other Essays*, translated by Ted Humphrey (Indianapolis: Hackett, 1983).

Conclusion

This chapter set for itself the goal of constructing general principles to guide decision-makers in the post-intervention moment, and beyond into the near future. It did this by observing, first, that AHI is a kind of armed conflict, and then by looking at the two major rival post-armed conflict policies: those of retribution and rehabilitation. Many historical cases were examined, ranging from World War II to today's Iraq and Afghanistan. The account then looked for inspiration from the RtoP doctrine, witnessing its development from the ashes of Rwanda to its more recent application in Libya. The chapter concluded by offering 12 substantial principles to guide our sense of post-intervention justice, noting that the RtoP doctrine concurs in general with the author's own endorsement of the post-war paradigm of rehabilitation.

14

Rethinking responsibility to protect

The case for human sovereignty

DAVID RODIN

The rise of universal human rights is transforming the ethics of military action. The breadth and depth of this "rights revolution" is profound, and no aspect of military ethics will be left untouched. Nowhere has the transformative effect of rights been experienced earlier or with more force than in the way we think about military humanitarian intervention. In the last decade the doctrine of Responsibility to Protect has successfully entrenched a conditional understanding of state sovereignty that makes human rights the touchstone of sovereign rights. This has been a genuine advance.

But the current theory and practice of humanitarian intervention is at an unstable resting point in its development. It continues to suffer from significant conceptual and operational deficits. In this chapter I will ask a surprising question: why should we conceive of military humanitarian intervention as a form of *war*? I will argue that by doing so we deform key aspects of humanitarian intervention, which in turn underlies the significant political controversy that the practice continues to generate. Instead of conceiving of intervention as a form of war, I will suggest we approach it through the paradigm of what I will call "human sovereignty." This approach affirms the right of people to determine their own political settlements without violent coercive interference from either foreigners or compatriots. It thereby places significant strategic and operational constraints on the conduct of intervention, which I will explore in detail, paying particular attention to the 2011 intervention in Libya. In the final sections, I contrast the human-sovereignty approach with Mill's classic treatment of intervention and its latter-day reinterpretation by Michael Walzer. Finally, I will reflect on the sources of the obligation to intervene, suggesting that there are reasons why the duty to prevent atrocity is strong even when more lives could perhaps be saved through more traditional forms of aid.

Let us begin by reflecting on how we got to where we are now. In the old paradigm, foreign intervention to prevent mass atrocity was thought to reveal a deep tension between two different moral values, or sets of rights. On the one side was the moral value of state sovereignty, which enshrines the right against intervention in their internal affairs and their "inherent" right to defend against armed attack.[1] On the other side lay the human rights of individual persons. In an influential article, Kofi Annan referred to these competing values as "two concepts of sovereignty": the political sovereignty of states and the personal sovereignty of individuals.[2] When a state attacks its own people, then the two values were thought to come into a fundamental conflict, leading to what Annan referred to as "the dilemma of humanitarian intervention."[3] As Annan's language reflects, the conflict was often viewed as a tragic one: No matter what course of action is taken, some important moral value will be compromised.

The great conceptual leap out of this dilemma thinking was achieved by introducing what is, in essence, a conditionality argument. Sovereignty, in its normative sense, should not be viewed as an immutable and inherent attribute of states. Rather a state's possession of sovereign rights is conditional on the state's respecting and protecting the rights of its citizens. If a state fails in this responsibility, then its sovereignty becomes in part or in whole forfeited; and it is liable to external forceful intervention, provided such intervention is both necessary and proportionate.

Note how the conditionality argument differs from the dilemma view. If the possession of sovereign rights is conditional on respecting human rights, then there is no inescapable value conflict in situations of humanitarian intervention. The right against external intervention that the state would ordinarily enjoy has been forfeited, leaving an appropriately motivated intervener at liberty to act. The implied analogy is with cases of individual self-defense. There is no dilemma in a standard case of self-defense. Rather the attacker, by breaching his obligations toward the victim, forfeits his own right against attack, and the defender may use proportionate and necessary force against him without any color of wrongdoing. It had long been accepted that states could forfeit their right against intervention by attacking other states. The conditionality argument extended this line of reasoning to attacks made by a state on its own people.[4]

The conditionality argument was implicitly endorsed by the International Commission on Intervention and State Sovereignty (ICISS) in their seminal

---

[1] See *Charter of the United Nations*, Article 2(4) and Article 51.

[2] Kofi Annan, "Two Concepts of Sovereignty," *The Economist* (September 16, 1999).

[3] *Ibid.*

[4] In 2002, I deployed a variant of the conditionality argument as a *reductio ad absurdum* against the thesis that the right of national self-defense is grounded in rights of individual self-defense. If this were true, I argued, then far from being deeply opposed, as is usually assumed, humanitarian intervention and national self-defense would actually share an underlying moral structure, and indeed the right of humanitarian intervention could be derived from the right of national self-defense. It is a mark of how rapid has been the conceptual transition in this area, that an argument deployed as a *reductio* would soon be widely accepted as establishing a substantive positive claim about the justification for humanitarian action. See David Rodin, *War and Self-Defense* (Oxford University Press, 2002), 130–31.

report on Responsibility to Protect.[5] But it did not originate there. The basic form of the argument had already been well established in several earlier discussions including those of David Luban, Fernando Tesón, and Michael Walzer.[6]

Nonetheless, embedding the conditionality argument within the doctrine of Responsibility to Protect, and that doctrine's endorsement by the United Nations General Assembly in 2005, was a genuine advance. It enabled us to escape the loose and unsatisfactory image of a "trade-off" between competing values implied by the dilemma view, and to move toward a shared understanding of the concrete conditions for permissible intervention, most notably the four "Responsibility to Protect crimes" of genocide, crimes against humanity, ethnic cleansing, and war crimes.[7] It also reflected the clear truth that states possess rights *because* of the rights of their citizens, not *independently* of them.

However, even as the conditionality argument gained political traction and theoretical credibility, serious concerns remained. Many worries concern the seeming political nature of the current doctrine and practice of humanitarian intervention.[8] First, there has been deep unease about forcible regime change

[5] I say that the conditionality argument is "implicitly" accepted in the report, because this is one of two important matters on which the report maintains a consistent (and presumably intentional) ambiguity. Here is the key passage: "sovereignty implies a dual responsibility: externally – to respect the sovereignty of other states, and internally, to respect the dignity and basic rights of all the people within the state." *The Responsibility to Protect*, Report of the International Commission on Intervention and State Sovereignty (Ottawa: International Development Research Centre, 2001), 8; see also related passages under "Basic Principles," xi.

The term "implies" can mean two things. First, is a forward-looking sense: Sovereignty is *the source of*, or generates, the two responsibilities. Second, is the backward-looking sense that I have been discussing: The possession of sovereignty is *conditional* on observance of those two responsibilities. The report does not clarify whether it intends to invoke one or both of those senses, and neither does the *2005 World Summit Outcome Document* of the General Assembly. Despite its reticence, we cannot make sense of the basic argument of the report without assuming that it embraces at least the conditional sense of this claim. Without a conditionality claim, it would be impossible to understand how the Responsibility to Protect can sometimes include the responsibility of third parties to respond in ways that intervene in the internal affairs of a state. The second matter on which the report is studiously ambiguous is whether the "responsibility" of the international community to respond to atrocity is in fact a "duty." I discuss this in the final section of this chapter.

[6] David Luban, "Just War and Human Rights," *Philosophy & Public Affairs* 9, no. 2 (1980), 160–81; Fernando Tesón, *Humanitarian Intervention: An Inquiry into Law and Morality* (New York: Transnational Publishers, 1997). Even Michael Walzer, who, as we shall see, adopted an ambivalent stance concerning humanitarian intervention, argued that "a state (or government) established against the will of its own people, ruling violently, may well forfeit its right to defend itself even against a foreign invasion." See Michael Walzer, *Just and Unjust Wars*, 4th edn. (New York, Basic Books, 2006), 82n.

[7] See *2005 World Summit Outcome*, UN General Assembly Resolution, UN document A/60/1 (October 24, 2005), para. 138.

[8] For an excellent overview of the contemporary debate, see articles by Alex J. Bellamy, Simon Chesterman, James Pattison, Thomas Weiss, and Jennifer Welsh in *Ethics & International Affairs* 25, no. 3 (2011), 251–92.

in the course of humanitarian intervention, as can be seen in the reaction of many states and commentators to the NATO intervention in Libya. More broadly, there have been significant worries about the permissibility of intervening militarily to support one side of an ongoing civil conflict. This was the de facto status of the Libya intervention, and is clearly implicated in proposals, current at the time of writing, to arm rebel forces fighting against the regime of Bashar al Assad in Syria. Some commentators have been concerned at the apparent weakening or abandonment of the traditional doctrine of impartiality in United Nations practice that this seems to reflect.[9] These reservations have been exacerbated by the apparent selectivity of the practice of intervention by Western forces. Why are some cases singled out for intervention, when other, perhaps more, serious cases are not? And of course the background to much of this unease has been the 2003 invasion of Iraq. There is considerable consensus among commentators that this intervention was not justified and, indeed, was without just cause. Yet the operations there were at various points justified as a form of humanitarian intervention. Moreover, the brutal and dictatorial Saddam regime clearly lacked the moral legitimacy required to claim full sovereign rights.

These factors are a source of considerable disquiet for advocates of Responsibility to Protect. They are interlinked in that they all concern problems with the way that intervention may improperly disrupt the indigenous politics of a community. Precisely this concern was, of course, one of the central motivations for the original conception of state sovereignty as a non-conditional right. Perhaps it was after all a mistake to move to a conditional understanding of sovereignty?

My diagnosis is different. I believe that all of these issues stem in different ways from the same basic error: that of conceptualizing, resourcing, and operationalizing humanitarian intervention as a form of warfare. This error can be corrected by rooting the doctrine and practice of humanitarian intervention in a richer notion of sovereignty that I will call "human sovereignty."

Conceiving of humanitarian intervention as a particular kind of war was a natural step because most commentators have approached the issue of intervention squarely from within the framework of just war theory. The Responsibility to Protect report is a case in point. By structuring their argument around classical just-war principles (including a full-throated discussion of "just cause") ICISS strongly implies that the responsibility to respond to humanitarian crisis, is, at the limit, a responsibility to engage in humanitarian war.[10]

---

[9] See especially Jennifer M. Welsh, "Civilian Protection in Libya: Putting Coercion and Controversy Back into RtoP," *Ethics & International Affairs* 25, no. 3 (Fall 2011), 255–62.

[10] The report divides the traditional *jus ad bellum* criteria into a "threshold" criterion of just cause, and "other precautionary criteria" that include right intention, last resort, proportional means, and reasonable prospects of success. Gareth Evans and Mohamed Sahnoun (co-chairs), *The Responsibility to Protect*, Report of the International Commission on

Conceiving of humanitarian intervention as a form of war is significant because, as Clausewitz rightly identified, war is deeply and inherently political: "war is not merely an act of policy but a true political instrument, a continuation of political intercourse, carried on with other means."[11] To conceive of humanitarian intervention as a form of war, particularly when combined with the conditionality argument, is therefore to see it as encompassing a permission to engage in deep intervention in the political processes of the target community.

True, many commentators have emphasized the limited scope of permissible humanitarian intervention. For example, the ICISS report insists that "The primary purpose of the intervention must be to halt or avert human suffering" and that the "overthrow of regimes is not, as such, a legitimate objective."[12] However, these warnings are presented in the context of a discussion of the "precautionary" criterion of "right intention" in which it is quickly acknowledged that intentions of interveners are most commonly mixed, and frequently permissibly so. Moreover, the report leaves open the possibility that overtly political forms of interference in a community may be a necessary means to achieve civilian protection. The practice of intervening states in Libya following UN Security Council Resolution 1973 (which explicitly references the Responsibility to Protect) suggests that the norm was interpreted by the interveners themselves as permitting steps to engage in deep political interference amounting to forcible regime change.[13]

Limits on the political character of intervention have shallow roots within the conditionality account of humanitarian intervention. After all, if as the conditionality argument suggests, a state has forfeited its sovereign right against intervention, how exactly ought we to conceive of restrictions on political interference within that community? What is the normative source and content of such restrictions? What we require is a deeper account of the moral limits on the political conduct of humanitarian intervention, without falling back on the earlier dilemma view that attributes a non-conditional status to state sovereignty.

I think this account can be provided by reflecting more deeply on the way that sovereignty connects with human rights. As is well known, sovereignty

Intervention and State Sovereignty [ICISS] (Ottawa: International Development Research Centre, December 2001), 32–37.

[11] Carl von Clausewitz, *On War*, edited and translated by Michael Howard and Peter Paret (Princeton University Press, 1976), 87.

[12] *The Responsibility to Protect*, ICISS Report, 35.

[13] On March 21, 2011, President Obama stated, "It is US policy that Gaddafi needs to go." The following month Barack Obama, David Cameron, and Nicholas Sarkozy confirmed this position by jointly publishing an article entitled "The Bombing Continues till Gaddafi Goes" stating that "it is impossible to imagine a future for Libya with Gaddafi in power." *The Telegraph* and *The Times* (April 15, 2011).

was originally conceived as an attribute of states. The original conception of sovereignty, as developed by theorists such as Jean Bodin and Thomas Hobbes, meant that there could be only one supreme source of authority within a territory. As we have seen, Kofi Annan proposed that the concept of state sovereignty be complemented with a notion of individual sovereignty – the rights and freedoms of individual persons. However, it is crucial to understand that in a normative sense, it is the sovereignty of individuals, not of states, that is primary. The legal notion of state sovereignty is a descriptive concept: It means simply that a state is de facto capable of asserting supreme authority within its territory. But the de facto exercise of power tells us nothing about a state's moral right to assert that power. Sovereignty in its normative sense refers to a moral and political right; it means the right to manage one's own affairs without violent or coercive intervention by others. But this right of non-interference is possessed, first and foremost, by individual persons and only derivatively by states.

But why do individual persons possess this morally primary right to non-interference? Ever since the Enlightenment, we have conceived of persons as being capable of possessing moral rights because of their status as free, equal, and rational moral agents. This trio of moral attributes constitutes what we might call "the Enlightenment conception of the human subject." It still provides the best account of why persons can bear rights; and, as I will suggest below, it informs also the content and limit of those rights.

States and social entities can also possess the sovereign right to non-interference, but they do so only derivatively. Political sovereignty is a synthetic attribute; it is created when individuals join together in just political relations. Without an appropriate connection to a community engaged in just political relations, state sovereignty is simply a de facto monopoly of force that imposes no special obligations on others.[14]

How should we conceive of just political relations that are capable of grounding the collective sovereign rights enjoyed by states? That is a central question of political philosophy and a full account is beyond the scope of this discussion. But it is clear that a basic condition of just political relations is that they respect the sovereignty of individual persons – that is to say, the right of individuals to manage their own affairs without unjustified violent or coercive intervention by others.

All of this I take to be familiar and, I hope, uncontroversial. However, there is a corollary of this principle that is little noticed and of great importance. If just political relations that stand at the source of state sovereignty must respect the sovereign rights of individuals, then it is clear that just political relations must

---

[14] This account follows the reinterpretation of the social-contract tradition elaborated in somewhat different terms by Michael Walzer and David Luban. See Walzer, *Just and Unjust Wars*, chap. 4; Luban, "Just War and Human Rights," 160–81.

exclude the conduct of politics through violence. Just political relations are necessarily non-violent. Why? Because political violence is the attempt to compel the will of others through force. In doing so, it overrides or negates their status as free, equal, and rational moral agents. Debate, persuasion, compromise, negotiation, horse-trading, and majoritarian voting are all characteristic modes of politics that engage with and recognize the rational will of others. But politics conducted through violent coercion is different. It treats the will of the other as an object to be acted on or overcome through force.

As Clausewitz explained, the attempt to overthrow the will of an enemy through force is the defining characteristic of that archetypal form of political violence, war: "physical force ... is the means of war; to impose our will on the enemy is its *object*."[15] Political violence and war are in this way antithetical to the most minimal standards of just political relations because they fail to recognize the status of persons as rights-bearing moral agents. And it is precisely such relations that stand at the normative root of all political sovereignty.

Crucial to this claim is a distinction between different ways in which violence can be employed by political actors or state agents. Political violence is best understood as violence that is constitutive to the formation of collective decisions or outcomes. But not all violence employed by political actors or agents of the state is political violence in this sense. Consider a court of law that employs violence to enforce a legitimate sentence. Court officials do not thereby engage in "political violence," and they need violate no rights of the condemned man. What is crucial is the distinction between what we might call "input-violence" and "output-violence." Political violence employs violent coercion as an *input* to a collective decision process. An example would be if the prosecution used violent threats to influence the decision of judge or jury. Legitimate law enforcement, in contrast, employs violence as an *output* of decision procedures that are morally justified because they take proper account of the rights of subject persons (crucially of course by excluding violence from those decision procedures). Political violence – that is to say violence employed as a constituent of a decision procedure – always contravenes rights, whereas violence that is the output of morally justified decision procedures need not.[16]

The fact that political sovereignty emerges from the rights-respecting interactions of individual persons explains *why* political sovereignty is conditional in the first place. A state cannot claim the moral protection of political sovereignty when it is engaged in acts of political violence against members its community. This is because the moral right of political sovereignty only exists because of the mutual practice of just political relations – a practice that I have argued excludes political violence.

---

[15] Clausewitz, *On War*, 75 (italics in the original).
[16] A related distinction between political violence and violence employed in defense of rights will be discussed below.

But the conditionality argument is only half the story. It is crucial to understand that in a situation of humanitarian intervention we have to deal not only with the negative aspect of sovereignty identified in the conditionality argument – the forfeiture or absence of sovereign rights on the part of those who perpetrate political violence or atrocity. We have to account also for the positive aspects of political sovereignty – the fact that members of a community who are not engaged in violent or otherwise unjust political action retain the sovereign right to manage their own affairs without interference. They possess this right as much against the political action of external interveners, as they do against the internal perpetrators.

This observation lies at the core of the notion of "human sovereignty," as I am using it. A humanitarian intervention conducted under principles of human sovereignty would combine the negative account of the forfeiture of state sovereignty found in the conditionality argument, with a positive account of the right of people to forge their own political settlements free from violent interference by either insiders or outsiders. Crucially, members of a community may continue to possess this positive right even when their government has forfeited its right against forceful foreign intervention.

The argument so far has been highly abstract. What would a humanitarian intervention informed by human sovereignty actually look like? And how would it differ from the more traditional conditionality approach? All accounts of humanitarian intervention begin with the imperative to prevent grave human-rights abuses. But an intervention conducted under the conception of human sovereignty would insist on a complementary strategic objective that informs and supports the primary objective. The complementary objective is to respect and to facilitate a tolerably just and non-violent indigenous political process within the community subject to intervention. Human sovereignty recognizes the fact that people have the right to forge their own political settlement through just political relations, unimpeded by violent interference by either compatriots or foreigners. Even when a government has forfeited its sovereignty by engaging in atrocity, the right of human sovereignty may still be held by significant elements of the community. This residual human sovereignty places significant constraints on the action of interveners.

In particular, two constraints are of fundamental importance. First, there is a general prohibition on providing sustained military support to one belligerent within a civil conflict. Interveners should not be in the business of "picking winners" among competing political factions. Even when one community or faction bears overwhelming responsibility for abuses, this does not justify providing sustained military support to its enemies. Humanitarian interveners must not become participants in a civil war.

This principle has three practical corollaries. First, in almost all circumstances, interveners may not provide direct military aid to one faction in a civil conflict. They may not provide weapons, training, communications, intelligence, or logistical support. Second, interveners should not integrate or coordinate their operations with those of a particular faction, for example by providing close air support, even when it may be operationally advantageous to do so. Third, interveners should explicitly declare their readiness to use force to interdict atrocities or other criminal acts, irrespective of who are the perpetrators. This may entail carrying out operations, when necessary, against both government and opposition forces, which must itself rule out close operational coordination.

The principle of no sustained coordination does not preclude ad hoc cooperation with a particular faction to thwart an imminent massacre or atrocity. What is precluded, however, is a sustained campaign of support in which interveners integrate themselves militarily and politically with one particular side of a conflict. Interveners may use force to defend rights, but they are not entitled to become participants in a civil military conflict over the political destiny of the community.

These operational principles are supported by both pragmatic and moral reasons. It is pragmatically perilous to support an armed faction in a civil conflict about whom we may know very little. It is a profound error to believe that the enemy of the bad guys must be the good guys. The opponents of an abusive regime might indeed be virtuous freedom fighters, struggling to establish a just civil order. But they may equally be disempowered perpetrators-in-waiting, preparing to settle old ethnic or sectarian blood-scores. It is particularly difficult to assess the moral status and true intentions of rebel actors who typically have no previous record of government. To provide direct military assistance to one political actor in circumstances of such uncertainty involves moral and political recklessness at best, and at worst it may involve complicity in international crimes.

But there is also a deeper moral reason for the prohibition on providing sustained military support. The notion of human sovereignty implies that people have the right to determine their own affairs and political destiny without the violent or coercive interference by others. This right is most obviously violated by a state or other actor that commits the four Responsibility to Protect crimes. But the right is also violated by rebels or insurgents who employ force of arms against the state in order to forge a new political settlement – and by those who give them military support. Human sovereignty encompasses the right to a political process compatible with our status as free and rational moral agents. And that, as I have argued, entails at the minimum a political process not conducted through means of political violence.

This leads naturally to the second implication of the human sovereignty account. An explicit goal of intervention should be to positively facilitate and foster an indigenous and non-violent political process consistent with the right of human sovereignty.

Analytically, we may think of a hierarchy of four processes by which political transformation can be achieved within a community. By "transformation" I mean profound political change such as regime change or altered constitutional arrangements.

(1) Political transformation may be achieved through participatory constitutional mechanisms. Most notable are democratic processes, but we may envision other forms of legitimate participatory politics that are not fully or exclusively democratic.

(2) Political transformation may be achieved through popular, non-violent but extra-constitutional means. These are classic strategies of non-violent political resistance: strikes, civil disobedience, mass mobilization, sit-ins, boycotts, and the like. These are all strategies by which a community (or significant components of it) withdraws consent from current political arrangements.

(3) Political transformation through violent military means: civil war, coup, insurgency, military revolution and their counter-measures; military repression and counter-insurgency.

(4) Political transformation achieved through atrocity, including the four Responsibility to Protect crimes of genocide, crimes against humanity, ethnic cleansing, and war crimes. These crimes are characterized by an attempt, not merely to violently coerce a political opponent, but to eliminate or destroy that opponent entirely.

The first thing to note is that there is a clear hierarchy in the moral legitimacy of these processes from the first to the last. Categories 1 and 2 represent the "green zone" of tolerably just political processes. Categories 3 and 4 represent the "red zone" of political processes that, to varying degrees, violate the right of human sovereignty. Moreover, the legitimacy of practices within the green zone is interlinked. Thus extra-constitutional civil disobedience is permissible to the extent that participatory constitutional avenues are either absent or deficient.

Humanitarian intervention is best conceived as forceful action required to protect persons from atrocity, and conducted in such a way as to push actors out of the red zone and into the green zone of political interaction. It can achieve this first by providing credible security guarantees for those citizens who seek to participate in green-zone political processes and, second, by seeking to marginalize and restrain those on both sides who engage in red-zone acts. Fortunately, in many circumstances there will be considerable synergy in these two overlapping goals.

This can clearly be seen when we examine these principles in an operational context. Consider the 2011 NATO intervention in Libya. Note first that the human sovereignty account is entirely consistent with the reasoning employed by the United Nations Security Council. UN Security Council Resolution 1973 banned all non-humanitarian flights and authorized member states "to take all necessary measures … to protect civilians and civilian populated areas under threat of attack in the Libyan Arab Jamahiriya, including Benghazi, while excluding a foreign occupation force of any form on any part of Libyan territory."[17] Although the Council did not employ such terms, this mandate seems well calibrated to the demands of human sovereignty. Interveners are authorized narrowly to protect civilians and the areas in which they live, and overt political interference is constrained by a ban on the occupation of territory.

In reality the intervention was conducted in very different terms. Early in the campaign, leaders of intervening states declared that the Gaddafi regime must end and strongly suggested that this was an objective of the operation.[18] This impression was strengthened by close coordination with, and military support offered to, the rebels. In effect, NATO became the air-combat wing of the Free Libyan Army. Sorties were undertaken against loyalist forces in rear positions that were not posing an imminent threat to civilians or to civilian populated areas.

The intervention was de facto an act of forcible regime change. This had two significant negative consequences. The first is that it gave the victorious Libyan military factions a strong hand in forging the post-crisis political settlement. It is reasonable to assume that these factions included some of the more extreme actors of Libyan politics, whether or not they included full-fledged members of Al Qaeda.[19] Second, it tainted the notion of Responsibility to Protect in the eyes of many states. The perception that Western forces grossly exceeded their mandate in Libya, by transforming a civilian-protection mandate into a political-transformation operation, has made it much more difficult to achieve consensus in the Security Council for action to avert ongoing atrocity in Syria.[20]

In light of the way the intervention was actually conducted, Resolution 1973 looks like a stillborn precedent for the concept of human sovereignty. Was there an alternative?

Imagine that the campaign in Libya had been conducted on principles of human sovereignty. How might it have proceeded? Recall that the crisis began, not with an armed insurrection, but (following the examples of Tunisia and Egypt) with peaceful protest and a civil-resistance movement in major cities. A human-sovereignty-based doctrine would have made this peaceful protest

---

[17] UN Security Council Resolution 1973, UN document S/Res/1973 (March 17, 2011), para. 4.

[18] See note 13.

[19] In the aftermath of the Libyan revolution, protests have occurred against the continuing influence of the militia brigades who fought against the Gaddafi regime. Some brigades are widely perceived to be implementing fundamentalist policies out of touch with the majority of the population, and some are suspected of being complicit in the murder of US Ambassador Christopher Stephens in Benghazi in September 2012.

[20] Though the self-interested obstructionism of Russia and China should not be either underestimated or exonerated.

movement – not the nascent armed insurgency – the center of gravity of the operations. The overarching strategy would have been to use airpower to create a perimeter of tolerable safety around those engaged in peaceful protest in the urban centers. A clear and explicit message would be sent to the citizens of Libya: You have the right to attempt political transformation through peaceful protest; and if you exercise that right, then the NATO force will take steps to protect you from attack.

At the same time, armed insurgents would be marginalized through a refusal to provide military assistance to a broader insurgency campaign. Additionally, NATO would make clear that they interpret the UN mandate to also authorize strikes against rebel forces should they threaten civilians or civilian areas. Of course, as noted above, this would not preclude ad hoc coordination with citizens from either faction collectively defending themselves against ongoing or imminent unjustified attack from opposing forces.

Two questions about this proposal are key: Could such a strategy have been effective in narrowly military terms? Second, what would have been the impact on the broader political context? The truth is that it is impossible to know the answer to the first question. Enormous advances have been made in the ability to conduct aerial surveillance and precision strikes, but urban areas remain an extraordinarily challenging operational environment. Presumably a combination of fixed-wing, rotary, and drone aircraft deployed in a situation of air-superiority would have been sufficient to deny the regime the ability to use artillery, armored vehicles, and massed columns of troops against a body of civilian protesters. But it is clear that airpower alone could have provided scant protection from snipers hidden in civilian buildings or against non-uniformed agents of the regime mingling within a crowd. Moreover, airpower can do nothing against a state's security apparatus used to terrorize and torture protesters and those associated with them. Using airpower in crowded urban environments would also inevitably have led to the accidental killing of civilians.[21]

Would such a precarious operational effect have been sufficient to achieve the objective of enabling a peaceful, indigenous, political process to run its course in Libya? Again, this is an imponderable question. What is striking, however, is that airpower would likely have been sufficient to prevent the regime from using large-scale military assets to bodily remove or dissipate a mass of protesters, while leaving undisturbed its ability to use lower-grade forms of violence to terrorize or coerce. This suggests that the key determinant would be the moral strength and cohesion of the protesters themselves. What gives hope is that, throughout the various "Arab Spring" movements, young men and women have demonstrated a moral courage in the face of violence and state terror that is in equal measure humbling and awe-inspiring.

---

[21] I am grateful to Air Commodore (ret.) Peter Gray for his advice on the capabilities and limitations of contemporary airpower.

Let us assume, then, that the strategy outlined could indeed have achieved a "tolerable" degree of safety for those engaged in civilian protest, at least sufficient to sustain that movement in the face of government opposition.[22] What would have been the effect? There can be little doubt that if the civilian protest movement had been allowed to run its course in Libya, then the Gaddafi regime, devoid of internal legitimacy, would have gone the way of the Mubarak and Ben Ali regimes before it.

But now we might have a different worry. If intervention of the kind here advocated would also have led to regime change, then are we not just back with the problem of improper political intervention? What has become then of the right of communities to determine their own affairs free from violent or coercive interference implied by the notion of human sovereignty?

There is a clear answer to this charge. An intervention that removes criminal violence from the political process of a community is not an improper interference in the politics of that community. On the contrary, it is a means to enable a more legitimate politics process.

It makes all the difference how intervention leads to political transformation. We must distinguish between justified violent acts that have political consequences and acts of political violence. The latter are ruled out by human sovereignty, whereas the former need not be. To see this, consider the following hypothetical case. If I am summoned for an interview in the Oval Office and the US president suddenly and inexplicably flies into a violent rage and tries to kill me, then I may kill him in self-defense if such action is both necessary and proportionate. My killing of the president would be a violent act with profound political consequences. But it would not be an act of political violence. The political consequences of the killing play no intentional or justificatory role in my defensive action. Similarly, if a humanitarian intervention removes the ability of a regime to sustain itself by murdering and intimidating its own citizens, then the political transformation that results will clearly be a consequence of the intervention. But this does not mean that the intervention is an act of "political violence," in any objectionable way.

Consider an analogy: Killing an aggressor in self-defense or defense of another is not an act of murder (it is not a violation of the right to life). Rather, it interdicts a violation of the right to life. Similarly, an intervention that removes the capacity of actors to deploy political violence is not itself an improper political intervention (it is not an act of political violence). Rather, it is an interdiction of political violence.

This might seem a casuistic distinction, but it is a crucial one. Permissible intervention is proportionate action to defend human rights from imminent attack and that simultaneously creates the possibility of a more legitimate

---

[22] "Tolerable," of course, does not mean morally tolerable but merely that those subject to it would be capable of bearing up under it.

political process within the community. The permissible political objectives of humanitarian intervention is nothing less – and, crucially, nothing more – than to open up and defend a space in which a non-violent indigenous political process consistent with the right of human sovereignty can take place.

By way of conclusion, I would like to first distinguish my view from a rival to which it may appear superficially similar, and second to reflect on whether, and to what extent, halting atrocity through military intervention is obligatory as well as permissible.

I have argued that interveners are morally required not to give sustained political or military support to one faction in a civil war. John Stuart Mill, in his famous essay on intervention, similarly argued that foreign powers must remain neutral in a civil conflict; but for Mill the requirement of neutrality is much stronger: it grounds a general prohibition on humanitarian intervention itself.[23] His reasoning is an interesting mix of virtue ethics and consequentialism. Free institutions will only be sustainable if the community possesses a deep commitment to freedom and is willing to sacrifice for it. "The only test possessing any real value, of a people's having become fit for popular institutions, is that they, or a sufficient portion of them to prevail in the contest, are willing to brave labor and danger for their liberation." "If a people ... does not value [freedom] sufficiently to fight for it, and maintain it against any force which can be mustered within the country ... it is only a question in how few years or months that people will be enslaved."[24] Foreigners should not intervene in a civil war, because the conflict has a morally important epistemic function (it tells us whether the people are fit to be free) and a generative function (fighting for freedom is itself a "school" which teaches the virtues of freedom).[25]

Whatever we think of this argument, Mill was clearly wrong to believe that only enduring in a *violent* struggle could perform these epistemic and generative functions. Recent protest movements, including the Arab Spring, have demonstrated, beyond doubt, that non-violent action can also play these roles. The Kalashnikov-wielding fighter in an anti-government brigade demonstrates no greater commitment to freedom than the woman who repeatedly risks detention, torture, and death through peaceful protest. We do not need to protect the domain of military struggle in order to provide opportunities for braving labor and danger. Those opportunities are regrettably common enough.

The question is whether the process of violent struggle by members of a community possesses a moral value sufficient to outweigh the goods that might be achieved by external intervention (including the prevention of murder). Michael Walzer, who adopts and reinterprets Mill's argument, thinks

[23] John Stuart Mill, "A Few Words on Non-Intervention" [*Fraser's Magazine*, December 1859], in *Essays on Politics and Culture by John Stuart Mill*, edited by Gertrude Himmelfarb (Garden City, New York: Doubleday Anchor Books, 1963), 381–382.
[24] *Ibid.*   [25] *Ibid.*

that it does. This is because he believes that indigenous violent struggle is a form of morally valuable communal autonomy. A community whose political arrangements are forged through the competition of internal military force is self-determining, whereas a community that experiences external intervention is not.[26] So important is the value of communal autonomy for Walzer that he endorses Mill's claim that if a foreign power intervenes on one side of civil war, then other states would be justified in undertaking a counter-intervention, not to determine the outcome of the war, but only to preserve the underlying domestic balance of power.[27] The bizarre nature of this position is not lost on Walzer who provides an analogy that brings it sharply into relief: "It is as if a policeman, instead of breaking up a fight between two people, should stop anyone else from interfering or, if he cannot do that, should give proportional assistance to the disadvantaged party."[28]

Walzer is apparently willing to accept this peculiar implication. But the problems with the communal-autonomy account are familiar and deep. If violent struggle is a legitimate, and indeed protected, form of political process in the domestic sphere, then why not also in the international sphere? If one replies that genuine communities have an intrinsic unity that makes violent struggle an appropriate mechanism for deciding internal arrangements, but not for deciding interstate disputes, then one faces a different problem. What would be the objection to replacing or supplementing certain constitutional functions of the Supreme Court with forms of violent contest that reflect the domestic balance of power? One might answer, in a consequentialist vein, that deliberation through violence would be more costly and less efficient than a judicial process. But that response entirely misses the point. Even if the process were a kind of formalized gladiatorial contest in which resulting harms were tightly constrained and only suffered by consenting participants, such a process could not possibly be just. This is because of a fundamental point that I have emphasized repeatedly in this chapter: Violence is never a morally appropriate mechanism of political or collective deliberation. While people can become liable to defensive violence because they are responsible for an unjust threat to the rights of others, political decisions and outcomes must be determined by deliberative processes that recognize and respect the status of persons as rights-bearing subjects. Political violence of any form manifestly fails to do this.

The difference between the rival positions can be succinctly summarized: Mill and Walzer think that intervention should protect a space *for* indigenous violent politics. I believe that intervention should protect a space *from* violent politics. If people have the right to determine their own political affairs without violent coercion by others, then they possess this right against the violent

[26] Walzer, *Just and Unjust Wars*, 88–89.
[27] *Ibid.*, 97. Mill, "A Few Words on Non-Intervention," 123–24.
[28] Walzer, *Just and Unjust Wars*, 97.

coercion of compatriots as much as they possess it against foreigners. That is the essence of the approach that I have been calling "human sovereignty."

One potential objection to my approach is that by placing constraints on the political character of intervention, it implicitly makes intervention more onerous. If such a norm were generally accepted, then this may have the effect of reducing the readiness of foreign powers to undertake interventions, which may in the long run be worse for the victims of atrocity themselves. This raises the difficult question of whether humanitarian intervention to stop atrocity is morally obligatory, and if so what is the strength of the obligation. If intervention is sometimes obligatory, then these additional burdens may simply be costs that interveners are morally required to bear.

The original ICISS report is ambiguous on this issue. The term "Responsibility to Protect" sounds like a synonym for "Duty to Protect"; and when the authors discuss the responsibilities of governments to protect their own citizens, it is clearly being used in this way. But when the report discusses the "responsibility" of international agencies and states, it is much less clear that they are attributing a duty. For example, duties are often enforceable; but would a state that culpably fails to intervene in a clear Responsibility to Protect situation be liable to violent remedial action if that were both necessary and proportionate to force it to fulfill its obligations?[29]

A further challenge comes from reflecting on opportunity costs. Humanitarian intervention requires the expenditure of significant financial, human, and political capital. But in narrow welfare terms, this expenditure could certainly realize greater good if it were instead directed toward providing basic food or medical aid for the world's poor. Why direct resources to atrocity-prevention through military intervention, when we could save more lives through aid? For consequentialists like Peter Singer, the answer is simple: We shouldn't.[30]

---

[29] I discuss these issues in David Rodin, "The Responsibility to Protect and the Logic of Rights," in Oliver Jütersonke and Keith Krause (eds.), *From Rights to Responsibilities: Rethinking Interventions for Humanitarian Purposes*, PSIS Special Study 7 (Geneva: Programme for Strategic and International Security Studies, 2006).

[30] Peter Singer, "Bystanders to Poverty," in N. A. Davis, R. Keshen, and J. McMahan (eds.), *Ethics and Humanity: Themes from the Philosophy of Jonathan Glover* (Oxford University Press, 2010).
   In one sense, of course, the consequentialist challenge negates itself by proving too much. If we were really obligated always to maximize aggregate welfare, then the vast majority of the state's activity could not be justified. Cultural and education programs, minority-rights initiatives, environmental protection, and philosophy research all get government support yet generate less aggregate welfare than spending on food and medical aid. Still, the question has bite because both humanitarian intervention and foreign aid are forms of assistance for foreigners, so it is appropriate to ask whether such assistance should not be administered so as to maximize the welfare of the recipients.

RETHINKING RESPONSIBILITY TO PROTECT

However, many people intuitively believe that there is a stronger reason to intervene to prevent atrocity than to alleviate poverty. One potential reason is that giving aid to the poor averts harm, but intervening to stop atrocity averts harm and, in addition, averts heinous wrongdoing. However, Jeff McMahan and Victor Tadros have recently argued that this consideration provides only a weak reason to privilege the prevention of wrongs over equivalent harms.[31] One ought to rescue even a modestly greater number from natural harm in preference to a smaller number from the wrongdoing of others.

My tentative proposal is that the greater duty to prevent atrocity may in part be explained by the differing moral status of regimes of self-help in the provision of economic goods and security goods respectively. Consider economic goods first. A regime based primarily on self-help for the provision of economic goods is morally justified, because it produces positive externalities for other members of the community. When people take primary responsibility for their economic welfare and seek to further it through competitive economic interactions, they tend to produce increases in efficiency and innovation. These increases in productivity generate greater aggregate wealth compared with regimes that attempt the central coordinated provision of welfare goods. Call this the "Adam Smith thesis."[32]

Now consider security. In contrast to economic goods, a self-help regime for the provision of security generates substantial externality harms. When people take primary responsibility for their own security and seek to further it through competitive security interactions, this generates further risks and insecurity for other members of the community, making everyone worse off. This is, of course, a central observation of social-contract theory: By independently seeking our own security, we degrade the security of all. Without the shared and socially coordinated provision of security, we would be in a state of nature in which the life of man is "solitary, poor, nasty, brutish and short."[33] Call this the "Hobbesian thesis."

Neither the Adam Smith nor the Hobbesian thesis is attractive in a pure or absolute form. We know that regimes of economic self-help create negative externalities (such as inequality, and environmental degradation) even as they produce aggregate benefits. For these reasons, even the most libertarian societies recognize a role for collective and centralized provision of certain economic and regulatory goods, including mandatory social insurance,

---

[31] Jeff McMahan, "Humanitarian Intervention, Consent, and Proportionality," in Davis *et al.*, *Ethics and Humanity*, 60ff.; Victor Tadros, *The Ends of Harm: The Moral Foundations of Criminal Law* (Oxford University Press, 2011), 105–8, 122–23.

[32] Of course, this thesis has not always been uncontroversial; but the contrasting experiences of North and South Korea, and East and West Germany, strongly suggests that it possesses considerable truth.

[33] Thomas Hobbes, *Leviathan*, edited by R. Tuck (Cambridge University Press, 1991), chap. XIII, paras. 9, 89.

redistributive taxation, aid, and social funding. Moreover, certain kinds of aid can generate important positive externalities. Conversely, every sovereign recognizes certain rights of private-security provision, such as the right to use necessary and proportionate defensive force against imminent unjust threats.

But these provisos do not blunt the normative force of the two theses. The grain of economic and security goods clearly run in different directions. A presumption in favor of self-help for the provision of economic goods is justifiable, because such regimes tend to create positive externalities for others. A presumption in favor of shared and collective provision of security goods is not justifiable because self-help security regimes create substantial negative externalities for others. The greater obligation we have to intervene against atrocity than to provide aid to the poor should be understood in this context.

Let me straightaway acknowledge the limitations of this argument. To talk of the positive externalities of economic self-help can seem inappropriate, if not perverse, in the face of the extreme need experienced by many of the global poor. The force of this point is well taken. It demonstrates that there can be no lexical priority for the obligation to provide security goods over welfare goods. What is more, no single actor, or group of actors, in isolation can realize the positive externalities of replacing a self-help system with an effective, shared, and coordinated security regime. If that is so, then how can these considerations be normative for actors in an international environment still largely structured around self-help security arrangements?

This later point shows that, contrary to appearances, the externalities argument is not best interpreted in consequentialist terms. It may, instead, be better understood in contractualist terms, as suggested by my allusion above. An agent in the state of nature has a moral reason to undertake actions that conduce to the development of an effective, sovereign-governance system, even if these actions on their own will not be sufficient to bring this structure about. In a similar way, the obligation to intervene against atrocity is partially grounded in our recognition that security is different from economic goods: It cannot be appropriately provided under a primary regime of self-help.[34] This difference helps to explain why we have greater reason to be our brother's keeper in matters of security than in matters of economic welfare.

---

[34] This obviously raises the question of why self-help is generally accepted as the principle remedy for international security. I discuss this question in Rodin, *War and Self-Defense*, 181–88.

SELECT BIBLIOGRAPHY

UN documents and reports

(by date)

Annan, Kofi, *The Question of Intervention: Statements by the Secretary-General of the United Nations Kofi Annan* (New York: United Nations, Department of Public Information, 1999).

Two Concepts of Sovereignty, Annual Report to General Assembly, Press Release SG/SM/7136, GA/9596 (September 20, 1999).

We the Peoples: The Role of the United Nations in the Twenty-first Century, Millennium Report of the Secretary-General, UN document A/54/2000 (March 2000).

A More Secure World: Our Shared Responsibility, Report of the Secretary-General's High-level Panel on Threats, Challenges and Change (New York: United Nations, 2004).

In Larger Freedom: Towards Development, Security and Human Rights for All, Report of the Secretary-General, UN document A/59/2005 (March 21, 2005).

2005 World Summit Outcome, UN General Assembly Resolution, UN document A/60/1 (October 24, 2005).

UN Security Council Resolution 1674, UN document S/Res/1674 (April 28, 2006).

Implementing the Responsibility to Protect, Report of the Secretary-General, UN document A/63/677 (January 12, 2009).

Early Warning, Assessment and the Responsibility to Protect, Report of the Secretary-General, UN document A/64/846 (July 14, 2010).

UN Security Council Resolution 1970, UN document S/Res/1970 (February 26, 2011).

UN Security Council Resolution 1973, UN document S/Res/1973 (March 17, 2011).

Reports and studies

Amnesty International, *The Battle for Libya: Killing, Disappearances and Torture* (London: Amnesty International Ltd., September 13, 2011).

Bell, Anthony and Witter, David, *The Libyan Revolution: Roots of the Rebellion*, Parts I, II, and III (Washington, DC: Institute for the Study of War, September 2011).

Bell, Anthony, Butts, Spencer, and Witter, David, *The Libyan Revolution: The Tide Turns*, Part IV (Washington, DC: Institute for the Study of War, November 2011).

Evans, Gareth and Sahnoun, Mohamed (co-chairs), *The Responsibility to Protect*, Report of the International Commission on Intervention and State Sovereignty (Ottawa: International Development Research Centre, December 2001).

The US Army Stability Operations Field Manual: US Army Field Manual No. 3–07 (US Government: US Army, 2008).

US Special Inspector General, *Hard Lessons: The Iraq Reconstruction Experience* (Washington, DC: US Independent Agencies and Commissions, 2009).

Waxman, Matthew C., *Intervention to Stop Genocide and Mass Atrocities*, Council Special Report No. 49 (New York: Council on Foreign Relations, October 2009).

Books

Abiew, F.K., *The Evolution of the Doctrine and Practice of Humanitarian Intervention* (The Hague: Kluwer Law International, 1999).

Allard, K., *Somalia Operations: Lessons Learned* (Washington, DC: National Defense University Press, 1995).

Altman, Andrew and Wellman, Christopher Heath, *A Liberal Theory of International Justice* (Oxford University Press, 2009).

Anghie, Antony, *Imperialism, Sovereignty and the Making of International Law* (Cambridge University Press, 2005).

Annan, Kofi, *The Question of Intervention: Statements by the Secretary-General* (United Nations, 1999).

Annan, Kofi (with Nader Mousavizadeh), *Interventions: A Life in War and Peace* (New York: Penguin Press, 2012).

Barnett, Michael N., *Eyewitness to a Genocide: The UN and Rwanda* (Ithaca, New York: Cornell University Press, 2003).

Bellamy, Alex J., *Global Politics and the Responsibility to Protect: From Words to Deeds* (London and New York: Routledge, 2011).

  A Responsibility to Protect (London: Polity Press, 2009).

Blair, Tony, *A Journey: My Political Life* (New York: Knopf, 2010).

Bodin, Jean, M.J. Tooley (trans.), *Six Books of the Commonwealth* (1576) (Oxford: Basil Blackwell, 1967), Book I, Chapter 8. Available at: www.constitution.org/bodin/bodin.htm

Bridoux, Jeff, *American Foreign Policy and Post-War Reconstruction: Comparing Japan and Iraq* (London and New York: Routledge, 2012).

Brownlie, Ian, *International Law and the Use of Force by States* (Oxford: Clarendon Press, 1974).

Principles of Public International Law, 6th edn. (Oxford University Press, 2003).

Buchanan, Allen, *Human Rights, Legitimacy, & the Use of Force* (Oxford University Press, 2010).

Caney, Simon, *Justice Beyond Borders: A Global Political Theory* (Oxford University Press, 2005).

Carlton, Eric, *Occupation: The Politics and Practices of Military Conquers* (London: Routledge, 1992).

Cassesse, Antonio, *International Criminal Law*, 2nd edn. (Oxford University Press, 2008).

Chatterjee, Deen K. and Scheid, Don E. (eds.), *Ethics and Foreign Intervention* (Cambridge University Press, 2003).

Chesterman, Simon, *Just War or Just Peace? Humanitarian Intervention and International Law* (Oxford University Press, 2001).

Chirot, Daniel and McCauley, Clark, *Why Not Kill Them All? The Logic and Prevention of Political Mass Murder* (Princeton University Press, 2006).

Clark, Wesley K., *Waging Modern War: Bosnia, Kosovo, and the Future of Combat* (New York: Public Affairs Press, 2001).

Clarke, Walter and Herbst, Jeffrey, *Learning from Somalia: The Lessons of Armed Humanitarian Intervention* (Lexington, Massachusetts: Westview Press, 1997).

Shake Hands with the Devil: The Failure of Humanity in Rwanda (New York: Carroll & Graf Publishers/Random House, 2004)

Coady, C.A.J., *The Ethics of Armed Humanitarian Intervention*, no. 45 (Washington, DC: United States Institute of Peace, 2002).

Connor, R.W., *Thucydides* (Princeton University Press, 1984).

Cook, Martin L., *The Moral Warrior: Ethics and Service in the US Military* (Albany, New York: State University of New York Press, 2004).

Dallaire, Lt. General Roméo, *Shake Hands with the Devil: The Failure of Humanity in Rwanda* (New York: Carroll & Graf Publishers/Random House, 2004).

Damrosch, Lori F. (ed.), *Enforcing Restraint: Collective Intervention in Internal Conflicts* (New York: Council on Foreign Relations Press, 1993).

Damrosch, Lori F., Henkin, Louis, Murphy, Sean D., and Smit, Hans, *International Law* (St. Paul: West Group, 2001).

Danspeckgruber, Wolfgang F. and Tripp, Charles (eds.), *The Iraqi Aggression Against Kuwait: Strategic Lessons and Implications for Europe* (Boulder, Colo.: Westview Press, 1996).

Davidson, Eugene, *The Death and Life of Germany: An Account of the American Occupation* (St. Louis: University of Missouri Press, 1999).

Dinstein, Yoram, *War, Aggression, and Self-Defense*, 4th edn. (Cambridge University Press, 2005).

Dobbins, James and Jones, S. (eds.), *The United Nations' Role in Nation-Building* (Washington, DC: RAND, 2007).

Dobbins, James and Lal, Rollie, *America's Role in Nation-Building: From Germany to Iraq* (Washington, DC: RAND, 2003).

Dobos, Ned, *Insurrection and Interventions: The Two Faces of Sovereignty* (Cambridge University Press, 2012).

Donald, David H., Baker, Jean Harvey, and Hold, Michael F., *Civil War and Reconstruction* (New York: W.W. Norton, 2000).

Downes, Alexander, *Targeting Civilians in War* (Ithaca, New York: Cornell University Press, 2008).

Doyle, Michael W., *Liberal Peace: Selected Essays* (London and New York: Routledge, 2012).

   Striking First: Preemption and Prevention in International Conflict, edited with commentaries by Stephen Macedo (Princeton University Press, 2008).

   Ways of War and Peace (New York and London: W.W. Norton, 1997).

Drumbl, Mark, *Atrocity, Punishment and International Law* (Cambridge University Press, 2007).

Elster, Jon, *Closing the Books: Transitional Justice in Historical Perspective* (New York: Cambridge University Press, 2004).

Evans, Gareth, *The Responsibility to Protect: Ending Mass Atrocity Crimes Once and For All* (Washington, DC: Brookings Institution Press, 2008).

Fletcher, George P. and Ohlin, Jens David, *Defending Humanity: When Force is Justified and Why* (Oxford and New York: Oxford University Press, 2008).

Frowe, Helen, *The Ethics of War and Peace: An Introduction* (London and New York: Routledge, 2011).

Garrett, Stephen A., *Doing Good and Doing Well: An Examination of Humanitarian Intervention* (Westport, Conn.: Praeger, 1999).

Gehring, Verna V. and Galston, William A. (eds.), *Philosophical Dimensions of Public Policy*, Policy Studies Review Annual, Vol. 13 (Piscataway, NJ: Transaction Publishers, 2002).

Gierycz, D., *Responsibility to Protect: A Legal and Human Rights Based Perspective* (Oslo: NUPI, 2008).

Gross, Michael L., *Moral Dilemmas of Modern War: Torture, Assassination, and Blackmail in an Age of Asymmetric Conflict* (Cambridge University Press, 2010).

Grotius, Hugo, *The Rights of War and Peace*, 3 vols., edited by Richard Tuck (Indianapolis: Liberty Fund, 2005).

Hamilton, Alexander, Madison, James, and Jay, John, *The Federalist Papers*, edited by Clinton Rossiter (New York: Penguin Group, 1961).

Hilsum, Lindsey, *Sandstorm: Libya in the Time of Revolution* (New York: Penguin Press, 2012).

Hippel, Karin von, *Democracy by Force: US Military Intervention in the Post-Cold War World* (Cambridge University Press, 2000).

Hirsch, Andrew von, Bottoms, Anthony E., Burney, Elizabeth, and Wikstrom, Per-Olof H., *Criminal Deterrence and Sentence Severity: An Analysis of Recent Research* (Oxford: Hart Publishing, 1999).

Hobbes, Thomas, *Leviathan*, edited by R. Tuck (Cambridge University Press, 1991).

Hoffman, Stanley, *The Ethics and Politics of Humanitarian Intervention* (South Bend, Ind.: Notre Dame University Press, 1996).

Ignatieff, Michael, *Virtual War: Kosovo and Beyond* (New York: Metropolitan Books, 2000).

Johnson, James Turner, *Morality and Contemporary Warfare* (New Haven: Yale University Press, 1999).

Johnstone, Ian, *The Power of Deliberation* (Oxford University Press, 2011).

Jones, Adam, *Genocide: A Comprehensive Introduction* (London and New York: Routledge, 2010).

Kant, Immanuel, *Groundwork for the Metaphysics of Morals (1785)*, translated by Lewis White Beck (New York: Macmillan, 1990).

The Metaphysics of Morals (1797), translated by Mary Gregor (Cambridge University Press, 1991).

Perpetual Peace and Other Essays, translated by Ted Humphrey (Indianapolis and Cambridge: Hackett Publishing, 1983).

Knight, Andy W. and Egerton, Frazer (eds.), *The Routledge Handbook of the Responsibility to Protect* (New York: Routledge, 2012).

Lamani, Mokhtar and Momani, Bessma (eds.), *From Desolation to Reconstruction: Iraq's Troubled Journey* (Waterloo, Ontario: CIGI, 2010).

Lindenmayer, E. and Kaye, J.L., *A Choice for Peace? The Story of the Forty-One Days of Mediation in Kenya* (New York: International Peace Institute, 2009).

Linklater, Andrew, *The Transformation of Political Community* (Cambridge: Polity Press, 1998).

Lucas, George R. Jr., *Perspectives on Humanitarian Military Intervention* (Berkeley Public Policy Press, 2001).

Lucas, George R. Jr. and Rubel, W. Rick (eds.), *Case Studies in Military Ethics*, 3rd edn. (Boston: Pearson/Longman, 2010).

Luck, Edward C., *UN Security Council: Practice and Promise* (New York and London: Routledge, 2006).

Maga, Timothy P., *Judgment at Tokyo: The Japanese War Crimes Trials* (Lexington, Kentucky: University Press of Kentucky, 2001).

Mamdani, Mahmood, *Saviors and Survivors: Darfur, Politics and the War on Terror* (New York: Pantheon, 2009).

May, Larry, *After War Ends: A Philosophical Perspective* (Cambridge University Press, 2012).

May, Larry and Forcehimes, Andrew (eds.), *Morality, Jus Post Bellum, and International Law* (Cambridge University Press, 2012).

McPherson, James M., *Battle Cry of Freedom: The Civil War Era* (Oxford University Press, 2003).

Mee, Charles L., *The Marshall Plan* (New York: HarperCollins, 1987).

Melvern, Linda, *A People Betrayed: The Role of the West in Rwanda's Genocide* (New York: Zed Books, 2000).

Moellendorf, Darrel, *Cosmopolitan Justice* (Boulder: Westview Press, 2002).

Noueihed, Lin and Warren, Alex, *The Battle for the Arab Spring: Revolution, Counter-Revolution and the Making of a New Era* (New Haven and London: Yale University Press, 2012).

Orend, Brian, *Human Rights: Concept and Context* (Peterborough, Ontario: Broadview Press, 2002).

Introduction to International Studies (Oxford University Press, 2012).

The Morality of War (Peterborough, Ontario: Broadview Press, 2006).

War and International Justice: A Kantian Perspective (Waterloo, Ontario: Wilfrid Laurier University Press, 2000).

Pattison, James, *Humanitarian Intervention and the Responsibility to Protect: Who Should Intervene?* (Oxford University Press, 2010).

Persico, Joseph E., *Nuremburg: Infamy on Trial* (New York: Penguin, 1995).

Pogge, Thomas, *World Poverty and Human Rights*, 2nd edn. (Cambridge: Polity Press, 2008).

Prunier, Gérard, *Rwanda: History of a Genocide* (New York: Columbia University Press, 1995).

Ramsey, Paul, *The Just War: Force and Political Responsibility* (Lanham, Md.: Rowman & Littlefield, 2002).

Rawls, John, *The Law of Peoples* (Cambridge, Massachusetts: Harvard University Press, 1999).

Reiff, David, *Slaughterhouse: Bosnia and the Failure of the West* (New York: Touchstone, 1995).

Roberts, A. and Guelff, R. (eds.), *Documentation on the Laws of War*, 3rd edn. (Oxford University Press, 2000).

Rodin, David, *War and Self-Defense* (Oxford: Clarendon Press, 2002).

Schabas, William A., *An Introduction to the International Criminal Court* (Cambridge University Press, 2001).

Schonberger, Howard B., *Aftermath of War: Americans and the Remaking of Japan, 1945–1952* (Kent, Ohio: Kent State University Press, 1989).

Segal, Leon V., *Fighting to the Finish: The Politics of War Termination in America and Japan* (Ithaca, New York: Cornell University Press, 1989).

Shaw, Malcolm N., *International Law*, 5th edn. (Cambridge University Press, 2003).

Shue, Henry, *Basic Rights: Subsistence, Affluence and US Foreign Policy*, 2nd edn. (Princeton University Press, 1996).

Sidgwick, Henry, *The Elements of Politics* (New York: Macmillan, 1908).

Geoffrey L. Simons, *The Scourging of Iraq: Sanctions, Law and Natural Justice*, 2nd edn. (London and New York: Macmillan/St. Martins, 1998).

Singer, P.W., *Wired for War: The Robotics Revolution and Conflict in the Twenty-first Century* (New York: Penguin Press, 2009).

Singer, Peter, *One World: The Ethics of Globalization*, 2nd edn. (New Haven and London: Yale University Press, 2004).

Snider, Don M., Nagl, John A., and Pfaff, Tony, *Army Professionalism, Military Ethics, and Officership in the 21st Century* (Carlisle, Pennsylvania: Army War College Strategic Studies Institute, 1999).

Solis, Gary D., *The Law of Armed Conflict: International Humanitarian Law in War* (Cambridge University Press, 2010).

Tadros, Victor, *The Ends of Harm: The Moral Foundations of Criminal Law* (Oxford University Press, 2011).

Teitel, Ruti G., *Transitional Justice* (Oxford University Press, 2002).

Tesón, Fernando R., *Humanitarian Intervention: An Inquiry into Law and Morality*, 3rd edn. (New York: Transnational Publishers, 2005).

A Philosophy of International Law (Boulder, Colorado: Westview Press, 1998).

Todorov, Tzvetan, *Hope and Memory: Lessons from the Twentieth Century*, translated by David Bellos (Princeton University Press, 2003).

Tondini, Matteo, *Statebuilding and Justice Reform: Post-Conflict Reconstruction in Afghanistan* (London and New York: Routledge, 2010).

Valentino, Benjamin, *Final Solutions: Mass Killing and Genocide in the Twentieth Century* (Ithaca, New York: Cornell University Press, 2004).

Waley, Arthur, *Three Ways of Thought in Ancient China* (London: George Allen & Unwin, 1939).

Walzer, Michael, *Arguing about War* (New Haven and London: Yale University Press, 2004).

Just and Unjust Wars: A Moral Argument with Historical Illustrations (New York: Basic Books, 1977).

Spheres of Justice: A Defense of Pluralism and Equality (Oxford: Basil Blackwood, 1983).

Thick and Thin: Moral Argument at Home and Abroad (New Haven: Yale University Press, 1994).

Weiner, Antje, *The Invisible Constitution of World Politics* (Cambridge University Press, 2008).

Weiss, Thomas G., *Humanitarian Intervention* (Cambridge: Polity Press, 2007).

Welsh, Jennifer, *At Home in the World: Canada's Global Vision for the 21st Century* (New York: HarperCollins, 2004).

Welsh, Jennifer M. (ed.), *Humanitarian Intervention and International Relations* (Oxford University Press, 2003).

Wheeler, Nicholas J., *Saving Strangers: Humanitarian Intervention in International Society* (Oxford University Press, 2000).

Woodward, Bob, *Plan of Attack* (New York: Simon & Schuster, 2004).

Zakheim, Dov S., *A Vulcan's Tale: How the Bush Administration Mismanaged the Reconstruction of Afghanistan* (Washington, DC: Brookings Institute, 2011).

Zartman, William, Deng, Francis M., Kimaro, Sadikiel, Lyons, Terrence, and Rothchild, Donald, *Sovereignty as Responsibility: Conflict Management in Africa* (Washington, DC: The Brookings Institution, 1996).

Articles and essays

Annan, Kofi, "Two Concepts of Sovereignty," *The Economist* (September 16, 1999).

Applbaum, Arthur, "Forcing a People to be Free," *Philosophy & Public Affairs* 35, no. 4 (2007), 359–400.

Baker, D.-P. and Pattison, J., "The Principled Case for Employing Private Military and Security Companies in Interventions for Human Rights Purposes," *Journal of Applied Philosophy* 29 (2012), 1–18.

Barnett, Michael N., "Building a Republican Peace: Stabilizing States After War," *International Security* 30, no. 4 (2006), 87–112.

Bass, Gary J., "Jus Post Bellum," *Philosophy & Public Affairs* 32, no. 4 (fall 2004), 384–412.

Bellamy, Alex J., "International Law and the War with Iraq," *Melbourne Journal of International Law* 4, no. 2 (2003), 497–521.

  "Kosovo and the Advent of Sovereignty as Responsibility," *Journal of Intervention and Statebuilding* 3, no. 2 (2009), 163–84.

  "Libya and the Responsibility to Protect: The Exception and the Norm," *Ethics & International Affairs* 25, no. 3 (Fall 2011), 263–69.

  "Motives, Outcomes, Intent and the Legitimacy of Humanitarian Intervention," *Journal of Military Ethics* 3, no. 3 (2004), 216–32.

  "The Responsibility to Protect – Five Years On," *Ethics & International Affairs* 24, no. 2 (2010), 143–69.

  "The Responsibility to Protect and the Problem of Military Intervention," *International Affairs* 84, no. 4 (2008), 625–30.

  "Responsibility to Protect or Trojan Horse? The Crisis in Darfur and Humanitarian Intervention after Iraq," *Ethics & International Affairs* 19, no. 2 (2005), 31–54.

Bellamy, Alex J. and Williams, Paul D., "The New Politics of Protection? Côte d'Ivoire, Libya, and the Responsibility to Protect," *International Affairs* 87, no. 4 (2011), 825–50.

Blake, Michael, "Collateral Benefit," *Social Philosophy & Policy* 23 (2006), 218–30.

  "Reciprocity, Stability and Intervention: The Ethics of Disequilibrium," in D. K. Chatterjee and D.E. Scheid (eds.), *Ethics and Foreign Intervention* (Cambridge University Press, 2003), 53–71.

Buchanan, Allen, "The Internal Legitimacy of Humanitarian Intervention," *Journal of Political Philosophy* 7, no. 1 (1999), 71–87.

  "Justice and Charity," *Ethics* 97, no. 3 (1987), 558–75.

Buchanan, Allen and Keohane, Robert O., "The Preventive Use of Force: A Cosmopolitan Institutional Proposal," *Ethics & International Affairs* 18, no. 1 (2004), 1–22.

Caney, Simon, "Human Rights and the Rights of States: Terry Nardin on Non-Intervention," *International Political Science Review* 18, no. 1 (1997), 27–37.

Cook, Martin L., "Immaculate War: Constraints on Humanitarian Intervention," *Ethics & International Affairs* 14 (2000), 55–65.

Copp, David, "The Idea of a Legitimate State," *Philosophy & Public Affairs* 28, no. 1 (Winter 1999), 3–45.

Daalder, Ivo H. and Stavridis, James G., "NATO's Victory in Libya: The Right Way to Run An Intervention," *Foreign Affairs* 91, no. 2 (2012), 2–7.

Dobos, Ned, "International Rescue and Mediated Consequences," *Ethics & International Affairs* 26, no. 3 (Fall 2012), 335–53.

Doyle, Michael W., "A Few Words on Mill, Walzer and Nonintervention," *Ethics & International Affairs* 23, no. 4 (Winter 2009), 349–69.

Dubik, James M., "Human Rights, Command Responsibility and Walzer's Just War Theory," *Philosophy & Public Affairs* 11, no. 4 (Fall 1982), 354–71.

Evans, Gareth and Sahnoun, Mohamed, "The Responsibility to Protect," *Foreign Affairs* 81, no. 6 (November/December 2002), 99–110.

Evans, Mark, "Selectivity, Imperfect Obligations and the Character of Humanitarian Morality," in Alexander Moseley and Richard Norman (eds.), *Human Rights and Military Intervention* (Aldershot: Ashgate, 2002), 132–49.

Fabre, Cécile, "Mandatory Rescue Killings," *Journal of Political Philosophy* 15, no. 4 (2007), 363–84.

Falk, Richard, "Humanitarian Intervention: A Forum," *The Nation* (July 14, 2003).

Farer, Tom J., "The Ethics of Intervention in Self-Determination Struggles," in D.K. Chatterjee and D.E. Scheid (eds.), *Ethics and Foreign Intervention* (Cambridge University Press, 2003), 143–67.

Finnemore, Martha, "Constructing Norms of Humanitarian Intervention," in Peter J. Katzenstein (ed.), *The Culture of National Security: Norms and Identity in World Politics* (New York: Columbia University Press, 1996), 153–85.

Finnemore, Martha and Sikkink, Kathryn, "International Norm Dynamics and Political Change," *International Organization* 52, no. 4 (1998), 887–917.

Florini, Ann, "The Evolution of International Norms," *International Studies Quarterly* 40, no. 3 (1996), 363–89.

Franceschet, Antonio, "Kant, International Law, and the Problem of Humanitarian Intervention," *Journal of International Political Theory* 6, no. 1 (2010), 1–22.

Frey, R.G., "The Doctrine of Double Effect," in R.G. Frey and Christopher Heath Wellman (eds.), *A Companion to Applied Ethics* (Oxford: Blackwell, 2003), 464–74.

Gheciu, Alexandra and Welsh, Jennifer, "The Imperative to Rebuild: Assessing the Normative Case for Postconflict Reconstruction," *Ethics & International Affairs* 23, no. 2 (Summer 2009), 121–46.

Gifkins, Jess, "Syria and the Responsibility to Protect," *Global Responsibility to Protect* 4, no. 4 (2012).

Gilbert, Alan, "Marx on Internationalism and War," *Philosophy & Public Affairs* 7, no. 4 (1978), 346–69.

Glanville, Luke, "The Antecedents of 'Sovereignty as Responsibility'," *European Journal of International Relations* 17, no. 2 (2011), 233–55.

Glover, Jonathan, "Responses: A Summing Up," in N.A. Davis, R. Keshen L, and J. McMahan (eds), *Ethics and Humanity: Themes from the Philosophy of Jonathan Glover* (Oxford University Press, 2010), 37–281.

Goodman, Ryan, "Humanitarian Intervention and Pretexts for War," *American Journal of International Law* 100 (2006), 107–41.

Graham, G., "The Justice of Intervention," *Review of International Studies* 13 (1987), 133–46.

Gvosdev, Nikolas, "R2P: Sovereignty and Intervention After Libya," *World Politics Review* (June 28, 2011).

Harrington, Joanna, "R2P and Natural Disasters," in Andy W. Knight and Frazer Egerton (eds.), *The Routledge Handbook of the Responsibility to Protect* (New York: Routledge, 2012), 141–51.

Holzgrefe, J.L., "The Humanitarian Intervention Debate," in J.L. Holzgrefe and Robert O. Keohane (eds.), *Humanitarian Intervention: Ethical, Legal, and Political Dimensions* (Cambridge University Press, 2003), 15–52.

Hubert, Don and Blätter, Ariela, "The Responsibility to Protect as International Crimes Prevention," *Global Responsibility to Protect* 4 (2012), 33–66.

Huntington, S.P., "New Contingencies, Old Roles," *Joint Forces Quarterly* 2 (Autumn 1993), 38–43.

Kahn, Paul, "The Paradox of Riskless Warfare," *Philosophy & Public Policy Quarterly*, 22, no. 3 (2002), 2–8.

Lango, John W., "Is Armed Humanitarian Intervention to Stop Mass Killing Morally Obligatory?" *Public Affairs Quarterly* (July 2001), 173–92.

Lauterpacht, Hersch, "Kelsen's Pure Science of Law," in Elihu Lauterpacht (ed.), *International Law: Being the Collected Papers of Hersch Lauterpacht* (Cambridge University Press, 1975), 404–36.

Lefkowitz, David, "On a Samaritan Duty of Humanitarian Intervention," in Paolo Tripodi and Jessica Wolfendale (eds.), *New Wars and New Soldiers: Ethical Challenges in the Modern Military* (Farnham: Ashgate, 2011), 87–101.

Litz, Brett T., King, Lynda A., and King, Daniel W., "Warriors as Peacekeepers: Features of the Somalia Experience and PTSD," *Journal of Consulting and Clinical Psychology* 65, no. 6 (1997), 1001–10.

Luban, David, "Intervention and Civilization: Some Unhappy Lessons of the Kosovo War," in Ciaran Cronin and Pablo de Greiff (eds.), *Global Justice and Transnational Politics: Essays on the Moral and Political Challenges of Globalization* (Cambridge, Massachusetts: MIT Press, 2002), 79–115.

  "Just War and Human Rights," *Philosophy & Public Affairs* 9, no. 2 (Winter 1980), 160–81.

Luban, David and Shue, Henry, "Mental Torture: A Critique of Erasures in US Law," *The Georgetown Law Journal* 100 (2012), 823.

Lucas, George R. Jr., "Agency After Virtue: A Defense of Kantian Constructivism," *International Philosophical Quarterly* 28, no. 3 (September 1988), 293–311.

"From *Jus ad Bellum* to *Jus ad Pacem*: Re-Thinking Just-War Criteria for the Use of Military Force for Humanitarian Ends," in D.K. Chatterjee and D.E. Scheid (eds.), *Ethics and Foreign Intervention* (Cambridge University Press, 2003), 72–96.

"Moral Order and the Constraints of Agency: Toward a New Metaphysics of Morals," in Robert C. Neville (ed.), *New Essays in Metaphysics* (Albany, New York: State University of New York Press, 1987), 117–39.

May, Larry, "The Principle of Just Cause," in Larry May (ed.), *War: Essays in Political Philosophy* (Cambridge University Press, 2008), 49–66.

Mbeki, Thabo, "What the World Got Wrong in Côte D'Ivoire," *Foreign Policy* (April 29, 2011).

McMahan, Jeff, "Humanitarian Intervention, Consent, and Proportionality," in N.A. Davis, R. Keshen, and J. McMahan (eds.), *Ethics and Humanity: Themes from the Philosophy of Jonathan Glover* (Oxford University Press, 2010), 44–72.

"The Just Distribution of Harm Between Combatants and Noncombatants," *Philosophy & Public Affairs* 38, no. 4 (Fall 2010), 342–79.

"Pacifism and Moral Theory," *Diametros* 23 (2010), 3–20.

Mennecke, Martin, "Punishing Genocidaires: A Deterrent Effect or Not?" *Human Rights Review* 8, no. 4 (2007), 319–39.

Mill, John Stuart, "A Few Words on Non-Intervention," *Fraser's Magazine* (December 1859). Reprinted in *Essays on Politics and Culture by John Stuart Mill*, edited by Gertrude Himmelfarb (Garden City, New York: Doubleday Anchor Books, 1963). Available at: www.libertarian.co.uk.

Miller, David, "Distributing Responsibilities," *Journal of Political Philosophy* 9, no. 4 (2001), 453–71.

Mueller, John, "War Has Almost Ceased to Exist: An Assessment," *Political Science Quarterly* 124, no. 2 (2009), 297–321.

Nagel, Thomas, "Agent-Relative Morality," in P.A. Woodward (ed.), *The Doctrine of Double Effect: Philosophers Debate a Controversial Moral Principle* (Notre Dame, Indiana: University of Notre Dame Press, 2001), 41–49.

Onuf, Nicholas G., "Humanitarian Intervention: The Early Years," *Symposium on the Norms and Ethics of Humanitarian Intervention* (University of California–Irvine: Center for Global Peace and Conflict Studies, May 2000).

Orend, Brian, "Jus Post Bellum," *Journal of Social Philosophy* 32 (2002), 117–37.

"Justice After War," *Ethics & International Affairs* 16, no. 1 (2002), 43–56.

Øverland, Gerhard, "High-Fliers: Who Should Bear the Risk of Humanitarian Intervention?" in Paolo Tripodi and Jessica Wolfendale (eds.), *New Wars and New Soldiers: Ethical Challenges in the Modern Military* (Farnham, UK: Ashgate, 2011), 69–86.

Parekh, Bhikhu, "Rethinking Humanitarian Intervention," *International Political Science Review* 18, no. 1 (1997), 49–69.

Pattison, James, "The Ethics of Humanitarian Intervention in Libya," *Ethics & International Affairs* 25, no. 3 (Fall 2011), 271–77.

"Just War Theory and the Privatization of Military Force," *Ethics & International Affairs* 22 (2008), 143–62.

"Outsourcing the Responsibility to Protect: Humanitarian Intervention and Private Military and Security Companies," *International Theory* 2 (2010), 1–31.

Pogge, Thomas, "An Institutional Approach to Humanitarian Intervention," *Public Affairs Quarterly* 6 (1992), 89–103.

Rodin, David, "The Responsibility to Protect and the Logic of Rights," in Oliver Jütersonke and Keith Krause (eds.), *From Rights to Responsibilities: Rethinking Interventions for Humanitarian Purposes*, PSIS Special Study 7 (Geneva: Programme for Strategic and International Security Studies, 2006).

Schachter, Oscar, "The Legality of Pro-Democratic Invasion," *American Journal of International Law* 78 (1984), 645–50.

Scheffer, David, "Atrocity Crimes Framing the Responsibility to Protect," *Case Western Reserve Journal of International Law* 40, no. 1 (2008), 111–35.

Shue, Henry, "Conditional Sovereignty," *Res Publica* 8, no. 1 (1999), 1–7.

"Eroding Sovereignty: The Advance of Principle," in Robert McKim and Jeff McMahan (eds.), *The Morality of Nationalism* (New York and Oxford: Oxford University Press, 1997), 340–59.

"'Let Whatever Is Smoldering Erupt'? Conditional Sovereignty, Reviewable Intervention, and Rwanda 1994," in Albert Paolini, Anthony Jarvis, and Christian Reus-Smit (eds.), *Between Sovereignty and Global Governance: The State, Civil Society and the United Nations* (New York: St. Martin's, 1998), 60–84.

"Mediating Duties," *Ethics* 98, no. 4 (July 1988), 687–704.

Singer, Peter, "Bystanders to Poverty," in N.A. Davis, R. Keshen, and J. McMahan (eds.), *Ethics and Humanity: Themes from the Philosophy of Jonathan Glover* (Oxford University Press, 2010), 185–201.

Smith, Michael J., "Humanitarian Intervention: An Overview of the Ethical Issues," *Ethics & International Affairs* 12, no. 1 (1998), 63–79.

Snyder, Jack and Vinjamuri, Leslie, "Trials and Errors: Principle and Pragmatism in Strategies of International Justice," *International Security* 28, no. 3 (2003/2004), 5–44.

Tan, Kok-Chor, "The Duty to Protect," in Terry Nardin and Melissa S. Williams (eds.), *NOMOS XLVII: Humanitarian Intervention* (New York and London: New York University Press, 2006), 84–116.

Tesón, Fernando, "The Liberal Case for Humanitarian Intervention," in J.L. Holzgrefe and Robert O. Keohane (eds.), *Humanitarian Intervention: Ethical, Legal and Political Dilemmas* (Cambridge University Press, 2003), 93–129.

Todorov, Tzvetan, "Right to Intervene or Duty to Assist?" in Nicholas Owen (ed.), *Human Rights, Human Wrongs*, The Oxford Amnesty Lectures 2001 (Oxford University Press, 2003), 28–48.

Valentino, Benjamin A., "The True Costs of Humanitarian Intervention," *Foreign Affairs* 90, no. 6 (November/December 2011), 60–73.

Verwey, Wil, "Humanitarian Intervention in the 1990s and Beyond: An International Law Perspective," in J.N. Pierterse (ed.), *World Orders in the Making: Humanitarian Intervention and Beyond* (London: Macmillan, 1998), 200.

Vinjamuri, Leslie, "Deterrence, Democracy, and the Pursuit of International Justice During Conflict," *Ethics & International Affairs* 24, no. 2 (2010), 191–211.

Vossen, B. Van der, "The Asymmetry of Legitimacy," *Law and Philosophy* 31 (2012), 565–92.

Walzer, Michael, "The Case Against Our Attack on Libya," *The New Republic* (March 20, 2011).

"The Moral Standing of States: A Response to Four Critics," *Philosophy & Public Affairs* 9, no. 3 (Spring 1980), 209–29.

Weiss, Thomas G., "Halting Atrocities in Kenya," in *Great Decisions* (New York: Foreign Policy Association, 2010), 17–30.

"The Sunset of Humanitarian Intervention? The Responsibility to Protect in a Unipolar Era," *Security Dialogue* 35, no. 2 (2004), 135–53.

Welsh, Jennifer M., "Civilian Protection in Libya: Putting Coercion and Controversy Back into RtoP," *Ethics & International Affairs* 25, no. 3 (Fall 2011), 255–62.

"Who Should Act? Collective Responsibility and the Responsibility to Protect," in Andy W. Knight and Frazer Egerton (eds.), *The Routledge Handbook of the Responsibility to Protect* (New York and Oxford: Routledge, 2012), 103–14.

Western, Jon and Goldstein, Joshua S., "Humanitarian Intervention Comes of Age: Lessons from Somalia to Libya," *Foreign Affairs* 90, no. 6 (November/December 2011), 48–59.

Wheeler, Nicholas J. and Morris, Justin, "Justifying the Iraq War as a Humanitarian Intervention: The Cure is Worse Than the Disease," in Ramesh Thakur and Waheguru Pal Singh Sidhu (eds.), *The Iraq Crisis and World Order: Structural, Institutional and Normative Challenges* (Tokyo: UN University Press, 2006), 444–63.

Williams, Robert E. and Caldwell, Dan, "*Jus Post Bellum*: Just War Theory and the Principles of Just Peace," *International Studies Perspective* 7 (2006), 309–20.

Wolfendale, Jessica, "Performance-Enhancing Technologies and Moral Responsibility in the Military," *The American Journal of Bioethics* 8, no. 2 (2008), 28–38.

INDEX

Abdelaziz, Maged A., 205
Abdul Jalil, Mustafa, 54
Abu Ghraib, 158
Afghanistan
    US-led war in, 5, 84, 142, 234, 236
African Union, 9–24, 52, 53, 204
    2001 Constitutive Act of the African
        Union, 212
aggression
    definition, 226
Al Jazeera, 51
Al Qaeda, 5, 38, 53, 229, 253
American Civil War (1861–1865), 232
Angola, 169
Annan, Kofi A., 13–14, 78, 199, 200,
        204, 244, 248
    Two Concepts of Sovereignty, 13, 244
Aquinas, Thomas, 98
Arab Emirates, 204
Arab League, 24, 52, 204
Arbour, Louise, 222
Arkes, Hadley P., 197
armed humanitarian intervention
        (AHI)
    challenge to state sovereignty, 12,
        64–65, 71
    concept of, 3–5, 61, 96, 224, 252, 256
    consent to, 110–1
    criteria for
        extreme emergencies, 210
        four key crimes, 211, 213–14, 245
    duty of, 33, 40, 64, 78, 122, 258, 259
    government relationship, 92–94
    history of, 27, 28–36, 38–41,
        149–54
    human rights, 243
    legal authority, 16–17, 182, 200

Libya, 22–25
moral basis for, 5–10, 61, 63–64,
        65–66, 67, 76, 95, 100, 107–8,
        109–10, 256
    natural disasters, 212
    as pretext, problem of abuse, 16, 24,
        29, 54, 148, 149, 154–62, 167,
        173, 175, 186, 199
    problems with, 43, 45, 46–47
    within Responsibility to Protect
        doctrine, 15
    right of, 33, 46–47, 64, 78
    selectivity, 47, 49, 55, 246
    strict neutrality, 44
    as war, 246–47
armed intervention
    civil wars, 246
    legal authority, 16–17, 200
    regime change, 169, 170
    right of, 46–47, 48, 196–97
Armitage, Richard L., 133
Ashton, Catherine, 52
Assad, Bashar al, 246
Athens, 193
Augustine (of Hippo), 98, 104, 178
Australia, 26, 87

Bangladesh, 197
Ban, Ki-moon, 18, 172, 212, 220
Barnett, Michael N., 184
Belgium, 237
Belhadj, Abdelhakim, 54
Bellamy, Alex J., 35, 95, 96, 97–106,
        107, 108, 109, 111, 158
Bilmes, Linda J., 81, 84
Blair, Anthony (Tony) C. L., 199
Blake, Michael, 35

Blätter, Ariela, 213
Bodin, Jean, 10, 248
Bosnia/Yugoslavia, 227
  intervention in, 3, 13, 32, 39
Bowden, Mark R., 31
Brazil, 166
  intervention in Libya, 204
  Responsibility while Protecting, 209
Brezhnev, Leonid Ilyich, 195
  Brezhnev Doctrine, 194
BRICS countries, 52, 53, 166
Buchanan, Allen, 30
Bush, George H. W., 29, 143
Bush, George W., 56, 143, 146, 235

Cambodia
  Vietnam's intervention, 107, 181
Canada, 26, 199, 238
  intervention in Afghanistan, 236
  intervention in Libya, 239
Caney, Simon, 178
Catherine the Great (of Russia), 50
ceasefire
  in Libya, 51–52, 56, 204
Chile, 153, 160, 167, 169
China, 166, 212, 226
  Côte d'Ivoire, 218
  intervention in Libya, 24, 38, 177,
    187, 204
  intervention in Syria, 153, 154,
    159, 204
  state of Chu, 149
  state of Qi, 149
  state of Song, 149
Chirac, Jacques R., 146
Chomsky, A. Noam, 205
civil war, 4
  in Libya, 37, 53
  in Syria, 38
Clark, Wesley K., 31
Clausewitz, Carl von, 247
Cleomedes, 193
Cleon, 193
Clinton, Hillary Rodham, 21, 160
Clinton, William Jefferson, 29, 198
cluster munitions, 157, 158
Coady, C. A. J. (Tony), 30
Cold War, 46, 187

colonialism, colonial powers, 16, 50,
  55, 57
Cook, Martin L., 85, 86, 87
Côte d'Ivoire, 166, 172, 218
crimes against humanity, 18, 24, 188
  as justifying armed intervention,
    200, 213–14

Dafur Janjaweed militia, 214
Dallaire, Roméo, 31, 44, 238
Damrosch, Lori, 191
Des Jardins, Joseph R., 88
Dinstein, Yoram, 191
Diodotus, 193
Ditchley Foundation, 13
Dobbins, James F., 234, 235
double effect
  doctrine of double effect, 72–77, 98,
    105, 107, 111
  intent and foresight, 73–74
Doyle, Michael W., 17, 35
Drumbl, Mark A., 213, 219

economic sanctions, 227
  definitions, 228
Egypt, 19, 253, 255
Escoto Brockmann, Miguel d', 190, 205
ethical responsibility, *see* moral
  responsibility to strangers
ethnic cleansing, mass expulsion, 17,
  18, 29, 81, 188
  as justifying armed intervention, 15,
    200, 214
European Union, 21, 52, 157
Evans, Gareth J., 14, 35, 36, 56, 173,
  188, 199, 212
Evans, Mark, 90

Fauchille, Paul Auguste Joseph, 176
Feinberg, Joel, 93
Fichte, Johann Gottlieb, 176
force protection, 44, 85, 184
France, 26
  intervention in Iraq (1991), 129
  intervention in Libya (2011), 23, 24,
    50, 55, 202, 239
  intervention in Rwanda (1994),
    173, 238

Frederick the Great (of Prussia), 50

G-77, 199
Gaddafi, Muammar, 19, 20–24, 48, 51,
    54, 129, 159, 201, 202, 219, 220,
    221, 239
Gaddafi, Mutassim, 24
Gaddafi, Saif al-Islam, 24
Gbagbo, Laurent, 166, 218
Geneva Conventions (1949), 11, 225
genocide, 17, 18, 29, 188, 190,
    see also Rwanda
    Armenian genocide, 28
    definition, 237
    Genocide Conventions of 1948, 37,
        90, 190, 203
    Holocaust, 29, 38, 226
    as justifying armed intervention,
        200, 203, 214
    Srebrenica, 183
Germany, 228
    Blitzkrieg of 1939, 227
    Holocaust, 29, 38, 226
    intervention in Afghanistan, 236
    intervention in Libya, 204
    invasion of Czechoslovakia
        (1939), 173
Ghoga, Abdul Hafiz, 22
Global Centre for the Responsibility to
    Protect, 215
Goodman, Ryan, 161
Good Samaritan, 9, 42
    legislation, 41
Goya, Francisco, 58
    Disasters of War, 58
Grotius, Hugo, 148, 150, 154, 158, 163
    The Rights of War and Peace,
        148, 154
Guatemala, 167, 169

Hague Conventions, 225
Haiti, intervention in, 32, 41, 44
Heller, Hermann, 176
Hegel, Georg Wilhelm Friedrich,
    43, 176
Hitler, Adolf, 173, 228
Hobbes (of Malmesbury), Thomas, 248
Hoffmann, Stanley, 30
Hubert, Don, 213

humanitarian aid, 46
    definition of, 4
humanitarian intent, 99, 101, 103, 104,
    105, 106, 182–85, 186
human rights, 10, 11–12, 175, 176,
    179, 187, 209, 243, 244, 255,
    see also universal moral rights
    Universal Declaration of Human
        Rights, 11
Human Rights Watch, 19, 20, 25, 57,
    78, 157
human sovereignty, 243, 250, 251,
    see also sovereignty
    and humanitarian intervention, 253,
        255, 256, 258
Hussein, Saddam, 72, 97, 129, 143, 229,
    234, 235

Ignatieff, Michael G., 81
Ihering (Jhering), Rudolph Ritter
    von, 176
imperfect duty, 8–9, 34, 36, 37, 41, 79,
    88, 90
Independent International
    Commission of Inquiry on the
    Syrian Arab Republic, 216
India, 152, 177
    Côte d'Ivoire, 218
    intervention in Libya, 204
    invasion of East Pakistan (1971), 197
Indonesia (East Timor), 169
International Commission of Inquiry
    on Darfur (2003), 203
International Commission on
    Intervention and State
    Sovereignty (ICISS), 14, 41, 78,
    151, 200, 203, 210, 238, 244, 246
    The Responsibility to Protect, 14, 78,
        238–39, 247, 258
International Court of Justice (ICJ),
    175, 190
    Statute of the International Court of
        Justice, Art. 38, 190
International Covenants on Human
    Rights, 175
international crimes, 213,
    see also transnational crimes
International Criminal Court (ICC),
    21, 191, 220, 221, 222, 223

China non-party, 192
India non-party, 192
Russia non-party, 192
United States non-party, 192
international customary law, 17, 163,
  190, 206
international ethics, 192–98,
  see also moral responsibility to
  strangers
  Liberals, 195–98, 207
  communitarians, 172, 195, 198
  cosmopolitans, 197–98
  Realists, 5, 193–94, 207
  Socialists, 194–95, 207
international law, 11, 36, 61, 159,
  163, 189–92, 194, 198,
  see also international
  customary law
  jus cogens, 191
  opinio juris, 190, 206
intervention, *see also* armed
  humanitarian intervention
  concept of, 3–4, 192
  state consent, 3
Iraq
  intervention in 1991, 129, 145,
  169, 229
  US-led war in 2003, 5, 72, 81, 84,
  87, 133, 137, 142, 143, 151,
  157, 159, 162, 173, 183, 234,
  235–36, 246
Islamic Conference, 52
Italy
  intervention in Libya, 239

Japan, 226
Jefferson, Thomas, 179
  Declaration of Independence, 179
Johnson, James Turner, 30
Joseph II (of Austria), 50
Juppé, Alain, 51
jus ad bellum, 62, 75, 99, 109, 133, 224,
  225, 226
jus ad pacem, 114
jus in bello, 103, 114, 133, 224,
  225, 226
jus post bellum, 133, 134, 136, 184,
  224, *see also* post-intervention
  justice, post-war justice

just war, 10, 181, 200, 246
  just cause, 72, 74, 75–77, 111, 200
  last resort, 10, 209
  legitimate authority, 10, 200
  proportionate means, 10, 68, 69–70,
  71–77, 200
  reasonable prospects, chance of
  success, 10, 39
  right intention, 10, 104, 200

Kaldor, Mary H., 161
Kambanda, Jean, 226
Kant, Immanuel, 36, 37, 40, 163,
  174, 178
  Perpetual Peace, 163, 174
Khmer Rouge, 167
Kosovo Commission, 199, 203
Kosovo/Yugoslavia
  intervention in, 3, 13, 16, 17, 31,
  32, 39, 44, 46, 104, 113, 142,
  151, 198
Kouchner, Bernard, 212
Kuwait, 229

Lango, John W., 30
La Rochefoucauld, Francois duc
  de, 57
last resort, 197, 209, *see also* just war
Lemaire, Luc, 31
Leninism, 194
Libya
  civil war, 37, 218, 220, 221,
  239, 255
  Free Libyan Army, 253
  intervention in, 3, 17, 19–25, 37,
  47–48, 51–54, 56, 113, 148, 153,
  156, 159, 162, 166, 172, 179,
  200–203, 209, 246, 252, 253
Longuet, Gérard, 51
Luban, David J., 30, 197,
  216, 245
  debate with Walzer, 198
Lucas, George R. Jr., 114, 117, 128

MacArthur, Douglas 231
Mahbubani, Kishore, 142
Marshal Plan, 232,
  see also reconstruction of
  Germany and Japan

Martin, Ian, 203
Marx, Karl Heinrich, 194
mass atrocities, 166, 170–71, 251,
    see also crimes against
    humanity, ethnic cleansing,
    genocide, war crimes
deterrence of, 220–22
May, Larry, 146
McCall, John J., 88
McMahan, Jeff, 104, 114, 115, 116, 117,
    120, 123, 127, 128, 259
Melos, 193
Mencius, 149
messianic zeal, 55, 57
military forces for humanitarian
    missions, 89–90
Mill, John Stuart, 28, 32, 174, 195, 196,
    243, 256, 257
"A Few Words on Non-intervention"
    (1859), 28, 196, 256
Milosevic, Slobodan, 226
moral reasoning, see moral
    responsibility to strangers
moral responsibility to strangers,
    5–10, see also human
    rights, international ethics,
    utilitarianism
duty of beneficence, duty to aid, 8–9
    79–80, 124–25
    cost proviso, 8, 81, 82–84, 85–88,
        89–90, 91
    distribution of costs, 116–29,
        see also "Pottery Barn" rule
duty of non-maleficence, 7
Good Samaritan, 9
government relationship, 92–94
graduated responsibilities, 6
imperfect duty, 8–9, 34, 36, 41, 79,
    88, 90
third-party self-defense, 7
universal moral rights, 9–10
Moreno-Ocampo, Luis G., 24
motives, intentions, 96–107, 182,
    see also humanitarian intent
double intent, 98, 104–6, 111
intent and foresight, 73–74
Moussa, Amr, 24
Mueller, John E., 161
Muñoz, Heraldo, 148, 155

Myanmar
    Cyclone Nargis emergency (2008),
        206, 212
Mytilene, 193

national interest, see state interest
National Transitional Council (Libya),
    22, 54, 166, 201, 203
New York Times, 113
Nigeria, 177, 198
non-interference, non-intervention, 12,
    61, 163, 171, 174, 176, 179, 181,
    192, 194, 195–96, 209, 210
    as derivative right of states, 248
    as right of individuals, 248
North American Treaty Organization
    (NATO), 26
    intervention in Afghanistan
        (2001), 236
    intervention in Former Yugoslavia
        (Bosnia, 1995), 39
    intervention in Former Yugoslavia
        (Kosovo, 1999), 17, 39, 44, 46,
        84, 104, 113, 151, 198
    intervention in Libya (2011), 17, 19,
        23, 37, 53, 113, 148, 153, 156,
        159, 162, 166, 179, 200–203,
        209, 239, 246, 252, 253

Obama, Barack H., 56, 201,
    202, 235
Operation Provide Comfort, 143
Orend, Brian, 33, 35
Øverland, Gerhard, 114, 116, 117, 120,
    122, 128

Parekh, Bhikhu C., 96, 97
Pattison, James, 35
Petraeus, David H., 235
Philippines, 169
Plato, 43
    Republic, 43
Pogge, Thomas W. M., 129
political transformation, 252, 255
Pol Pot, 107, 181
Ponds, Linda, 36
Popular Will argument, 70
post-intervention justice, 239–41,
    see also jus post bellum

post-war justice, 224, 225–36, 241,
    see also jus post bellum
post-war Rehabilitation Model, 229,
    see also reconstruction of
    Germany and Japan
  application to Afghanistan and Iraq,
    233–36
    Afghanistan economy, 236
    Afghanistan regime change, 234
    Afghanistan security, 235
    Iraq economy, 235–36
    Iraq regime change, 234
    Iraq security, 235
  forces regime change, 230
  rehabilitation principles, 232–33
  rejects reparations, compensation
    payments, 229
  rejects sweeping sanctions, 229
post-war Retribution Model, 225–29
  aggressor gives up unjust
    gains, 227
  aggressor is demilitarized, 227
  aggressor to suffer further
    losses, 227
  apology from aggressor, 226
  exchange of prisoners, 226
  public peace treaty, 225
  war-crimes trials, 226
"Pottery Barn" rule, 134–47
  fault-based conception, 135–39
  strict-liability conception, 140–45
Powell, Colin L., 133, 134, 146
Powell Doctrine, 39
prevention
  of mass atrocities, 3, 67
  of deadly conflict, war, 14–15
proportionality principle, 10,
    68, 69–70, 71–77, 198,
    see also just war
psychological factors for war
  bias in interpretation of practices
    and norms, 141–43
  temporal-discounting bias, 143–44
psychological problems in military
    forces
  morale, 44
  psychological damage, 44,
    84–85, 91
Pufendorf, Samuel von, 150, 163

Qatar, intervention in Libya, 24,
    202, 204

Rasmussen, Anders Fogh, 113
"rational actor" framework, 218–19
reconstruction of Germany and Japan,
    230–32
  education systems, 231
  German and Japanese economies,
    231–32
  purging process, 231
  written constitutions or basic
    law, 231
Red Cross (International Committee of
    the Red Cross, ICRC)
  report on Libyan intervention,
    25, 201
refugees
  Libyan, 51
regime change, 166, 167, 172, 174,
    177, 179, 180, 185–86, 234,
    245, 247, *see also* post-war
    Rehabilitation Model
  agents of, 168
  definition of, 167
  following intervention in Libya, 24,
    38, 253
  normative quality, 167
  recent history, 168–71
  UN Security Council authorized, 180
reparations, compensation payments,
    227, 229
Responsibility to Protect (RtoP), 3,
    13–16, 27, 34–35, 48–49, 114,
    151, 159, 166, 177, 179, 187,
    188, 189, 243
  adoption and implementation,
    17–19, 37–38, 201, 204–5,
    206, 209
  criminalization of, 211
  evolution of, 198–200, 205–7,
    237–9
  four key crimes, 211, 213–4, 245
  *Implementing the Responsibility to
    Protect*, 18, 205
  interpretation of, 48–49, 158
  legal status, 192, 204, 207
  "Libya wound," 204, 253
  possible abuse, 205

Responsibility to Protect (RtoP) (*cont.*)
  precautionary principles, 15
  rationale for intervention in
    Libya, 239
  responsibility to prevent, 14–15, 200
  responsibility to react, 15, 169,
    200, 212
  responsibility to rebuild, 15, 200, 239
Rhodesia, 176, 191
"riskless" war, 84
Rodin, David, 34, 35
Rome Statute (1998), 191, 212, 220,
    222, 226
Roth, Kenneth, 157
Russia
  and Afghanistan, 236
  intervention in Georgia (2008), 153,
    156, 158, 161, 183
  intervention in Libya, 24, 38, 177,
    187, 204
  and Syria, 153, 154, 159, 204, 219
Rwanda, 129
  French 1994 intervention, 173, 238
  genocide/non-intervention (1994),
    3, 13, 31, 32, 39, 46, 102, 153,
    183, 237–38
  Hutus, 237, 238
  Tutsis, 237

Sahnoun, Mohamed, 14, 188, 199
Sarkozy, Nicolas P. S., 21
Saxon, Dan R., 221
self-defense, defense of others, 7, 16,
    62, 63–64, 65–66, 142
  preemptive/preventive, 33
self-determination, 174–79, 184,
    195, 197
self-help regimes
  economic, 259, 260
  security, 259, 260
Senussi, Abdullah al, 24
Shue, Henry, 30, 34, 92, 216
Sidgwick, Henry, 75, 77
Singapore, 153
Singer, Peter A. D., 258
Skinner, Quentin R. D., 156
Snider, Don M., 44
Somalia, intervention in, 3, 13, 29, 31,
    32, 38, 41

South Africa, 166, 176, 177, 191,
    204, 219
sovereignty, 10–12, 50, 171–79, 187–88,
    209, 243, 248, *see also* human
    sovereignty
  and culture, 70–71, 172, 174
  conditional sovereignty, 12–13, 34,
    103, 178, 198, 207, 211, 243,
    244, 249
  of the family, 42
  of individuals, 248, 250
  popular sovereignty, 179, 180
  sovereign equality, 78, 171, 172,
    181, 187
Soviet Union (USSR), 194
  Communist Party, 195
  intervention in Czechoslovakia
    (1968), 195
  intervention in Germany (1953), 195
  intervention in Hungary (1956), 195
Sri Lanka
  assault against Tamil Tigers, 215
Stalinism, 194
state interest, 5, 41, 142, 193
Stevens, J. Christopher, 38
Stiglitz, Joseph E., 81, 84
Syria, 154, 160, 204, 219, 246
  civil war, 38, 153, 166, 253
  massacre at Houla (May 2012), 216

Tadros, Victor, 259
Taliban, 5, 234, 235
Tesón, Fernando R., 97, 108, 245
Thakur, Ramesh, 215
Thucydides, 193
  *History of the Peloponnesian
    War*, 193
Tisias, 193
Togo, 177
transnational crimes, 213,
    see also international crimes
treaties
  *1991 Treaty ending the Persian Gulf
    War* (ceasefire UN Sec. Council
    Res. 687), 229
  Treaty of Versailles, 228
Treitschke, Heinrich Gotthard
    von, 176
Tunisia, 19, 253, 255

United Kingdom (Great Britain), 26, 160, 176
  intervention in Afghanistan (2001), 236
  intervention in Iraq (1991), 129
  intervention in Iraq (2003), 151
  intervention in Libya (2011), 23, 50, 55, 202
United Nations (UN), 11, 46, 50, 51
  mission in Bosnia, 39
  mission in Côte d'Ivoire, 166, 218
  mission in Kosovo, 39
  mission in Rwanda, 39, 238
United Nations Charter, 12, 163, 175, 180, 225
  Article 2, 17, 171, 189
  Article 24, 180
  Article 25, 180, 190
  Article 39, 189–191
  Article 42, 12
  Article 48, 190
  Article 51, 7, 12
  Article 103, 192
  Chapter VI, 18, 217
  Chapter VII, 12, 18, 150, 152, 189, 191, 203, 206, 217
Chapter VII determinations of threats to peace, 191
  Chapter VIII, 18
United Nations General Assembly, 48, 152, 160, 175, 176, 188
  Declaration on Principles of International Law concerning Friendly Relations and Co-operation among States (A/res/2625), 175
  Declaration on the Colonial Countries and Peoples (A/res/1514), 175
United Nations Peacebuilding Commission, 184
United Nations peacekeeping, 218
United Nations resolutions
  Security Council Res. 1441 (Nov. 2002), 137
  Security Council Res. 1674 (April 2006), 37, 190, 205
  Security Council Res. 1970 (Feb. 2011), 21, 24, 51, 220

Security Council Res. 1973 (March 2011), 22, 51, 153, 166, 177, 201, 217, 247, 252, 253
United Nations Security Council, 49, 150, 151, 164, 166, 176, 184, 188, 189, 191, 192, 204, 215–16
  approval of Res. 1970, 21
  arms embargo over Sudan (2005), 201
  authority for use of force, 12, 13, 16–17, 18, 151, 152, 153, 159, 172, 179, 182, 200
  authorization of intervention in Côte d'Ivoire, 172
  authorization of intervention in Libya, 22, 47, 172, 202, 216, 221–22, 239
  authorizing regime change, 180–81
  right of veto by permanent members, 49
United Nations World Summit (2005), Summit agreement, 48, 152, 159, 164, 172, 187, 210, 239, 245
United Nations 2005 World Summit Outcome Document, 188, 189, 211, 222, 239
  Responsibility to protect populations from genocide, war crimes, ethnic cleansing and crimes against humanity (paragraphs 138 and 139), 17, 188, 200, 211, 212, 223, 245
United States, 26, 160, see also United States military interventions
United States military interventions
  in Afghanistan (2001), 5, 84, 142
  in Bosnia (1995), 32
  in Grenada (1983), 173
  in Haiti (1994), 32, 41, 44
  in Iraq (1991), 129, 145, 169,229
  in Iraq (2003), 5, 72, 81, 84, 87, 133, 137, 142, 143, 151, 157, 159, 162, 173, 183, 246
  in Kosovo (1999), 16, 32, 113, 142
  in Libya (2011), 23, 239
  in Somalia (1992), 29, 32, 38, 41
universal moral rights, 9–10, 11–12
Urquhart, Brian, 90

utilitarianism, 6, 207

Vattel, Emer de, 150, 163
Verwey, Will, 97
Vietnam, intervention in Cambodia
     (1979), 107, 181
violence and political relations
   just political relations, 248–49
   political violence, 249, 255, 257
Vitoria, Francesco de, 175

Walzer, Michael, 29, 30, 32, 87, 97, 98,
     104, 105, 174, 184, 196, 197,
     203, 210, 243, 245, 256, 257
   debate with Luban, 198
   double intent, 98, 104–6, 111
   Just and Unjust Wars, 29
war
   decline of interstate wars, 161
   humanitarian intervention as war,
     246–47

war crimes, 17, 18, 188
   justifying armed intervention,
     200, 214
   war-crimes trials, 226
Weinberger Doctrine, Weinberger–
     Powell Doctrine, *see* Powell
     Doctrine
Weiss, Thomas G., 151
Welsh, Jennifer M., 35
Wheeler, Nicholas J., 156, 157
   Saving Strangers, 156
Wolfowitz, Paul D., 33
World War I (1914–1918), 228
World War II (1939–1945), 226
   Holocaust, 29, 38, 226
   World War II settlement, 230

Younis, Abdel Fatah, 54

Zinni, Anthony C., 31
Zuma, Jacob G., 53